"When the Scriptures say minds, souls, and strengtl of who we are before God ; fancy term for caring for th ing God to draw us closer to ....uras invitation to let Jesus into all of v .., ,u are, providing you with needed encouragement and practical tools, will be a trusted companion wherever you find yourself today."
—Terra Mattson, MA, LMFT, LPC, counselor, author, and founder of Living Wholehearted and Courageous Girls

"What a precious gift you hold in your hands! Laura brilliantly combines her own vulnerability, biblical truth, and creative practices for our struggles. Showing us how much Jesus loves us in our fear, anxiety, and depression, Laura encourages therapy, medicine, movement, healthy boundaries, and more. You will feel seen, heard, and loved. Our culture is in need of a book that points us to Jesus and to His gracious tools available to help our mental health."
—Amy Seiffert, author of *Starved* and *Grace Looks Amazing on You*

"This book is a balm for both mental and spiritual health. Laura's vulnerability and empathy create space for you to open up and consider a Jesus who not only loves you like you are today but has the power and willingness to mend your broken mindsets. Holding up the power of Scripture and prayer as well as the power of great therapy, Laura is a trustworthy guide to help you take a step forward on your mental health journey."
—Alli Patterson, author of *How to Stay Standing* and teaching pastor at Crossroads Church

HOLY
CARE
for the
WHOLE
SELF

**Biblical Wisdom for Mental
and Spiritual Well-Being**

LAURA L. SMITH

Our Daily Bread
Publishing.

Holy Care for the Whole Self: Biblical Wisdom for Mental and Spiritual Well-Being
© 2024 by Laura L. Smith

All rights reserved.

Requests for permission to quote from this book should be directed to: Permissions Department, Our Daily Bread Publishing, PO Box 3566, Grand Rapids, MI 49501, or contact us by email at permissionsdept@odb.org.

The persons and events portrayed in this book have been used with permission. To protect the privacy of certain individuals, some names and identifying details have been changed.

The author and publisher are not engaged in rendering medical or psychological services, and this book is not intended as a guide to diagnose or treat medical or psychological problems. If medical, psychological, or other expert assistance is required, the reader should seek the services of a health-care provider or certified counselor.

Scripture quotations, unless otherwise indicated, are taken from the Holy Bible, New International Version®, NIV®. Copyright © 1973, 1978, 1984, 2011 by Biblica, Inc.™ Used by permission of Zondervan. All rights reserved worldwide. www.zondervan.com.

Scripture quotations marked ESV are taken from the ESV® Bible (The Holy Bible, English Standard Version®), copyright © 2001 by Crossway, a publishing ministry of Good News Publishers. Used by permission. All rights reserved.

Scripture quotations marked MSG are taken from *The Message*, copyright © 1993, 2002, 2018 by Eugene H. Peterson. Used by permission of NavPress, represented by Tyndale House Publishers. All rights reserved.

Scripture quotations marked NLT are taken from the Holy Bible, New Living Translation, copyright © 1996, 2004, 2015 by Tyndale House Foundation. Used by permission of Tyndale House Publishers, Inc., Carol Stream, Illinois 60188. All rights reserved.

Interior design by Michael J. Williams

Library of Congress Cataloging-in-Publication Data

Names: Smith, Laura L., 1969- author.
Title: Holy care for the whole self : biblical wisdom for mental and spiritual well-being / Laura L. Smith.
Description: Grand Rapids, MI : Our Daily Bread Publishing, [2024] | Includes bibliographical references. | Summary: ""Jesus created us for abundant life, and that includes mental health and well-being. Through holistic practices such as memorizing Scripture, gratitude, prayer, and counseling, Laura Smith guides readers toward freedom and fullness"--Provided by publisher"-- Provided by publisher.
Identifiers: LCCN 2023017377 (print) | LCCN 2023017378 (ebook) | ISBN 9781640702776 | ISBN 9781640702783 (epub)
Subjects: LCSH: Mental health--Religious aspects--Christianity. | Spiritual exercises. | Christian life.
Classification: LCC BT732.4 .S65 2024 (print) | LCC BT732.4 (ebook) | DDC 261.8/322--dc23/eng/20230829
LC record available at https://lccn.loc.gov/2023017377
LC ebook record available at https://lccn.loc.gov/2023017378

Printed in the United States of America
24 25 26 27 28 29 30 31 / 8 7 6 5 4 3 2 1

To the phenomenal women—and man—who were willing to vulnerably share their stories, experiences, and expertise. This is your book. Betsy, Brenda, Chad, Elisa, Juiquetta, Kristan, Laura, L.C., Maddie, Mallory, Maryanne, Robin, Robin, Sharee, Sharon, Sherri, Sue, and Tammy, I am forever grateful. Jesus loves you more than you can fathom and cares immeasurably about every part of you, including your mental health.

CONTENTS

INTRODUCTION

I am not a mental health professional. I'm not a pastor. I'm just a regular girl, wife, mom of four, daughter, sister, friend, and Jesus lover trying to juggle my relationships and my writing and maintaining a home and tending to all the to-dos. Some days I'm living my best life. And some days I feel stressed, worried, fearful, overwhelmed, or plain tired. And then there are days when I get frozen in my tracks. When my heart races. When I have a zillion and eight thoughts and am terrified to speak any of them. When I jump at seemingly nothing or wake up screaming from my sleep. Rationally, I know Jesus is with me on those days, that He has my best interests in mind, that He protects me, loves me, and is so powerful He can take down anything that comes my way. But sometimes my body or mind forgets these truths and responds irrationally.

Psychologists have determined that our early years are formative years. As a little girl I craved love and approval from someone who mattered to me. So much. Turns out their actions made me feel like I wasn't good enough. I believed some bad choices they made were because of me. That's how my little-girl self saw things. This warped my views of relationships and of myself. I internalized a feeling that I was a walking, talking disappointment to those around me and to God.

It damaged my mental health. I didn't know it. Because that was just my life. The one I lived. The lens I looked through was the only one I had. I didn't know mine was all smudgy and the wrong prescription. I had no idea other people were looking through less distorted lenses.

At some point in my thirties, I realized damage had been done that impacted many of my decisions and perceptions. I started opening up with my husband, who is my most trusted friend. It was both terrifying and freeing to speak my thoughts out loud. Brett kindly and gently asked if I wanted to see a counselor, to which I responded, "No, I'm fine," and fully believed it.

I have such a happy life. Despite some scars from childhood, I've been over-the-top blessed with a loving husband and wonderful kids. I find peace and strength daily in Jesus and His unconditional love for me. I've done a lot of work digging into my Bible, spending hours in prayer, and having deep conversations with Brett (who sees my best and worst and loves me the same) to relearn who I am and what matters most. I've come a very long way from the fragile little girl and the teenage and college-aged young woman who was desperate for love and felt she had to prove herself to everyone all the time.

A handful of years back my close friend Shena started seeing a Christian counselor. While on a walk together one chilly morning, she shared with me how *free* she felt and proceeded to literally spin in a circle, arms extended. Shena knew some pieces from my past, and as we talked and walked along a trail littered with fallen leaves, she suggested counseling might also help me. Her words penetrated. Sure, my husband had suggested counseling before, but for some reason this time the idea stuck.

Maybe I should.

Now a few years into my counseling journey, I realize it is one of the best decisions I've ever made. Yes, I'd made progress, grown, and healed a lot over the years through prayer and confiding in my husband and learning how to care for myself. But there was so much *more* available to me. Like my friend, I now feel free. Not every day. Not all the time. But in a way I never knew was available before.

Counseling has given me language for events that happened to me, for things I've experienced, for ways I react and cope. Counseling has given me fresh ways to pray for my healing and my future. It's given me tools for when I get into situations that trigger unhealthy emotions and responses, and footholds to stand on when things feel unsteady. Counseling has opened my eyes, showing me things that were never my fault even though I'd been shouldering the blame. It is liberating. And this freedom makes my life feel so much fuller.

"I have come that they may have life, and have it to the full," Jesus tells us (John 10:10).

Mental health struggles can hinder us from living this full life.

Jesus wants better for us.

More.

Jesus is a healer. In Scripture we find Jesus healing *all* the sick (Matthew 8:16), *all* who were ill (Matthew 4:24), and *all* who touched His cloak (Mark 6:56). These accounts of Jesus's healings do not separate physical from mental illness but include healing to anyone and everyone with any kind of ailment.

Today, Jesus still restores broken bodies, hearts, and minds. Sometimes through inexplicable miracles. Sometimes slowly during daily time with Him. Through repeated prayers. Through gradual discovery of what affects us and what we need to function better. And sometimes through the doctors, nurses, counselors, and therapists God created. Just like Jesus empowers medical doctors to help us heal from fractured bones and diseases, Jesus also equips mental health professionals to help us heal from emotional wounds, anxiety, depression, trauma, and other mental health disorders.

Christians struggle with their mental health just like non-Christians. But talking about mental health in the church isn't always simple. I have too many Christian friends who were told their faith wasn't "strong enough" because they were unable to manage their spiritual and emotional well-being solely by leaning on God's strength. And even if they weren't flat out told their faith wasn't up to par, they internalized those feelings. These friends were given Bible verses by well-intentioned members of their communities, such as "Do not be anxious" (Philippians 4:6), as the only remedy for their anxiety. And when they had a panic attack, they felt guilt or shame because they were told the Bible tells them not to panic. Listen, I love Philippians 4:6. I hold on to it and claim it. But it's not always that easy. Mental health struggles, just like a physical injury or disease, aren't always something we can snap our fingers or say a verse out loud or pray to make them go away.

Hear me out: reading the Bible, praying, and all the other aspects of a faith-filled life are incredible resources to give us strength and hope in our mental health challenges. For me, these things saved me from many downward spirals and honestly kept me afloat for decades. I'm also a firm believer in miracles. Yes, there have been instances when someone has prayed for a mental health ailment to be healed and it vanished! That is so glorious! But mental health, just like physical health, often requires a lifetime of attention and care. Mine does.

When our youngest was diagnosed with a hole in his heart at birth, my husband and I begged God for healing, opened the Bible, and filled our heads and hearts with His promises. We reached out to a small group of friends and asked for prayer. *And* we took our boy to see a pediatric cardiologist. When the doctor suggested an ultrasound for our baby, we had it done. When we were told to come back in two weeks, we found childcare for our other three littles and made the hour-long trek back down to the children's hospital with our newborn. Nobody told us we weren't trusting God or weren't praying hard enough during those hospital visits and tests. Seeking medical care was important and necessary as a complement to prayer.

I approach my mental health this same way. I pray, cling to Scripture, call out to Jesus, ask trusted friends to pray for me, *and* see a counselor. I take her expert advice. I read the books she suggests and attempt to incorporate the practices she recommends into my life.

My journey is just that: one person's journey and the observations, revelations, and chains that have been broken along the way. My journey has made me want to shout from the rooftops, "Jesus cares about your mental health!" Because He does. So deeply. But just hearing that from me, a woman you don't know, might not be enough for you. Because my experiences could be totally different from yours, I talked to over a dozen friends as well as some Christian mental health professionals. With their permission I'll also share pieces of their journeys, how they've struggled and triumphed, how their faith has been integral to both their everyday well-being and their hardest mental health battles. I'm not alone. And you're not alone.

Maybe you, like me, could benefit from counseling. Maybe you could just use some tips on how to relieve your stress or get out of a funk. Or maybe you're not reading this for yourself but for someone you care about. Wherever you're at, here's the bottom line: Jesus loves you. Every part of you. He made you, and He longs for healing and a full life for you. I'm praying this book inspires you to realize that your mental health matters, that Jesus cares about it. That it's not something to ignore or hide or try to manage by yourself. Jesus doesn't want you or me to be anxious or depressed or overcome by false narratives or past memories. He doesn't want us to withdraw from others or unnecessarily carry burdens we were never meant to bear. Christ doesn't want us to be enslaved to anything or anyone. And He doesn't want us to be alone.

Jesus invites us into abundant life. Free life. I'm praying this book helps you find the abundance and freedom that Christ came to give us.

So if the Son sets you free, you will be free indeed. (John 8:36)

Ready to find some freedom and fullness? Let's go!

1

Woven Together

How God Created You

In elementary school my class took a field trip to the Ohio Village, a replica of a nineteenth-century pioneer village. Throughout are actors posing as townspeople running the shops and homes as they would have in the 1890s, dressed in period dress. We stopped in a building set up to mimic a turn-of-the-century home to see how fabric was made. The woman donning a bonnet and calico apron inside explained how wool was sheared from sheep and then cleaned. She let us take turns carding the wool—passing around a large lump of fuzz and two paddle-like brushes called carders.

The wool was more of a vanilla caramel swirl than the white fleece of sheep depicted in storybooks. I can still hear the *thweh thweh* sound of the cards going through the dense wool, smoothing it, softening it. The woman explained how this carded wool was next rolled into a thick yarn, then showed us her spinning wheel, like the ones I'd only seen in fairy tales like "Sleeping Beauty" and "Rumpelstiltskin." She spun the yarn from the cards to refine it into thread. Lastly she took some of her freshly spun thread and walked us over to her wooden loom, where she demonstrated how the thread could be woven to create the fabric she would then cut and sew into clothing for her family. No wonder pioneer women only had a couple of dresses! Makes me extremely thankful for the luxury of clicking and adding to my cart whenever one of my kids needs new socks or a dress for prom.

The Bible tells us that before we were born, God intentionally crafted us together stitch by stitch:

> For you created my inmost being;
>> you knit me together in my mother's womb.
> I praise you because I am fearfully and wonder-
>> fully made;
>> your works are wonderful,
>> I know that full well.
> My frame was not hidden from you
>> when I was made in the secret place,
>> when I was woven together in the depths of
>> the earth.
> Your eyes saw my unformed body;
>> all the days ordained for me were written in
>> your book
> before one of them came to be.
> (Psalm 139:13–16)

The psalmist uses the words "knit" and "woven," which take me back to my field trip and the extensive process of knitting or weaving together something from scratch. Knitting or weaving a piece of clothing—or if you're God, a person—isn't something you decide to throw together on a moment's notice. It isn't something you do absentmindedly or because you're bored. It is a careful, intentional, time-consuming act.

I picture God whistling while He shears sheep and picks cotton, dyeing the fluff into a variety of colors, carding the thick fibers over and over until they're soft and subtle, smiling as He spins the thread on His spinning wheel until it's the perfect consistency. Once God has an assortment of threads to choose from, I imagine He patiently deliberates between fuzzy wool or sleek silk for this part of our body and that part of our mind. I envision Him choosing a combination of soothing neutral hues accented by bright, bold ones to make us strong or passionate about some things and more subtly inclined toward others.

God knew who we would be because He took so much thought and time to specifically design us before He ever started weaving—you and me, him and her, and every single human on earth. God considered what we'd need to stand up to the things that would come our way, to add the beauty and richness He wanted us to add to the earth, to navigate the relationships He knew we'd be involved in, to find joy, to feel His love, and to shine His light to the world. Then He wove it in, stitch by stitch, thread by thread.

God loves you so much! He put all this awesomeness in you.

And yet this world is a broken one. Where people leave us and let us down. Where tragedies and disasters take place. Where we get hurt or frightened or overwhelmed. And sometimes negative thought patterns get wonky or spiral or actually take over our minds. Just like our bodies are susceptible to physical ailments outside of Eden, our minds are susceptible to struggles too.

So you and me? We have days when we feel stressed, fatigued, anxious, depressed, overwhelmed, or like we could never face that thing or person. We might cry tears we didn't see coming, have a panic attack that freezes us mid-step, feel anger bubbling up unexpectedly, experience depression that keeps us in bed, or feel like we don't have enough of ourselves to go around. There are days we'll be downright scared or confused. But Jesus sees us in our struggles—nothing is hidden from Him. Nothing. Psalm 139 declares our frames weren't hidden from God in that secret place where He made us.

So now what?

1. God made us intentionally and wonderfully to inspire awe.
2. Sometimes we're a hot mess.

How do we remember who God made us to be when life is hard and our emotional well-being is fragile or shaky?

With God's grace and love. That's how.

Interestingly this psalm that declares how marvelously we were created by God ends like this:

> Search me, O God, and know my heart;
> test me and know my anxious thoughts.
> Point out anything in me that offends you,
> and lead me along the path of everlasting life.
> (vv. 23–24 NLT)

King David, who wrote this psalm, knew that God created him in amazing ways. But David was also aware he had anxious thoughts, worries, cares, and pain. He asked God to help him address those anxious cares, to help direct his feet back onto a glorious and everlasting path. One where he could flourish as God intended him to.

We can too.

God created us brilliantly. But our broken world brings mental health struggles our way. This isn't something new. It dates back at least to King David's time. And the way God's people dealt with it then is still the way God's people (that's you and me) can deal with it today. By going to God and talking to Him about our struggles, by allowing Him to point us where we need to go next.

God could lead some of us to Bible verses that calm our souls or simple practices to improve our mental health like breathing exercises or journaling. He could lead some of us to seek prayer or see counselors or take medication prescribed by a doctor or any combination of the above. But God *will* lead you back to His glorious, everlasting ways. He wants that for you. Because He loves you.

We can start right here and right now by inviting God to search our hearts. And our Maker, the one who wove you and me into beautiful tapestries, works of art designed to make people catch their breath, will lead us to ways to care for ourselves, inside and out.

Jesus Cares

> Search me, God, and know my heart;
> test me and know my anxious thoughts.
> (Psalm 139:23)

What mental health struggles have you experienced? List some of them here. Not for anyone else to see but just to get them out of your brain and into the open.

Ask Jesus to search your heart, to sift through your anxious cares and pain, and show you the next step you should take to get back to the glorious life He's always intended for you.

2

Allergies Are Real

So Are Your Mental Health Issues

"Achoo!"

"God bless you," my daughter Mallory said.

"Thank you," I said.

Our family continued watching *Jumanji* on the couches of the condo we'd rented. We'd had a lovely day at the beach and made pasta topped with olive oil and tangy Parmesan cheese for dinner. Now that the dishes were cleaned up, everyone was in their pj's (some of us with freshly applied aloe on bright red spots of skin that had gotten more than a bit too much sun). We were winding down after a full day.

"Aaaa—chhoo!" I sneezed again.

"God bless you," Max said this time.

And then I sneezed again and again, and my eyes started watering.

"You okay?" Brett looked me right in the eyes.

I glanced around, assessing the situation: the blue-striped couch, the smooth white-tiled floor, the bumpy beige knit blanket I'd draped across my lap. I tossed the blanket off, stood up to get a tissue, and sneezed again. "I think it might be this blanket. Or maybe the couch. Somebody probably had their dog in here."

"Pause the movie," Mallory said.

"Mom, you okay?" Maguire asked.

"Here, trade seats with me," Maddie suggested.

"Do you want to shower? Or maybe change?" Brett asked.

Everyone else in our family was totally fine. None of them had sneezed even once. None of their eyes were watering. Yet everyone acknowledged that I needed help. That my problem was valid. I'm allergic to fur, any animal with fur, actually the dander that clings to an animal's fur. And although we were in a pet-free unit, if the owner had taken a blanket from his home where his cat lived, or a maintenance person had brought along her dog while fixing the sink, or any other furry interaction had taken place in this condo, I could be sneezing all week.

Because my family knows me and loves me, they recognized I had a real situation going on. They stopped what they were doing to acknowledge my personal needs and help get me out of harm's way.

When you're allergic to something it affects your personal body chemistry. For whatever reason my body senses animal dander as poison and my immune system reacts accordingly. It's similar with our mental health issues. A crowd might trigger an anxiety attack for you but not for your friends who walked into the same jam-packed restaurant. A setback in your budget could cause an onset of depression for you while your sister calmly starts crunching numbers to find a way to make dollars stretch. Seeing a certain object or hearing a specific song could trigger a memory of past trauma for you while the rest of the world seems oblivious to the fact that you sense danger. But here's the thing: your mental health triggers are as real as my allergies are. Just because no one else in the room is experiencing those same symptoms does not mean that they're not valid or that they don't deserve attention. They are. And they do.

Your needs are real to Jesus too. He sees you. Right where you are.

Let me show you.

As Jesus and his disciples, together with a large crowd, were leaving the city, a blind man, Bartimaeus (which means "son of Timaeus"), was sitting by the roadside begging. When he heard that it was Jesus of Nazareth, he began to shout, "Jesus, Son of David, have mercy on me!"

Many rebuked him and told him to be quiet, but he shouted all the more, "Son of David, have mercy on me!"

Jesus stopped and said, "Call him."

So they called to the blind man, "Cheer up! On your feet! He's calling you." Throwing his cloak aside, he jumped to his feet and came to Jesus.

"What do you want me to do for you?" Jesus asked him.

The blind man said, "Rabbi, I want to see."

"Go," said Jesus, "your faith has healed you." Immediately he received his sight and followed Jesus along the road. (Mark 10:46–52)

The large crowd dismissed Bartimaeus and told him to be quiet. They didn't have time for him and his problems. They didn't see Bartimaeus's needs as urgent.

But Jesus did.

He heard Bartimaeus's cries. He believed Bartimaeus's needs were valid. He answered the call of this blind man everyone else ignored. Jesus healed Bartimaeus in the midst of a crowd. Was this so everyone could see how much Bartimaeus mattered to the Lord? That we all matter to our Savior? That no one should be ignored when they're struggling? I like to think so.

Jesus asked Bartimaeus what he wanted. This sounds odd at first glance. Clearly the blind man screaming for mercy at the top of his lungs on the side of the road wanted to be healed, wanted sight. But Jesus asked Bartimaeus what he wanted. Which I *love*. How personal. How intimate.

Jesus sees us too. And He longs for us to call out to Him in our need. In a quiet moment of prayer, listen for His whisper in your ear, in your heart, in your fragile mind, "How can I help? What is it you *truly* want?"

Sometimes we might be crying out that what we want is revenge or to be left alone or to numb our pain. But Jesus knows our hearts. He offers us so much more. And so He comes up close, so we can feel His loving presence, and says, "I know your hurt, panic, fear, depression, OCD, or addiction is real. What do you really want me to do for you?"

If you visualize looking into the eyes of the Prince of Peace, you can see the peace that emits from His gaze, feel the warm, safe love of His embrace. Ask Him to take you by the hand and help you see what you cannot on your own.

Jesus simply uttered the words "Your faith has healed you" to Bartimaeus. And it was so. Jesus saw him. Loved him. Healed him without asking for anything in return. And Jesus wants to guide you and me on the path to healing too. This doesn't usually mean that our mental health issue is forever resolved, although I have on rare occasions seen that take place. It's usually a way back to stability, a step toward recovery, a breath to calm us down.

Bartimaeus wasn't a one-off. This is what Jesus does. This is who He is.

> Jesus entered Jericho and was passing through. A man was there by the name of Zacchaeus; he was a chief tax collector and was wealthy. He wanted to see who Jesus was, but because he was short he could not see over the crowd. So he ran ahead and climbed a sycamore-fig tree to see him, since Jesus was coming that way.
>
> When Jesus reached the spot, he looked up and said to him, "Zacchaeus, come down immediately. I must stay at your house today." So he came down at once and welcomed him gladly. (Luke 19:1–6)

Zacchaeus was up in the branches of a tree. Sure, he was short, so it was hard to see what was going on. But the Bible also tells us he was a chief tax collector, which means he was disliked, probably despised. I'm guessing the crowd didn't make way for Zacchaeus to get to the front or to a place where he could see. Nobody would want to help a chief tax collector. I imagine Zacchaeus glancing left and right, hoping no one would notice him, climbing the branches of that sycamore tree, grateful for a safe spot to check things out, hidden from public view.

But Jesus saw Zacchaeus. Jesus stopped in His tracks and delayed whatever He was on His way to do. Jesus knew Zacchaeus needed healing. Not physical healing like Bartimaeus, but heart healing. Zacchaeus was a social outcast. Inviting Himself to Zacchaeus's house would change the way others saw Zacchaeus, give him a new chance, a new identity, and a renewed heart. Zacchaeus had been greedy before. Tax collectors were notorious for cheating people out of their money.

But that day, seen, noticed, invited, included, Zacchaeus was healed. His heart changed.

> Zacchaeus stood up and said to the Lord, "Look, Lord! Here and now I give half of my possessions to the poor, and if I have cheated anybody out of anything, I will pay back four times the amount."
>
> Jesus said to him, "Today salvation has come to this house, because this man, too, is a son of Abraham. For the Son of Man came to seek and to save the lost." (Luke 19:8–10)

Jesus invited Himself to Zach's house for dinner and announced that Zacchaeus was saved in front of the crowd. Because Jesus knew all the trials of Zacchaeus's heart without being told. Because Jesus noticed this troubled man when no one else did. Because Jesus understood what Zacchaeus was experiencing was real and that he needed help. Because Jesus came to seek and save the lost. He came to seek and save you and me.

Jesus sees me and knows I startle easily. Not just in scary situations. I get jumpy at things that are not at all threatening. Jesus doesn't judge me for this or ask me to get over it or dismiss it as dumb or not real. No. Jesus looks at me. Asks me what I need. Calls me down from my tree. And then guides me to more abundant life.

Jesus led me to a therapist who explained, "It makes perfect sense that you get startled easily. You lived through a time of past trauma when you were always on edge and on guard. You had to be. When things take you by surprise now, your instinct tells you to worry about what will happen next. Therefore, you startle."

I sat there listening to her with my jaw wide open.

My whole life I'd thought I was overly sensitive, easily frightened. I thought it was a flaw of mine. Something bad about me, like a personal blind spot. Turns out my body and psyche are trying to protect me. This is normal behavior for people who have been through what I've been through. It's not a weird quirk but a natural reaction. This is so freeing! And if Jesus hadn't connected me to my counselor, hadn't prompted her to explain things to me in this way, I wouldn't know. I'd still be judging myself for being hypersensitive and startling at inconsequential things. But Jesus sees us—Bartimaeus, Zacchaeus, me, you. He comes to seek and save the lost.

My friend Sherri gets claustrophobic. At funerals. At church. She describes having nausea, tunnel vision, a racing heart, and whooshing in her ears. She knows the people around her are not experiencing these same things. Sherri said, "God pointed me toward help, and I'm so thankful for it. My counselor helped me figure out my triggers and gave me some tools. If the thought of feeling trapped ever happens, I just pull out my tools. I love how God brings you a way out and a rescue!"[1]

Jesus wants to do this for you too. Bring you a way out. Bring you a rescue. When the insecurities rise. When your hands start to shake or your vision blurs. When you feel the tightness in your chest. When she calls. When he walks in the room. When you smell that thing that reminds you of what you'd rather not remember. Jesus is the one who always sees you in your distress. He acknowledges what you're going through is valid and never wants you to go through this alone. He loves you right where you are.

He might call you over or down like He did for Bartimaeus and Zacchaeus. He might lead you to the right counselor or make sure you get prescribed the right medication. Jesus might make sure that toxic person is a no-show. He might connect you to healthy friends who support you or give you the right words at the right time to protect you. Jesus could even cancel a meeting or obligation on your calendar to give you some much-needed rest. Jesus wants to help you heal from fear, shame, need, worry, panic, or sadness. He longs to guide you toward an abundant life, full of love, grace, and joy. That could look a million and ten ways. But our loving God will cater His care to you specifically.

If you think your problem is yours alone, or that Jesus wouldn't understand, that's simply not true. Jesus came down from heaven to walk this earth, so He could fully feel what humans experience. Betrayal by a trusted friend? Jesus experienced that with Judas Iscariot. Abuse from an authoritative figure? Jesus was whipped and hung on a cross by a government who should have been protecting innocent citizens. Childhood trauma? Jesus was born in a stable, abruptly moved to the foreign land of Egypt as a toddler because King Herod was having baby boys slaughtered, and just as abruptly moved to Nazareth approximately three years later. Poverty? Remember that born-in-a-stable part? Grief? Jesus mourned and wept over the loss of His dear friend Lazarus (John 11:35). Depression? The night before He was crucified, Jesus told His disciples, "My soul is overwhelmed with sorrow to the point of death" (Matthew 26:38).

Not only does Jesus see you in your mental health struggle, but He also went through similar situations so He would know how you feel, so He could love you even better in these moments.

Your issues are real. They are worth noting. You are worthy

of care. Just like my family saw me sneezing on vacation and knew I needed help. Just like Jesus saw Bartimaeus and Zacchaeus when no one else would give them the time of day, drew them close, and healed them on the spot. Jesus sees you. He loves you. He cares.

Jesus Cares

> When Jesus reached the spot, he looked up and said to him, "Zacchaeus, come down immediately. I must stay at your house today." So he came down at once and welcomed him gladly. (Luke 19:5–6)

Do you have any tendencies, habits, or impulses that others might not always take seriously, or that you might not offer grace to yourself about, like startling easily, claustrophobia, or needing to wash your hands more frequently than others?

Set a timer for five minutes. Get in a safe place and close your eyes (keep them closed until your timer goes off) and ask Jesus to help you claim these problems, that they happen to you, that you are worthy of care in those moments. Then ask Him to heal you, to bring you peace and clarity even if the healing is a long journey.

Share this struggle with someone you trust. Ask them if they'll be a go-to person for you when you have an episode or experience.

3

A Tale of Two Grandmas

You're Not Alone

My grandma was gentle, sweet, and kind. I remember her getting down on the floor to play paper dolls with me, sharing her secret dream of becoming a Rockette doing high kicks at Radio City Music Hall, her voice gravelly from countless cigarettes. I can feel the weight of the tiny pair of bronze slippers she had as a decoration on her coffee table, so tiny I could put my fingers in the feet and walk them across the table. Although her name was Mary Margaret, she went by Peggy. "Short for Margaret," she told me, although I never exactly understood how. She made me feel seen, like my stories and opinions mattered. I never heard Grandma say an unkind word about anyone.

My grandma was also an alcoholic.

When Grampa left Grandma for another woman and moved to California, she was left alone in Chicago. One brutal winter, Grandma slipped on the ice, broke her hip, and decided she'd had it. Both her cousin and her daughter (my aunt) lived in Sarasota, Florida. My grandma moved there, trading snow for sunshine, got a job at the local department store, and lived near two of her favorite people. She'd always had "her bourbon" before bed, but none of us thought anything of it. At least I didn't.

One afternoon Grandma's cousin called my dad and told him he had to come to Florida ASAP. Dad discovered Grandma passed out in her apartment surrounded by piles of empty bottles of bourbon and two liters of 7 Up. Apparently this mixture was her drink of choice. No one's sure when she started drinking too much. She'd lived alone for years. Had she always drunk so much? Too much?

How deep was Grandma's pain when Grampa left? What had my grandma endured as a child, as a young wife and mom whose husband went off to fight in World War II and then returned, and as a grown woman that I never knew about? Our family visited Grandma a couple of times a year, but as a little girl—and eventually a junior high and high school girl—I asked my grandma about her adorable cats that she treated like queens and the shells she found on the beach near her apartment, not about her mental health.

I never met my other grandmother, Violet. She died of breast cancer long before the medical advances of our time, when my mom was only a freshman in college. When someone mentions Violet, I picture either the photograph of this dark-haired beauty at my mom's house or the newspaper clipping my mom kept of her mother: "Mother of Three Earns PhD," the headline reads. In the late 1940s a woman getting her PhD—a mom no less—was remarkable. Violet went on to have two more babies, making her a mother of five. Also remarkable.

Similar to my grandma, my grandmother's husband left her for another woman. Grandad moved to Florida (not California), leaving her with five kids and no husband. I'm not sure when she started feeling the effects of her cancer, but she suffered for years. Violet also struggled with schizophrenia, often experiencing hallucinations and paranoia. As a little girl I'd look at her photograph and wish I had met her. I wanted to know her. I still would love to have known her.

When my mom was a girl she had to ride downtown on the bus with her mother to escort her to the Columbus State Mental Hospital (also known as the Hospital for the Insane—that was its actual name) for electroshock treatments. This was before they used anesthesia. She was wide awake for the whole thing, making this an extremely painful and traumatic experience. Can you imagine?

What did my beautiful, intelligent grandmother suffer? Who did she talk to? Anyone? How was she treated in a day and age when women were not encouraged to get PhDs, when divorce was considered scandalous, and when mental health issues were publicly labeled as "insanity"?

My heart breaks for both these women—my mom's and dad's mothers, my grandmothers. Women who were abandoned and suffering. Who lived in a time when no one openly discussed their troubles. Both my grandmas were churchgoers. But did anyone tell them that Christ was with them in their suffering? That He wasn't judging them but loving them? That it was okay to ask for help? That Jesus wanted to make people and doctors and resources available to ease their pain? Or did my grandmas suffer alone and afraid?

The two women never met. Which surprises me. My parents started dating when they were thirteen and were on and off all through high school. They only lived a couple of blocks away from one another. Certainly their mothers' paths should have crossed. But things were different then. There were no giant gatherings for prom pictures where parents chattered while snapping photos of their kids in gowns and tuxes. Even if Peggy had been at a school football game or a play cheering on my dad, Violet's hands were too full to attend school events when my mom was younger, and by the time my mom was in high school, Violet was too sick. If my grandmothers had met, would they have been able to confide in one another? Bear a bit of each other's burdens? Pray for one another?

I'll never know.

But I know about you and me. We live in a day and age where people are talking about mental health—praise Jesus! Where there are books and podcasts and social media accounts promoting awareness and care for our mental health. We live in a time when a football player like Ohio State's Harry Miller declares on *The Today Show* that he is giving up playing for one of the top five college teams in the nation to care for his mental health. We live in a day and age when Olympian Simone Biles withdraws from the Olympics, publicly stating the reason is to care for her mental health. These superstars didn't hide their mental health struggles—they spoke about them on national television!

It's commonly known in our culture that chemical imbalances, trauma, and genetics can literally mess with our minds, and that there are safe and proven ways to help. We are not only permitted but encouraged to care for our mental health.

Maybe you're not there yet. Maybe you're still nervous about what people will think, concerned about the stability of your job or marriage or friendship or leadership role if you're open about your mental health struggles. I get it. The gospel calls us to be brave and bold, but society doesn't always make it that easy.

But caring for our mental health is possible in God's

kingdom. Jesus is a healer. He's full of unfailing love and faithfulness (John 1:14 NLT). Jesus doesn't stigmatize anyone. He never did.

In Jesus's day leprosy was considered extremely contagious. No one wanted to get close to a leper no matter what. Lepers were outcasts forced to live in permanent quarantine. If lepers were anywhere near other people, they had to ring a bell and shout "Leper!" or some other obvious announcement that their contagious self was in the vicinity.

But Jesus didn't stigmatize those people suffering from leprosy.

> A man with leprosy came and knelt before [Jesus] and said, "Lord, if you are willing, you can make me clean."
>
> Jesus reached out his hand and touched the man. "I am willing," he said. "Be clean!" Immediately he was cleansed of his leprosy. (Matthew 8:2–3)

Did you see that?

In Jesus's time no one would touch a leper. But Jesus didn't hesitate. He saw the person behind the stigma, the human behind the illness. Jesus does the same for you and me. He reaches out when it seems no one else could possibly understand how we're feeling, when it feels scary to share with anyone what ails us, when we're worried about how people might treat or see us if "only they knew." And in those moments, in all moments, Jesus who is faithful offers us love and freedom. He might reach out to us by having us read an article or book that speaks to our exact situation, reminding us we are not alone. Jesus might reach out to us by having a friend call or text or ring the doorbell in the midst of a dark moment. He might reach out by having a stranger ask us a question or say hello, reminding us that we're seen. Jesus reaches out because He loves us.

When my grandmothers were going through their struggles, it was all hush-hush, because to announce what was going on was like ringing a bell or shouting out loud as they entered the room, "Depression! Schizophrenia! Alcoholism!" Which was not who they were, just an ailment they had. And it's certainly not what Jesus wanted for them or for us. Just like Jesus loved on those lepers then, He also loves people struggling with mental illness. He loved my grandmothers. I hope they knew. He loves you. I pray you know. And He doesn't want you to go through this alone. Jesus is on a mission to free us all from what ails us. And sometimes that freedom begins when we share our struggles with others.

In the process of writing this book, I became more aware than ever of the amazing women around me and how so many of them were also struggling with their mental health.

One friend messaged me, asking for prayer because she was anxious. Another told me on a walk that she had tried counseling before and it hadn't worked, but she was going to try again. I witnessed someone I love have a full-on panic attack. Another friend posted something on social media about her struggle with depression. All these women love Jesus, talk to Him, believe in Him, trust in Him. But life is hard, and struggles are real. What I saw and learned is that so many people around us are fighting mental health battles. Oh, I wish my grandmas knew this!

That woman you look up to? Her husband might be a high-functioning alcoholic and you would never guess it, but his addiction affects your friend and her mental health every single day.

That greeter at church who always wears the biggest smile and says something kind to you every week as you walk through the door? He might have experienced something traumatic long before you ever met him. He's never brought it up, because why would he mention that he was sexually assaulted as a child or survived a horrific accident or something else that he can't even bring himself to speak? But that thing caused damage and scars. His body and mind created methods of defense—some healthy, some not. He deals with triggers and flashbacks and lies he's believed and reactions he's had.

Your neighbor's daughter might be battling depression and in counseling. And your friend? She's trying to care for her daughter, the rest of the family, and her small business all by herself. She's stretched thin and so very worried about her girl.

A man on your committee might be bipolar. He faithfully takes his prescribed mood stabilizers, which makes his disorder undetectable to you, but they also make him consistently tired and upset his stomach. He puts on a brave face and always pitches in, acting like everything is great, but it's not.

Basically, we're not alone. According to the CDC, 50 percent of people in the United States will be diagnosed with a mental health disorder in their lifetime.[1] Half. Of all people.

I'm not for a moment saying your battle isn't painful or hard or unique. I'm simply saying that unlike my grandmothers, we don't have to deal with our mental health struggles in isolation. Statistically every other person you encounter could empathize with some of the things you're experiencing.

My sister-in-law told me, "The most impactful thing my mother ever did for me as a mom was articulating her mental health journey with me. It calmed my mind about what I was going through with anxiety. Talking with my mom took away all the stigma."

What if instead of keeping to ourselves, not wanting to "bother" anyone with our problems, not wanting anyone to think badly of us, putting on a happy face every time we went out and about, posting only sunshine and roses, and automatically answering that "everything's fine," we were honest when people asked how we're doing?

What if I was honest and you were honest and she was honest? Not telling the whole world about our dark days and compulsions but sharing with people we know are safe, who we trust will love and honor us. I'm not advocating pity parties, constantly complaining about all our woes, but I am inviting us to confide in people we trust, to shine light on dark places, to encourage each other in our challenging seasons.

Mental health issues tend to run in families, and as you can see my family has experienced both schizophrenia and addiction. So where does that leave me? Not cursed or doomed but seen by a beautiful Savior who loves me and walks each day of my life with me. Free to talk about my mental health struggles with caring family and friends. You are too! Whatever you or someone you care about is dealing with, you're not alone, they're not alone, we're not alone. We have Jesus who promises, "Surely I am with you always, to the very end of the age" (Matthew 28:20).

Jesus Cares

Jesus reached out his hand and touched the man. (Matthew 8:3)

Have you shared your mental health issues with anyone? Why or why not?

Close your eyes and picture Jesus reaching out and touching you. He has zero judgment about your mental health. He loves you as you are. He's reaching out to you.

Is there someone safe who you could share your struggle with today? A sister? Spouse? Small group member? Trusted colleague? Start with something small like "I'm feeling a little anxious." Or "I've been feeling kind of sad lately." Or "I'm struggling with my mental health." Or "I could really use some prayer." And go from there. Maybe even write down what you want to say ahead of time. If there's something specific your friend can do to help, ask them. You could say, "Would you mind checking in on me?" or "Could you listen for a few minutes?"

4

The Beehive

Community

If bees find nectar, they come back to their hive and do a dance to let the other bees know how far away, what direction, and what kind it is. If it's dark out and the bees can't see their bee friend dancing, it's not a problem; they can smell the pattern of this "waggle dance."

That's not all bees do for each other. They huddle together to keep warm, taking turns being on the outside of their cluster so every bee gets a chance to be on the inside where there's more heat. Bees clean each other off (honey can be quite sticky), care for one another if they're sick, and even create bridges by intertwining their legs with one another to help other bees over gaps in the hive that are too large to cross by foot and too small to fly across.[1] Bees thrive in community. And they set a beautiful example for us.

Community. We need it. God designed us for it.

Back when God was creating the world He created the heavens, earth, dark, light, sky, water, land, plants, fish, birds, and creatures. After God created all these things He paused, looked over His creation, and said, "This is good." Then God created the first human, Adam. And then, for the first time in history, we hear God saying something isn't good: "The LORD

God said, 'It is *not* good for the man to be alone. I will make a helper suitable for him'" (Genesis 2:18, emphasis added).

God knew it wasn't good for humans to be alone, but God knew how to fix that problem in a jiffy. He created helpers, partners, and relationships to get us through. People to listen to us, support us, laugh and cry with us, people who point us back to God and who He created us to be, and who we, in turn, point back to God's love when they stray.

Throughout the Bible we see God giving His people community to help them along their journeys. God gave Noah his family to help him endure the flood, Moses his brother, Aaron, to travel the wilderness together, and Ruth and Naomi each other to start a new life. Jesus gathered a group of friends around Himself, the disciples, so He didn't have to go about His three-year ministry alone. Jesus traveled, dined, and prayed with His disciples. It's like they were on a tour bus for three years together, only on foot, going from town to town to teach and heal the crowds. And when Jesus sent the disciples out to do good work, He didn't send them alone but in pairs to go into villages, perform healings, and tell people that the kingdom of heaven was near (Luke 10:1).

Jesus wants you to have community too. To have people in your life who help you get through whatever you're facing, help you process your pain and struggles, bring you joy and hope, point you back to Jesus, and travel your mental health journey with you.

Community is biblical and also scientific. My friend Dr. Robin Warner, a psychiatrist in California, told me, "Community is essential for mental health in a medical, concrete way. Being in community releases oxytocin, which protects our hearts." The Mayo Clinic says friendships increase our sense of belonging, give us purpose, boost our happiness, relieve our stress, improve our self-confidence, remind us of our self-worth, help us cope with trauma, and encourage us to have healthier habits.[2]

This makes so much sense! God knew having special people in our lives would be good for us, so He gave Adam a companion in Eve and kept giving people throughout history communities so we could be happier and healthier, both physically and mentally. Yet three out of five Americans describe themselves as lonely.[3]

Wait! God said it wasn't good for man (or woman) to be alone.

We need community. Even when we think we can do it on our own. Even when we're introverts (*raises hand*). Even when we're hesitant to approach someone else. Because life can be hard and messy, and when it is we need others to help us through the rough patches, see us through the muck, and point us back to the glorious life Jesus intends for us.

"My friends are my lifelines!" my mom exclaims when I ask her how community informs her well-being. "When I was going through my divorce, my friends and I went on walks together every day and talked about everything that was going on. It was so helpful. They were incredibly supportive. I went to see a counselor later, but as the divorce was taking place, my friends were what got me through." Mom nods, emphasizing how valuable her friends are for her. "Now I'm in a really good place, but on any given day my friends will shoot me an upbeat text or check to see how I'm doing. If one of them is sick or busy, I'll make a big batch of soup or a giant salad and take some to them so they don't have to worry about a meal. We celebrate each other's birthdays, swap books, pick one another up from the airport. We're a team. It's something really special!" Mom flashes her beautiful smile. "My friends and I often comment how God brought us all together here in this neighborhood at the same time. How we are so very blessed because of it."

I thank God my mom has these amazing people around her, loving her and holding her up. She does the same for all of them. I pray everyone reading these pages can find the kind of community my mom has. Mom and her group of friends call themselves "the Beehive."

If you have people around you who care, reach out to them, connect with them, allow them into your mental health struggles. Ask for help when you need it. Jesus didn't intend for you to brave this alone.

If you feel alone, start small and right where you are to find a healthy friend or two to connect with. Look around—who do you volunteer, work, play pickleball, or go to class with? My mom's friends met each other over a two-year period as one by one they all moved into the same neighborhood of condos. One of my best friends and I met when she was hired by my publisher to edit my first book. Through the process we exchanged a zillion emails and phone calls and became steadfast friends. I met another close friend when we were asked to teach a Bible study together at our local church. My sister-in-law's crew consists of the other parents from her son's baseball team. My friend Laura met her community in a college small group. Even though they graduated years ago and none of them live near their college town anymore, they're all still super close.

Who do you bump into at church, the pool, the grocery store? Who of these people do you think might be a good friend? Sit next to them. Engage in conversation before or after the game or meeting. Invite someone to join you on a walk. Invite another over for tea. If it all sounds like too much, try texting one friend you can trust. Engaging this way can be a beautiful stride toward connection. Take it one step at a time. But take that first step. And then the next.

Our communities might not do waggle dances or clean honey off of us, which is probably a good thing. But maybe, like my mom's group of neighbors, they'll pop in for a visit, drive us to a doctor's appointment, listen when we need to talk, give us a hug, or pray for us when we need comfort. If you ask Him, Jesus will put people around you to help you on your journey. It's what He wants for you and your emotional and spiritual well-being. He's been doing it from the beginning of time.

Jesus Cares

> The LORD God said, "It is not good for the man to be alone. I will make a helper suitable for him." (Genesis 2:18)

Do you have a supportive community (this could be family, friends, neighbors, people from your church, etc.)? Take a moment to thank Jesus for them. Then take a moment to thank them personally. Shoot a text, write a card—something to let someone who supports you know how much you appreciate them.

If you've struggled to find community, you can start today. Ask Jesus to help you find the right people, to help you find a place to start.

Consider joining a group, study, or class at a nearby church, library, or community center. You could invite neighbors over for brunch, coffee, or charcuterie, or join a recovery or support group like Al-Anon or a grief group. Volunteering is an amazing way to meet people. You could chair the pie-eating contest on the Fourth of July, pass out blankets to people experiencing homelessness with a local charity, or plan the end-of-year party for your granddaughter's preschool class. The goal is to connect with kind, caring people with some physical proximity to you and with a common interest.

Make a goal to get together with someone this week and a different person next week.

5

What's in a Name?

Naming Our Struggles

When you don't know the name for something, the truth gets complicated. If my husband says, "Let's go to that Italian restaurant we love," I might picture Via Vite, the trendy Italian spot with an outdoor patio overlooking downtown Cincinnati's Fountain Square. Brett might be referring to Nicola's, the cozy restaurant in the Over-the-Rhine neighborhood with an enclosed outdoor courtyard covered in twisty vines and tiny fairy lights. We love both of these scrumptious spots, but they are not the same thing. By not using the name of "that Italian restaurant we love," there could be confusion. I might meet my husband at the wrong spot or have false expectations of what our evening will look like or make a reservation at the wrong restaurant. Names are important.

As my kids were learning to talk, I'd narrate our lives nonstop, giving everything a name. "We're going to put on your blue jacket now. First one arm—your right arm. Good job! Now the other. This one is your left arm. Oops, your hand is stuck. Can you get it? Let Mama help you. There's your hand. That's right. Let's zip it up. Oh, the zipper is being stubborn. There we go. All set!"

Just by putting their jacket on I'd given my child names for the jacket, the color blue, their arm, their hand, me, left and right, and a zipper, even a word for when something doesn't work—*stuck*. Over hours and days and weeks they'd learn these words. Mimic them. Then learn to use them to communicate back to me and with others.

Names help us talk about things.

Names have always mattered. God thinks so too: "Now the LORD God had formed out of the ground all the wild animals and all the birds in the sky. He brought them to the man to see what he would name them; and whatever the man called each living creature, that was its name. So the man gave names to all the livestock, the birds in the sky and all the wild animals" (Genesis 2:19–20).

Back in the garden of Eden God let the first man, Adam, name every single creature. When Adam called the four-legged critter with a white stripe running down its long, wide black tail a skunk, it was a skunk. From that day forward if Adam or Eve saw a skunk, they could tell each other, "Careful, there's a skunk over there. Let's not scare him." And they would both know what they meant. Because they also knew when you scared the creature with the name "skunk," it would cause a big stink.

Names are helpful for understanding who or what we're talking about.

This holds true when naming our mental health issues.

My friend Sharee had been in a horrible car accident and struggled ever since with both a fear of dying and anxiety while driving, including panic attacks. Sharee knew something was wrong but didn't connect the dots until she was diagnosed with post-traumatic stress disorder (PTSD). Once she had a name for what was happening, it was so clear. Having a name for her PTSD allowed her to seek the correct treatment to address its effects on her life and eventually heal so she could comfortably drive and live again without fear.

Names matter.

My sister-in-law L.C. told me of a night she woke up feeling impending doom. "I felt dread, like I was going to die. I had chest pain, was nauseated, couldn't catch my breath, and had a fear I'd never felt before. Rationally I could say, 'I'm in bed in my home with my husband. The house is quiet.' I could tell my reaction did not match my reality—which was terrifying. I didn't know what to do and was completely paralyzed with overwhelming terror. I woke up my husband but couldn't find words to describe what was happening. I told him I might be having a heart attack."

Later L.C. was able to define what had happened as a panic attack. Having a name for what she'd experienced was priceless. The words *panic attack* enabled her to get more understanding and help from her doctor.

Naming our situations can be super helpful, just like naming poison ivy or a sunburn helps us soothe our red itchy arm. Sunburns and poison ivy get very different treatments. One you moisturize. One you dry out. If you don't know the name of what you're dealing with, you could actually make it worse. Knowing the name for a sunburn or a poison ivy rash gives you power—power to know what to do, how to handle things—both in the moment and in case your body should get that same uncomfortable red sensation again. Similarly, naming our mental health struggles helps us know how to treat and respond to what's happening in our minds and bodies. It can direct us to Bible passages that address certain issues, friends who have been through similar situations, and resources that discuss and provide solutions for our struggles. The National Alliance on Mental Illness explains that a diagnosis is an "important tool for you and your doctor" and a "starting point for learning more" ways to help yourself.[1]

Keep in mind that naming a mental health struggle is not the same as naming ourselves. L.C. is not a panic attack or panic. Sharee is not trauma or PTSD. Just like if you have poison ivy, you aren't poison ivy. You also *aren't* depression or anxiety or OCD or addiction or any other malady. You are still you. Even more important than knowing the name of our struggle is knowing *our* name. The name God Himself gives us.

In Genesis 17 God gives Abram and Sarai new names. Prior to their name changes they were senior citizens with infertility struggles. But God changed their names. Abram became Abraham, meaning "father of many nations," and Sarai became Sarah, meaning "princess." (Sarai also meant "princess," but God wanted to mark a change in Sarai's identity— that forever more she would be different.) Their new names were a symbol of a new identity. With their new names came a new destiny. Abraham and Sarah's new names were both a confirmation and reminder that they had more potential than they could imagine, that God had enormous, marvelous plans for them. They, who had struggled to get pregnant for decades, would become the parents of many nations.

Jesus gave His disciple Simon a new name: "Jesus looked at him and said, 'You are Simon son of John. You will be called Cephas' (which, when translated, is Peter)" (John 1:42). Cephas or Peter means "rock." Jesus gave Simon this new name to indicate that he would go from being a fisherman to being a rock for the church. And this same Peter, who was one of Jesus's best friends, tells us who we are, how God views us: "But you are a chosen people, a royal priesthood, a holy nation, God's special possession, that you may declare the praises of him who called you out of darkness into his wonderful light. Once you were not a people, but now you are the people of God; once you had not received mercy, but now you have received mercy" (1 Peter 2:9–10).

You and me, no matter what we've experienced or what we're struggling with, are chosen by God. Handpicked. He chose us before He even created us and meticulously put all our characteristics in us. God knows our thoughts and actions, and after seeing us at our best and worst says, "You over there with the scars on your wrists. You with the secret you don't want anyone to know. I choose you. I want you to be with me always."

We are royal. Maybe not with flowing robes and people obeying our orders, but worthy of the beauty and riches God offers—not gold and jewels, but life and love everlasting, healing and wholeness that are priceless.

We are holy. Yes, even despite everything we've been exposed to or attempted or been addicted to. When Jesus died on the cross, He took all our sins. And He didn't just clear our slates; He elevated our status beyond what we could ever deserve. Pastor and theologian Tim Keller says, "In the gospel we discover that Jesus has taken us off death row and then has hung around our neck the Congressional Medal of Honor. We are received and welcomed as heroes, as if we had accomplished extraordinary deeds."[2]

Amazing, isn't it?

We are God's special possessions. Think of your favorite possession—a family heirloom, a historic coin, a letter from someone you love, your most expensive piece of jewelry. Where do you keep it? How do you treat it? How much value do you put on it? That's how God sees you. Priceless.

If you've struggled with mental health, you've experienced darkness. But God has "called you out of darkness into his wonderful light." This doesn't mean you'll never have a dark day again, but it does mean that the light of Jesus is always with you, always guiding you to something better, to the calm after a storm, peace after chaos, healing after harm. Even when things feel heavy or scary, the gentle glow of Christ's light is there to comfort you, provide you warmth, or light a path to a safer place.

You are a child of God. You have received Christ's mercy. Nothing can change that—not a relapse or an attack or a trigger or an episode. You will always be God's beloved child. His mercy is always available to you. Forever.

This is the truth of who you are. This is your real name. *Child of God.*

Names matter.

When we don't have a name for a mental health struggle we're battling, it's so much harder to know how to handle it. With names for our issues and ailments we can seek help, gather the correct tools, start the healing process, continue to grow, and move forward. And when we understand our names, our true names—*Chosen, Royal, Holy, Special, Child of God*—it changes everything.

Jesus Cares

But you are a chosen people, a royal priesthood, a holy nation, God's special possession, that you may declare the praises of him who called you out of darkness into his wonderful light. Once you were not a people, but now you are the people of God; once you had not received mercy, but now you have received mercy. (1 Peter 2:9–10)

Do you have names to describe your mental health struggles? If not, consider talking to a mental health professional about what you're experiencing to help you name or pinpoint some of your struggles.

What are some negative labels that have been put on you throughout your life (by you or others)?

Cross those out and write over them *Chosen. Royal. Holy. Child of God.* Sit with Jesus for a few minutes and ask Him to show you how these words are true about you. Ask Him to let these real names for you sink into your soul.

6

Time for an Upgrade

Replacing Old with New

This year it feels like everything in our home needs to be replaced. The cookie sheets I got as a wedding gift twenty-six years ago are warped. When I bake cookies, the dough balls slide to the middle of the pan and morph into one giant cookie. The towels we bought for our first home have holes and their ends are frayed. The skillet I've used to sauté countless vegetables, make an incalculable number of grilled cheeses, and brown taco meat for endless Taco Tuesdays has lost its nonstick coating.

And so one by one we've replaced these things. I asked for new cookie sheets and a skillet for Christmas. Glamorous, right? But the new cookie sheets are large and flat and even have an edge that keeps vegetables from sliding off the pan when roasting them. My new skillet is easy to clean because nothing sticks to it. I shopped a clearance sale on towels and was able to get new ones for 65 percent off. They are thick and plush and feel like they belong in a palace. Quite the upgrade compared to our old threadbare ones.

And you know what I've said as each new item arrived and I've either pitched the old items or put them in a donate pile?

"What an upgrade!" Immediately followed with "Why did I wait so long?"

I waited because it felt expensive. I waited because it felt unnecessary. I waited because it felt like one more thing to do on an already long list. But it was past time. And the replacements were so worth it—actually even better than the originals when they were new.

The same holds true when it comes to our mental and spiritual well-being. God invites us into new. To get rid of old lies, habits, feelings of shame, or fears or worries that consume us.

> See, I am doing a new thing!
> Now it springs up; do you not perceive it?
> I am making a way in the wilderness
> and streams in the wasteland. (Isaiah 43:19)

Just like God told the nation of Israel it was time to move forward out of the wilderness, He invites us out of old negative beliefs and coping mechanisms into new, healthier thought patterns and behaviors.

And we hesitate. Because investing in a conversation with a counselor, mentor, trusted friend, or pastor feels expensive—like we'll use up our time and their time and it will cost us vulnerability.

We put off exchanging old unhealthy habits for new healthy ones because it feels easier to keep going in the same toxic relationship or with the old way of processing things, the one we've known for so long, or to stay in denial because then we don't have to face our problems, even though they might be overtaking us. We rationalize that even though the way we're doing things doesn't work well, we know how long to metaphorically cook things on the pan that's lost its stick or the warped cookie sheets. We know what to expect.

Sometimes tending to our mental health feels like an additional thing we need to do when we already feel overwhelmed, possibly to the point of anxiety or depression. We might wonder, What if adding steps to care for ourselves or trying a new process overwhelms us even more?

But according to *Psychology Today*, the best way to get rid of bad habits is by learning and replacing them with new and different ones.[1] It's not just stopping the old way of doing something—that can be super hard to do. But replacing old ways of thinking or doing with new thoughts or actions actually trains our brains to make a permanent switch.

Sometimes replacing the old with new feels hard, but Jesus will do this with you. He loves you so much; He says He's doing a new thing; He's making a way. It doesn't all depend on you. You have a Savior who wants to clear the path for you. Will you let Him?

What could that look like?

For me, Jesus cleared a path by having my therapist help me pinpoint a particular memory that had traumatized me and made me feel powerless for decades. She and I walked through that instance using a psychotherapy method called eye movement desensitization and reprocessing (EMDR). It's a process that gets your right brain and left brain working back and forth together to take an old bad memory and reprocess it with new thought patterns. By taking that incident from the past through EMDR, I'm now able to see that what happened that day no longer has power over me. I traded old for new. Instead of experiencing the extreme fear and panic I used to have when triggered, I now visualize myself kicking my trigger down and watching it crumble while I fly away.

For my friend Betsy, Jesus also made a way through EMDR. Her ex-husband unexpectedly and traumatically left her and her daughter. "There was a part of that evening that I had a visceral response to every time I talked about it," she says. "Taking that memory through EMDR taught me to stop focusing on what my ex did and instead to focus on the beauty of the Lord meeting me there, on what God did for me in that moment." Betsy upgraded from the threadbare actions of her ex-husband to the plush love of Jesus. (Please note that EMDR should only be done under the direction of a certified therapist.)

Jesus gave new approaches to a friend of mine who struggles with OCD through her counselor challenging her to each day leave at least one thing that she really wanted to move or straighten where it was, to not touch it even though it was driving her bonkers. Another friend keeps a strict routine to help her feel more in control, but when plans change, anxiety sweeps in. Jesus helped create a new pathway for her by having her counselor suggest she change things up a bit, intentionally altering her routine some days so when an unexpected change comes it doesn't throw her as much.

Replacing old habits and reactions with new. It's good for our souls, even if it's challenging. Walking through that memory with my counselor was h-a-r-d. She was kind and attentive, making sure I stayed mentally and emotionally safe throughout the process. She helped me find peace and pauses if things got too intense. It was still painful, but the result? So worth it. My friends I mentioned don't like letting things be messy or changing up their schedules. It's difficult for them.

But it's also teaching them to let go of trying to be in control and to trust God more fully so they can find more peace.

When the Israelites were freed from slavery, they whined and complained about their new free life. Why? Because change is hard. "The Israelites said to [Aaron and Moses], 'If only we had died by the LORD's hand in Egypt! There we sat around pots of meat and ate all the food we wanted, but you have brought us out into this desert to starve this entire assembly to death'" (Exodus 16:3).

God knew this was difficult for the Israelites. And because He is a good and loving Father, He provided them with food day and night in the desert.

> The LORD said to Moses, "I have heard the grumbling of the Israelites. Tell them, 'At twilight you will eat meat, and in the morning you will be filled with bread. Then you will know that I am the LORD your God.'"
>
> That evening quail came and covered the camp, and in the morning there was a layer of dew around the camp. When the dew was gone, thin flakes like frost on the ground appeared on the desert floor. When the Israelites saw it, they said to each other, "What is it?" For they did not know what it was.
>
> Moses said to them, "It is the bread the LORD has given you to eat." (vv. 11–15)

Just like God saw the struggling Israelites, Jesus sees you as you're trying to heal. He sees you as you ache to leave the slavery of your struggles behind, as you're taking steps to new, healthier practices. Jesus hears you as you confide in someone you trust. He sees you when you faithfully take the prescription your doctor has prescribed. Jesus is right next to you when you choose whispering a prayer, breathing deeply, or practicing self-care over the way you used to handle your triggers. Jesus says, "I hear you. I see you. I'm going to send what you need. I'll take care of you in the mornings and the evenings. I'll clear a path for you. It might be different than how things were before. The process might take a while. That's okay. I'll be with you through it all. I want to make you new."

Jesus probably won't have a flock of quail fly over your kitchen in the evenings or have a layer of manna appear on your floor, but He might provide a friend or therapist who is the best listener. He might have your doctor prescribe a medicine that is life changing. He might create a healthy distraction that keeps you from reaching for the thing you know you shouldn't grab. Jesus might help you discover how therapeutic bike rides or journaling or making homemade pasta or sitting on your back deck with a neighbor is for you. I don't know what new things He'll want to do in your life, but I do know Jesus wants us to be renewed and restored.

That might include some of the treatments or practices above, or it might be replacing unhealthy eating habits with healthy ones or replacing doing something harmful every time you feel worried with petting your dog when you get that same anxious feeling. Jesus is all about doing things in new and improved ways.

> Neither do people pour new wine into old wineskins. If they do, the skins will burst; the wine will run out and the wineskins will be ruined. No, they pour new wine into new wineskins, and both are preserved. (Matthew 9:17)

> Therefore, if anyone is in Christ, the new creation has come: The old has gone, the new is here! (2 Corinthians 5:17)

Jesus invites us into new, better, and healthier ways to care for our physical, spiritual, and mental well-being. Jesus urges us to pick up new life-giving habits and rhythms, to take off any damaging or toxic old practices and put on our new, healthier selves that deserve new wineskins. Jesus's new ways far exceed the plushness of a new towel or the reliability of a new pan. He'll upgrade your life in ways you never dreamed possible and maybe even prompt you to ask, "Why did I wait so long?"

Jesus Cares

> See, I am doing a new thing!
> Now it springs up; do you not perceive it?
> (Isaiah 43:19)

Ask Jesus if there is anything old in your life that you could get rid of to care for your mental health.

Is there anything stopping or impeding you from stepping into some healthier practices?

Close your eyes and ask Jesus to make you new. Give Him anything you mentioned that might be in your way. Ask Him how you can let go, move forward, step out of whatever is holding you back or down. Sit still for five minutes and note anything you sense Jesus might be sharing with you.

Take that first step today. I'm praying for you as I write this that you'll have the courage to do it, that you'll lean into Jesus as you go, that you'll remember He's with you, making a way in your wilderness.

7

Skyline Dip and Brownies

Memorizing Scripture

"Mom, do we have the stuff to make Skyline dip?" my youngest asked when I picked him up from school. "We're supposed to bring food into homeroom tomorrow."

"Of course. We can make it when you're done with your homework."

As a mom of four I'm often called on at the last minute to produce a snack, side dish, dip, or dessert—for the pregame event, banquet, picnic, class party, you name it. And I'm happy to do it. But sometimes I get very little notice. Like none. So I've learned to be prepared. I try to always have the ingredients on hand needed to make Skyline dip or to whip up a batch of brownies. This arms me with a savory and a sweet option.

Both these foods take barely any time, use few ingredients, and allow me to ensure my kids with food allergies have something safe to eat. I prepare both dishes nut and gluten free. If I send brownies with one of my kids to a sleepover, I add unsweetened chocolate to my cart the next time I'm at the store. If I bring Skyline dip to the cross-country picnic, the next time I get groceries I add cream cheese, Skyline chili, shredded cheddar, and Fritos (the scoopy kind) to my cart.

When I get home, I have to hide the Fritos so no one randomly snacks on them, leaving me without this essential ingredient. And the next time there's a bring-a-dish emergency, I'm restocked and ready.

The brownies are my favorite, rich and fudgy, way better than from a box and just as simple. I don't even like the cheesy chili dip, but my kids do, and it always gets polished off.

Just like I have a couple of recipes ready to whip up at any given time, I also have some Scripture memorized to pull out at a moment's notice. Not for a banquet or potluck, but for when I'm confronted with something that might compromise my mental health. You might want to have some at the ready for when you find yourself experiencing a panic attack or sense a wave of depression coming on, or for when your will power wanes and you're reaching for something or someone you know is unhealthy, maybe even toxic for you. Maybe you need these verses when you think you might do something out of control or feel yourself retreating. In desperate times, our thinking isn't always sharp. We may go into fight-or-flight mode, but if we have a few powerful verses memorized, then we will be armed and ready for our mental health battles. We're not called to fight them on our own.

The apostle Paul describes the struggles of our fallen world in Ephesians 6:12: "For our struggle is not against flesh and blood, but against the rulers, against the authorities, against the powers of this dark world and against the spiritual forces of evil in the heavenly realms." If you've ever wrestled with your mental health, you might agree that sometimes it feels way beyond your control, and that Paul had it right when he talked about there being "powers of this dark world" and "forces of evil" against us. Sure, we might have a bad day or episode simply because we're tired or hangry, but sometimes there's something more powerful working against us.

I love that Paul doesn't leave us hanging with this threat of spiritual warfare but instead shows us how God equips us to handle the evil forces against us:

> Therefore put on the full armor of God, so that when the day of evil comes, you may be able to stand your ground, and after you have done everything, to stand. Stand firm then, with the belt of truth buckled around your waist, with the breastplate of righteousness in place, and with your feet fitted with the readiness that comes from the gospel of peace. In addition to all this, take up the shield of faith, with which you can extinguish all the flaming arrows of the evil one. Take the helmet of salvation and the sword of the Spirit, which is the word of God. (vv. 13–17)

I've always loved this passage. And I cling to every piece of that armor. But the last bit is what we're going to focus on here: "Take . . . the sword of the Spirit, which is the *word of God*" (emphasis added). In Scripture, the "Word of God" refers to both Jesus and the Bible, which is super cool. We can take the Word of God (Jesus, who is our defender and protector) and the Word of God (the Bible and all the truth it holds about who God is and who we are in Him) and use it as a sword to fight the evil forces against us. Pretty awesome.

> All Scripture is God-breathed and is useful for teaching, rebuking, correcting and training in righteousness. (2 Timothy 3:16)

> It is the same with my word. I send it out, and it always produces fruit. It will accomplish all I want it to, and it will prosper everywhere I send it. (Isaiah 55:11 NLT)

All Scripture is God-breathed. All of God's Word accomplishes what He wants it to. But which Bible verses should we have on hand to whip out in the moment of battle?

That depends on you. God says *all* of it is useful. Which verses in Scripture help *you* cling to the truth, joy, love, strength, and grace Christ offers? Everyone needs different standbys. It's just like how my friend Beth sends in potato skins to any potluck or event because they're affordable to make for a crowd while my friend Michelle takes veggie trays to her church dinners or a volleyball banquet because she doesn't like to cook, and I stick with my Skyline dip and brownies. We all have different standbys for different reasons. All effective and helpful.

My dad left us several times while I was growing up. Little-girl Laura equated his leaving with me not being lovable. This created long-term wounds that I'm working through with Jesus and my counselor. When the Enemy tries to tell me, "Your dad didn't love *you* enough to stay," or "Why would anyone want to stay with you?" I pull out Matthew 28:20 where Jesus declares, "And surely I am with you always, to the very end of the age," reminding myself that Jesus will never walk out on me. Or I go to Isaiah 43:1–4 where God says,

> I have summoned you by name; you are
>   mine.
> When you pass through the waters,
>   I will be with you;
> and when you pass through the rivers,
>   they will not sweep over you.
> When you walk through the fire,
>   you will not be burned;
>   the flames will not set you ablaze.

> For I am the LORD your God,
>   the Holy One of Israel, your Savior;
> I give Egypt for your ransom,
>   Cush and Seba in your stead.
> Since you are precious and honored in my sight,
>   and because I love you.

And suddenly those lies from the Enemy don't hold any weight.

These verses are ultrapowerful *for me*. On days I'm shaky, on days when I'm not thinking clearly, I return to these verses from Scripture again and again. They are my go-to armor. And they cut my doubts like a sword.

These verses might not hit you hard. Sure, they matter. But you have other things you're grappling with. My friend Chad had an addiction God has helped him overcome. He clings to these verses: "You were taught, with regard to your former way of life, to put off your old self, which is being corrupted by its deceitful desires; to be made new in the attitude of your minds; and to put on the new self, created to be like God in true righteousness and holiness" (Ephesians 4:22–24). It reminds Chad that his past doesn't define him. Jesus does. And Jesus says Chad is righteous and holy. He doesn't have to slip into old patterns. He is being renewed.

My friend Elisa Morgan has been seeing a counselor on and off for almost forty years to help her maneuver "adoption, parenting, grandparenting, identity issues, career and life changes, loss, and grief—you know, the things of life." She has a favorite verse to help her when she feels overwhelmed: "I have told you these things, so that in me you may have peace. In this world you will have trouble. But take heart! I have overcome the world" (John 16:33). Elisa finds peace in these words Jesus spoke. He said flat out that we will experience trouble. Life isn't going to be easy breezy all the time. But Jesus doesn't want us to freak out or get overwhelmed. He's stronger, more powerful, wiser. If we cling to Jesus, we'll be okay. We'll find peace.

You get the idea.

Clinical psychologist Dr. Regina Josell also talks about how helpful this practice of speaking truth and encouragement over ourselves can be. She says, "Write down encouraging words you can read to yourself during a panic attack."[1] She suggests you tuck these words or statements of affirmation "in your pocket or purse or type it into your smartphone notes so it's easy to access."

Having Bible verses written out as our "scripts" or even a few words from a verse as a phrase to repeat doesn't solve every problem. But it does diminish the power of darkness. Because you know what knocks a lie off its feet every time?

Truth.

Scripture is what Jesus used when Satan tempted Him in the desert. Satan threw out some twisted temptations based on lies that God wasn't enough and that Satan offered something better. And Jesus flung back truth from Scripture He'd memorized (Matthew 4:1–11). This went on for a while, and after Jesus spoke truth out loud three times, "then the devil left him" (v. 11). That's right. Truth makes Satan run away.

For me, Scripture doesn't erase the wounds I have from my childhood, but it brings comfort. It helps me change my focus from my fears to my calming, loving God, from lies to truth. Speaking Scripture out loud, whispering it in prayer, writing it down, or opening to the pages where it's printed in my Bible makes me less shaky, reminds me who I actually am (a beloved child of God), and helps me take the next breath or step.

There will be situations where even though you're recalling Scripture, you will also have to do something about your surroundings, your companions, what's in your hand. If you require treatment or physical protection of any kind, please seek that quickly. Just know that you can continue to whisper truth from the Bible as you walk out of the room, as you wait for someone to answer the phone, as your medication kicks in, or as you regain your breath.

I often go to Psalm 23 when I wake up from a nightmare, repeating in my head over and over, *The Lord is my shepherd. I shall not want. He makes me lie down in green pastures. He leads me beside still waters. He restores my soul* (see vv. 1–3).

When we speak Scripture, it doesn't matter if we get the words one-hundred-percent right. It's the fact that we're turning to God in a time of trouble. That we're believing His promises are true. When I recite this psalm I learned as a little girl, I'm saying out loud that I believe God will protect me and give me what I need. That He will help me get rest from my troubles, even when I can't get rest for myself. That He will lead me to refreshing stillness. That God will restore me.

He can restore you too.

These go-to verses are wonderful tools to recalibrate, just like go-to brownies and Skyline dip are wonderful dishes to always have up my sleeve. But I'm not always making snacks and appetizers on the fly. I enjoy planning out meals for my family for the week, making a grocery list to get the right ingredients, spending time stirring and simmering. I'm also not always flinging out Bible verses in a challenging moment.

I'm a huge fan of reading my Bible every morning and seeing what God has in store for me on the pages. I love doing Bible studies to dig deep into themes or books of the Bible. But sometimes I need to bring food on a moment's notice, and sometimes we have little or no warning when we need to pull out Scripture to help fight our mental health battles.

Some situations call for something sweet—verses to soothe, calm, and reassure us, like fudgy brownies. And in others we need something salty—verses to help us get fired up, stand strong, and fight our battles, like spicy Skyline dip. Having a few verses memorized is like having the right ingredients stocked in your pantry ready to go, so you can fight the Enemy, renew your energy, remember who you are in Christ, celebrate something amazing God has done, discern which way to go, or hold on when you feel like you're slipping.

The best way to find the verses you need is by regularly engaging with your Bible. Asking friends, pastors, or your counselor for some passages is also a great idea. But find two or three verses that arm you for battle. Post them on your mirror, desk, fridge, or steering wheel. Write them on the inside of your journal or make them the wallpaper on your phone. My oldest daughter has "I can do all things through Christ who strengthens me—Philippians 4:13" tattooed on her forearm. Just put them somewhere you can access them easily. Before you know it, these verses will be written on your heart.

Because I've made my brownies and Skyline dip so many times, I no longer need a recipe for either. I just know what to do. In the same way, the more you read and speak the Bible verses that hold you up, the more these words from God's living Word will automatically pop into your mind. You'll throw that truth out and the Enemy will flee. Light will shine in a dark space. You'll have a chance to catch your breath. A Bible verse won't solve all our problems, but it knocks the Enemy off his feet, gives us a foothold where we can steady ourselves, and positions us to climb to safety.

Jesus Cares

It is the same with my word. I send it out, and it always produces fruit. It will accomplish all I want it to, and it will prosper everywhere I send it. (Isaiah 55:11 NLT)

Do you have a go-to verse memorized that you can pull out in a mental health crisis or when things just feel off?

If so, take time to learn another verse this week. If not, use this week to memorize one. It can be a passage we talked about in this chapter (Isaiah 43:1–4; Matthew 28:20; Ephesians 4:22–24; John 16:33; Psalm 23; Philippians 4:13) or an entirely different one. Try writing it out every day or saying it out loud every morning and night—whatever helps you commit these words of truth to memory.

8

The Forgotten Moka Pot
Rediscovering Lost Goodness

My older son, Max, liked coffee before, but his part-time job as a barista sparked a deeper love and appreciation of coffee in him. He was gifted some fancy beans from the coffee shop where he worked, but they were of little use in our coffee maker at home that uses pods. Max was so excited about those beans, though. He showed them to me, explained in detail about their tasting notes, and let me smell their rich aroma. He shrugged, saying he guessed he'd take them into work sometime to grind them there and bring them back home to use in his Mr. Coffee that he usually only plugged in for larger gatherings.

"We have a grinder here," I offered.

"What?" He looked astonished.

"Sure. It's in that cupboard." I pointed. "The little white thing with the cord and the clear top."

Max pulled down the coffee grinder, amazed that we'd had that hiding in our kitchen all this time. I showed him how it worked, and he started grinding. "I wish we had a French press," he remarked over the whirr of grinding beans.

And as he said it, I pictured my little silver pot. Not a French press, but similar—a moka pot. I'd gotten it decades ago when I was young and studied abroad and wanted to recreate that European cup of coffee back stateside. I hadn't used it in years. I'd considered throwing it in the giveaway pile a time or two but could never bring myself to do it. I knew right where it was, pulled it down from its shelf, and handed it to Max.

"I have this," I said.

At that point he started laughing. "I wouldn't be surprised if you pulled a full-on espresso machine down next."

I cleaned the dust out of my moka pot—hot water only, no soap—and dried it with a red-and-white kitchen towel. The next morning I googled how to use a moka pot, thinking I remembered but wanting to be sure. I put water in the bottom and some ground coffee my husband had received as a gift in the aluminum filter, screwed on the top, and set it on the stove. I couldn't remember how long it took. I couldn't remember how I would know when it was ready. But I watched and waited. And then my pot sang to me, a gurgling tune of water steaming, coffee brewing and climbing up into the top of the pot. I peeked a couple of times, and when it was ready it poured so prettily in a thin arching stream into my mug. I added a splash of almond milk and one spoonful of sugar.

That first sip took me immediately to a café in Paris with a cane-backed chair facing the boulevard, a tiny white bowl with sugar cubes sitting in front of me. Chill in the morning air as tourists and Parisians shuffled by along the cobblestone side street. Me with nowhere to go but this café and wherever I wandered that day.

I'd remembered I liked the coffee from this pot, but I'd forgotten that I *loved* it. That it tugged at something deep inside me. That it stirred memories of a place I feel so connected to.

How could I have forgotten about something I loved so much? How could I have stopped using it?

Throughout the years of my life, jobs, moves, relationships, interactions, raising kids, and taking classes, a bazillion new memories from each phase had entered my brain. The moka pot was pushed back into long-term memory somewhere and apparently not needed until now. There are other beautiful parts of our lives, ourselves, our personalities that are buried back in our minds from a time before. We'll talk plenty in this book about getting rid of false narratives and stepping into new truths. But taking care of our well-being isn't all about fixing broken pieces; it's also about reclaiming some beautiful parts of ourselves that we may have forgotten.

My friend Laura tells me, "I have a playful side to myself, but mental health and life circumstances made walls close in on that. For a period of time, several years, I felt super serious, and my silly side was hidden. Through therapy I rediscovered play and fun and laughter." Laura continues, "I also love to travel solo. But my anxiety and depression made me fearful of taking trips alone. Through caring for my mental health, I've remembered that I'm strong and independent and that I can do this! I don't have to be limited by my mental health issues. I feel like these parts of me have been redeemed. I can enjoy the things that make me me."

Perhaps you used to be more brave or social or creative or adventurous. Maybe you used to laugh more easily, but hard things or unkind people or social comparisons or lies of the Enemy or of this world have come your way and you've developed coping mechanisms to, well, cope. Taking care of your mental health can restore these beautiful parts of yourself that God put in you in the first place and reinstate living to the full.

As Miriam Smolover, a therapist, says in regard to mental health recovery from abuse, "It takes great courage to work through problems caused by the abuse. Your body may feel like a battleground over which you fight ghosts who have great power, reclaiming territory which is your birthright."[1]

I love that she says "reclaiming" something that's our "birthright." I equate our birthrights to all the things God gave us when He created us, the things He always intended to bring us joy, the parts of our personality that He always wanted us to embrace that may have been buried or stifled by assaults on our well-being, like my friend Laura's playful side.

Jesus wants to restore us. To return us to who we were always intended to be. To bring back the beautiful memories, the endearing qualities, the freedom and joy He always intended for us to have, the things He considers our birthrights. Matthew 9, Mark 5, and Luke 8 all recount the day a woman who had been bleeding for twelve years sought Jesus in a crowd. This physical ailment would have marked this woman as unclean according to Jewish law. She would have had to quarantine. And if she touched anyone—yikes! That person would be considered unclean as well. For her to go out in a crowd was audacious. To reach out and touch Jesus was the move of a woman in complete desperation. She would be shamed and punished and ridiculed and chastised for such irresponsible, dangerous, and unholy behavior. But she was so very desperate. Who wouldn't be after twelve years of isolation?

The Bible tells us as soon as she touched the edge of Jesus's cloak, "immediately her bleeding stopped and she felt in her body that she was freed from her suffering" (Mark 5:29). She was instantly restored. To a woman who wasn't bleeding. Who wasn't unclean. Who wasn't ostracized and forced to stay away from everyone else. She had been healthy and free to socialize before this twelve-year period began. And once again she was free. "[Jesus] said to her, 'Daughter, your faith has healed you. Go in peace and be freed from your suffering'" (v. 34).

Jesus healed her. Freed her.

Jesus wants to do the same for you and me.

How? The bleeding woman had to take some risks. She had to leave where she was quarantining and go out in the open, which she wasn't supposed to do. People knew who she was. She was probably known as "the bleeding lady" or some other negative nickname or label. Getting through the crowd unnoticed with that kind of notoriety would have been tricky. Like the woman, if we want healing, we have to be willing to take risks and step into them. Scripture tells us there was a large crowd pressing on Jesus. To get up to Jesus, the woman would have had to be both intentional and bold. But she did it. Because she wanted healing. Because she believed Jesus could give it to her.

I also want healing. You?

I believe Jesus can heal me because I believe the Bible is true. And it tells of Jesus healing the blind, the lame, and the lepers, casting out demons, raising the dead, and stopping this woman's bleeding. He can heal us too.

So how do we boldly step into the crowd?

The first step is declaring that our mental health matters, that it deserves attention. We're told the woman had seen many doctors and spent all her money on treatments (Mark

5:26). She wanted healing. She was doing what she could to heal. She was willing to invest her time and money. We also need to be willing to invest some of ourselves into our healing—whether that's carving out time to exercise, take a nap, and meditate on the Bible, or spending money on foods that are healthy for us or counseling or something as simple as seed packets if gardening is good for our souls. And we need to step toward Jesus. To push our way toward Him. Even when there are things in our way. Even when it feels easier not to.

And when we do, Jesus reminds us who we are. He called the woman "daughter." That's who she had always been. A child of the one true King. But she'd probably forgotten. She'd been banished and most likely felt unwanted and unseen. Jesus restored her, reminded her she wasn't an outcast but royalty. Always had been. But the circumstances of her ailment had made others dismiss this truth. And after years of suffering, perhaps she forgot also. You, too, are a son or daughter of the one true King. You are royalty in God's kingdom. He calls you "daughter" or "son," with all the love a perfect, loving father would speak those endearing names. You always have been, but maybe you've forgotten a piece or two of that identity.

I wonder what that woman did next? Did she start giggling, surprised by the sound of her own laughter? Or dancing, delighted that she remembered how? Did she remember the dream she'd been chasing prior to her ailment and decide now was the time to start her own business or open a shelter for other afflicted women? Did she remember how much she loved hosting and have a huge party, inviting everyone she knew who she hadn't been able to see in years?

You are worthy of dancing and laughter and delight in your day-to-day existence. You were created for goodness. For love. For grace. Maybe even for delicious coffee that tastes like France. What amazing parts of you have been tamped down, buried in the rubble, dismissed, or tucked away on a shelf? Intentionally take action toward wellness today and rediscover that you have always been cherished by Christ, that He has always and will always love you, that you are royalty who can hold your head up high and live out the incredible calling God has on your life.

I love *The Message* paraphrase of Paul's instructions to the church of Galatia: "Make a careful exploration of who you are and the work you have been given, and then sink yourself into that. Don't be impressed with yourself. Don't compare yourself with others. Each of you must take responsibility for doing the creative best you can with your own life" (Galatians 6:4–5).

Who are you? What are the things you're good at? That delight you? Do you remember? Sink yourself into those—if they were part of you once, they're still a part of you. Live this beautiful life of yours creatively, fully, like only you can do. Stretch out your hand, take the pot down from the shelf, reach out for the hem of Jesus's robe, and experience His love and restoration.

Jesus Cares

[Jesus] said to her, "Daughter, your faith has healed you. Go in peace and be freed from your suffering." (Mark 5:34)

Describe your favorite parts of yourself from a previous time.

Are there any of those things you miss doing, miss being? Ask Jesus to help you remember how free He always intended you to be.

Ask Jesus how you might reconnect with some of your previous joy or delight. If you loved riding bikes around your neighborhood, maybe He'll prompt you to start biking again. Did you love to sing? Put on some tunes; maybe even sign up for your church choir or worship band. Were you great at making people laugh? Jesus might nudge you to invite a friend to coffee and tell her some hilarious stories.

9

Pajama Pants and EpiPens

Prayer

My friend Betsy tossed and turned. There was an unexpected family decision she needed to make within the next twenty-four hours. It was late. She was exhausted, but her mind couldn't let go, racing with what-ifs of all the ways this decision could affect her family. Her body fought sleep, doing that thing where she nodded off for a moment only to be abruptly awakened by a leg or arm going herky-jerky.

Then, in the dark of her room and the midst of her concerns, her lip felt all tingly, like it might be swelling. Betsy had experienced an assortment of unexplained allergies lately—a long-lasting rash and her lip swelling two other times. If her lip was indeed swelling, Betsy knew this could be the start of anaphylaxis (think about anyone you know with a peanut allergy). Panic rose in her chest. Her thoughts spiraled rapidly.

Why was her lip swelling?

Did she eat something weird?

What if it was a severe reaction and her throat swelled shut?

What if her throat swelled shut and she died?

Should she wake her husband?

What if it was nothing?

Shouldn't she try to sleep?

How was she going to make this decision?

What choice was best for their family?

What was wrong with her?

What if she couldn't breathe?

Deciding it was pointless to stay in bed anxious and fearful, Betsy tried not to disturb her sleeping husband, grabbed the EpiPen she'd been prescribed to use in emergencies, and tiptoed downstairs. Even though everything felt out of control, she knew there was one thing she could do.

Betsy knelt on the fuzzy carpet of her family room in her cozy flannel pajama pants and sweatshirt and prayed. Soon she realized her lip was okay; it wasn't swelling. She wasn't having an allergy attack, just misplaced worry. Such a relief! Then Betsy felt God prompt her to talk to her body out loud, to tell her body it was all right. Betsy had never done this before. It felt weird, but she followed God's directions, saying to her body, "You're fine. There's no swelling. You're doing a good job. Since everything is okay, you can rest now." And it calmed her.

Betsy surrendered her body, thoughts, and emotions to God. First by grabbing medicine in case it was needed. Then by praying. She heard from God and was obedient. It certainly wasn't normal for her to crawl out of bed late at night, pray out loud on the floor downstairs, and speak to her body, but neither was the decision she was facing or this strange fear of swelling and the anxiety that came with it. After ten minutes of proactively talking to Jesus and caring for her mental health, Betsy felt peaceful. Her thoughts stopped nose-diving. She was reassured that she was healthy *and* that God would be with her family no matter what she decided. Back under the covers, Betsy hugged herself, reminding her body that it was safe and loved by God, and soon fell asleep.

Prayer is powerful.

When our minds swirl, when we don't know what to do, when we're frozen in our tracks, we can talk to Jesus and ask for help. Prayer can sustain, change, and save us. It can help us process everything on our minds, get us through rough spots, strengthen us, and encourage us. Prayer can also help our mental health.

"Imagine carrying a backpack hour after hour," Elizabeth Bernstein says. "It will start to feel impossibly heavy. But if you can hand it off to someone else to hold for a while, it will feel lighter when you pick it up again." Amy Wachholtz, associate professor and clinical health psychology director at the University of Colorado Denver, says that this is exactly "what prayer can do. . . . It lets you put down your burden mentally for a bit and rest."[1]

What are you trying to carry on your own right now? What could you hand over to Jesus to carry?

As we touched on in the chapter about memorizing Scripture, when Paul explained to the Ephesians how to fight their battles against evil, he gave them the picture of a Roman warrior dressed in armor. After Paul went through all the powerful pieces of the armor of God, he said, "And pray in the Spirit on all occasions with all kinds of prayers and requests" (Ephesians 6:18).

Pray.

On all occasions.

With all kinds of requests.

This means we can pray when something shouts in our heads or when something triggering affronts us. We can pray for peace, courage, and healing when the tension builds, before or after opening an important email that contains information that could change things, and before and after counseling sessions. We can pray when everything feels off or when we're exhausted or when we just feel a little edgy. We can stop when we feel that nudge or tug and listen to what God wants us to hear or know about that person, this situation, the decision or road ahead. This means Betsy can pray when she fears she might be having an allergic reaction or is stressed by a weighty decision she needs to make. My friend Kristan says she uses prayer to slow down her mind when it's racing—to breathe in Jesus.

And by praying, Betsy, Kristan, you, and me are all reminded that God is with us. That He is on our side. He is always there to talk to, no matter where we are or how we feel. Praying reminds us someone bigger than us, way bigger, is in control—whew! God reassures us when we pray that He's not disappointed in us and that we're not alone. Prayer might help us feel Christ's protection, find a way out, or discover the first step to safety. God might remind us that He loves us and will always love us even if we can't get out of bed or if we made a bad choice or took a step backward. Or Christ might nudge us to talk to our bodies. The possibilities are endless.

Paul knew how powerful prayer is and instructed the church in Thessalonica: "Rejoice always, pray continually, give thanks in all circumstances; for this is God's will for you in Christ Jesus" (1 Thessalonians 5:16–18). These instructions hold true for us today. So, yes, we can pray when anxiety and depression flare up, and also we can pray continually. This habit of consistent prayer builds peace and trust in our lives, so when we're faced with something taxing, we have a strong foundation to stand on.

When I was a girl, we prayed before dinner and before bed. The prayers were short and rote: "God is great" and "Now I lay me down to sleep." It wasn't a bad thing. It just wasn't taking advantage of the open line of communication God offers us. Now I pray in the morning, thanking God for a new day and asking Him for whatever I think my family or I might need. I pray through my journaling when I take quiet time with my Bible. Midday I pray, preferably in my closet, shutting the door to distractions in attempts to reset. I also pray with my husband at night, using prayer together as a punctuation mark for our day.

I also praise God throughout the day for the blessings He showers me with, everything from tasting something delicious—*Thank You, God, for fresh corn on the cob from the farmers market, sweet and crisp, perfectly buttered and salted*—to an idea for a chapter to write—*Thank You, Jesus. Please guide my words and let them glorify You.* This kind of daily, consistent prayer strengthens our faith and our trust. The more we listen to God telling us how much He loves us, meditate on the truths from the Bible, and acknowledge how good He's been to us, the more we remember that God is on our side no matter what's going on around or inside us.

You get the idea. Prayer can be anytime, anywhere, about anything. It can be proactive and reactive. This continual turning to God in conversation keeps us from floundering and sets us back upright when we stumble.

God gave us the gift of prayer to talk to Him, and He's so good, so loving, He also uses prayer to calm our nervous systems. Research from Dr. David Rosmarin, a professor of psychology at Harvard Medical School, has demonstrated that prayer "can calm your nervous system, shutting down your fight or flight response. It can make you less reactive to negative emotions and less angry."[2] My sister-in-law L.C. agrees: "Talking to God one-on-one empties my mind of all the noise." Prayer quieted Betsy's anxiety that night. If you've ever prayed as you've felt your emotions taking over, you've probably felt it's calming power too.

Prayer doesn't necessarily make mental health struggles vanish. It can. I've seen it happen. But typically our mental health issues require a journey of healing. Betsy still suffers from anxiety after that beautiful evening when God comforted her. But not only did she feel relief that night, her experience of praying and receiving God's peace also strengthened her for future episodes. Praying through the highs and lows allows us to travel our mental health journeys freer, lighter, and more grounded.

Mental health issues are sometimes genetic or chemical or caused by trauma or grief that was imposed upon us. Prayer is not a substitute for medical care or self-care but a complement to them. Prayer is a weapon that continues to erode the walls that block us in. Prayer takes the Enemy down notch by notch.

Time spent talking with God is never wasted. He always hears us. "How bold and free we then become in his presence, freely asking according to his will, sure that he's listening. And if we're confident that he's listening, we know that what we've asked for is as good as ours" (1 John 5:14–15 MSG).

God is always listening. He heard Betsy's prayers that night. She didn't get a neon sign telling her what to choose for her family, and her mysterious allergies weren't figured out. But God washed calm and love over her. Betsy's panic subsided. She found rest.

Jesus cares about us so much that He's created this perfect way for us to communicate with Him. He wants to take your burden and lighten your load. Turn to Him in prayer and allow Christ's power to comfort, console, calm, encourage, and strengthen you. Let Jesus remind you that everything you need is in Him.

Jesus Cares

And pray in the Spirit on all occasions with all kinds of prayers and requests. (Ephesians 6:18)

How often do you pray?

Try setting a timer for ten minutes, closing your eyes, and praying the entire time—no peeking. You can talk to Jesus about anything and everything. Commit to doing this at least three days this week.

Make a conscious effort to turn to God in prayer in the midst of a mental health struggle. Sometimes our struggles are so overwhelming that we're anything but rational. If that's the case, you can simply say "Jesus" or "Jesus, help!" It makes a difference. There's power in His name. If you are too distracted or emotional to pray during an episode, that's okay. Give yourself grace. Jesus does. Turn to Him as soon as you can. He's waiting to take your burden from you.

10

4,048 Gold Stars

The Cost of Freedom

A t the World War II Memorial in Washington, DC, there is a massive navy-blue wall decorated with 4,048 gold stars. Each star represents one hundred American servicemen or servicewomen who lost their lives (or who remain missing) in the war. Along the edge is an inscription carved in all caps that reads, "HERE WE MARK THE PRICE OF FREEDOM."

When my youngest, who is a World War II buff, and I were touring DC, we made a point of visiting this wall sandwiched between the Washington Monument and Lincoln Memorial. When I read this inscription, my eyes welled up, because, of course, there is a price to freedom. And for me to be able to wander around the nation's capital on a sunny July day with my fifteen-year-old without fear of all the things the Nazi regime stood for and enforced and were on their way to implementing across the globe during that Second World War, somebody had to pay a price. Apparently 404,800 American somebodies. Not to mention all the millions of people from other countries. People I never knew, am not related to, whose paths I will never cross, gave up their lives so mine would be free. So I can practice freedom of speech and religion. So I have the right to vote. So my blond-haired, blue-eyed boy will never ever have to join the Hitler Youth.

All freedom is costly.

Freedom from tyrants and dictators.

Freedom from slavery.

Freedom from debt.

Freedom from addiction.

Freedom from anything that shackles us.

Freedom is attainable. It's just pricey. Including freedom from mental health issues.

I speak from experience.

Every time I make the forty-five-minute drive to my counselor's office, I'm a little shaky. I spend most of the way there listening to worship music and in prayer. Why? Because going to counseling is hard. I need to intentionally ask God to come into the appointment and give me the courage to say the things that are hard to say, to admit the places where I'm weak and broken and damaged, to allow someone else into the parts of me that I really don't want anyone to see, the parts I've buried for decades. If I want freedom from the scars of my past, I have to dig deeper than I want to. I have to revisit painful memories and share uncomfortable thoughts. Sure, I could walk in and tell my counselor that everything's great, but that wouldn't gain me any freedom.

I spend the drive home processing what my counselor and I discussed. What she says always makes sense in her office. I understand why she asks the questions she does and why I answer how I do, but still sometimes I'm alarmed to hear my own responses and thoughts. Sometimes her diagnosis is so spot-on and helpful but also a bit jarring. I do what? Because of why? But I don't want to. That person will never change? Never? Deep down I knew that, and yet I was holding out hope.

I know this doesn't sound like the most convincing ad to make an appointment to see a counselor, but here's the reason it's actually an incredible idea. All that work I do before, during, and after counseling brings me freedom.

Freedom to know that I'm not alone. Freedom in discovering my responses are not only normal but expected considering what I've been through and been exposed to. Freedom in the fact that I'm making progress. That I'm loosening old chains and slowly learning how to pull them off and walk away. Freedom in having words to describe my feelings and reactions. Freedom that comes from gaining control over things that have made me feel helpless for too long. Freedom in the knowledge that if I keep at it, there's even more freedom in sight for me. All of this is so liberating! It helps me breathe more deeply and feel more known. I understand myself better. It helps me fight for this human (me) that God created in His image and her mental health all the more.

But it costs me something.

Time. Dollars. And sometimes even opening Pandora's box, which I've been fighting for years to keep bolted shut.

My friend Elisa says caring for her mental health costs her vulnerability. My friend Chad had to give up old habits as he fought for his mental health, and it felt costly. On her road to mental wellness, my friend Maryanne had to distance herself from someone she loved, which was emotionally expensive for her. But when we keep all the pain, false expectations, old ways of doing things, and fears under lock and key, we miss out on freedom. And freedom is something Jesus wants us all to have.

The apostle Paul tells us, "It is for freedom that Christ has set us free. Stand firm, then, and do not let yourselves be burdened again by a yoke of slavery" (Galatians 5:1).

Jesus has set us free. I've always loved the first half of this verse. Because, yes please, I want to be free. But the second part of this verse matters too. Jesus calls us to stand strong and fight to hold on to that liberation. I watch *Hamilton* or *Les Misérables*, musicals that strike a deep chord in me, and witness the protagonists fight for their freedom like it's the most valuable thing in the world. Just like those young Americans and French during their revolutions doing anything they could for freedom, we can intentionally peel off what's weighing us down, what's holding us back, what's caging us in and fight for the freedom Jesus offers.

Jesus doesn't want us to be burdened by the scars of our pasts, the anxieties or fears that take over, or the depression or impulses that try to wrestle us to the ground. Our Savior wants us to be free. Jesus knows all about paying for freedom because He paid for it dearly on the cross. For you and me.

> But he was pierced for our transgressions,
>   he was crushed for our iniquities;
> the punishment that brought us peace was on
>   him,
>   and by his wounds we are healed.
>   (Isaiah 53:5)

Which was part of the reason my voice got thick when my son asked me if I was all right, and a hot tear spilled out of my left eye and down my cheek that day at the World War II Memorial. The price of my actual freedom—my freedom from an old way of life, from past sins, from who other people told me I was, from fear—was paid outside the city of Jerusalem over two thousand years ago by my beautiful Savior, Jesus Christ. He paid the highest price of all—the price of His very life—so that we could be free. He wouldn't have done that for us if He wanted us to stay in a state of unhealth, restlessness, or fear.

Paul reminds us: "Now the Lord is the Spirit, and where the Spirit of the Lord is, there is freedom" (2 Corinthians 3:17).

There is ultimate freedom in Jesus. He calls us deeper and deeper into it every day, into a life where we can be ourselves, unclench our fists, roll back our shoulders, stop running and hiding and obsessing—a life filled with joy and light. He knows it might cost us something—time, money, discomfort, work, facing our monsters. Jesus felt the glaring pain of nails being driven into His feet and hands. The sharp sting of a sword thrust into His side.

And Jesus also experienced the freedom of stepping out of the grave three days later. Walking lightly on feet that had previously endured so much pain. Freedom not just for Himself but for all His beloved children—you and me—for all our days. Our Lord invites us into this freedom—to walk out of our graves, to push back the stones that hold us in, and to experience new life for our souls.

Sure, it will cost us something. Freedom always does. But it will be so worth it.

Jesus Cares

> Now the Lord is the Spirit, and where the Spirit of the Lord is, there is freedom. (2 Corinthians 3:17)

How free do you feel today?

What is holding you back from living a free and animated life full of Christ's love and peace?

Ask Jesus what is one intentional thing you can do today to step toward freedom, even if it costs you time or sharing something that feels easier to keep inside.

Thank Jesus for offering you ultimate freedom in Him!

11

Move and Groove

Exercise

My head is a tangle of thoughts—my college-age son is moving out of our home and into a house with friends sometime this summer. He hasn't given us a date. He's bad at asking for help, but I'm a planner who really wants to help, without being pushy. I long for the transition to go well for him, for us, for his roommates, for everyone.

Also, I have a counseling appointment this afternoon, and I have the choice to talk about anything I want. There's something I should bring up, but it's painful and hard. It would be so much easier not to. Is today the day? Or should I wait?

And . . . we have ants in our cupboard, which is disgusting, and I've called the exterminator and left a message but haven't heard back. I can't do anything until they return my call. But the bugs are creeping me out!

Plus, I want to get a card for my mom for Mother's Day *and* get it into the mail today, so it gets to her on time, but don't know when that's going to happen.

Not to mention I've written three partial chapters I can't figure out. Should I combine two of them? Are they strong enough to stand alone? Are they repetitive of something I've already written? How should I close the one and start the other?

Each thought bounces off the next. None of them landing anywhere.

Then I step outside.

A mourning dove coos in the distance. Our lilac bush is in full bloom. I inhale the heady fragrance, then take off to walk a loop around our neighborhood. With the first few steps the barrage of thoughts continues to bang against my brain rapid-fire. I'm unable to process any of them and still feel overwhelmed by all of them. But as I pass Snickers, the cocker spaniel who lives on the corner, running around his front yard, I'm somehow able to focus on my counseling appointment. God reminds me of a quote from *The Boy, the Mole, the Fox and the Horse* that I was reading last night:

"What is the bravest thing you've ever said?" asked the boy.
"Help," said the horse.[1]

When I saw that last night, it hit me hard. I just sat with the book open to that simple sentence for a few moments, letting it sink in. I felt like the horse was giving me permission and encouragement to ask my counselor for help, actually like God had me read that page specifically the night before an appointment to nudge me to ask for help. But by today I'd decided I could keep handling this issue on my own. Wasn't I doing all right?

As my feet hit the asphalt, *slap, slap, slap,* I picture the drawing of the back view of the boy riding the horse. Getting away from my desk and letting my body move and my mind unwind, I allot space in my brain for Jesus to put this image back in front of me. He reminds me that He is a healer. That He wants to heal me of this thing too. That asking for help from my counselor is a great way to start.

Halfway through the walk God hasn't written out the chapters for me or rewritten them for that matter. But He reminds me that the writing is just supposed to be like me talking to a friend, that I'm overthinking these chunks of words, that I just need to write them down and they'll eventually fall into place. Which gives me motivation to start again instead of finding distractions to work on anything except those chapters, as I had been doing before.

You get the point.

This sorting out of my thoughts and worries and hopes and questions and dreams happens when I intentionally take time to walk around my neighborhood. But not just there. It also happens on dreary, rainy days when I go to the rec center and run countless circles around the track that overlooks the basketball courts. I'll be listening to a sermon on my earbuds and be reminded that Jesus loves me right where I am. It happens on bike rides on the beach when the crash of waves and hum of the sea breeze make it too difficult to hear my daughter I'm biking alongside, so I get lost in my thoughts, and the soundtrack of the ocean is soothing, and the stress of getting everyone ready for the trip that I haven't yet let go of dissolves. It happens on walks uptown and jogs through the wooded trails near my house. This movement of my body detangles my thoughts, puts things in perspective, and helps me hear God more clearly.

But it isn't just me who thinks so.

"I'll wake up angry or stressed about something and go on a long bike ride. By the time I get home I don't even remember what I was so worked up about," my friend Brenda tells me.

"My biggest trick for caring for my mental health is going running," my friend Maryanne says. "If at all possible, I'll run outside. I can run in silence and let my thoughts turn around and around in my head until they quiet down."

"I recommend exercise of some form for all my patients," my psychiatrist friend Dr. Robin Warner says. "Increasing strength in any major muscle group is as good as an antidepressant." She goes on to tell me, "That's not a knock on antidepressants. I'm one-hundred-percent behind prescribing them for my patients who can benefit from them. I've seen them be life changing. This is just a huge testament to the power of exercise."

God created our bodies. And He created them to move. Jesus walked miles upon miles. Sure, He didn't call it exercise. At the time it was just how you got places. But also at that time everyone who was physically able walked everywhere, farmed, fished, hauled heavy buckets of water from wells. They didn't need to fit exercise into their routines; it was organically built into their daily rhythms.

God delights when we move our bodies, because He knows that keeping that heart He put inside of you pumping is good for both your physical and mental well-being.

Don't you realize that your body is the temple of the Holy Spirit, who lives in you and was given to you by God? You do not belong to yourself, for God bought you with a high price. So you must honor God with your body. (1 Corinthians 6:19–20 NLT)

Our bodies are precious. We should do our best to take care of them. If you google "the number one way to take care of yourself," exercise comes up on every single list. Exercising is honoring to God because you're caring for the body He made for you. It's part of God's original design.

If you have aches, pains, or limitations, of course, those need to be tended to, and you should speak with your doctor about what kind of movement is and isn't good for you. But Dr. Warner also explained to me, "Any kind of movement is helpful. I teach micro exercise like doing ten squats between meetings or using an exercise band while watching television."

You don't have to compete in Ironman races. If that's your thing—amazing. But you can also walk your dog, do wall sits or calf raises while you brush your teeth, go dancing, do yard work—whatever gets your heart beating and your body moving.

The Mayo Clinic tells us, "Physical activity stimulates various brain chemicals that may leave you feeling happier, more relaxed and less anxious."[2] Additionally the Mayo experts have proved exercise improves your confidence, increases your self-esteem, boosts your energy, and helps you fall asleep easier and get better, deeper sleep (bonus—sleep also helps our mental health).

Wow! I want all of that! What if we could use these words to describe ourselves? Happy. Relaxed. Less anxious. Confident. Energized. Rested.

A-ma-zing!

So what's stopping us? Sometimes we're tired or exercise seems too hard, or it's been quite a while since we tried. Sometimes our schedules are so full that we can't imagine squeezing one more thing in or the thought of lifting weights makes us cringe. That's okay. We can still make this work. How?

1. Pick something you enjoy doing. If you love sports, pick up a racket, bat, or ball. If you love the outdoors, go hiking or kayaking. If you crave time by yourself, go on a solo jog or bike ride. Do you adore your nieces and nephews, grand-kids, or neighbor kids? Play tag; chase; duck, duck, goose; or ring-around-the-rosy. What a great way to engage with those kiddos while moving your body. Plus, it's downright fun. There are no wrong answers here but so many options. If you enjoy the exercise you're doing, you're way more likely to stick with it.

2. Find something great to listen to. Love music? Make a play-list of your favorite songs. Music is proven to make workouts easier, increase your endurance, distract from fatigue, and boost your mood. People can go farther and longer during exercise if they're listening to music.[3] I'm a music fanatic, so I tend to think everyone is, but if you're not, that's okay—we can still be friends. There is also great nonmusic content out there to listen to. I typically have an audiobook downloaded on my phone, because listening to a book I wanted to read while I work out at the same time? Brilliant. Podcasts are also a great option. There are podcasts on just about everything under the sun—you can learn something new, be inspired, or simply be entertained all while working out. Listening to something while you exercise makes the time go by faster.

3. Grab a friend. Enlist a friend to join you on a walk, hit the gym or tennis court, or enroll in a fitness class. We've already talked about how community is important for our mental health. Having a friend to exercise with is doubly good for you. Personally, I love running with my husband or daughter, or walking with any of my kids or a dear friend. These jaunts are great ways to be together, share stories, and talk through things. But I also love time to myself to run or walk to process all the things in my head with God. On any of these suggestions, you don't have to be one-hundred-percent this or one-hundred-percent that. You can go with whatever fits your mood or schedule on any given day or season.

4. Try something new. Are you stuck in a rut? Did you dislike your previous fitness routine? My mom started rollerblading with her friends when she was in her mid-fifties, and they had a blast zooming around their neighborhood. In her seventies my mom started doing Pilates. My friend Beth had always been a runner but attended a Zumba class and fell in love. The dancing that got her heart rate up didn't feel like work at all. She wanted to share the fun with others, so Beth got certified to teach Zumba.

Any step forward with your exercise routine is progress. Did you do sit-ups today or walk up and down the stairs a couple of times when you didn't yesterday? Count it as a win! Did you try something new and didn't like it? That's okay—you ruled something out. Again, this counts as progress. God created our bodies for movement, but God isn't keeping score. That's not the kind of God He is. He just wants goodness for you.

God always intended for us to move about, so it makes sense that it's good for not only our physical but also our mental well-being. We owe it to ourselves to get out and move today.

Jesus Cares

Don't you realize that your body is the temple of the Holy Spirit, who lives in you and was given to you by God? You do not belong to yourself, for God bought you with a high price. So you must honor God with your body. (1 Corinthians 6:19–20 NLT)

What kind of exercise routine do you currently have or not have?

Take a moment to thank Jesus for your body, then ask Him how you can best take care of your body to care for your mental health.

Using the four suggestions in this chapter, write out:
1. An exercise you might enjoy
2. Something you could listen to while exercising
3. Someone you could enlist to exercise with you
4. A new form of movement you'd consider trying

Commit to doing at least one of those things today.

12

Repairing Holes

The Healing Process

"Laura! Did you see this?"

"Just a sec!"

I found my husband staring at the ceiling in our hallway. Water dripped from a small hole, forming a puddle on our dark walnut wood floor. I grimaced.

"What's it from?" Brett asked.

As if I had any idea. Let's just say neither of us are in the running to host the next HGTV show. But that didn't stop us from taking turns guessing.

"The roof?"

"A leak?"

"The kids' bathroom is right above this."

"From that storm the other night?"

We were clueless. But we knew who to call. I left a message for Russ, our trusty, talented contractor. Later, when one of our daughters went upstairs to shower, water poured from the growing hole. And . . . we figured out where the water was coming from.

For days the three kids who still lived at home showered in our shower. Five people. One shower. Two of them teenage boys. Fun times. Then, thankfully, Russ arrived and found the leak. Turns out all we needed was some caulk between a couple of tiles in the kids' shower. *Whew.* This was way cheaper and easier than expected. Still, Russ had to cut a really big hole around the original small hole in our ceiling before he could diagnose our problem. And due to a series of unexpected events, Russ couldn't get back to our house for three weeks to repair the drywall. Which was harmless, but we had this giant cavity in our ceiling.

It's interesting. A crack in the tile of the upstairs shower led to a small hole in our downstairs ceiling, which led to a gaping hole that anyone who entered our home would see.

This happens sometimes. Someone else's words or actions, or maybe an unexpected event, cause pain, confuse us, or make us feel ashamed in the moment. Over weeks, months, or years of internalizing, a small hole grows into a gaping one—it forms a wound.

My friend Brenda has a reoccurring dream of her playing high school basketball. Brenda is tall and athletic, but for her final game senior year, her coach didn't play her. His reasoning was, "You're too small. I want you to play center, and you're not big enough."

Reflecting on that time, Brenda says, "I should never have been a center. I'm not built for it. But even today when I am rejected for who I am, I have that nightmare. I never addressed that rejection then, and it's become a fear in my life: not being what someone else wanted me to be. It was a wound that I never paid attention to, so it never healed."

Or maybe we do something we regret. In that season we might be embarrassed or experience pain due to the consequences of our choice. If we internalize our guilt or fail to address our mistake, it grows into a large leak dripping onto other surfaces of our lives. It evolves into something bigger than our initial mistake.

Sometimes we experience something traumatic—something that frightened us, robbed us of safety or peace or assurance or security. And, yes, that moment was scary, but it spilled into other moments, other situations, soaking normal occurrences with damaging memories.

But there is healing available. Jesus is a healer.

When Russ returned, he filled the hole in our ceiling and painted over it. Today we have to squint to see where the damage was, and we live here. Yes, there was a hole—first a quarter-sized hole, then a one-and-a-half by three-foot rectangular hole revealing wood beams and dark, empty spaces. Some days our family might remember the time there was a leak in our ceiling. But honestly, we've pretty much forgotten about it. There's just a small shadowy mark where there used to be a fairly big problem.

Jesus can do this for our hearts and souls, find the source of the problem, and help us learn how to deal with and move forward from the damage. After all, He was a carpenter. And not just the kind that builds or restores houses—the kind that builds and restores hearts. Jesus doesn't just "fix" our problems or heal our pain or forgive us from sin. He *can* do all of that, sure. But when we trust Him and turn our lives over to Him, Jesus can renew and restore us from whatever unspeakable or unimaginable thing happened.

> Another time Jesus went into the synagogue, and a man with a shriveled hand was there. . . . Jesus said to the man with the shriveled hand, "Stand up in front of everyone." . . .

He . . . said to the man, "Stretch out your hand." He stretched it out, and his hand was completely restored. (Mark 3:1, 3, 5)

Jesus can do the same for you and me. He can take the shriveled things in our lives, the things that don't work how we want them to, the things that feel flappy and embarrassing and like they make our everyday existence harder, and restore them. I don't know what that means for you. For me, I still have PTSD and all the not so fun things that come with that. But Jesus helped me find the source of my anxious thoughts, defensive actions, and attempts at self-preservation—the emotional abuse I endured as a little girl that made me feel abandoned, like anything out of place could cause my walls to crumble down around me. Jesus has restored my heart, reminding me that nothing can separate me from His love. I don't have to keep all the balls spinning, appear perfect, or ensure that everyone else's life is going perfectly. Jesus reminds me I don't have to because He is the one actually in control. He loves me despite my flaws. He loves the people I love even more than I do. And these truths, both from the Bible and from conversations with the Lord, heal me, restore me, and repair that gaping hole in my heart.

Still, some days these truths are hard to believe. Maybe they're hard for you too?

How could Jesus forgive me for that?

I've endured too much to ever be whole again.

The abuse lasted so long; I don't know if I'll ever be "normal."

The trauma was too intense.

I did the most horrible things.

Yeah, me too.

But our God sees things differently.

> Whoever did want [Jesus],
>> who believed he was who he claimed
>> and would do what he said,
> He made to be their true selves,
>> their child-of-God selves. (John 1:12 MSG)

If Russ can find the source of a leak and patch is so well, don't you believe that Jesus—the Creator of the universe, the one who holds our feet to the ground with gravity, the one who created cows, cantaloupes, capillaries, and cacti, the one who crafts fog and starlight—could help you identify the source of your pain, give you tools to begin healing, forgive that mistake, get to the other side, shape you into your true child-of-God self?

He can. He longs for you to be whole.

Like we called Russ, all you have to do is give Jesus a call— just call out His name. Jesus already knows about your hole. He knows what caused it, when it got there, and how it has made you suffer. Still, Jesus wants you to tell Him about it. How it makes you feel. When it bothers you. Why it's so hard to get past. Not so you have to relive it but because Jesus longs to be in a relationship with you, and part of the healing process involves talking to someone you trust. Then Jesus can help you start healing—finding the root of your pain or worry or fear, seeing what needs to be cut, what needs to be smoothed out, what rough parts need to be sanded. And step-by-step, together, the restoration starts to take place.

I'm not trying to diminish scars of abuse or trauma, or say they're the same thing as a home fixer-upper project. I know firsthand emotional scars aren't cleared up by a brushstroke of paint. It's not an easy or quick fix. It can be a long, drawn-out, emotional process. Be patient with Jesus. Be patient with yourself. Celebrate the small wins and steps forward. Hold tightly to Jesus as you go. Then if you slip, He can pull you back up. Give yourself grace. Jesus does. Never be afraid to ask Him for help.

Brett and I knew we couldn't fix this hole in our ceiling on our own. We didn't even try. But we did have to take action. We had to pick up the phone and call for assistance from someone who we knew had the resources, knowledge, and skills to help. And once we did, there were many steps in the extended process. Russ had to find time in his schedule. In the weeks we waited, we were inconvenienced by sharing our shower. When Russ arrived, he had to cut that hole much bigger to dig around and see what was going on. He had to caulk the actual damage. We had to wait another day for the caulk to dry before the kids could move back to their shower. Then it was several more weeks of waiting before Russ could return to repair the hole. When Russ came back, he had more work to do. He needed a ladder and drywall and paint and a brush. The whole configuration also had to dry.

The same is true with our wounds. Our journey to mental health healing might include calling a counselor, trying to get into their schedule, waiting for weeks to get in, or waiting again between appointments. We might read some helpful books or meet with a pastor or trusted friend. We might need to revamp our sleeping schedule or eating routine or give something up. That might be hard. It might take several iterations. Years of appointments. Months of journaling. Trial and error. At times along our journey, parts of us might need to air out or dry out before we can take the next step.

Wounds might feel open and exposed, like everyone can see them. We might need to talk to another friend or try a different prescription or find a new counselor. I always need to pray. And then pray some more.

There are stages and steps to healing, some big, some small. There might be pauses in between—discoveries and recoveries. But in the end Jesus is a healer. We get to that point where although the wound still happened, we think about it less and less; we develop tools to help us manage it more and more. Where it was once a big concern, like water pouring out of our ceiling, it might become something we could go days, weeks, or eventually months without considering.

Jesus has the most miraculous paint. It's miraculous because it's red—His blood that He shed for you and me on the cross. But when Christ uses His blood to paint over our pain and loss and fear and shame, we don't turn red. We turn pure, dazzling white. His repair work is so perfect that even though we know the hole was there, and on some days we recall what we went through, the hole no longer defines us. It doesn't impair our decisions or relationships. It was there, but now it's not.

Jesus doesn't want us to remain in our suffering or pain. He recognizes that we might have mental health struggles, addictions, trauma, or chemical imbalances. But Jesus longs to heal us. In the end, Jesus will make everything right: "'He will wipe every tear from their eyes. There will be no more death' or mourning or crying or pain, for the old order of things has passed away" (Revelation 21:4).

Like a repaired hole in the ceiling, bright white and smooth, our past pain will all be settled by the great I Am, and it won't harm us anymore. It will probably take time and work and multiple phases, but Jesus promises to be with you every step of the way. He wants to heal you. From all the pain and fear and worry and sadness and confusion and unsettled moments. Call out to the Master Carpenter, *Jesus*. Invite Him to use His tools of love and grace to restore you.

Jesus Cares

"He will wipe every tear from their eyes. There will be no more death" or mourning or crying or pain, for the old order of things has passed away. (Revelation 21:4)

Call out to Jesus right now—say His name and ask Him for healing.

Sit in silence, making space for God to speak to you. What is He saying?

What's one step you can take today toward healing? Can you confide in one trusted person that you're struggling? Send a text? Make a call? Set up an appointment? Pray?

13

The Boy on the Bridge

Helping Others Helps Us

Jogging along my usual trail, I spied the tall bridge ahead. I'm drawn to bridges. Something about the echo of my feet along the wooden boards, the whisper or rush of water beneath my body, the elevated view of things. But as I made my way across this bridge, I noticed a teenage boy sitting alone atop the high rail, gazing down at the rocky streambed, wearing dark jeans and a thick black hoodie, hood pulled around his face despite the ninety-five-degree July morning.

He looked contemplative yet out of place. Dressed way too warmly. Too alone. On too precarious of a perch. I hoped he wasn't considering anything dangerous. I hoped he wasn't thinking sad, lonely, or desperate thoughts. As a mom of four I instinctively called, "Be careful up there."

"I will," he answered.

But as my feet hit the trail again, God shouted in my head, "Did you see that boy? Tell him."

"I just told him," I protested silently.

"Go back. Tell him that I love him. Let him know he has value. Don't let this opportunity slip by." I sensed the urgency in God's prompting.

But:

1. I had already crossed the bridge.
2. I'd already awkwardly spoken to the boy I didn't know.
3. I was so not equipped. I'm not a mental health professional. I'm just me, a mom on a trail.
4. A group of high school girls jogged past me and toward the bridge while this inner dialogue with God took place. If I did an about-face, followed the girls, and then called up to the random boy on the bridge, the girls would most likely think I was bonkers.

"Tell him for me," God insisted.

And so I pivoted, sprinted back to the bridge past the girls, approached the boy, and jogged in place while saying, "Hey, sorry to be a pest, but as I ran by God told me to come back and tell you that He loves you. That He thinks you're amazing. And that He wants you to be careful."

I expected hoodie boy to grunt, ignore me, or get a little ticked off by the weirdo lady—*ahem*, me—talking to him about God. But he didn't. He looked at me and smiled.

"Thanks. I promise. I will."

I don't know, and will probably never know, how God used those words. Maybe the young man was questioning God's existence or if anyone noticed or cared about him or if his life was worth living. Maybe the simple act of turning around showed the boy somebody saw him. Maybe the words "God loves you" changed his life. Or maybe he already had an amazing relationship with the Lord, was in a healthy space, and was just gazing at the water waiting for a friend or even praying. But I do know that God asked me to say something, that I was obedient, and that therefore God used it.

I'd started my run with a lot on *my* mind. My day was too

full, my week was too full, which meant my brain was beyond too full. I was stressed and overwhelmed. I had specific prayers for my kids about things I knew were out of my control. I wanted to fix things and help them. I'd tried. And fallen short. I needed to hand it all over to God, which isn't always easy for this mama bear. My shoulders were tense. My chest felt tight. I had that sensation bubbling up inside me that I was on edge and might cry or retreat or yell at any moment because I was trying to do it all and simply could not. But when I saw the boy, my concerns faded to the background. Here was somebody with potentially bigger problems than mine.

And something in me shifted.

The sight of the boy in the black hoodie, who was maybe totally fine but also maybe not fine at all, took my focus away from my worries and swung my attention to him. The conversation with God in my head was such a concrete reassurance that God sees all of us. He sees me, you, my kids, and this boy whose name and story I didn't know. God cared so much about this young man that He directed me to not only say something the first time I jogged by but also go back and say more. When I was hesitant, God practically shoved me toward the bridge. If I'd refused, I'm guessing God might have used those jogging girls in some way I can't speculate. But it was clear that God saw that young man and wanted him to know God loved him.

If God would do that for this stranger, isn't He also caring for the needs of my kids that I'm praying for? Wouldn't He do something similar for you and me? This boy's parents were nowhere in sight, but God sent me. And since God tended to all the details—that I chose to run this direction on this specific morning, that I got out of my car when I did so I'd pass this boy's path at this exact moment—couldn't God also manage all the things I was worried about? Couldn't He make sure the important things were taken care of? I ran away from the bridge lighter and in a healthier mental space than when I approached it. Not because I did anything for myself. But because I did something small for someone else.

Jesus instructs us over and over again to love others. One of His most famous stories is about a guy attacked by robbers and left at the side of the road. A priest and then a Jewish man walked right past, staying on the other side of the road, as far as possible from the bleeding guy, who was considered unclean. And then a dreaded, despised Samaritan man not only stopped but cared for the guy, took him to an inn, paid for his food, medicine, and lodging. This story is known as the parable of the good Samaritan.

> Jesus said: "A man was going down from Jerusalem to Jericho, when he was attacked by robbers. They stripped him of his clothes, beat him and went away, leaving him half dead. A priest happened to be going down the same road, and when he saw the man, he passed by on the other side. So too, a Levite, when he came to the place and saw him, passed by on the other side. But a Samaritan, as he traveled, came where the man was; and when he saw him, he took pity on him. He went to him and bandaged his wounds, pouring on oil and wine. Then he put the man on his own donkey, brought him to an inn and took care of him. The next day he took out two denarii and gave them to the innkeeper. 'Look after him,' he said, 'and when I return, I will reimburse you for any extra expense you may have.'" (Luke 10:30–35)

Everyone in the crowd listening to Jesus's story was shocked by the fact that the person they looked up to (the priest) and the person they identified with most (the Jewish man) did the wrong thing. The person who Jesus uses as an example of doing the right thing—of loving our neighbors—is the Samaritan, who they all disliked from the moment Jesus said the word *Samaritan* because of centuries of ethnic bigotry. This flipped their idea of who they should be kind to and what kindness looked like upside down.

Here's the kicker. After telling this parable, Jesus instructed the crowd, "Go and do likewise" (v. 37).

Meaning we're supposed to stop when we see someone in need. Help others. Not worry about getting dirty or what someone else might think. Show some love, kindness, and compassion. Don't we hope someone would stop and help us?

Of course we do.

But sometimes we have our own stuff and helping someone else can feel like a lot. Here's the secret sauce—helping others can both aid someone else *and* be the exact medicine we need to take our minds off our troubles for a moment and be reminded that we matter, that we have the power to make someone else feel loved, seen, and noticed.

Jesus doesn't ask us to spend 24-7 helping others. Yes, the Samaritan stops what he's doing, makes sure the injured guy is all right, and gets him the care he needs. And then the Samaritan goes on his way with a promise to return. He has some other things to tend to—work? Family? A doctor appointment? We don't know what else was on the Samaritan's calendar, but Jesus makes sure to put this detail in the story. We can help others *and* still care for our own responsibilities and needs. It's not one or the other. It's a balance. We can do this. We can stop and hold the door open for someone or shoot a text to that friend who is traveling today or going in for a procedure. We can take five minutes to write out a card or make a call or say a prayer. If we're baking a pie, we can double the recipe and give one to a friend. We don't have to do all these things every day. Jesus still calls us to rest, care for ourselves, and do the work He's equipped us to do, but when we see someone in need, that *is* the work He's put in front of us. It's our chance to help another. And ourselves.

My daughter Maddie told me she was feeling particularly anxious at work one day. She's a special ed teacher, and there had been a lot of pressure at her school that week. When taking some one-on-one time with a student to read an Elephant and Piggie book, the boy lit up and got so excited. "This was a book he *could* read!" Maddie explains, "He'd struggled so much with reading, but in this childlike moment, it all clicked for him. I got to witness him realize that he could succeed at reading! This moment totally took me away from my undercurrent of anxiety and into a joyful place."

My friend Kristan, who has been in ministry her entire adult life, shared with me a time when she saw God restoring her well-being through serving others. Her family had a trying season of church hurt and was pushed to leave the church where they served. They struggled with betrayal, loss of longtime friends, and the death of dreams.

Kristan explains, "In that time God sent us to the inner-city streets where we had the opportunity to establish a house of prayer and worship in the red-light district. We didn't feel like we had much to give because we were so drained, but we felt God telling us to just show up. Week after week we did. We loved people who were hurting, prayed with drug addicts and prostitutes, and held worship nights and prayer events.

"Our family is where we are now because of what God did for us then—because He called us to serve others in that season. Mentally we were a mess. If I would have kept to myself in my pain, I would have missed so much. My encounter with Jesus at the old, broken-down building changed me forever. My daughters were both baptized there. My family was restored there. My husband's heart was healed there. My heart was transformed there."

My friend Dr. Robin Warner, who is a psychiatrist, explains one way she helps her patients care for their mental well-being: "I encourage people to look at their giftings and see where they might help other people. If you can help others, you can find a way to use your pain for good."

We hear a lot about self-care, and self-care *is* an important part of tending to our mental health. But caring for others *also* helps our mental health. Caring for others can reduce our problems from a boil to a low simmer and sometimes take them completely off the stove.

The Mayo Clinic states, "Kindness can positively change your brain. Being kind boosts serotonin and dopamine, which are neurotransmitters in the brain that give you feelings of satisfaction and well-being, and cause the pleasure/reward centers in your brain to light up. Endorphins, which are your body's natural pain killer, also can be released."[1]

Being kind can reduce our pain, bring us pleasure and a sense of well-being. Jesus can use our serving others to heal us. Yes please. To all the above.

Both sides of Jesus's parable can inspire and comfort us. Jesus cares about us both when we're in a position to help others and when we're in need. He cares about us when we feel beaten up and abandoned. When we're physically or mentally battered or knocked out. He doesn't want us to be isolated or to feel lonely. Jesus will send people to help us— maybe a Samaritan man or a jogging middle-aged woman or a special ed teacher or a pastor or someone else altogether. Jesus made a point to highlight how the man in distress deserved help because He doesn't want us left alone on the side of the road or on top of a bridge.

And the other side is that of the helper. Jesus calls us to love our neighbors and gifts us with a sense of mental well-being when we extend kindness. Jesus created this beautiful circle out of the whole thing. He helps those in need *and* those who help others. We benefit no matter which one of those roles we fit into today. Those in need get cared for. And those who help receive a bonus feeling of satisfaction and purpose. It's beautiful. Just like a summer run along an old wooden bridge and all the possibilities God has in store along the path.

Jesus Cares

"Go and do likewise." (Luke 10:37)

Recall a time recently that someone extended kindness to you. How did it make you feel? Thank Jesus for that moment.

Sometimes the opportunity to be kind springs up on us like a boy on a bridge, but we can also plan acts of kindness. Ask Jesus to highlight someone you could show a little extra love or intentional care to today, and then follow through. Repeat tomorrow.

Measuring, Stirring, and Tasting

Creativity

Some days I feel the tug. It's a bit of an emptiness but also a restlessness. It's a something-is-missing feeling, but I'm not sure what. Almost instinctively, I reach for the giant glass bowl. This is step one to help me calibrate. I know the recipe by heart and start gathering the ingredients on my counter. I grab the canisters with dark green lids—flour, sugar, brown sugar. From the fridge I retrieve butter and eggs. And from the tall skinny cabinet above the microwave where I keep mugs, vitamins, and essential baking ingredients, I grab vanilla, salt, and baking powder. Oh right, and from my actual baking cupboard, the one with sweetened condensed milk, gluten-free cornbread mix, and coconut, I grab chocolate chips. I always have chocolate chips on hand. Always. Because this ritual of baking chocolate chip cookies is good for my soul. And I know it.

It dates back to my high school days when the words *mental health* and *self-care* weren't in my vocabulary. When I felt that everything was out of control—that I could study like a maniac (and I did) but couldn't ensure that I'd get into the college of my dreams. That I could follow the skin-care routines described in my *Seventeen* magazine to a tee, but my face might still break out. That I could wait for my boyfriend by his locker and pass him a note in the hallway of school, but I could not keep other girls from flirting with him. That I could follow the rules and keep curfew and keep my voice down (because my dad got angry if I was "too loud" or "too shrill"), and still he might be gruff or dismissive and make me feel like I'd disappointed him. Again.

I never articulated that those things made me feel shaky and alone, but when it all seemed like too much, I baked chocolate chip cookies. It was something I could do. Something I could mostly control. If you put the right ingredients in the right order and baked them for the right amount of time at the right temperature, you got cookies. And they tasted delicious. And made the whole house smell good. And made other people happy.

I've been baking chocolate chip cookies ever since. I literally made a batch last night. There is something soothing about mashing butter with sugar and brown sugar and getting a whole new creamy caramel-colored substance. The scent of vanilla is calming. Not just to me. It's a real thing. Scientists tell us the scent of vanilla reduces startle reflexes and anxiety and also has a calming effect.[1] Ritually I open the lid, inhale, exhale, and repeat before measuring it into a teaspoon. Then one more breath of the intoxicating scent before replacing the lid. If I'm baking with my kids, which I often do, we pass around the dark brown bottle and each take a whiff as if it were a magic elixir.

I nibble on chocolate chips as I bake. Treating myself. This counts as self-care, right? And when the dough is officially dough, I taste it. Yes, I know you're not supposed to because of the raw eggs, but I do it at my own risk, and the sweet, sticky bite with the rich accent of semisweet chocolate is heavenly. Confession? I like the dough better than the cookies.

I spend time in our kitchen daily making everything from stromboli stuffed with veggies and gooey mozzarella to PB&Js with my favorite French strawberry preserves to spicy turkey pumpkin chili on cold winter days. But baking chocolate chip cookies is different. I don't make them because I have to but because I want to. I bake cookies when I have time. There's no rush. Cooking other things can also soothe me, spreading homemade pizza dough on a pan, simmering chicken noodle soup. But chocolate chippers are my sweet spot.

What does this for you?

An article in *Forbes* explains that creating things reduces anxiety, depression, and stress, helps us focus, releases dopamine (the happy chemical), has a calming effect (just like vanilla), and actually boosts immunity and makes us smarter.[2] Basically, making things is super good for our mental health.

Which makes total sense. Because God, the original Creator, designed us to also be creators. The first sentence of the Bible shows God creating, and His creating continues through the whole first chapter. We see God create heavens, earth, water, sky, land, plants, trees, sun, moon, stars, fish, birds, animals, and finally us—humans. God created liquids, solids, and gases. God created things that fly, swim, crawl, run, and think. He also created things that don't move and have no thoughts but still have important purpose. God created with such variety! Think of a jellyfish, a kangaroo, and a Venus flytrap—all so completely different in shape, movement, and function.

Then God said, "Let us make mankind in our image, in our likeness, so that they may rule over the fish in the sea and the birds in the sky, over the livestock and all the wild animals, and over all the creatures that move along the ground."

> So God created mankind in his own image,
>   in the image of God he created them;
>   male and female he created them.
>   (Genesis 1:26–27)

You and I are created in God's own image. He put some of His creativity in us. Creating things—whether that's a flower arrangement, a pencil sketch of the tree in your front yard, a melody on the piano, a poem that captures your feelings, a wood carving, or a handmade greeting card—is good for us. Because when we step into who God designed us to be, we flourish.

And, yes, you are creative. We all are. God put this in all of us. Curiosity2Create, an entire online platform on creativity, states, "Everyone is inherently creative, we've possessed this power since we were born."[3] You don't have to like arts and crafts. Coming up with methods of communication and lesson plans and computer codes and systems for storing things are all creative. I'm guessing you're more creative than you think.

My friend, whose name is also Laura, thrives when she creates. So does anyone who gets to view her creations. She's a photographer, videographer, video editor, and incredibly cool, strong woman battling anxiety and depression. When I asked her what it feels like when she's behind the camera, she said, "I don't care if it's hailing or the most beautiful sunset. If it's the best or worst interview. It's about taking my brain and asking, 'How can I see beauty in this *and* how could somebody else see beauty in this?' What a privilege that I get to do this thing I love that at the same time allows me to share with someone else. It's a double whammy of thankfulness. In this creation process my brain opens, and I feel so completely my true self."

I love that! It does feel like my brain opens to something different when I create, when I'm baking those cookies. And I do feel more like me—like actual me, not manufactured me. I hum or sing and giggle. I let my mind wander. I'm not trying to prove myself or impress anyone. Sure, I hope my family likes the cookies, but I'm pretty sure they will. I'm just doing something that makes me happy, that taps into something joyful inside.

Creating is something all of us can do any day. I have friends who make wreaths, signs, and Christmas ornaments, who cross-stitch, knit, and sew stuffed animals, who have their own blogs or podcasts, who teach entrepreneurship, accounting, and spin classes, who build high-end kitchen tables out of wood, and who create earrings, beaded headbands, and lacy scarves.

I bake cookies.

I'll also pull out my watercolors and paint. When the kids were little, I'd create with them using crayons and markers and buttons and yarn. We'd make sock puppets and Lego houses and form Play-Doh into bright blue pretzels and neon orange cats.

What do you like to create?

The possibilities are endless.

"My practice of painting and making leads me directly to worship," says Makota Fujimura, a leading contemporary artist in a recent interview. "The voice of Jesus matched perfectly with the flow of energy going through me when I painted. The studio is the most sacred place I know."[4]

People throughout the Bible created things. Some for their businesses, like Paul, Aquila, and Priscilla, who sewed and assembled tents as their trade (Acts 18:1–3). There are numerous incidents in the Bible where God's people create meals for sustenance. Jesus made breakfast for the disciples (John 21:9). Lot prepared a feast (Genesis 19:3). We read in Exodus of God gifting Bezalel, Oholiab, and other skilled artisans with wisdom and ability to construct the tabernacle (Exodus 36:1). Mattithiah was in charge of baking the offering bread in the temple (1 Chronicles 9:31). These people created things for worship. In the Bible we also see people using their creativity to celebrate, like Deborah and Barak writing and singing a song (Judges 5:1).

As I said, it's cookies for me. I've baked them for decades but only recently actually identified them as a kind of therapy, a really healing kind. You'll need to do some self-exploration to find your go-to creative space that heals you in a special way. Think of something that calms you and brings you joy when you make it—a salad with vegetables you grew in your own garden, or black-and-white photographs taken with your good camera, not the one on your phone, or creative drills for the players on the team you coach.

"In the beginning God created the heavens and the earth" (Genesis 1:1). This is the very beginning of the story of mankind—God creating. There's something to that. It's part of our DNA to create. Something that lives deep within us that delights in creating, that brings God glory when we create. Something that smells and soothes like vanilla, gives our hands purpose, and tastes sweet to our souls. Something that brings us back to the people our Creator intended us to be when He created us.

What will you create today?

Jesus Cares

> So God created mankind in his own image,
>   in the image of God he created them;
>   male and female he created them.
>   (Genesis 1:27)

Write out some things you like to create. (If you don't think you're creative, think again. Coming up with alternate routes to get somewhere is creative. Putting together outfits is creative. Organizing a party or a fundraising campaign takes creativity. Creating a fitness plan uses creativity.) Thank Jesus for allowing you to make these things and for the joy creating brings you.

Commit to do something creative this week. Get it in your calendar. Order supplies. Prepare a space. If it's better to do with a friend, invite someone to join you. It could be as simple as playing a game of charades with friends or family. You have to get pretty creative to act those words out!

Journal about how it felt to prepare for the creation, about how it felt during the actual creating, and about how you felt when the thing you were making was complete.

15

Field Trips, Fine Wine, and Fish

When You Don't Feel Like Enough

I got back from the field trip later than expected. As I entered the house through the laundry room, I saw the clothes needed flipped from washer to dryer. It would only take a minute, but I didn't feel like I had a minute. I did it anyway. Then robotically walked to our watercooler to refill my hot-pink water bottle covered in Jesus stickers. The red light flashed, indicating the jug was empty and needed replaced. So back to the garage to grab a new five-gallon jug of water and swap it with the empty one. I also needed to get the chicken out to thaw for dinner. Which I needed to start making in (I checked my phone) one hour.

Only one hour at my laptop wasn't what I'd planned or hoped for today, but that's what I had. I also hadn't prayed midday like I usually do because I'd been chaperoning a field trip. I could blow it off; Jesus would still love me. But that didn't seem like the best idea. My brain was so swirly. My body so tired. Tomorrow was also a full day. Just thinking about it made my heart beat a bit too fast. I needed to get something done. But there clearly wasn't enough of me to do so. And if I took the time to pray, I'd have even less time to accomplish anything.

I tossed my head back and actually sneered at myself, my lack of capability to do the things that needed my attention, my lack of capacity. As if failing my to-do list made me a failure. Still, I set the timer on my phone for ten minutes. I knew this prayer time was important to keep me balanced, plus I'm a rule follower and this was a rule I'd set for myself. Out of habit I got on my knees on the cute little turquoise-and-lilac throw rug in my writing nook, closed my eyes, and started praying.

Jesus, I am overwhelmed. There isn't enough of me.

I am a God of abundance, not scarcity, He reminded me somewhere inside that is deeper than words or sounds.

I wanted to go on about all the things I had to do, the things I hadn't gotten to, how busy tomorrow would be and this past week had been. That's what I'd come into this prayer session wanting to do—complain.

Today. Now. These words from my heavenly Father echoed in my soul. It had been gorgeous outside today. And the field trip I chaperoned was great, getting to escort my high schooler's acting class to see a college production of a popular musical. The show was spectacular, and my son had such a strong love of theater.

Thank You, God. It was warm and sunny and so welcome after the cold, dark, gray winter. The show was high energy and well-done, and with my youngest now in high school, there won't be many more field trips I get to chaperone. It felt like a gift.

I exhaled a long, slow breath.

It was a gift. And the nice weather made all that driving to the school and show and back again way easier. And there was no traffic. You know I'm not a great driver, God, and I wasn't even stressed. Thank You. Everything went smoothly.

I breathed again and felt my lungs expand and contract. I was definitely calmer than when I started praying.

The thought of driving bumped me to my next thought. *Thank You that I could give that boy from the field trip who missed his bus a ride home. For prompting me to ask if he needed a ride. For letting me be available. In the car he said he made new friends today. Thank You, God, for that. Please let that boy know he's loved by You. I feel honored I got to help in some small way. Thanks for letting me be a part of it.*

I continued like that, praying for the people who came to mind. Asking God what He wanted me to start working on first. This manuscript was one of many projects open on my laptop. God didn't so much as say, *Work on the mental health book*, but He did nudge me to write about the prayer time we were having in a chapter, this chapter. I thanked God for my husband who had set a vase of yellow tulips, as bright as this sunny day in early March, on my desk yesterday.

And before I knew it, way before I was out of prayers, my timer went off. I slowly gathered myself off the floor, less frantic, more at peace. Because God's blessings were abundant. He had given me time and space to chaperone Maguire's field trip and give another boy a ride—things that were important, more important today than my laptop or anything on it.

Why had I sneered at myself before praying? Telling myself there's not enough of me? That is so unkind to me—to this girl God created. Have you ever done this to yourself? Called yourself a name in your head, been angry at or even cruel to yourself over a not perfect performance at a meeting or gathering, when you burned dinner or had to turn down a request? Made a face at yourself?

God says He crowned us with glory (Psalm 8:5), that we're more than conquerors (Romans 8:37), that we're His master-pieces (Ephesians 2:10).

God didn't tell me I didn't get enough done or that I couldn't get enough done. That I didn't have what it takes or couldn't complete the things He's called me to. So where did that idea come from?

For me it comes partly from my past when my dad repeatedly chose other women over our family. I felt like he was choosing that other home, that other life, over me, like it was all my fault because I wasn't enough. The Enemy loves to whisper in my ears that old lie that I didn't do enough, that I'm not enough, making the panic arise in my chest as I focus on to-dos that I wrongly think could prove my worth or make people love me instead of focusing on God's love that surpasses anything I could ever understand (Ephesians 3:19).

I'm working on changing these thoughts. God gives us the power to make this change.

My friend Kristan says, "When I feel like I'm not enough, I find myself defending my work or my worth—sometimes out loud and sometimes in my mind. If I notice I'm doing this, I know I have a problem. I try to counteract that feeling of not enough by spending time in silence and solitude, reminding myself that my value doesn't come from what I get done but from Jesus."

When we don't feel like enough—not enough to get out of bed, not enough to stand up for ourselves, not enough to say no to the temptation, not enough to call for help—we have the beautiful truth that we don't have to be enough. Jesus tells us, "My grace is sufficient for you, for my power is made perfect in weakness" (2 Corinthians 12:9).

We don't need to be everything because Jesus is.

Maybe you're asking, "But is He enough for me?"

He is. I promise. Here's the kind of abundance Christ offers.

Jesus was at a wedding where they ran out of wine, not a drop left.

Nearby stood six stone water jars, the kind used by the Jews for ceremonial washing, each holding from twenty to thirty gallons.

Jesus said to the servants, "Fill the jars with water"; so they filled them to the brim.

Then he told them, "Now draw some out and take it to the master of the banquet."

They did so, and the master of the banquet tasted the water that had been turned into wine. He did not realize where it had come from, though the servants who had drawn the water knew. Then he called the bridegroom aside and said, "Everyone brings out the choice wine first and then the cheaper wine after the guests have had too much to drink; but you have saved the best till now." (John 2:6–10)

This equates to about 750 bottles of wine! The wedding party didn't have enough wine. Jesus didn't provide a couple of bottles of cheap wine for them. He provided a lavish supply of the very best wine. Jesus doesn't offer us a little of Himself or a cheap, watered-down version of Himself. He offers us all of His perfect love, all of His amazing grace. He won't half listen to our problems while scrolling on His phone. Jesus gives us the best of Himself—His full attention.

He didn't die on the cross to save us from some sins but not others. He gives us complete salvation. This is the kind of abundance Jesus steps in and offers when we think we aren't enough.

Another time Jesus had been teaching a crowd all day. The crowd consisted of five thousand men, about twenty thousand people when you include the women and children, and they were getting hungry. When Jesus told the disciples to feed the crowd, they looked at Him like He was crazy and said, "We only have five loaves of bread and two fish. We don't come close to having enough."

> "Bring them here to me," [Jesus] said. And he directed the people to sit down on the grass. Taking the five loaves and the two fish and looking up to heaven, he gave thanks and broke the loaves. Then he gave them to the disciples, and the disciples gave them to the people. They all ate and were satisfied, and the disciples picked up twelve basketfuls of broken pieces that were left over. (Matthew 14:18–20)

Twenty thousand people. Two fish. Five loaves of bread. And twelve baskets of leftovers. That is a God of abundance. That is a God who doesn't care how much we have to offer as long as we trust Him. He takes what we have—jugs of water, one person's lunch box—and turns it into abundance. It's always enough. It's always more than enough.

This might mean in a bout of depression when it feels like we don't have enough energy to make a meal that God has a neighbor drop off a casserole. It might mean when we can't calm our anxious thoughts alone, Jesus puts an encouraging friend in our life who always picks up the phone when we call. Or perhaps we have some dangerous spirals we don't feel equipped to stop. Jesus might make sure we connect with a therapist who teaches us methods to assist us in halting those thought patterns. It might even mean Jesus prompting someone to place a vase of yellow tulips where we can see them, reminding us we're loved in the moment we were doubting if that was true. It means we don't have to fight for our mental wellness alone. When we don't feel like we have the capacity to stabilize our well-being, Jesus is on our side—filling in cracks, multiplying what we have, equipping us in our struggles, and creating avenues for peace and joy.

King David tells us in Psalm 23:1, "The LORD is my shepherd, I lack nothing." The New Living Translation translates this sentence, "The LORD is my shepherd; I have all that I need."

I know it doesn't always feel like it. In fact, it often doesn't. Many days I feel like I *don't* have enough courage to speak up, set that boundary, voice my opinion, or tell my counselor the hard thing. On the day I wrote this, I didn't feel like I had enough time, and I didn't feel like I was a good enough mom or writer to simultaneously pull off these two callings.

This scarcity mentality actually spirals downward. Two professors from Harvard and Princeton did a study on scarcity and concluded, "Scarcity produces a kind of tunnel vision, and it explains why, when we're in a hole, we often lose sight of long-term priorities and dig ourselves even deeper."[1]

But we don't have to worry about our limits. We don't have to have enough. Because Jesus does.

In a world that expects us to always do more, achieve more, earn more, buy more, it takes intentional effort to sit in contentment with what we have. Sometimes God will drop that contentment in our laps—an encouraging text will flash across our screens, a friend will give us the sweetest hug, the meeting we're stressed about gets canceled. Other times we might have to seek contentment through proactive practices like prayer, gratitude, meditation, reaching out to someone who loves us well, or journaling. We might want to light a candle, put on our coziest sweatshirt, focus on our breathing, or read a passage from the Bible that calms us. As we intentionally do things to help our well-being, Jesus steps in and multiplies our efforts, giving us more peace than our actions alone could bring.

During a mental health struggle, we can feel depleted and insufficient. But we have all we need. We lack nothing because we have the perfect love of Jesus that turns our tangled thoughts of not enough time into gratitude for sunny days and field trips, turns well water into the finest wine, takes the few things we have in our fridge and turns them into a feast, and takes our weary souls and leads them to green pastures and still waters. Christ's grace is sufficient. It's all we need.

Jesus Cares

My grace is sufficient for you, for my power is made perfect in weakness. (2 Corinthians 12:9)

The LORD is my shepherd; I have all that I need. (Psalm 23:1 NLT)

Where do you feel lacking today? Like you don't have enough?

Write out 2 Corinthians 12:9 and Psalm 23:1. Ask Jesus to help you see and believe that His grace is all you need—that you have everything you need because He is with you, because He is a God of extravagance and abundance who loves you faithfully.

Put the verses you wrote out somewhere you'll see them often this week.

16

Sunsets Are Free Therapy

Getting Outside

My daughter is slightly obsessed with sunsets. She told me her class was instructed to write down ten things they knew were true, and one thing she wrote was *Sunsets are free therapy.* "That is simply a fact," she insisted.

I think she's onto something.

Our family has been stepping onto our back porch for years to gaze as the violet, magenta, and marigold strips across the sky deepen, expand, and finally dissolve as the sun sets along the horizon. We also love to go for evening walks planned specifically in hopes of catching glimpses of God's sunset artistry on summer evenings. Because it's good for our souls.

But it's not just sunsets.

It's the roar of the ocean. The feel of soil in your hands or soft grass between your toes. The scent of lilies in bloom, lavender, fresh-cut grass, or pine trees. It's the sound of birds singing to one another in the morning, a cheery trill, or the hush of stars, so far away yet so comforting and bright in the evening sky. It's the rush of wind through your hair or the splash of cool water on your toes. It's pausing to watch the current of a stream moving onward or the way a hummingbird flits from flower to flower, gathering nectar while its wings beat about eighty times per second. It's an undoing of the ways we think things need to work and the things we think we need to do and instead observing how God takes meticulous care of the things He creates.

Being out in God's creation, experiencing it firsthand away from screens and fluorescent lighting and temperature-controlled rooms, loosens some of the thoughts and ideas inside that feel too tight and unravels the ones that feel all tangled.

Runs and walks in the woods near our home are a saving grace to me. The fresh air fills my lungs. The warmth of the sun shining on my face feels life-giving. Those wooded trails are a staple in my life that I frequent several times a week. In the freezing cold winter months, the crisp air and sparkle of snow crystals provide a pristine beauty that soothes me. In the springtime everything bursts and blooms and comes alive as the once-brown bare trees sprout billions of tiny bright green leaves while wildflowers wave colorful petals on long stems. In the summer the awning of branches provides a cool canopy of relief from the beating sun. And in fall, the golds, scarlets, and vivid oranges of the leaves, along with their sweet scent, create a scene worthy of postcards and paintings.

There's something about nature that really does feel therapeutic.

As my friend Laura posted on social media, "Mental health is gross and it's been kicking me down lately. Being outside and using my creativity reminds me that I exist."[1]

My friend Sue recalls being a little girl and seeing her grandmother on her hands and knees planting pansies. Sue asked her, "Are you having fun, Grandma?"

Her grandma answered, "The older I get, the more I love digging in the dirt. It brings me closer to the Lord."

Sue says she feels the same thing every morning when she sees the sun rise over the water by her home or the moon shining above it in the evening. "I feel so blessed by the beauty God has provided."

Which makes total sense. God created the world and all that's in it. When we go out into God's creation, we feel His presence more tangibly. The psalmist explained that the heavens and earth and sea and fields and forests (and everything in them) rejoice in God:

> Let the heavens rejoice, let the earth be glad;
>   let the sea resound, and all that is in it.
> Let the fields be jubilant, and everything in
>   them;
>   let all the trees of the forest sing for joy.
> Let all creation rejoice before the LORD.
>   (Psalm 96:11–13)

Psychologists have proven that being outside boosts your mood and energy, reduces stress, fights anxiety and depression, and helps you get your mind back on track.[2] Scientific studies also show that visiting blue spaces (lakes, oceans, and rivers) has a "psychologically restorative effect" and "induce[s] a positive mood."[3] I'm pretty sure that's because we feel closer to God when we're outside. Because we can pull away from everything else and draw closer to our Creator in His creation.

I'm not advocating for living outside or moving into caves. I really enjoy sleeping in my bed, thank you very much (without any bugs or bears). But research shows the average

American will spend forty-four years of their life in front of a screen—yikes![4] Meanwhile scientists tell us it's good for our mental health to get outside. So, you see, we have a problem. We're stuck to our screens when outdoors is healing for us. You don't have to be strong at math (thankfully) to figure out this equation. There's a way to fix this.

Get outside.

This can be as simple as taking your morning coffee or the book you're currently reading (maybe even this one) out to your porch when the weather allows. Grab a cozy throw if there's a chill in the air or a glass of ice-cold lemonade if it's hot. It could mean walking your dog, planting flowers or watering them, or setting up a weekly date with friends to play cards or checkers on someone's deck or at a park. Pack a picnic. Make a snowman. Build a fire in your firepit and roast marshmallows or hot dogs. Or take your Bible somewhere beautiful—spread your towel on the sand, sit down on a rock by a stream, find a bench in a public park and read God's love story to you. Journal about it. While you're outside, put away your phone. You can have it with you for safety, but tuck it in a pocket and if possible silence your messages.

Focus on what's out there. Open your senses in wonder. What do you smell? How does the air feel on your face? What do you hear? Do you notice something you haven't before— a nest high in a branch, the way the leaves are shaped on a familiar tree, a picture in the clouds?

God created light, the sky, land, seas, plants, the sun, the moon, stars, fish, sea creatures, birds, animals, and then us. And then he told mankind, "Look! I made all this for you" (see Genesis 1:2–30).

And here we are stuck to our screens (me too—I'm not

throwing stones but reminding myself). I'm all for climate control, but also I sense a change in me, a calm, a release, when I'm outside. If sunsets and for that matter sunrises, flowers blooming, squirrels gathering nuts, leaves wafting in the wind, geese honking, and raindrops gently falling are free therapy, let's take advantage of them. Let's get out and notice and savor and experience all these wonderous things God created. Let's start today.

Jesus Cares

> Let the heavens rejoice, let the earth be glad; let the sea resound, and all that is in it. (Psalm 96:11)

Get outside today. Even if the weather is less than ideal, grab an umbrella and/or coat and find a way to spend at least fifteen minutes outside. While you're out there, thank Jesus for rain or sun, for warm or cold, and for a plant or animal you encounter.

Be mindful of what's around you—try to use all five of your senses. When you return indoors, jot down what you noticed or experienced and take time to marvel that God created it all.

Note how you feel before you go out compared with how you feel after being outside. Commit to repeating this exercise at least two more days this week.

17

When You See
a Storm Coming

Proactive Care

"They're saying eight to twelve inches of snow on Thursday," Brett told me as we were walking around our neighborhood. "That could totally mess up our flights."

"It could," I answered. "But who knows, we might not even get snow. Nothing to worry about."

"We're going to get snow. Lots of it. It's just a matter of when it hits," Brett insisted. "We need to talk about what we're going to do."

"We can look at flights but not do anything until tomorrow. Let's just keep our eye on the weather." These were the optimistic words coming out of my mouth, but the words inside my head were, *Stop! No! I don't want to change this. I don't like change. We have flights. We have plans. Maybe if we don't look at the weather the snow won't come, and we can keep things how they are.*

Did I mention my husband loves the possibilities that come with change, and I really struggle with change?

But a snowstorm was on its way. And even if I didn't want to acknowledge it, it was still coming. I needed to plan accordingly. Or I wouldn't get to go on the beach getaway my husband and I had planned. Our flight might get canceled, or my mom might not be able to navigate the snowy roads to our house, meaning she wouldn't be able to watch our kids. I had to accept the incoming storm and prepare for it. I didn't have to do it alone. I had Brett. And I always have Jesus. But I did have to take action.

The same is true with our mental health. There are days we won't see a mental health struggle coming. But sometimes we see a storm on the horizon before it hits. When we do, we have ways to prepare for it. We don't have to get ready for that storm alone. God is on our side and promises to always be with us. But we do need to take action.

If getting your blood drawn, flying, or giving a presentation makes you anxious or has previously evoked an episode, there are strategies to make it less overwhelming next time it pops on your calendar. If winter always brings on seasonal affective disorder, you could start planning ways to integrate little lunchtime walks so you get some daylight into your schedule. If the holidays trigger bad memories or a conversation with *that* person always makes you feel trapped, you can plan ways to proactively care for yourself prior to these events so you can better cope when they occur.

Bringing up this incoming storm with Jesus in conversation (prayer) is a great place to start. Tell Him it's coming up. Jesus knows this already. He knows everything. But He loves to hear from you. Tell Him the things about it that concern you. Sometimes just voicing them gives us perspective. Maybe Jesus will bring a Bible verse to mind or have a friend text one that encourages and strengthens you. Write it out. Read it aloud. Make it your phone wallpaper.

Maybe Jesus will play a song for you in your car or at church or even in a coffee shop that calms you or gears you up or infuses you with strength and hope. Download it on your phone. Listen to it. On repeat.

Maybe God will prompt a friend to ask if there's anything they can be praying about for you. This is your opening. Ask them to pray for you ahead of and during the triggering event; give them specific days and times if you have them.

Maybe Jesus will remind you to rest or that you won't be alone because He'll be with you, or that you really should eat something, or that you should schedule an appointment with your pastor or counselor.

Getting ready for a storm is practical and it's biblical.

In Genesis 6 humans had turned away from God and become wicked. But Noah was righteous and walked with God (v. 9). God planned a flood, but before the rain started to fall, God instructed Noah on how to keep himself and his family safe during that incoming storm: "So God said to Noah, '. . . Make yourself an ark of cypress wood; make rooms in it and coat it with pitch inside and out. This is how you are to build it'" (vv. 13–15).

Sure, it sounded weird. There was no rain falling and Noah was supposed to build a boat. A giant boat the length of one and a half football fields. Typical day. But God wanted Noah to be ready for the incoming storm. It rained for forty days and nights, which not surprisingly flooded the entire earth. Noah, who had prepared ahead of time for the storm, along with his wife, sons, their wives, and the animals God instructed Noah to bring on board, all remained safe in their floating hotel. When the waters subsided many months later, they all walked safely onto land (8:18–19). God didn't ask

Noah to figure it out by himself. God gave Noah specific instructions ahead of time on how to prepare for this flood, and Noah obediently followed them.

God can help you prepare for your mental health storms too if you ask Him.

You might want a guaranteed phrase or trick, but usually the way God prepares us is less obvious or not how we might think preparation for a storm should look. I'm guessing Noah thought God's idea was pretty far out there.

When you pray to Jesus about your upcoming storm, He might not get you out of the flood or dreaded doctor's appointment, but He may give you a friend to accompany you for moral support. God might not cancel your spouse's business trip if you get on edge when they go out of town, but as an answer to your prayer He may arrange for your book club or Bible study or girls or guys night out to be rescheduled for that very night so you have something to look forward to and won't be alone.

God created counselors who can give you tools or methods to help you prepare for your incoming storm and all the emotions that come with it. My therapist has me write out flash cards to better process why I might be worried about a future situation. Going through the steps of her flash cards helps me identify what specifically might upset me. This advanced preparation helps me strategize how I can react to an upcoming storm in ways that protect my mental health.

If there's a difficult conversation or confrontation I know I need to have and I'm worried about how it will impact me, my counselor practices that conversation with me through role-playing. She gives me different scenarios: "If someone says this, how will you answer? What if they say this? How about this?"

It doesn't mean I'll be at ease when that conversation takes place, but I will be better equipped.

My friend Brenda knew spending Easter with her family after the recent loss of her mother was going to be emotionally taxing. Brenda was grieving, but so were all the people she was going to be around. To prepare herself before taking the trip home, she spent hours in silence and solitude with God. This time fortified her. Gave her peace and strength to handle what was up ahead. "I need that margin," she told me. "When I create this space with the Lord before heading into something challenging, I'm a better person, a healthier person."

Prayer is awesome, but there are all kinds of other things you can do that are also proactive rather than reactive. You might read a book that helps you understand your emotions and feelings, follow an encouraging social media account, call or grab coffee with a friend and confide in them what's going on, or go for a walk. Practicing breathing on a regular basis helps you calm your central nervous system when storms hit. Journaling your feelings about the upcoming storm can help you process and prepare for the situation. Journaling also gives you a consistent way to process your feelings, what's blaring in your life and what's simmering under the surface. Journaling lets your right brain talk to your left brain, which helps balance your overall mental health. Making sure you're consistently taking prescribed meds is yet another way you can remain more stable when a predicted storm hits.

These proactive practices are like carrying an umbrella

when the forecast calls for rain. Or unplugging your laptop and having candles and matches ready if you suspect the power might go out. Or building an ark that's 450 feet long, 75 feet wide, and 45 feet high (Genesis 6:15) when God tells you a flood is coming.

I mentioned prayer is my favorite way to prepare for a situation I know in advance will challenge my mental health. Praying Scripture can be especially helpful if I'm struggling to find words. I pray Psalm 16 over and over before having to interact with a recurring triggering situation in my life.

> Keep me safe, my God,
> for in you I take refuge.
>
> I say to the LORD, "You are my Lord;
> apart from you I have no good thing." . . .
>
> LORD, you alone are my portion and my cup;
> you make my lot secure.
> The boundary lines have fallen for me in pleas-
> ant places;
> surely I have a delightful inheritance.
> I will praise the LORD, who counsels me;
> even at night my heart instructs me.
> I keep my eyes always on the LORD.
> With him at my right hand, I will not be
> shaken.
>
> Therefore my heart is glad and my tongue rejoices;
> my body also will rest secure,
> because you will not abandon me to the realm of
> the dead,

nor will you let your faithful one see decay.
You make known to me the path of life;
   you will fill me with joy in your presence,
   with eternal pleasures at your right hand.
      (vv. 1–2, 5–11)

This psalm anchors me to the truth and safety God offers. God is my refuge. He makes my lot secure. He counsels me. I won't be shaken. He won't abandon me. I will find joy and pleasure with Him. No matter what comes at me. *Whew.* These reassurances are for you too.

Jesus knew storms would come our way. He didn't want us to face the biting winds, torrential rains, and numbing cold alone. Jesus told us how to stand strong in them—by building our foundations on Him.

> Therefore everyone who hears these words of mine and puts them into practice is like a wise man who built his house on the rock. The rain came down, the streams rose, and the winds blew and beat against that house; yet it did not fall, because it had its foundation on the rock. (Matthew 7:24–25)

Rain will fall. Streams will rise. Winds will blow and beat against us. But we can keep from falling by building our lives on Jesus, His grace, and His strength. When possible, we should prepare for the storms ahead of time. The very best way we can do that is to spend time with Jesus. That's how we build our foundations on Him. Faithfully reading our Bibles. Talking to God through prayer about everything: the way we feel, the things that freak us out, the upcoming flight or gathering or decision or diagnosis. And spending time listening to His responses. Asking Jesus, in the quiet, to fill us with His peace, to keep us safe from the storms.

By the time Brett and I had circled the neighborhood on the walk where we were discussing that incoming snowstorm, I'd conceded to having him change our flights. When Brett called the airline, they moved both our departing and returning flights forward two days with zero fees and no problems. Wow. The condo we'd rented accommodated us as well. Somehow the change in plans saved us a hundred dollars on the rental car—go figure. My mom's calendar, which is always booked, was open, and she was grateful to make the two-and-a-half-hour drive to our house *before* the threat of snow. Brett and I flew to South Carolina. After we landed, as both Brett and the weather app predicted, twelve inches of snow hit Ohio. Our kids got two fun-filled snow days off school, sledding and icing sugar cookies with their awesome grandma. My husband and I got our time away together.

It was as if God orchestrated the whole thing.

My original instinct, pretending the storm wasn't going to happen, was not a good strategy. I'm thankful for my husband who was thinking more clearly than I was and was willing to nudge me toward reality—the reality that when we can, we should prepare for storms.

Jesus cares so much about you. He wants to help you breathe His peace in and out when you see a storm coming, remind you of what you can do to prepare for the storm, and encourage and show you how to do that, so that during the storm you'll be able to stand.

Let's turn to Jesus ahead of time, assemble our arks, and build our lives on Him, our "shelter from the storm" (Isaiah 25:4).

Jesus Cares

Keep me safe, my God, for in you I take refuge. (Psalm 16:1)

Therefore everyone who hears these words of mine and puts them into practice is like a wise man who built his house on the rock. The rain came down, the streams rose, and the winds blew and beat against that house; yet it did not fall, because it had its foundation on the rock. (Matthew 7:24–25)

Do you have any upcoming storms on your calendar? Or maybe one that will most likely occur even if you're not exactly sure when?

Read Psalm 16 and Matthew 7:24–25 again. Thank God for being your rock in your storm, for keeping you secure.

Ask Jesus how you can be preparing for the upcoming storm to guard your mental health. Sit in silence with a journal and jot down anything that comes to mind.

Take action: text that friend, make that appointment with your counselor, journal your thoughts, or commit to praying in advance about the upcoming situation.

18

When a Storm Takes You by Surprise

Reactive Care

As my friend Juiquetta waited to get her ultrasound, she saw something in the doorway of the room that reminded her of a white stencil sketch of an angel. She felt God with her before it all started—His reassurance that He was there with her, that she wasn't alone.

The ultrasound showed that her little girl had trisomy 13, a rare genetic syndrome caused when a baby gets an extra thirteenth chromosome. The doctor explained that her baby would have multiple birth defects and most likely not survive. This is the stormiest of storms a mama can have come at her. And it took her completely by surprise.

But Juiquetta in her fierce faith told everyone in the room, "I don't know if you all want to stay and pray with me. You can if you want. But I'm about to get on my knees and pray because I don't know what else to do."

Juiquetta told me the medical team excused themselves, and then she got down on her knees on that cold floor of the examining room in her gown, asking God to help her live through this, breathe through this. She told God, "I can't do this without you."

Juiquetta went full term with her pregnancy. Haneh was born with a fully formed face and brain despite the odds. Juiquetta calls the precious thirty-eight minutes they shared together "a blessing, a miracle." Juiquetta also told me God gave her a dream of her own mother, who had passed away, pushing a stroller in heaven—such a sweet assurance that her mother was healed and restored and that her daughter was loved and cared for in heaven.

As we talked about in the previous chapter, sometimes God gives us ways to prepare for incoming storms. Other times God steps in, saves the day, and takes down a storm before we ever feel the effects of it. But sometimes in this broken world of ours we'll feel a storm hitting like a giant wave crashing over us, knocking us off our feet, choking us with mouthfuls of salty water, stinging our eyes, and leaving us temporarily disoriented and sometimes battered and bruised. But our God promises to never leave us. In these times God shows up, picks us up, and pulls us out of the water and safely to shore. Sometimes Jesus even invites us into the calming of the storm, standing by our side and giving us what we need so there will be another victory for heaven. Jesus put power in us when He sent the Holy Spirit, and that power comes in incredibly handy when we're up against a tempest.

Let's unpack that a bit.

First off, any storm that comes your way? Jesus has the power to calm it.

A furious squall came up, and the waves broke over the boat, so that it was nearly swamped. Jesus was in the stern, sleeping on a cushion. The disciples woke him and said to him, "Teacher, don't you care if we drown?"

He got up, rebuked the wind and said to the waves, "Quiet! Be still!" Then the wind died down and it was completely calm.

He said to his disciples, "Why are you so afraid? Do you still have no faith?"

They were terrified and asked each other, "Who is this? Even the wind and the waves obey him!" (Mark 4:37–41)

This was no ordinary thunderstorm. This was a furious squall. Water was pouring into the boat, threatening to pull it under. But Jesus only had to say three words and the whole thing went completely calm.

I love that God made sure this story was in the Bible. I find reassurance that the disciples were terrified, even though Jesus was with them. This consoles me when I struggle to heed the Bible's instructions of "do not be afraid" and "do not be anxious" (John 14:27; Philippians 4:6), which are awesome commands but way easier said than done. Sometimes I lose sight of the fact that powerful, loving Jesus is with me. And some days I struggle to tap into the peace of this truth even when I try. I fear when the roads are icy and one of my kids is out driving. I fear when someone I love has bad news from a doctor. I worry when I see someone I care about do something unhealthy or dangerous for them. I know Jesus is mighty. I've seen Him do miracles. But seeing that I'm not the only one who struggles with fear is a reassuring reminder that these feelings are normal reactions to storms.

The disciples called out to Jesus for help. So did Juiquetta. And we can too. He's right here with us, just like He was in the boat with His disciples and that hospital with Juiquetta.

Prayer is how we call out, and when we do, Jesus always hears our prayers.

Sometimes Jesus will do as He did in that boat and shout, "Be still," and presto! Storm averted. But other times Jesus asks us to tap into the resources He gives us and the power He puts in us to calm a mental health storm.

The apostle Paul tells us that God's great power is on our side. "I also pray that you will understand the incredible greatness of God's power for us who believe him. This is the same mighty power that raised Christ from the dead and seated him in the place of honor at God's right hand in the heavenly realms. Now he is far above any ruler or authority or power or leader or anything else—not only in this world but also in the world to come" (Ephesians 1:19–21 NLT). We're packed with God's holy power, and Jesus wants us to use it to help calm our mental health storms.

Juiquetta tapped into God's power by turning to Him for help. By intentionally getting down on her knees, Juiquetta overcame an anxiety attack and received the strength from God to carry on and the desire and courage to take her baby full term, even knowing the potential danger. A desire and courage she doesn't believe she could have mustered on her own.

You might tap into Christ's power when you're tempted by an old toxic response or behavior by asking Him to help you say no or get you out of there. Or you might tap into God's power by asking for courage to say the brave thing, to turn around, or to set the boundary in the midst of an unexpected storm.

My psychiatrist friend Robin Warner has some more tips for how we can care for our well-being in an unexpected situation that compromises our mental health, suggesting, "In the moment you can ground yourself with deep breathing. The nervous system God designed automatically calms down when you take deep breaths. You can also look around the room you're in and find everything rectangular—a window, a desk, a book. Or you can find something to touch— a nubby corduroy jacket, soft sweater, bumpy chair. These things help your prefrontal cortex (which helps us make well-thought-out decisions) get a little of its power back. Adrenaline from something unexpected can override logic, but by engaging in a logical brain exercise, or by touching something that brings you to the present, you can slow down the adrenaline and the spiraling thoughts or emotions of panic."

I don't know what storms will take you by surprise, but I do know that Jesus will be with you in that boat or crowd or hospital. He might put an end to your troubles with a phrase, He might show you His presence to remind you that He's there, or He might invite you into the fight. He'll give you all you need for that battle, even if it feels small. With God, it will be exactly what you need.

Jesus equipped one friend of mine to fight her storms with a prescription she can take when she feels a mental health storm rising. This action on her part effectively calms her storms. Jesus connected another friend to a therapist who taught her to dunk her head quickly in and out of a large bowl of ice water to distract her from spiraling thoughts when a storm hits. She can now fight anxious thoughts by getting out that bowl and filling it with cold water. God equipped my friend Betsy by having her read an article that taught her rhythmic leg tapping is a way to halt panic attacks. When anxiety starts to unexpectedly flutter in her chest, she fights her storm by intentionally tapping a rhythm on her legs: one tap, two taps, then two taps, one tap. It centers her, calms her, brings her back to the present, to something she can control.

God will give us tools to help us out of trouble, to cope, to get through the storms. He offers anyone who believes in Him access to His mighty power. So when the unexpected storm hits, we can have faith that Jesus will help us calm it. Maybe with a word from our Protector, maybe with our own hands gripping the supplies and resources He's gifted us, maybe by someone God sends to help us in our moment of need, or maybe with courage or strength or willpower He provides when we don't have enough on our own. In any of those situations, the winds can be calmed, the waves can cease, and we can find peace in Jesus, the Prince of Peace.

Jesus Cares

> You, dear children, are from God and have overcome them, because the one who is in you is greater than the one who is in the world. (1 John 4:4)

Do you have any tricks up your sleeve you use when unexpected mental health storms hit? Like leg tapping, breathing exercises, or smelling something lovely like a candle or raspberry-scented soap?

Spend some time in prayer asking Jesus how to equip yourself for unexpected storms. Write down what you sensed or heard from Him. If you didn't hear anything, that's okay. Ask Him again tomorrow and the day after that. All time you spend with God is helpful.

Practice praying in unexpected situations—it doesn't have to be a storm. Someone cancels plans? Ask God to help you use the time that's now open in your schedule. Your adviser asks you to switch tasks or locations or groups at the place you work or volunteer? Ask God to help you learn from and embrace your new responsibilities. If we rehearse turning to prayer in times that aren't tumultuous, we'll be in the habit of praying in more dire storms.

19

Apple Suits, Robes, and Other Outfits

Shame

My mom sewed me an apple suit when I was a girl. It's exactly what it sounds like—a pair of pants and matching jacket made from brown fabric with a pattern of bright red apples on it. Possibly part of the reason I was such a nerd in third grade. Anyway . . . I remember walking home from school one day and really having to go to the bathroom. I probably should have gone before I left school, but there was this whole end-of-the-day thing with gathering books and jackets and getting in line, and one was expected to do all those things in a timely, orderly fashion. I was a girl who did what was expected of her. Always. Still usually am.

I thought I could make it the short fifteen-minute walk home and resorted to all the things one does to not wet their pants along the way. I shifted my weight back and forth at the red light, bent down to pretend to tie my shoe, held my breath, and walked faster, but by the time I made it up our front doorstep I was running out of time. I had to dig in my backpack for my house key tied to a white shoelace, slide it in both the normal lock and the dead bolt, and make it turn. My bladder didn't make it. I had an accident on our front porch, leaving a shameful puddle on the concrete. I was mortified!

I know I changed pants and cleaned myself up. I'm sure I tried to hide the puddle. How? I have no recollection. What did I do with the apple pants? I also don't remember. But I vividly recall the horrible, embarrassing realization that as a third grader I'd wet my pants. Did the neighbors see? Would everyone know? They would all think less of me than they already did. My brother would taunt me. My dad would yell at me. My mom would be disappointed, especially because it all happened while I was wearing the pants she'd sewn for me. Any friends I might have sort of had would disown me if they knew.

This wasn't the first time I'd felt shame. And it certainly wasn't the last.

Shame. It's a horrible, haunting thing.

Brené Brown is a leading expert in the study of shame. She states that everyone has shame: "It's the most human, primitive emotion that we experience." Brown defines shame as "the intensely painful feeling that we are unworthy of love and belonging."

Brown's research has shown that secrecy, silence, and judgment are the three ingredients to make shame grow. But the good news, Brown says, is that shame cannot survive if you speak about it and receive empathy. Shame depends on the belief that we are alone.[1]

We don't have to let our shame grow. We can speak about it. Jesus will listen. He will empathize. He doesn't want us to feel shame. He tells us, "I did not come to judge the world, but to save the world" (John 12:47).

Jesus didn't come to point out all the things we do wrong.

We're usually pretty good at doing that ourselves. Sure, He'll give us a nudge when we're offtrack, help us realize if we've been unkind or judgmental. Jesus will convict us when we fall away from the beautiful lives He intends for us, but shame? That's not His MO. Jesus came to save us. To love us. To care for us. And we can start by talking to Him about anything we're ashamed of right now.

We see the process of shame play out with the very first people. Adam and Eve were living in paradise where there was no shame. Zero. Adam and Eve were naked. They spoke their true feelings. They weren't nervous or concerned about how they looked or what they would say. They never second-guessed what the other one would think of them. They were just living their literal best lives.

But then Satan came along and started manipulating words and suggesting half-truths. The Enemy convinced Eve that the one fruit she shouldn't eat (which is interestingly enough often represented by an apple) was actually awesome. And Eve fell for that snake's sneaky con. "So she took some of the fruit and ate it. Then she gave some to her husband, who was with her, and he ate it, too. At that moment their eyes were opened, and they suddenly felt shame at their nakedness. So they sewed fig leaves together to cover themselves" (Genesis 3:6–7 NLT).

Did you see it? The first time shame showed up was after Adam and Eve listened to Satan instead of God. The first thing they did afterward? Try to hide. The shame was not from God. The Bible doesn't say God was ashamed of Adam and Eve. It says Adam and Eve suddenly felt shame.

When the cool evening breezes were blowing, the man and his wife heard the LORD God walking about in the garden.

So they hid from the Lord God among the trees. Then the Lord God called to the man, "Where are you?" (vv. 8–9 NLT)

God was going for a walk in the evening. This seems to be a usual thing because Adam recognized those footsteps. God knew what had happened and was looking for His kids. Not because He was mad at them but because He liked being with them and it was time for their evening walk. But Adam and Eve were hiding. Their actions separated them from God, created shame. Then Adam and Eve fostered the shame by trying to keep it a secret, by keeping it silent, by hiding.

God wanted to put an end to the shame. He wanted Adam and Eve to speak about it, knowing that would get it out in the light where it could not survive. So God called to them. Adam sheepishly waved from behind the bushes, "Over here," and explained why they were hiding.

God asked, "Who told you that you were naked?" (v. 11).

Not because God didn't know what happened but because God loved those naked bodies He created. They were works of art like Michelangelo's statues of David or Moses, perfectly chiseled out of marble, stunning, but even better! And Adam and Eve were covering up God's craftsmanship. God was concerned. I imagine He wanted His creations to know they were beautiful exactly how He made them (Genesis 1:27; Psalm 139:14)—that there was nothing that needed covering up.

In Genesis 3:21 we read, "The Lord God made clothing from animal skins for Adam and his wife." What? God loved the way He'd created these people. He never intended Adam and Eve to be in this state of sin and shame. But God also knew that from the day of the forbidden fruit forward, Adam and Eve would recognize their nakedness and worry about it. God needed them to understand that they had defied God by listening to the snake instead of Him, and there were repercussions for that. But God didn't want them to feel shame.

God never wants us to feel shame. It's not in His nature.

And so our loving God made Adam and Eve the very first clothes—no, not apple suits but animal skins. Those made more sense at the time.

Who does that? Who has someone defy them and hide from them, and then tenderly makes them something to diffuse their worry? Our loving God, full of compassion and slow to anger. That's who.

That's how God treated Adam and Eve when they disobeyed Him.

Pause to consider how much He longs to comfort and care for us when we're trying but not quite getting there or downright failing, even when things are hard, even when we mess up.

This is how God described Himself to Moses: "The LORD, the LORD, the compassionate and gracious God, slow to anger, abounding in love and faithfulness, maintaining love to thousands, and forgiving wickedness, rebellion and sin" (Exodus 34:6–7).

Whew! What a comfort to know how compassionate, gracious, and abounding in love our God is! In all situations. No matter what we've done or where we've been. No matter what has caused us to feel shame and how that has affected our overall well-being.

Although it's getting better, there is still stigma around mental health. If you feel any shame because you have OCD or an eating disorder or struggle with any mental health issue, our compassionate, gracious, and loving God says, "Who told you that's something to be ashamed about?" God says, "What do you need? What's at the root of your worry? Let me clothe you."

And yet, sometimes we hide in the bushes full of shame.

Shame is dangerous for our mental health. Shame can cause depression and anxiety.[2] But our God is not a God who wants us to feel shame. Not about any mental ailment we might be experiencing or about anything we've done or had done to us. Yes, if we've made a mistake, God wants us to learn from it. Sure, God wants us to know right from wrong. We might feel convicted when we run away from God's loving will for us, but that's just to draw us back to Him, to His love, not to evoke shame.

There was a woman who carried some stigmas. She had the stigma of being a Samaritan, a people group the Jews despised. She also had the stigma of being married five times. What's your first thought if you hear someone has been married five times? Probably not super positive.

We don't know the woman's circumstances. Possibly she was infertile, and her husbands handed her certificates of divorce for not being able to produce heirs, which were the currency of their culture. Perhaps all five husbands died. Any way you look at it, she'd been through a lot. Sadly, she was probably thought of as "that" woman. It was likely because of the way the woman had been shamed that she came to the well at noon each day when no one else would be there, when she wouldn't have to endure the stares or eye rolls or whispers.

And yet Jesus came to her. He stopped at her town at the well she frequented at the time of day He knew she'd be there. He sat and chatted with her and looked her in the eyes. He said, "I know your story. You don't have to hide it or try to explain it to me. You don't have to crave attention or acceptance, aching for people to understand what actually happened. I have something that will satisfy all your cravings. Living water. Me."

It changed her life. The woman went from avoiding people to immediately going into town where all the people were. "The woman left her water jar beside the well and ran back to the village, telling everyone, 'Come and see a man who told me everything I ever did! Could he possibly be the Messiah?'" (John 4:28–29 NLT).

She must have been convincing. Whatever the townspeople had thought of her previously was cast aside by the way the woman was empowered after encountering Jesus. Because as soon as they heard her words, "the people came streaming from the village to see him" (v. 30 NLT).

My friend Tammy grew up with a brother with disabilities. Because her parents had so much extra on their plates caring for him, she tried to play the perfect little girl who would never cause her parents problems. Because she was incapable of living up to this impossible standard she'd set for herself, Tammy felt ashamed. Like she'd let herself and her parents down.

For decades she kept those emotions in the dark, where they festered. Tammy says, "That shadow of shame cast itself on so many decisions, actions, and reactions in my life." Jesus didn't want any of that for her! By sharing her stories with her counselor, Tammy has brought the shame into the light and received empathy. Tammy states, "Through therapy I'm learning to step out of that shadow."

My friend Chad had a pornography and sexual addiction

all throughout high school. He says, "I kept it completely hidden—no one knew about it. When my parents found out about this alter ego of mine, they were shocked. They didn't know how to handle it. At one point my dad looked me straight in the face and said, 'You're nothing but a liar.' There was so much shame at being defined as a liar. That that's all I was."

Chad shares that it's been a process of months and years to help him step out of that shame. "Having accountability partners and getting counseling have taught me that the number one thing that gets rid of shame is knowing that I'm not the only one with this problem—there are others. I met other men who are leaders in their churches, who came from Christian homes and went to Christian schools like I did, who also struggled with sexual addiction and hid it. Hearing their stories of where they'd been and how Jesus redeemed them showed me I'm not alone."

Chad added, "Spending time in the Bible has helped me learn that it's not in Jesus's nature to make us feel shame. I still have to deal with my issue. I still have to do the work, but I don't need to go back into my shell and hide. This is now my testimony, that Jesus loves me and doesn't want to shame me. It helps me with my own recovery, but by sharing I also hope to help others and bring them out of shame."

We can have false shame in our lives like Tammy or shame about something we regret like Chad. We might feel ashamed of the state of our mental health and how that makes us act or react, or we might feel shame for something in our past or something we're trying to undo, but Jesus loves us no matter what.

Jesus told the story of the prodigal son who left his father and home and spent his inheritance (while his dad was still alive, which is horrible) on "wild living" (Luke 15:13). Penniless and hungry, the son returned home.

> But while he was still a long way off, his father saw him and was filled with compassion for him; he ran to his son, threw his arms around him and kissed him.
> The son said to him, "Father, I have sinned against heaven and against you. I am no longer worthy to be called your son."
> But the father said to his servants, "Quick! Bring the best robe and put it on him." (Luke 15:20–22)

The father didn't shame the son. He didn't ask, "Why did you run away? Why did you squander what I had for you?"

No one would have blamed the dad if he had. The son was hoping to be able to be a mere servant. He was filled with such shame for his actions that he didn't dare ask to be treated like a son or to live in the family home again. But God is compassionate and gracious. He is "slow to anger, abounding in love and faithfulness, maintaining love to thousands, and forgiving wickedness, rebellion and sin" (Exodus 34:6–7). So the father ran out to his son, held him tight, clothed his son in his own robe, covering any shame, and threw him a party.

By speaking of his shame with his father, by not hiding anymore in secrecy, the son received his father's empathy, and his shame had to subside.

It was Satan, not God, who told Adam and Eve they weren't enough. The Samaritan village put a stigma on the woman that Jesus erased. Satan twisted Tammy's desire to be good into undeserved shame. Jesus didn't want shame for Chad; He just wanted His son to walk into the light. The world, not the father, told the prodigal son that he was worthless and unforgivable after his mistakes. And my mom didn't shame me when I wet my pants that day back in third grade. She wasn't even home. All that shame jumped in my head before I ever saw a soul. That slippery snake is still telling God's perfect creations (you and me) that we're not enough in Christ. He does it all the time. I bet you've heard him hiss.

But Jesus wants to clothe you in His love and compassion, give you living water to drink. He wants to clothe you in joy. In hope. In strength. He wants to wrap His royal robe around your shoulders and remind you that you are His beloved son or daughter, His treasured creation made in His very image.

When our mental health issues flare up and shame tries to creep in, we need to consider who we're listening to. When we have a panic attack in front of friends. When we have a relapse. When we have to cancel. When we take ten steps backward. When we feel out of control. We are not what we've done or where we've been or what they've called us or our mental health issues. We are children of the one true King, of a good Father who loves us the way we are, who makes us clothes way better than apple suits (sorry, Mom)— garments of love. Jesus finds us where we're hiding, runs out to us, welcomes us back home without shame but instead with grace and love.

Jesus Cares

And I pray that you, being rooted and established in love, may have power, together with all the Lord's holy people, to grasp how wide and long and high and deep is the love of Christ, and to know this love that surpasses knowledge—that you may be filled to the measure of all the fullness of God. (Ephesians 3:17–19)

What shame are you shouldering today?

Tell Jesus about it. He already knows. But telling the One who is full of kindness and compassion and slow to anger is the beginning of dissolving that shame. Remember, shame can't survive when it receives empathy, and Jesus empathizes.

After you pray about your shame, share it with someone you trust, someone you know will offer you compassion. You're doing it! You're dissolving shame!

20

Saint Bernards, Lasagna, and Border Control

Boundaries

When I heard about the Alps growing up, I always thought of Switzerland. But when my parents came to meet me in France at the end of my study abroad program the summer between my junior and senior years of college, that all changed. Now when I hear "the Alps," I think of Saint Bernards, the best lasagna I've ever tasted, and border control.

My parents and I spent a couple of days in Paris, then headed to the French Alps. Yes, it was summer, but my folks had a time-share week in North Carolina that they were able to trade for a French ski resort in summertime, which makes me laugh just typing it out. Since my parents and I didn't know if we'd ever make it back to Europe, we planned a day trip from the ski resort to neighboring Italy—just to say we'd been there, and of course for the extra stamp on our passports.

We had no idea what any of the foreign traffic signs meant as my dad drove our silver Renault rental car toward the village of Petit Saint-Bernard, France. The tiny town wasn't named for the big fluffy dogs with barrels around their necks, although there were plenty of doggy souvenirs, but after Saint

Bernard of Menthon, the patron saint of skiing, snowboarding, hiking, backpacking, and mountaineering, which was fitting. The town is so small, if you drive one more minute you're in Piccolo San Bernardo, Italy, but to officially get to the Italian side, we had to go through border control.

The checkpoint was just like in the movies. There was a guard hut and a barricade going across the road. Two very stern Italians, which for the record are the only stern Italians I've ever encountered, came out in full uniform and approached our car. My heart started pounding and I sat up straighter in the back seat. I felt as if we were trespassing or breaking the law, even though we weren't. Maybe this impression came from watching too many James Bond films. Not knowing any Italian at the time, we didn't understand a word the police said, but we handed them our passports, smiled, nodded, stated our names when they gestured to us, and kept eye contact as they matched faces with passport photos. The guards took our passports and disappeared in their hut for what felt like a very long time. Mom, Dad, and I whispered, wondering what was going on. Eventually the guards returned, raised the gate, and waved us through.

The guards were just doing their job. Keeping their country safe. Keeping danger out of their community, lives, and homes. And they took this assignment of protecting their border seriously.

We need to do the same. Protect the boundaries of our hearts and minds. We're told in Proverbs, "Above all else, guard your heart, for everything you do flows from it" (4:23).

Why? Because we live in a broken world where memories or circumstances might threaten our hearts. We can't stop the things that might trigger us, but we can make a conscious effort to avoid some of these things by setting boundaries for our hearts, for our well-being, like uniformed sentinels keeping watch.

How do we do this?

Just like we'd set boundaries for other areas of our lives, like locking the doors of our home or car because not just anyone is welcome to enter, or having an electric fence in our yard so our dog won't wander off, or installing a baby gate in our home to make sure our little one doesn't tumble down the stairs. We take inventory of what threatens us, and if there's something specific we identify as potentially dangerous, we set up a barrier for protection.

Dr. Henry Cloud and Dr. John Townsend, the authors of the *New York Times* bestseller *Boundaries* (it is so good— please go read this book!), explain, "A helpful way to understand setting limits is that our lives are a gift from God. . . . When we say no to people and activities that are hurtful to us, we are protecting God's investment."[1]

Are you protecting God's investment of your precious life?

One friend of mine struggled with an eating disorder in college. To ensure she takes care of her body and mind, she decided to never diet again. A family member of mine experiences anxiety riding on elevators. Whenever possible, she takes the stairs. Another friend is a gifted speaker, but something funky goes on inside when she talks in front of a crowd, something unsafe and dark. And so, even though she gets invited to speak at all kinds of events, she won't do it. She knows danger lurks for her in those invitations, so she turns them down.

My friend Brenda wants children but doesn't have them. She was repeatedly recruited to volunteer in kids' ministries at church. After years of doing what she thought was the "right thing" but was actually emotionally draining for her, she decided to no longer serve in this way. Brenda now volunteers at an adult ministry, which allows her to give of her time and talents while protecting her well-being.

If your mental health gets shaky when you don't get enough sleep, you can set a specific bedtime each night. Social media has been linked with intensified senses of loneliness, anxiety, and depression. If this is a dangerous space for you, perhaps you need to set some social media parameters. Does that account create a bad feeling, jealousy, sarcasm, or a desire to do something you know isn't good for you? You have the power and the right to unfollow, unfriend, or mute that potentially harmful account. You could delete an app that consumes you, set a timer for how long you're on social media, or have certain days or hours that you don't allow yourself on social media at all.

If crowds make you anxious, you can avoid places with big groups whenever possible. Does a certain person consistently take advantage of, manipulate, or criticize you? How can you minimize contact with that person? My friend Sharee drew a line in her life and "got out of relationships with a few people who were super negative." She told me this negativity from others brought her down to dangerous places.

Unfortunately, we can't avoid all the things that might threaten our mental health. Some are unavoidable. But we *can* be mindful of things that throw us off and do our best to manage those situations.

Jesus's disciple Peter instructed his readers to be on the lookout for evil: "Stay alert! Watch out for your great enemy, the devil. He prowls around like a roaring lion, looking for someone to devour. Stand firm against him, and be strong in your faith" (1 Peter 5:8–9 NLT). Peter is referring to the schemes of the devil. Of course, many things that ail us aren't of Satan. Crowds are innocent in themselves. But if they cause panic for you, Satan might try to use a crowd to make you believe that you're not in control or that you're less than, or maybe even to doubt Jesus's presence in your life. To prevent that sneaky snake from getting the upper hand, we can watch out. Be alert.

Our boundaries need to be flexible because we can't control everything that takes place around us. But we can be alert. You can't avoid every crowd, but if you find yourself in one, you might be able to navigate away from a congested area to find more space—maybe an aisle seat or the back of a room away from the fray. You might have a late meeting or flight that disrupts your designated bedtime. Could you compensate by napping on the plane or sleeping in the next day?

What can you say no to in order to protect yourself?

Jesus set all kinds of boundaries.

"The crowd that gathered around [Jesus] was so large that he got into a boat and sat in it out on the lake, while all the people were along the shore at the water's edge" (Mark 4:1). Apparently Jesus needed some room. He didn't shirk His responsibility to teach the crowd but protected Himself and His needs.

"[Jesus] did not let anyone follow him except Peter, James and John the brother of James" (5:37). Jesus was about to perform a mega miracle. He was going to raise Jairus's daughter from the dead, but Jesus didn't want the crowd to follow. I'm not sure why, but He had His reasons. And to protect them Jesus stood firm and did not let the crowd follow.

"Immediately Jesus made his disciples get into the boat and go on ahead of him to Bethsaida, while he dismissed the crowd. After leaving them, he went up on a mountainside to pray" (6:45–46). The disciples probably could have helped Jesus dismiss the large crowd, but Jesus knew it would be better if the disciples went ahead and He stayed back, so He separated Himself from them. Jesus then created another physical boundary, this time between Himself and the crowd, by going up a mountain for prayer time alone with God.

I just scanned through Mark 4, 5, and 6 and found Jesus setting distinct boundaries in each chapter. You get the idea. Jesus knew what He needed and wasn't afraid to ask for it. Not in a bossy or needy way, just in an honest way. "You go ahead. I'll stay back. I could use some space. I'm going over here." Why did Mark so intentionally put these details in his account of Christ's life? Maybe to show us how we can follow suit.

Stressful situations will occur. Sometimes the circumstances aren't even toxic, but a combination of things going on inside our heads puts us at risk. One way we protect our mental wellness is by setting boundaries.

We don't need to draw lines around everything in our life. I can drive from my home state of Ohio to Kentucky or Indiana without border control. There are no barricades or enforcement officers. No one asks to see my papers or passport or license. I don't get stopped or glared at. There are some people and activities in our lives like this. We trust them so much and know them so well that we can be ourselves, take our time, and never have to worry. But there are some things in our lives—and they're different for all of us—that are helpful to set limits around. Remember, Jesus taught crowds *and* sent crowds away. He was sometimes in the midst of large groups *and* sometimes physically set Himself away from them. Jesus asked people to follow Him *and* sometimes made sure no one was following Him.

Boundaries aren't bad things. They don't confine us. They make us safe. They actually give us freedom in the places we are.

Our Savior has designed us for an abundant life. Why not take our cues from Him and set up a few boundaries of our own to keep threats out and pleasant living in?

Once my parents and I got through the checkpoint and over to the Italian side of the border—Piccolo San Bernardo—we found a small restaurant with tables and chairs in the midday sun. We pointed to a few menu items and were delighted by the heaps of delicacies brought to our table. I don't recall what else we ate, but I can still taste the lasagna with dense noodles doused in tangy red tomato sauce. We sat and laughed and ate until we were so full we thought we would bust. We paid with lire, which was the Italian currency prior to the euro. One thousand lire equaled approximately fifty cents, so we paid with thousands of lire that felt like Monopoly money. After lunch we walked the cobblestone streets of the village and bought postcards with gorgeous photos of the snowcapped Alps and a fuzzy Saint Bernard key chain.

Then we got in our car and crossed back into France.

At the time it felt strange that we, an innocent American family, would be stared down at that Italian border. But now it makes so much sense. Nobody wants danger in their lives. So France and Italy guard their borders. As new things (cargo, trucks, or tourists) come in and out, they monitor them. And if something seems suspicious, they don't let it into their country.

We can also draw some lines to protect ourselves. Some long-term relationships, patterns, or expectations in our lives could be unhealthy. If we've never taken action against these things, or just recently realized the damage being done, we can evaluate them to protect our emotional well-being. If we realize they are toxic or harmful, it is never too late to start creating boundaries. And as new people and circumstances enter our lives, we can evaluate them too—is this healthy? Does it pose a threat? And after assessing the situation, we get to decide if it can come in or if our life will be safer if we keep it out. Setting boundaries can protect us from some obvious dangers and free us to enjoy new things—like authentic Italian lasagna and a view of one of the most beautiful mountain ranges in the world.

Jesus Cares

> Above all else, guard your heart,
> for everything you do flows from it.
> (Proverbs 4:23)

Take a quick assessment of your life. Ask Jesus if there are any places you could set some boundaries that would protect your mental health.

Take action to put at least one boundary in place. Is there someone you need to distance yourself from? How about not answering their phone calls but only responding to them over text, where you have time to process what they've communicated and think through your response? Do you need protection from your screen time? How about going to Settings on your phone and creating limits on the amount of time you spend there? Ask Jesus for guidance and courage to protect your new (and old) boundaries.

21

Toppling Shelves and Cleaned-Out Drawers

Creating Order

The shelves in my closet are totally fine.

Until they are one-hundred-percent not.

They start out neat and orderly. Then one day I'm in a rush and shove a sweater on a shelf less than folded, only for it to topple askew. A few days later my daughter will borrow a hoodie and put it back-ish on top of that sweater. Or there will be a day when I can't find the leggings I'm looking for and I rummage through my entire shelf of workout clothes not finding them until the moment my husband calls for the second time, "Honey? You ready?"

I pop the leggings on, leaving that shelf topsy-turvy. So it goes. And it's not a problem. Until one day I scream, "AH-HHHH, these shelves are driving me bonkers!" and proceed to pull everything off every shelf, sit down on the floor of the closet amid my heap o' clothes, fold each item, and put it neatly back in place.

What's the tipping point? Why do I go from "no big deal" to "how could anybody be expected to live in these conditions"? For me, it's always when something else feels out of control—maybe my schedule is too crammed or someone I love is being treated poorly. Subconsciously, organizing my shelves helps me feel in charge of at least one area of my life. There's something soothing about folding a T-shirt in a perfect square, sleeves tucked back, neckline in view, and then stacking it flatly on top of the previous tee just like I learned when I used to be a manager at a clothing store in the mall. The actual folding is tactile—smooth T-shirts, fuzzy sweatshirts, thick, bumpy denim. It gives my brain a break from my laptop and my work. Just me. And clothes. And shelves. In my quiet closet. Simple. Basic. Rhythmic. And orderly.

It's not just me who finds calm in organizing. My mom says, "When I'm feeling overwhelmed or anxious, I'll attack a project—like clean a drawer out."

My friend Sharee says when things feel out of control, she goes for "a healthy, productive distraction, like cleaning my place. It's something I can control, and I have more peace when things are clean."

My daughter Maddie says, "I always keep my own space, my own room, clean. I feel calmer there. Even if the other areas of the townhome I share with my roommates are cluttered, even if my life is hectic, I know my room is organized in a way I like it—that I have that calm, controlled space."

According to mental health experts, cleaning and organizing can decrease anxiety and depression and increase creativity. Decluttering can help us focus and refresh our mental space.[1] Sigh, that sounds lovely.

It also makes sense.

Our God is a God of order, not of chaos. In Exodus 25 God gave detailed instructions to Moses on how to build the ark of the covenant, which would house the tablets God wrote the Ten Commandments on. God also gave specific details on how to build a table, lampstand, altar, tabernacle, and courtyard. Here's just a sampling:

Make upright frames of acacia wood for the tabernacle. Each frame is to be ten cubits long and a cubit and a half wide, with two projections set parallel to each other. Make all the frames of the tabernacle in this way. Make twenty frames for the south side of the tabernacle and make forty silver bases to go under them—two bases for each frame, one under each projection. For the other side, the north side of the tabernacle, make twenty frames and forty silver bases—two under each frame. Make six frames for the far end, that is, the west end of the tabernacle, and make two frames for the corners at the far end. At these two corners they must be double from the bottom all the way to the top and fitted into a single ring; both shall be like that. So there will be eight frames and sixteen silver bases—two under each frame. (26:15–25)

The tabernacle is a gorgeous example of the amazing order and symmetry of God and the things He designs.

This does not mean that God's mad at you if you're slightly unorganized or downright messy. Which is a relief to this girl who lets closets, drawers, and (I'll admit it) sometimes entire rooms get a bit cluttered.

I'm a creative and fully embrace that in the midst of a project I might have multiple Bibles, reference books, notepads, sticky notes, colored pens, and Ghirardelli 72-percent cacao squares littering my desk. It's how I access ideas and stories and flow. But I also know I can't keep my desk this way. At the end of a chapter or manuscript or assignment, I need to put those books back on my bookshelves, recycle the scraps of paper covered in scribbles, toss the shiny purple chocolate wrappers, tend to any family paperwork (bills, school forms, etc.) that has grown into a pile in the corner by the door, wipe down the whole surface, and start over. It clears my mind and creates fresh space to start anew.

Jesus loves you no matter what, and nothing you do or don't do can increase or decrease His fierce, faithful love for you. God doesn't love you more or less if you're neat or messy, but when we actively get things in order, it's one way God can help us tap into peace and calm.

We see God's desire to restore the beautiful design and order of His creation at the end of time on earth as we know it in the book of Revelation. In it, Jesus declares, "I am making everything new!" (21:5).

Like when I dumped out a drawer in our kids' bathroom, peeled off the old contact paper caked with remnants of blue minty gel toothpaste, a smear of waxy deodorant, and a squishy spot that might have once been lotion or maybe mousse (it kind of smelled like coconut), and threw it away. I rolled out a fresh white piece of contact paper and lined the drawer, making it look brand-new. There was such satisfaction in the smoothness, in the contrast before and after, in the clean slate, in having made this transformation with my own hands.

Obviously, when Jesus makes things new, it's way better than that! When Jesus creates the new Jerusalem, it will look like this:

> The city was laid out like a square, as long as it was wide. He measured the city with the rod and found it to be 12,000 stadia in length, and as wide and high as it is long. The angel measured the wall using human measurement, and it was 144 cubits thick. The wall was made of jasper, and the city of pure gold, as pure as

glass. The foundations of the city walls were decorated with every kind of precious stone. . . . The twelve gates were twelve pearls, each gate made of a single pearl. The great street of the city was of gold, as pure as transparent glass. (Revelation 21:16–19, 21)

Stunning. Right?

Pure gold with precious stones and gates made of pearls sounds breathtaking, almost too beautiful to imagine. And God in His sense of order and exquisite design makes the new city a perfect square with an even dozen gates. The number twelve shows up everywhere to represent the twelve tribes of Israel. Twelve thousand stadia long. Twelve thousand stadia wide. One hundred forty-four (twelve by twelve) cubits thick. Yes, God likes things to be organized and well laid out. And when He builds something, He builds it right.

God also built you specifically and intentionally. If He puts that much care into a gate, wall, or street, can you imagine how much more ornately and orderly He created you?

But just like my junk drawer that keeps getting more random things tossed into it until it's hard to open and close or find anything in, sometimes we, designed for beauty and order, get tangled and disheveled. It is here where Jesus wants to come in and clean house. Maybe that's through some serious prayer time with Him, where He can help you sort your thoughts into neater, easier-to-handle piles. Maybe that's through counseling, where a professional therapist can help you organize your feelings and reactions—kind of like California Closets assessing and organizing your closets but for your mind. And sometimes Jesus will bring you peace and clarity and hope in the simple act of tidying things up.

Jesus is waiting to come in and transform your entire life.

Therefore, if anyone is in Christ, the new creation has come:
The old has gone, the new is here! (2 Corinthians 5:17)

Jesus cares so much about us that He cleans out the closets and drawers of our pasts. He wants to get rid of our mental messes and give us new ways of handling hard situations and managing challenges. He makes us new, and He invites us into the makeover, to bring order to some of our chaos.

It can be as simple as changing your sheets and treating yourself to a soft, freshly scented pillow at bedtime or as elaborate as a full-on spring-cleaning of your living area top to bottom. If it feels too overwhelming, clearly that isn't helpful. You don't have to do it all, but committing to at least a small act of clearing off that shelf or getting rid of that pile or even putting your dirty coffee cups in the dishwasher brings a sense of accomplishment and order.

When we clean, the actual act of washing dishes in warm, lemon-scented suds or wiping smears off a mirror to give it a sheen brings us peace and satisfaction—things I could sure use. Things God wants for us. Tidying also gives our minds more space and less stress—more things I could use. This doesn't have to be another thing on your to-do list that overwhelms you. Instead, consider it free therapy. Invest a little time today to join Jesus into creating more order in this world and more peace in your mind.

Jesus Cares

Therefore, if anyone is in Christ, the new creation has come:
The old has gone, the new is here! (2 Corinthians 5:17)

What is one thing you have the time and resources to clean up today? If today is already overwhelming, plan to do it tomorrow.

Take a moment to journal or talk to Jesus about how you felt before, during, and after the cleaning process.

22
Tadpoles, Trips, and Tears
Grief

During a field trip in elementary school to COSI, the awesome, giant, interactive science museum in Columbus, Ohio, all the students received tadpoles. I named my tadpole Joey. I loved him. I carefully followed the instructions the docent at COSI gave me to nurture my tadpole as he grew into a frog. I stared at his odd little self for hours. Eventually he grew two tiny hind legs. And then one day Joey looked like he was floating on his back. I told myself he was just being silly, swimming upside down, but in my gut I knew something was wrong. The next day I hoped he would be right side up—I'd imagined the whole thing—but of course he wasn't. Which I knew meant Joey was dead, but I couldn't admit it. So I pretended to myself that I didn't see him. If I couldn't see it, maybe it wasn't real.

The following day my brother or mom (I forget which one) saw Joey floating and "broke the sad news" to me. I acted surprised, but I already knew. I'd been carrying around the sadness and fear and, honestly, the grossness of a dead tadpole in my room for days. Not to mention the guilt of being dishonest. I thrive on being honest, and the worry of being caught in my deceit made my stomach hurt.

189

Grief, even over a tadpole, is confusing and hard and unpredictable. We lose something we don't want to lose, and our bodies and minds seem to go into autopilot and react in the weirdest ways.

During March of 2020, my girlfriend Beth and I were scheduled to go on a "women of the Bible" tour of Israel with a local church. The trip of a lifetime we'd prayed about, invested in, and been ready to embark upon was canceled just a couple of days before departure. Even though the world was shutting down around us due to the COVID-19 pandemic, Beth and I schemed up ways we could still go. We texted the leader of the group, looked into individual flights, researched what it would look like to go without a tour guide—not the thoughts of sane women. Thankfully, none of our strategies worked or we may have been quarantined in Israel for months. Once again, I'd lost something I didn't want to lose, and I reacted uncharacteristically. I'm not a schemer. I don't like to break rules, go rogue, or confront a system, and yet that's how I reacted.

In the following days everyone I knew lost things. Our kids lost theater productions, soccer and track seasons, retreats, prom, graduation, attending class in person, living on campus. We all lost the privilege of attending church. And too many friends lost their health and loved ones to the pandemic.

Suddenly the whole world seemed to be grieving something or someone, some more severely than others. According to Harvard Medical School, "Chronic stress also is common during acute grief and can lead to a variety of physical and emotional issues, such as depression, trouble sleeping, feelings of anger and bitterness, anxiety, loss of appetite, and general aches and pains."[1]

My examples of a tadpole and a canceled trip are just blips on the radar compared to losing a loved one. I've experienced that kind of grief too, the heart-wrenching kind. The truth is all types of grief take a toll on our mental health in unexpected and unpredictable ways. The greater the loss, the greater the pain and the stronger the effects on the person mourning.

There are typically five stages of grief: denial, anger, bargaining, depression, and acceptance. But there is nothing typical about how we grieve. David Kessler, a world-renowned expert on grief, explains that the five stages are "tools to help us frame and identify what we may be feeling. But they are not stops on some linear timeline in grief. Not everyone goes through all of them or in a prescribed order. . . . At times, people in grief will often report more stages. Just remember your grief is as unique as you are."[2]

Your grief is going to be different than his or hers. And you have permission to go through it at your own pace, to feel the feelings, to ask for help in whatever way makes most sense for you. Grief is complicated and multifaceted and feels so stinking unfair. You lose something or someone you love, and then on top of it you suffer grief.

Jesus experienced grief when His friend Lazarus died.

When Jesus saw [Lazarus's sister Mary] weeping and saw the other people wailing with her, a deep anger welled up within him, and he was deeply troubled. "Where have you put him?" he asked them.

They told him, "Lord, come and see." Then Jesus wept. The people who were standing nearby said, "See how much he loved him!" But some said, "This man healed a blind man. Couldn't he have kept Lazarus from dying?"

Jesus was still angry as he arrived at the tomb, a cave with a stone rolled across its entrance. "Roll the stone aside," Jesus told them. (John 11:33–39 NLT)

When Jesus was confronted with His friend's death, Jesus got angry, was troubled, cried, and then returned to anger. His emotions were real.

So are yours.

Grief takes our emotions on a roller coaster. And since Jesus was fully human (while staying fully God—one of those mysteries I won't fully get my mind around this side of heaven), He experienced all these emotions in a matter of moments. If you are a follower of Jesus, you can take comfort in this. Jesus felt and expressed His emotions. Jesus got to have the final say in what was recorded in the Bible, and He cares so much about us that He wanted you and me to be able to read about His complicated emotions when faced with grief. Jesus wants us to understand that these emotions are not only okay but normal. He felt that way too.

My mom cried every day for a year after she and my dad got divorced. She filed for the divorce. She got most everything in the settlement because of my father's multiple acts of adultery, so finances weren't an issue. Mom knew she had to get out of that marriage, but still she mourned it.

My friend Brenda's mother passed away last November. She told me that grieving her mom has also made her grieve unfulfilled dreams, so when the grief from missing her mom comes up, all these other unfulfilled dreams rear up too.

These women are smart women. Women who love Jesus. Their brains knew one thing, but their hearts and minds felt something else. Grief will do that. Jesus knew He was about to raise Lazarus from the dead, yet still our Lord wept.

Your emotions and reactions during grief don't have to be rational. They probably won't be. You might pretend not to see something, try to overturn the system, cry uncontrollably, start lamenting seemingly unrelated things, or do none or all of the above. But you aren't alone. Jesus grieved too. And then He performed a life-giving miracle. He wants to bring hope and life and joy into your life after the mourning. That could be through the love of family and friends, a new puppy who makes you laugh and brings you companionship, or maybe a support group where you can safely share your feelings, learn from others, and slowly get stronger step-by-step.

The prophet Isaiah told the people of Israel God would

> provide for those who grieve in Zion—
> to bestow on them a crown of beauty
>   instead of ashes,
> the oil of joy
>   instead of mourning,
> and a garment of praise
>   instead of a spirit of despair.
>   (61:3)

Today, Jesus still wants to provide for you in your grieving. He wants to help you find beauty, joy, and praise again.

I felt a bit nauseous typing out the story of Joey, my tadpole. It's oddly all so vivid and somewhat sickening in my memory. Yet I never told anyone about it until now. About how I lied about not knowing my tadpole was already dead. There was such a longing in my heart for him to be alive. He was supposed to turn into a frog! I had big plans of releasing

Joey into the creek and watching him hop into a whole new life. What had I done wrong? Had I killed him? Was it my fault?

And I was so ashamed and sad that I lied about it. I let his little body float in his fishbowl for a couple of days, not tending to him. It was dishonest and irresponsible, which is the opposite of how this people pleaser operated as a little girl (and still today). My example is intentionally insignificant compared to some of the loss you may have experienced. But even grade school grief over a tadpole can be hard to grapple with. In my panic I never turned to anyone for help. I certainly didn't ask Jesus for help. But you can. We all can.

Grief isn't something you can just dismiss or even pray away. Prayer is great and definitely helpful, but it won't undo who or what you've lost. Jesus says, "Blessed are those who mourn, for they will be comforted" (Matthew 5:4). Grieving, mourning, is a healing process. Jesus will comfort you throughout this process. Be gentle with yourself. Make sure you're eating and sleeping and moving. Give yourself time. Ask for help.

Loss is hard. But Jesus is with you. He wants to provide what you need in your lament. He wants to help you find beauty again. He loves you and longs to hold your hand through this grief journey. He wants to turn your mourning into joy.

Jesus Cares

> [God will] provide for those who grieve in
>   Zion—
> to bestow on them a crown of beauty

> instead of ashes,
> the oil of joy
> instead of mourning,
> and a garment of praise
> instead of a spirit of despair.
> (Isaiah 61:3)

What are you mourning?

Ask Jesus how you can be gentle with yourself today. Write down at least two things you can do to take care of yourself. Follow through with them.

What emotions have you been holding back, ignoring, or stuffing? Talk to Jesus about everything you're feeling. He's the very best listener. And it will feel good to let out some of those emotions.

23

When You're Run-Down

Rest and Refuel

I love watching the runners at a track meet. No matter what event they're in—a sprint, relay, or long run—those athletes give it all they have. You see it in their faces and bodies—the determination, the drive, the intentional extending of their legs for the next stride and then the next, deciding when and if they should pass another runner, gearing up for it, powering through. And when they cross the finish line? Many of the runners collapse to the ground.

Three of our four kids have run track, so I've seen my share of races. But at the first event of the first meet I ever attended, I watched a young man crumple on the lane just two steps over the finish line, gasping for air. I immediately began praying in my head for that boy. Was he okay? *God, please be with him.* Race after race more kids did this. Some of them running so hard they threw up at the finish. Some reaching for their inhalers or curling up into a ball. I watched coaches and parents and trainers gather these strong teenage athletes in their arms and help them get off the track, regain their breathing, and eventually recover. Because they ran their races. Hard. They gave it their all.

And then they collapsed and had to rest.

So do you and I.

Jesus invites us into a balance of going full force and resting and recovering. Let's look at the running-our-races part first. Then we'll pick up with the resting.

"Never be lazy, but work hard and serve the Lord enthusiastically" (Romans 12:11 NLT). I love verses like this. They get me excited and motivated to go out there and give it all I've got. I want to go full throttle for Jesus. In my parenting, marriage, writing.

I am a lot of things—good and bad—but some of the qualities God put in me are passion and empathy. I feel everything my family is feeling, and I'm passionate about making their lives full of love and grace and joy. If one of them is waking up extremely early, I *want* to wake up to give them a hug before they leave. If one of them needs a ride, someone to listen, a fudgy brownie, I *want* to provide it for them. This also spills out into my writing—I pray over these words I type that as you read these pages you will feel the hope and undeniable love of Jesus down to your bones. I will sit in my writing chair day after day trying to find, as Hemingway would say, "*le mot juste*,"[1] the perfect word or words to illustrate Christ's amazing and forever love for you.

I also try to exercise regularly, make relatively healthy meals for our family, keep our house reasonably clean, and so on. But here's the thing. Giving it *all* I've got for *all* these things *all* the time eventually feels heavy. Not in a bad way but in a "I gave it all I had" way, and then I get tired. And just like those athletes, at some point I'll feel like I'm going to collapse. I'll start drinking too much coffee to "keep my energy up." I'll wake up extra early too many days in a row, cheating myself of sleep to "get it all done," and get grumpy or jittery or forget to breathe or cry too easily (yes, even more easily than typical, which is. a. lot.). Or that weird red spot will show up under my left eye that only appears when I'm spread way too thin. Or, if it's really bad, all the above.

My mental health suffers because I'm not taking care of myself. And I'm shaky and off and a prime target for the Enemy to slither in and shout some lies at me because my defenses are down.

So many other people feel the same. My friend Elisa was the primary caregiver for her mother and brother when she was just a teenager. Elisa felt like she lost part of herself during those years because she was exhausting her resources caring for them, saving nothing for herself.

Ever been there? Are you there now?

Jesus cares about our mental health. He does. Yes, He asks us to run the race. As Paul tells the church in Corinth, "So I run with purpose in every step" (1 Corinthians 9:26 NLT). Or as *The Message* paraphrases this verse, "I'm giving it everything I've got."

And we should too. God gifted us with family, friends, and functionality. He's given us responsibilities, skill sets, and missions, calling us to give it all we've got.

And also, God calls us to rest. I told you we'd get to the resting part.

The way *The Message* states that earlier verse from Romans is this: "Don't burn out; keep yourselves fueled and aflame" (12:11).

Paul is telling the Romans, Yes, run, but *also* don't burn out.

The Bible is packed with verses encouraging us both to fight the good fight with all we've got *and* to rest.

The story of Elijah illustrates this work-rest rhythm so beautifully.

God's prophet Elijah first shows up in the Bible in 1 Kings 17:1, boldly telling the evil King Ahab that for the next few years there is going to be a horrific drought in the land. Not the kind of message that's well received.

Elijah obediently follows God's directions and promptings for about three and a half more years after giving Ahab this bad news. This faithful work leads Elijah back in front of King Ahab in a kind of showdown where God uses Elijah to show the Israelites that the one true God is infinitely better than the false god Baal they have been worshipping. Elijah sets the terms of the challenge: "Get two bulls for us. Let Baal's prophets choose one for themselves, and let them cut it into pieces and put it on the wood but not set fire to it. I will prepare the other bull and put it on the wood but not set fire to it. Then you call on the name of your god, and I will call on the name of the LORD. The god who answers by fire—he is God" (1 Kings 18:23–24).

The Baal worshippers danced and shouted around their altar from morning until past noon, and absolutely nothing happened. Then Elijah had twelve giant jugs of water poured all over the bull on the altar to God and said:

> "Answer me, LORD, answer me, so these people will know that you, LORD, are God, and that you are turning their hearts back again."
>
> Then the fire of the LORD fell and burned up the sacrifice, the wood, the stones and the soil, and also licked up the water in the trench. (vv. 37–38)

Woo-hoo! God showed them who was who. God's fire couldn't be stopped by all that water—in fact it burned up rocks and dirt! Then giant rain clouds came, the skies opened up, and after three and a half years of drought God sent rain. So very much rain.

Talk about giving it your all. This was Elijah's fifteen minutes of fame. His biggest moment as a prophet. He'd been bold and brave and burned for the Lord. He stood up to a fierce king, not once but twice. Elijah declared that God was God in front of 450 prophets of the idol Baal. And then Elijah courageously directed the showdown where God's spectacular power dominated. God did something mighty in this man.

Not surprisingly King Ahab was furious. He told his wife, Jezebel, who was even nastier than Ahab, and she put a death warrant on Elijah's head. Terrified, Elijah ran away to the wilderness, and next thing we know, this is what Elijah tells God: "I have had enough, LORD. . . . Take my life; I am no better than my ancestors" (19:4).

Elijah went from one hundred to zero. He was spent. He'd given it all he had, and now he was empty. He was suicidal, asking God to take his life. Many biblical scholars believe Elijah suffered from depression, and after expending all his energy and then receiving a death threat, his depression flared up intensely, as it would. Immediately after asking God for death, Elijah lay down and fell asleep.

Did God cast a sleep over him, so His prophet would get the rest he needed? Or did Elijah's body literally have no more energy to run on? I like to think God forced this sleep. Because when Elijah woke up, an angel had baked some fresh bread for the prophet and gave him a jar of water. No lie. An angel of God does this for Elijah twice in a row (vv. 5–8). This is how personal our God is! This is how much God cares about our well-being! In our most desperate times, God invites us to sleep, eat warm bread, and drink cool, fresh water.

God doesn't just do this for His prophets. He does it for us too. My daughter is a teacher and had an especially stressful and exhausting week. That Friday, her district canceled school due to potential tornados in the area. It felt as if God gifted Maddie a day to get some extra sleep when she so desperately needed it for her well-being.

When my mom had foot surgery, she couldn't walk or drive for six weeks. She had to rest her foot to recover. God used her neighbors to make sure she was staying off that foot and being well-fed. Like angels, they waltzed into her kitchen with marinated chicken, bagel sandwiches, salad, and butter pecan turtle bars. One of them even baked her a fresh loaf of bread and brought it over still warm.

Our lives are so precious to God, and thankfully our good Father knows sometimes we're better off if He *doesn't* answer our prayers. God did not take Elijah's life. It was after this resting time that God spoke to Elijah in a still, small voice. And soon after that, God allowed Elijah to pass the baton to the next prophet, Elisha. Because Elijah was rested and refueled, he regained stability, a desire to live, and the drive, passion, and energy to interact with God, to hear God, and to do the work God called him to do.

Yes, God calls us to give one hundred percent.

And then God calls us to rest.

"Our bodies and minds are connected," explains my friend Robin Hostetler (who has an impressive list of letters after her name that means she is super certified in the counseling world). "When you burn out, it's a physical thing, but because it affects your body, it also affects your mental health. If you're not rested, things like anxiety and depression flair up. We can't keep going without rest."

God created our bodies. He's more aware than we are of what they're capable of, what they need, how long they can function, and what's necessary to refuel, recharge, and rest them.

According to the Sleep Foundation, our brains process emotions and memories while we sleep.[2] A lack of sleep can negatively influence our moods and emotions and increase the intensity of both depression and anxiety. Lack of sleep can also aggravate ADHD. And yet we as a culture tend to blow off sleep. The phrase "sleep is overrated" is thrown around as truth.

It's a lie.

Sleep is critical to our well-being.

My friend Sharee, who battles depression and is also a wellness coach, explains, "To take care of my mental health, I have to start with the basics. Am I sleeping and eating well? I can't regulate my emotions when I'm in survival mode and not getting enough sleep."

Jesus Himself emphasized the importance of rest. "Then, because so many people were coming and going that they did not even have a chance to eat, [Jesus] said to [the disciples], 'Come with me by yourselves to a quiet place and get some rest'" (Mark 6:31).

Jesus recognized when He and His dear friends were exhausted. They hadn't even taken time to eat. Have you ever been there? Running from this to that and realizing you never had lunch? Or maybe you did eat but it was shoving a taco down while driving to your next appointment or nibbling on a kind of stale granola bar you'd tucked in your bag who knows how long ago. Jesus doesn't want that for you. He invites you to come away with Him and get some rest.

How can you find rest?

My counselor friend Robin, who I mentioned above, encourages all her patients to create a designated place in their homes where they can rest. She suggests they put a cozy blanket there, have a candle nearby, and have access to calming music.

You might need to go to bed earlier or maybe wake up later. Maybe it means sleeping in on your day off or, if you're required to be awake both early and late, taking midday naps. When my kiddos were little, I often laid down and closed my eyes during their nap time. Resting also means taking days off, preferably a full day every week (God calls this Sabbath). If you have a busy season—say you're an accountant and tax-filing April is intense, or perhaps you're moving across the country—resting will be hard during that season but so very necessary after that season. And not just for an hour or two or a day but for several days to refuel your tank. Yes, rest refers to sleep but also to slowing down, cozying up in a chair with your Bible or a great novel, finding a spot in your sunroom or porch, closing your eyes, praying, sitting poolside and noticing the warm sun on your skin, listening to good music, enjoying a long, drawn-out, hot bath or meal, taking time to soak in or savor every note, bubble, or bite.

After track events, athletes rest. You'll often see them lying or sitting down for several minutes after a race. When their heart rate and breathing return to normal, they'll chat and laugh with their friends in their "team camps," hydrate, and snack on trail mix or protein bars. They may even run another event or two that day an hour or so later. Then they repeat the whole process over again. Running with all their strength and might. Their bodies temporarily shutting down to recover. Resting. Then returning to normal teenagers gulping blue sports drinks, showing each other funny photos on their phones, popping in their earbuds, and doing silly dance moves to the music playing in their ears.

This is how God made us. To run the races He's called us to. And then to rest, hydrate, eat, and recover. It's critical to our mental health. And it's critical to living the abundant lives Christ invites us into.

Jesus Cares

Come with me by yourselves to a quiet place and get some rest. (Mark 6:31)

Don't burn out; keep yourselves fueled and aflame. (Romans 12:11 MSG)

Ask Jesus to help you find a way to get fifteen more minutes of sleep every day this week—that's an hour and forty-five minutes extra by the end of the week. Maybe go to bed earlier by watching half rather than a full episode of that show, or simplify your morning routine, allowing yourself to sleep in. Pay attention—do you feel more rested? How does it affect you?

Are you drinking enough water? Doctors recommend on average men get 3.7 liters and women 2.7 liters each day.[3] Try filling a water bottle and carrying it around with you wherever you go.

What worked this week for getting more rest? What didn't? Thank Jesus for creating your body and commit to doing something that worked for the body He made for you again next week.

24

Music Is All Around Us

Gratitude

"Music is all around us. All you have to do is listen."[1]
This line from the movie *August Rush* tugs at me.
Maybe because I'm a music lover. Maybe because this movie
about an orphan who steps into his God-given gifts and destiny despite all odds makes me weep. But I think mainly I'm
moved by this statement because there's beautiful truth to it.

In Psalm 104:33 the psalmist declares, "I will sing to the
LORD all my life; I will sing praise to my God as long as I live."
The psalmist looks and sees that God's wonder is all around.
God set the earth on its foundation (v. 5), makes grass grow
(v. 14), directs the moon to mark the seasons (v. 19), and fills
the vast sea with countless creatures (v. 25). And because of
all these wonderful things and more that God created and all
the cool ways He makes them work for His glory, the psalmist reminds us we should sing for joy—joy about who God
is and what He's created! As I pause to think about streams,
creeks, waterfalls, and waves rushing and gurgling, crickets
rubbing their wings together, squirrels chattering, and foxes
barking, I realize two things that actually go hand in hand:

1. There *is* music everywhere if we listen.
2. Shouldn't we join in the chorus with praise?

Most days I think, How could I not?

Like on absolutely routine days like today, as I sit on the floor of our family room writing. It's early March and it's been cold for so long, but today? Today I went for a walk around the neighborhood, an audiobook about a photographer taking pictures of a French carousel whisking me to faraway Provence even though my feet walked along familiar streets. I noticed tiny green spikes in the flower beds that run along our driveway and the dirt around the neighbors' mailboxes and front walks too—early signs of daffodils sprouting, eager to grow to full height and bloom bright yellow blossoms. The vibrant green spears were promises of springtime and color and newness. When I returned home, the sunshine beckoned to me. And so, instead of sitting in my office, I sit on the floor by a giant window in the sunniest spot in the house, soaking in the warmth like a cat as I type. My heart is full of praise.

And on special days, like when I'm decorating the Christmas tree with my family, pulling out the reindeer ornament one of our kids crafted with layers of green and brown construction paper with globs of dried glue, Christmas music playing from somebody's phone, one of the kids belting out the lyrics, sipping steaming cocoa with a candy cane melting hints of peppermint into the warm chocolate, my heart is full of love and gratitude for my family and for Jesus being born and for the whole Christmas season. How could I not sing to the Lord and thank Him for all He is and all He does?

But I have dark days. Days when a friend is in tears as

she shares her suffering, or the news is bleak, filled with war and hate, or a migraine makes me nauseous and everything feels too bright, too loud, and too much. Or that thing that triggers me is front and center, staring me down, making my heart race and my chest tight and my mind malfunction. In these moments I feel as if I'm stuck in the quicksand of my situation, and as I'm sinking all I can think about is getting through or out or away, and praise feels so hard to muster, nearly impossible.

But here's the wonder of it all. Praise is exactly the thing that can get us out of the quicksand. We just have to look for one thing to praise God for. Just one.

My friend is in tears, but I am here with her. She is not alone. And neither am I. *Thank You, God, that we have each other, for this friendship over the years, for honesty and safety in our relationship, for the laughter we've enjoyed that paved the way for us to be able to share these tears.*

My head might be pounding, but the pain is temporary, and closing my eyes brings a moment's relief. *Thank You, Lord, for overall good health, for a minute to rest.*

I feel trapped. "Okay, okay," I tell myself, "look around, Laura, for something, anything." I grab the candle off the kitchen counter and inhale the scent of eucalyptus and lavender—sweet, peaceful. Inhale. Exhale. *But what about—?* "Look out the window, Laura, at the goldfinch, bright yellow, on the bird feeder." *Thank You, Jesus, for fragrance and feathers.*

See what happened? Even in my darker days and panicky moments? Finding one thing to be thankful for leads to another, not just that my friend isn't alone but also that I'm not alone, that we have each other. Afflicted with a migraine, I can still be grateful for how minor that is in the scheme of things, which leads me to be thankful for a healthy body. And even in panic, I can smell something, see something beautiful, and remember that God is good. That He wants good for me. You see, the music of God's love, something to be grateful for, really is all around. We just need to listen.

And when we do, something shifts inside us. According to positive psychology, expressing gratitude positively impacts our body functions and our psychological conditions, including depression, anxiety, and stress.[2]

It does? Yup! That's how it pulls us out of the quicksand. It's been scientifically proven that worry and gratitude cannot exist in the human brain at the same time!

As we think of something to be grateful for and intentionally thank God for it, our negative thoughts and emotions shrink, our worries flee. We're less sad or overwhelmed or panicky. Practicing gratitude builds trust and loyalty in relationships, can be an instant mood booster, reduces pain, increases energy, and helps us sleep better. In fact, consistently practicing gratitude can actually retrain our brains to be more permanently grateful and positive.[3] Amazing!

And logical.

God created us and all of creation and asks us to worship Him. When we do, we're expressing thanks for who God is and what He does. Worship = gratitude. Gratitude = worship.

Let the message about Christ, in all its richness, fill your lives. Teach and counsel each other with all the wisdom he gives. Sing psalms and hymns and spiritual songs to God with thankful hearts. And whatever you do or say, do it as a representative of the Lord Jesus, giving thanks through him to God the Father. (Colossians 3:16–17 NLT)

Let God's glory fill your life. Sing to Him with a thankful heart. Give thanks in all you say and do. Start with yourself. Can you walk? God created your feet. With ten toes. That all bend. And arches and heels and ankles and twenty-six bones in each foot! *Thank You, God, for making such intricate functioning parts that transport me from here to there.*

Maybe your feet aren't treating you right today. All right. Can you talk? God created two bands of muscle tissue (we call them vocal cords) and put them in your larynx, so as air passes them, they vibrate and make your distinct voice—no two voices are exactly alike! *Thank You, God, for my original voice that I can use to express my opinions and needs, my hopes, and my dreams. Thank You for the people I love, who I can identify from across the room simply by the sound of their unique voice.*

We could go on and on about how intentionally God designed the human body. We can also thank God for the smell of bread baking in the oven, or the warmth of a thick blanket, or the silky fur of our cat and how she purrs when we stroke her head. And as we're thinking of all this goodness, practicing this gratitude, we can marvel at the God who created all these good things.

Shauna Niequist puts it this way in her book *I Guess I Haven't Learned That Yet*: "The practice of gratitude keeps our hearts tender through the night."[4]

My friend Sharee says, "Journaling about the things I'm grateful for or even thanking God in my head for what He's done for me is one of my biggest tricks to taking care of my mental health."

Back when I was a girl and went to horseback riding camp in the summers, we sang a song around the crackling campfire. The lyrics came straight from John 16:33: "In this world you will have trouble. But take heart! I have overcome the world." When my junior-high self was full of doubt and insecurity, when the troubles at home of my dad leaving again and all the repercussions of those actions haunted me, this song brought me peace. It took me out of my swirling head for a moment and helped me savor sitting on a large wooden log, the smoky scent from the fire wafting through the night air, the miracle of fireflies flashing their golden glow, and the pureness of the sound of acoustic guitars and the voices of our camp counselors as they led us in song.

The song stayed with me because my heart needs the truth of John 16:33 that, yes, we'll have pain and grief and moments that feel out of control, but our good and gracious God is in control. Jesus offers peace. He overcomes trouble. I sang this song to my kids when they were little and struggling to fall asleep. "These things I have spoken unto you, that in me you shall have peace." I can't carry a tune, but weary toddlers aren't too critical. "In the world there shall be trib-u-la-tion."

"What does *tribulation* mean, Mommy?"

"Troubles. It means anything hard or scary or bad. Bad things happen, but wait, here's the good part." I'd snuggle them a little tighter before continuing in song: "But be of good cheer, be of good cheer, for I have overcome the world."

I'm not suggesting we can sing our mental health problems away. Jesus says flat out there will be troubles. You'll have mental health struggles. So will I. But:

1. Gratitude can flip a switch for us, literally changing our tune from worry to gladness.
2. In the end, we're going to be all right. Jesus overcomes

it all, all the problems of this world, even whatever ails us. We can be downright thankful, cheerful even.

You see, His goodness really is all around us. We just have to listen.

Jesus Cares

I will sing to the LORD all my life; I will sing praise to my God as long as I live. (Psalm 104:33)

Write ten things you're grateful to God for.

Stuck? Start with one thing you can smell, one thing you can see, one thing you can hear, one thing you can touch, and one thing you can taste. That should get you started.

Try infusing this practice into your days. When you feel sadness or worry coming your way, look around quickly for something you're grateful for. (Remember, it can be as simple as part of your body that works.) Tell Jesus thank you. Then thank Him for something else.

Thank Jesus for overcoming the world. Meditating on this truth can switch your brain from worry to calm.

25

What's Wrong with the Basement?

Setbacks

January in Ohio is f-r-e-e-z-i-n-g. Well, actually usually way below freezing. Today it was nine degrees. Yup, single digits. This presents a bit of a problem since my husband and I like to go on walks. Fortunately we live in a college town with some indoor options. There is the beautiful rec center, which we love, but sometimes walking a zillion tiny laps around the track just makes January seem extra January-y. So today we walked in the building where he teaches, which is practically empty during January while most students are away on winter break.

The red brick building is 210,000 square feet, housing countless classrooms, offices, and even two auditoriums. Still, walking the main hallway of any of the floors from one end to the other back and forth can feel monotonous. So Brett suggested, "We could go down a level."

"Great," I said. "That'll change things up a bit."

"It will," Brett answered, "but it *is* the basement."

"Okay," I said, not sure why he was stating the obvious, and headed down the steps.

The walls are a pretty pale yellow. The floors an elegant black-and-white checkerboard tile. Lovely light fixtures hang from the ceiling.

We walked and talked back and forth. And after about ten minutes something seemed off. I couldn't pinpoint it. I felt slightly dizzy or tired or both. Five or so minutes later it dawned on me. The basement felt dreary. Not at first. But the more time we spent down there, the darkness just kind of crept up on me. Slowly, steadily, hard to detect.

"Can we go back up a level?" I asked.

"See what I mean?" Brett asked, then nodded. "There aren't any windows."

"Right." I considered as we ascended the staircase. Even though it was a gray day, I was flooded with light as we stepped back onto the first floor. Washed-out daylight, muted by clouds, felt bright and glorious as it steeped in through the windows.

Light.

Even though I didn't realize it, I'd been missing the light, and it had affected me.

This is what darkness does sometimes. It creeps up on us, step-by-step, slowly but surely. We don't feel like we're in the dark because we can see. But we're not fully in the light either. Lack of natural light can cause headaches, fatigue, stress, and anxiety. Bad lighting can also reduce our productivity.[1] We humans need light to thrive.

And yet so many of us are walking around in spaces that are artificially lit. Yes, our offices, apartments, and shops—but also our perspectives. They're still tainted by the past. By lies we've been told. By expectations put on us that no one could actually live up to. We're going along with our days, thinking our mental health is a-okay. Everything seems stable in this season. Well, mostly. We had struggles, but we're good now. We've seen a counselor about *that*. We got out of the toxic job or apartment or situation. We've moved on. Right? But then sometimes slowly, and sometimes all at once, we realize something is dim. We feel a bit achy or antsy and can't put our finger on it.

It happened to me recently. My mom and I were chatting about my dad. He's not our favorite subject, but sometimes it's helpful for Mom and me to process the past together to get clarity on what actually happened, to remind ourselves that the inaccurate labels my dad assigned to us are not who we are in Christ. At first the conversation felt good, healthy. I was grateful to reinforce for Mom that she is amazing and valuable, beautiful and loved. One story led to the next, and what at first felt therapeutic got more intense. My chest felt tight, and I was jittery. I could hear in the back of my head my dad's voice criticizing me. I could see the look of disgust on his face.

It was fine.

I was fine.

And then I realized things were dim. I needed to find my way back into the light. I didn't want to stop my mom in the middle of her story, because maybe it was helpful for her. But I could feel my downward spiral starting. And getting worse. So I finally got the nerve to interrupt Mom and said, "I'm just going to pray for us right now." And I proceeded to thank Jesus out loud for who He is, for how He loves us perfectly, for how He freed us from the past. I prayed for continued healing for Mom and me, that the lies we'd been told wouldn't stick, that we would be reminded that we are not inadequate or less than just because one man said so. I prayed for Christ's peace and joy to flood us and thanked God for my relationship with my mom. As I said, "Amen," I felt better. The air felt lighter, the room brighter. And then I changed the subject and asked Mom if she wanted a chocolate covered caramel.

Inviting Jesus into the room, into our past, and into our pain pulled us out of the proverbial basement and back into sunlight.

Christ's light is illuminating. It's contagious. Healing.

And yet the Enemy really likes to keep things in the dark. Including when we slip up or have a setback. He'll try to get us to dismiss something that's bothering us, avoid telling someone how we feel, rationalize a toxic behavior or erratic thoughts, or push through something that's hard instead of reflecting on why it's so challenging. Because if we never address that we're slipping, how can we be restored again?

This is what happened while sitting on my mom's pale blue floral couch. I knew our conversation was going from good to bad, from healing to resurfacing painful emotions. And yet, I kept talking and listening. One voice in my head said, "This isn't healthy. Get out! Pray. Now." The other said, "Remember that other time? You should bring that up, too. Plus, wouldn't it be weird for you to start praying mid-discussion?" Even once I identified in my mind that things felt dark, it took me a couple of minutes to ground myself, to shake the shadow from my brain, and to reach for light. The Enemy would have loved to have Mom and I talk on and on, until we both reached points of old wounds flaring up, of feeling anger and resentment and shame. But Jesus doesn't want that for any of us.

Satan will distract us from the truth we already know, inviting us to numb an emotion or memory, to push it aside or bury it. Similar to how the pale artificial light of a basement slowly, discreetly zaps our energy and focus.

Jesus offers the opposite.

Christ is pure, bright, glorious light. He tells us, "I am the light of the world. Whoever follows me will never walk in darkness, but will have the light of life" (John 8:12). Jesus came so that we "may have life, and have it to the full" (10:10). I want this full life. I believe most people do. When Jesus shines a little light in this corner or a beam of sunshine in that crevice, illuminating for us that there's more healing to be had, it often requires some attention, some work. Like when He prompted me to pray to flip the tone of my convo with Mom.

Are we willing to step into Christ's bright light? Sometimes instead of handing our setback over to our loving Savior, we run and shut the blinds or flick the light switch back off, because we don't want to go there, because it takes effort, because it might hurt, because we don't like to be vulnerable. Maybe that snake whispers that people will think less of us if they know we still have issues, or that we're making too big a deal of something, or that we have a right to act out after what we've been through, or that it would be easier to go back to those familiar patterns . . . And before we can receive Christ's love and help, we've changed the subject. Or made a snarky comment. Or pretended we're totally fine. Or grabbed whatever our favorite numbing device is—food, drink, social media, Netflix, you name it—and avoided all the emotions. And things just gradually get darker or at a minimum stay dim.

But we can get out of the basement. And into the daylight. All we have to do is climb the stairs—be willing to acknowledge that we've slipped, share with someone that we're not okay, ask questions about how we're still being impacted or why we just reacted like that, or claim the emotion that feels erratic. Sometimes those steps back to well-being are steep and the climbing is exhausting, but this light?

It's glorious.

It's for you and it's for me. And it changes things. The gospel writer John tells us in his firsthand account of Jesus's life that Jesus, the true Light, gives light to *everyone*. No exceptions.

> In him was life, and that life was the light of all mankind. The light shines in the darkness, and the darkness has not overcome it. . . .
> The true light that gives light to everyone was coming into the world. (1:4–5, 9)

Christ's light is so very bright that the darkness can*not* overcome it. Even if the darkness has crept back up on you. Even if the darkness feels overwhelming again.

It may seem easier not to acknowledge the setback, the slipup, the lack of self-care, the lapsed boundary—let alone shine light on it. On that January day, the dark basement of a beautiful building seemed like a perfectly acceptable, even pretty, place to walk.

I'm not telling you any of this to make you freak out or feel guilty. Actually I'm saying the opposite. I'm telling you it's okay. It's okay if you've slipped into old behaviors or got stuck partway through your journey. We're all going to slip sometimes. You saw me on that couch with my mom, right? Yes, I halted the downward spiral through prayer and felt so much better for doing so. But that one conversation actually made me fragile for two weeks. I had three separate incidents where I unexpectedly broke into tears. So much of what I'd fought for, the boundaries I'd set, the lies I'd been working to unlearn, the truths I'd been focusing on started to un- ravel, just like the loose yarn on the edge of a sweater. When you pick at it, the string gets longer and longer, and the hole in your sweater gets bigger and bigger. I can't imagine what would have happened if I had let Mom's and my conversa- tion continue.

Our journeys to emotional and spiritual well-being are usu- ally more zigzagged than straightforward. We'll get really good at setting a boundary in our life—only to realize we're not get- ting nearly enough sleep. And the more exhausted we get, the more our mental health suffers. We'll blow it off, drink more caffeine, vow to catch up over the weekend, but not actually do it. And then one day in a bit of an edgy fog, we realize we need to make a change.

Perhaps we have a great counselor, but she moves or our insurance no longer covers her services, so our time together ends. We're fine, we think. We've learned some ways to cope and manage. Plus it's such an effort to find a new therapist. So we don't. For weeks that become months that become years. And the work that we've done is still done. We still made prog- ress. But when we have a flare-up, we might not process it. The things we learned seem so distant.

Our current prescription might not be working as well as it once did. We know changing medication can be chal- lenging, so we put it off. But as a result our moods aren't as stable, and our symptoms become more intense and more frequent.

Maybe we were obsessive about shopping, and we've gotten it under control. But it's our brother's birthday, so we get him a shirt that would look great on him *and* one for us because they're on sale. And while we're at the store or on that site, we add a few other purchases to our cart. Which is fine. But we can't stop thinking about those shoes and buy them too. Soon we've racked up a credit card bill we can't afford, and the more obsessive tendencies we thought we'd gotten past are in full swing.

Or we'll be diligent about getting outside because it both calms and energizes us, but miserable weather blows in that lasts for days. When the weather finally clears, we have a bit of a cold and decide to lay low. Before we know it, we've found a new rhythm, one where we don't go outside. It feels smart at first, and then like self-care, and then just easier, but finally we notice our energy is low. Our mood scrambled. It might take a few days to even figure out that we're off and why we're off. Oh, yeah, we suddenly realize. We haven't been outside in ages.

But we can reset again. We can reacclimate ourselves to truth. We can hold our spiraling or dismissive thoughts captive and turn to Jesus. We can unplug our television and push ourselves to go to bed earlier. We can ask for recommendations for a good Christian counselor. We can avoid stores and shopping websites, maybe even ask a friend to go in on a gift for the upcoming baby shower and to do the shopping. We can ask our doctor for help figuring out our meds. We can open the front door and head outside. We can take the first step, and then the next, and climb back up the stairs, sometimes quickly two steps at a time and sometimes slowly one by one, into the light.

These climbing moments can be challenging, but they grow us.

The University of Michigan's Eisenberg Family Depression Center explains, "Experiencing a setback when you've managed to stay healthy can be extremely frustrating and alarming. However, relapses can be a great opportunity for self-exploration and personal growth. You may ask yourself a few of these questions during and after a setback: What have I learned from this? How would I deal with this differently next time?"[2]

That totally lines up with Scripture. Of course our setbacks can bring growth. Paul tells the church in Rome: "We also glory in our sufferings, because we know that suffering produces perseverance; perseverance, character; and character, hope" (Romans 5:3–4). And James (Jesus's brother) tells us: "Dear brothers and sisters, when troubles of any kind come your way, consider it an opportunity for great joy. For you know that when your faith is tested, your endurance has a chance to grow. So let it grow, for when your endurance is fully developed, you will be perfect and complete, needing nothing" (James 1:2–4 NLT).

Our setbacks are normal. They're building endurance and perseverance in us. Each time we move toward Christ's light, it builds hope in us. Jesus is the Light of the World, and He wants to overcome any and all darkness in your life. It's so worth taking those steps upward—even when we have to blink in the sunlight, even if it hurts our calves—so we can thrive as God intended us to.

Are you ready? Let's get out of the basement and return to the Light.

Jesus Cares

In him was life, and that life was the light of all mankind. The light shines in the darkness, and the darkness has not overcome it. (John 1:4–5)

What darkness lurks in your life? Where have you faced a setback or let something slip?

Have you told anyone about it?

Whatever darkness is lingering, start climbing up the steps to the light right now. Close your eyes and tell Jesus about it. He already knows, but telling Him will get it off your chest and allow some light to shine in. Ask Jesus to help you see and feel His light. Ask Him for direction on next steps, on how to squelch this darkness with His loving light.

26

Point of Rocks

The Journey Is Worth It

The number one thing Tripadvisor told me we should do in Siesta Key was see Point of Rocks. I used a free airline companion ticket and booked a reasonable hotel within walking distance to this beautiful spot for a special mother-daughter trip with my girl her senior year of high school. The only trouble was there really isn't any good or normal way to get to Point of Rocks.

Point of Rocks is on the coast and public property, but a private home blocks access to it. There's no place to park because the place you're trying to get to is lodged between the Gulf of Mexico and someone's house. The lovely workers at the front desk of our hotel vaguely said something about going around the pier but couldn't describe how to do it. Wading and swimming from the beach out and around a precipice through some seriously jagged rocks looked scary and uncertain. The two men we saw attempting this route kept swearing and wincing as they repeatedly hurt their feet on sharp rocks and got knocked down by waves. Mallory and I were perplexed. Everyone agreed Point of Rocks was the place to go, but no one seemed to actually know how to get there.

Sitting on our beach chairs covered with striped cotton towels and breathing in the fresh, salty scent of the Gulf water mingled with the smell of the sunscreen we'd slathered all over ourselves, Mallory and I spied a dad with two children scaling the concrete seawall that protected the private property from the tide. Those folks were headed in the direction we wanted to go, so we paid careful attention as they took measured steps along the narrow ledge. Then they rounded the corner, out of view. What happened once they turned? Did they have access to the elusive Point of Rocks?

Mal and I decided we'd give it a try, but it felt like a scene out of an Indiana Jones movie. We waded waist deep over to the seawall. Once there, we hoisted ourselves up to the ledge, which was about four feet high, scraping our legs on the rough concrete as we did so. Facing the wall and using a metal rail as a handhold, we scooched along the eighteen-inch-wide ledge. Then we got to the mysterious corner where the family had disappeared.

What awaited us on the other side? Was this what we were looking for? I was in front of Mallory and peeked around the corner. The dad was trying to get his daughter to move. She was frozen along uneven, steep brown rocks. It was incredibly windy, and the waves thrashed against her body. Tears streamed down her cheeks. The dad asked his son, who had progressed a bit farther than the girl, to help get her back. I turned my head to Mallory and gave her the download. "We'll just wait here and let them get settled," I suggested. This was very much a single-file situation, and the dad and his kids were headed back our way on the one-way ledge.

At this point Mallory and I could have turned around. Clearly this wasn't an easy path. But here's the thing. Beyond the dad, the girl, the boy, and the waves was the most picturesque piece of America I'd ever seen. And it was calling to me.

And so I prayed in my head for peace for the girl around the corner and for that family's protection. Meanwhile, Mallory and I smashed our bodies against the seawall, making ourselves as flat as humanly possible as the dad and his kids inched past us and back to land. Then I leaned my head around the corner again and inhaled the sheer beauty. But we weren't there yet.

Mallory and I coached each other as we rounded the corner, stepped off the ledge onto a giant rough rock, and found our foot- and handholds. We kept calling out over the crash of waves, "You okay? Take your time. Lift your hand a little higher and you'll feel a good place to hang on. Got it?"

After a giant wave collided with my body, spraying salt water in my eyes, I had to wait a minute or two, maybe three, until I could see again, until my eyes stopped stinging. As I heard another wave coming, I called to Mallory, "Face the rocks so the next wave doesn't get in your eyes. Maybe put your right foot in that spot that's a little lower. There, see it?"

And step-by-step we treated these rocks like a climbing wall, taking our time, catching our breath, searching for safe, flat spaces to set our feet and decent spots to grab hold of—only we didn't have harnesses and the reward was way more exhilarating than reaching the ceiling of our local rec center.

The cove was pristine. The rocks to our back, the gorgeous turquoise waters of the Gulf to our front. And under our feet, not sand but shells, vibrant purple scallops, corkscrewed whelks, perfectly smooth spiraling olives, and conch shells completely intact. A few feet past the treasure trove of shells, a series of flat rocks like shelves, leading out to the seemingly endless ocean. It felt like our own private island. Just Mallory and me and so very much beauty. As if God had created this space and time just for us.

We stayed for an hour, maybe more, marveling at God's creation. Here in this space there was no clock, no phones, no social media, no to-dos, no comparisons, no stress. Just sunshine and seashells and the sparkling surface of the water.

Our mental health journeys can be like this.

Sometimes we're not sure where to start. There doesn't appear to be anywhere to park or access to what we need. The road ahead might look narrow or rocky or both. We might fear the unknown of what's around the corner. Even after we take the first step, once we decide to ask for help or tell someone we're struggling or maybe even pick up this book, there are still rocks to climb and salt water that might sting our eyes. We might get a little scraped up along the way or have to take more steps than we'd prefer, but the journey will be worth it—the peace and contentment priceless.

Honestly, I don't always look forward to my counseling appointments. I often consider canceling, asking myself, Do I really need this?

I don't *need* it. I could continue trying to navigate things on my own. But the reality is that it will be better; I will be better if I go.

I'm not alone in these thoughts. One friend shared that she often feels queasy on her drive to her therapist's office. Another admitted she has actually lied to her counselor, inventing excuses to cancel an appointment because it felt too hard on that particular day. Like when we first saw people scaling the seawall like Spider-Man to get to Point of Rocks and a voice inside me said, "Bail! You don't have to do this. It's too complicated."

But Point of Rocks was good for my soul and for my daughter's soul too.

Taking care of my mental health is also good for my soul. Healing. But sometimes it's hard. For example, my therapist is kind and wise. But she asks challenging questions like, "What percent true is that statement? What is a response you could give in that situation that protects your boundaries? What specifically were you afraid of? How does being assertive make you feel?"

Of course, I have the choice to skip through these questions and gloss over the answers. I can say what sounds right and give my therapist the answers I think she wants to hear. I can say "I had a great week" and "Yes, I did those things you asked me to do" and avoid talking about the episode from the week before that was painful or admitting to not having the courage to apply the tactics she suggested.

It would be easier that way. It would have been easier for Mallory and me to stay on our beach chairs too. But in both scenarios, I'd miss so much.

So during counseling I try to be honest and say the words I don't want to utter out loud, unleash the thoughts wreaking havoc on my mental health, get them out there, and feel the painful emotions that come with expressing them. If I don't feel them, don't go through the emotions, don't untangle the mess in my mind, then I don't get to the release, the freedom, the health on the other side.

My friend Laura shared that it's hard for her to ask friends for help when her mental health is poor. She says, "It can be painful letting others know I'm in a bad spot, but I need help to get out of bad spots." And so Laura does the hard thing, because her well-being is worth it. She asks.

My friend Sharee was apprehensive about trying a prescription to help with her clinical depression. She felt a stigma from her church that using medication was not trusting Jesus. She'd seen her church respond to a few of her friends with mental health issues by praying over them, saying that was enough, and discouraging them from seeking medical help. Sharee also knew of people who had been miraculously healed of their depression. But hers wasn't going away. It runs in her family and was plaguing her daily. She had to fight against the opinions and ideas of others. She had to wade through them and make a conscious decision to try medication despite all she'd heard. It was challenging, but Sharee shared, "I finally went on medication about a year ago, and it was one of the most helpful decisions for me."

Jesus knows better than anyone the pain of going through the hard stuff to get to the healing.

> Then Jesus went with his disciples to a place called Gethsemane, and he said to them, "Sit here while I go over there and pray." He took Peter and the two sons of Zebedee along with him, and he began to be sorrowful and troubled. Then he said to them, "My soul is overwhelmed with sorrow to the point of death. Stay here and keep watch with me."
>
> Going a little farther, he fell with his face to the ground and prayed, "My Father, if it is possible, may this cup be taken from me. Yet not as I will, but as you will." (Matthew 26:36–39)

Jesus knew crucifixion was excruciating. Humiliating. He knew His mom and best friends would see Him in the most pitiful and tortured state. Not to mention the physical anguish His body would endure. But after talking to God, even begging God for an alternate solution, Jesus realized the only way to healing and light and beauty was through this difficult journey. And so our Savior willingly went to be interrogated by the governor, Pilate, then by King Herod, and then back to Pilate again. Jesus allowed soldiers to mock, spit on, and scourge Him with a whip that ripped His flesh. Jesus agreed to have nails driven through His hands and feet, to hang in pain in a position so precarious it was impossible to breathe. Jesus chose to go through that—not because it sounded like a good time, not because it was the easiest way to go about things, but because Jesus knew that on the other side of His journey of suffering and sacrifice was resurrection. Salvation. Glory. Not just for Him but for all of us—you and me. He loves us *that* much.

As my friend Robin Hostetler, a certified trauma practitioner and clinical supervisor, puts it, "Jesus never gave up. Neither should we in regard to finding healing in our mental health."

So when I'm putting off making an appointment or considering canceling with my counselor because I'd rather not take the time from my day—rather not face the pain of my youth, thank you very much—I can remember that Jesus went through infinitely worse. When I'm sitting across from my therapist in the burgundy leather chair and she asks one of those questions I'd rather skim over, or when I'm faced with one of those situations she's helped equip me for and it's hard for me to speak up or set a boundary, I can find comfort in the fact that my Savior understands what walking through pain looks like.

Jesus also shows us what it looks like on the other side of the cross.

Victorious.

Wherever you're hesitating today—maybe to say no to something toxic, remove yourself from a situation, ask for help, confide in a friend, go for that walk, make modifications to your diet, schedule the appointment, fill the prescription—you too can find courage in the One who went before you, hope in the fact that Jesus goes in front of you and behind you on your journey. You can declare like King David,

> Before a word is on my tongue
> you, LORD, know it completely.
> You hem me in behind and before,
> and you lay your hand upon me.
> (Psalm 139:4–5)

My friend Maryanne says this about her journey: "I'd tell my younger self to avoid comparison, to steer clear of social media, to talk to someone about her struggles, to share her feelings with other people, that others do care." All things Maryanne has learned over the past couple of years of tending to her mental health. "But," Maryanne continues, "I don't know if my younger self would have listened. I think I had to go on the journey to get where I am."

My friend Betsy uses this metaphor for her journey with counseling: "Counseling is like cleaning out your closet. You have to pull everything out in a heap and make a mess. Then you get rid of the things you no longer need—false narratives, shame, guilt, regret, parts of your life that disturbed or harmed you. Then you can see what's left and reorganize and fold these things and put them back where they go. It gets worse before it gets better—the huge total mess before things get cleaned up. You might have to deal with the heavy and hard and sad things (the heap on the floor) before you can move forward on your journey. But it's worth it."

Getting to Point of Rocks *was* worth it. It felt like paradise, like this was maybe what Eden was like. What Mallory and I discovered there was far beyond our imagination and hopes for the adventure. In fact, we made the same treacherous trek back the next day. The gift at the end didn't diminish the taxing rock climbing and scrapes, but the reward was so meaningful, so stunning, that we would've powered through the challenges again and again to get back to it.

Your mental health is worth facing the challenges. It's worth the journey. Even over the rocks and through the waves. Jesus promises to walk with you every step of the climb. Beauty and peace and healing are waiting on the other side.

Jesus Cares

> Before a word is on my tongue
>> you, LORD, know it completely.
> You hem me in behind and before,
>> and you lay your hand upon me.
> (Psalm 139:4–5)

What is something you know you can do for your mental health that you've been putting off or avoiding?

Ask Jesus what one step you can take today to step forward in your journey (make a phone call, visit a website, text a friend, throw something out, etc.).

Ask Him what's another thing you can do by the end of the week.

Thank Jesus for protecting you and traveling with you, going before and behind you, hemming you in during your journey. You've got this. Jesus is with you! Your mental health matters so much! I'll be praying for you!

Closing Thoughts

IF YOU WERE WRITING THIS BOOK

I interviewed over a dozen friends to help with this book—single friends; married friends; friends in their seventies, sixties, fifties, forties, thirties, and twenties; mostly women friends but even one guy friend. Hopefully their stories helped show you that you are not alone in your story. The last question I asked each friend was, "If you were writing this book, what is the one thing you would want to make sure readers knew, something we haven't talked about yet?"

Their words were so brilliant, meaningful, and wise that I wanted to share some of their responses with you here as final thoughts as we wrap up our time together.

"Everything will be okay in the end. If it's not okay right now, it's not the end." —Brenda

"Your mental health isn't the only part of your identity. You are lovable, worthy, valuable, and righteous in whatever your mental health situation is. The lies of the world, ourselves, and the Enemy will try to tell you otherwise, but mental health does not limit us in the kingdom of God. You are seen. You are not alone." —Laura

"Don't discount your mental health or anyone else's mental health." —Sue

"When you read about the people in the Bible, you sometimes see what they've done and think they're awful, that they're nuts! Then they turn into individuals who do good for God. Saul killed Christians, then he totally changed, became known as Paul, and converted countless people to Christianity! I need this reminder that my bad things don't create bad things. That God uses the bad things for good. Whatever bad things are in your life, there's a fun part, the I-can't-wait-to-see-what-God-is-going-to-do-with-it part!" —Brenda

"Anxiety doesn't make you weak. It makes you dependent on the Lord. Anxiety is so common. You'd be surprised to know how many people are suffering just like you. There are so many people struggling with different mental health issues. This doesn't have to be a scarlet letter. It's okay. Please know you're not alone." —Betsy

"It's important for people to expect seasons, highs and lows, with your mental health. You won't be 'fixed.' Therapy is giving you tools to work through things more efficiently and effectively. It doesn't solve all your problems. It's okay that you're a work in progress. We all are." —Sharee

"Mental health is not less important than physical health. We don't think a thing about telling someone we're going to the eye doctor. Let's not hesitate to tell people we're caring for our mental health or seeing a counselor." —Sharon

"Therapy is like cleansing an old wound. Sometimes it feels worse before it feels better. Sometimes it stings. But it's important to remember, it is only after that cleansing that true healing can take place." —Tammy

"There's always hope in Jesus! And not just when we die and go to heaven. There's hope on this earth. Even when things don't go the way you want them to. If you're committed to Jesus, you can be content. You can find joy in any circumstance, maybe not right at this moment but at some point. Jesus is integral to the process of resilience." —Maryanne

"You're not alone. There is hope. Nothing can separate you from the love of Christ (Romans 8:28)." —Elisa

"Let's get rid of the stigma that Christians don't need mental health care. Jesus says He is our peace! He is a healer. He wants us restored!" —Chad

Have something you'd like to add? Something you'd say if you were writing this book? I'd love to hear from you. Fill out the contact form on my website at www.laurasmithauthor .com/contact-laura.html and let me know what you'd like for people to know about faith and mental health.

ACKNOWLEDGMENTS

Jesus, I am so grateful for your love and grace, for the ideas and words You flood me with, and for the experiences You've given me. I am grateful for how You created me and how You are healing me. All I am and have is due to Your amazing grace.

Jesus never intended for us to do anything alone. Including caring for our mental health. I could not have written this book without all these incredible people who shine Christ's light in my life.

I dedicated this book to the people who told snippets of their stories on its pages, but I acknowledge them here too: You are brave. You are beautiful. The sharing of your journeys is shining light in dark places and encouraging others to fight for their well-being. Thank you.

Brett, you have championed me along my mental health journey with such love and grace. So much of my healing is due to the beautiful, Christlike love you shower me with. You are my best friend and true love. There is no one I'd rather walk side by side through life with.

Maddie, thank you for your care and compassion. I am so blessed by how well you know me, get me, listen to me, and love me.

Max, I am so grateful for our conversations about Jesus

and His love. Your faith, pursuit of Jesus, and obedience to Him inspire me.

Mallory, thank you for sensing my needs and advocating for my joy. Your gift for understanding the people you love (including me) is invaluable.

Maguire, your peaceful presence and kind heart soothe my soul and bless our entire family.

The four of you are the best support network a mama could have. Thank you for hugs, laughter, and prayers. I learn so much from you and am blessed beyond measure to be your mom.

Mom, thank you for teaching me how to laugh and cry. Your consistent love, encouragement, attention, and support both while growing up and now have made all the difference.

Our Daily Bread Publishing, I am so thankful to you for believing in this book and making it a reality. You are a dream team! I am grateful for everyone at ODBP, but especially to my editor Joel Armstrong; your edits, suggestions, and brainstorming along the way made each page better. Thank you for taking my vision, stories, and words and fine-tuning them so beautifully into what the reader experiences, for knowing when I needed to say more or less, and for encouraging me throughout the process. Bill Crowder, thank you for your biblical wisdom. Dawn Anderson, your continued support and vision are a giant blessing to me. Patti Brinks, thanks for the beautiful cover. I adore the rocks representing the stones of travelers as we make our ways along our mental health journeys. Melissa Wade, Kat Needham, and Cathy Sall, thank you for all the ways you help get these words out into the world.

Bob Hostetler, thank you for championing this idea from start to finish. You are the very best agent. Your wisdom and support are pure blessing.

Barbara, thank you for giving me words for my struggles, tools to grow, and a safe place to work through it all. You are a gift.

Amy, the example you set of how to pursue God-given dreams and trust the Lord inspires me daily. My life is infinitely better because you are in it.

Shena, thank you for nudging me to spin joyfully in freedom. You make the Scripture "stir up one another to love and good works" (Hebrews 10:24 ESV) come to life. I feel stirred up for kingdom living every time I'm with you.

Tammy, thank you for always reading early versions of my writing and helping me shape and smooth these words. I'm so thankful for your contagious positivity that boosts my mood and soul.

Alli and Amy, I am stronger for having you two wise, faithful women of God in my corner. Thank you for your contagious pursuit of Jesus and for your friendship.

ADDITIONAL RESOURCES

As I said in the introduction, I am not a mental health expert, just a girl with her own mental health journey. But along this journey I've read all kinds of articles and books, watched countless TED Talks, and perused websites, eager to get my hands on material that would teach me how to heal in a way that Jesus would approve. In addition to all the ones cited throughout this book, here are some additional resources I recommend:

Hotlines for Help

Suicide Prevention Lifeline: suicidepreventionlifeline.org. 24-7 Hotline: 988

Rape, Abuse & Incest National Network (RAINN): www.rainn.org. 24-7 National Sexual Assault Hotline: 1-800-656-4673

National Eating Disorders Association (NEDA): www.nationaleatingdisorders.org. Help line (call or text): 1-800-931-2237

Books and Videos

Boundaries: When to Say Yes, How to Say No to Take

Control of Your Life by Dr. Henry Cloud and Dr. John Townsend

"Listening to Shame," by Brené Brown, www.ted.com /talks/brene_brown_listening_to_shame?language=en

Man's Search for Meaning by Viktor E. Frankl

Maybe You Should Talk to Someone: A Therapist, Her Therapist, and Our Lives Revealed by Lori Gottlieb

The Choice: Embrace the Possible by Dr. Edith Eva Eger

What If It's Wonderful? Release Your Fears, Choose Joy, and Find the Courage to Celebrate by Nicole Zasowski

Healing Verses

This book is packed with passages from Scripture, but here are a few verses that are especially healing to me.

A large crowd followed him, and he healed all who were ill. (Matthew 12:15)

People brought all their sick to him and begged him to let the sick just touch the edge of his cloak, and all who touched it were healed. (Matthew 14:35–36)

The LORD is with you, mighty warrior. (Judges 6:12)

For we are God's masterpiece. He has created us anew in Christ Jesus, so we can do the good things he planned for us long ago. (Ephesians 2:10 NLT)

The LORD watches over you—
    the LORD is your shade at your right hand;
the sun will not harm you by day,
    nor the moon by night.

The LORD will keep you from all harm—
    he will watch over your life;
the LORD will watch over your coming and
      going
    both now and forevermore.
      (Psalm 121:5–8)

PLAYLIST

I love music and find it quite healing. I've compiled a playlist of Christian songs that remind me of how much Jesus cares about our mental health and longs to help us on our healing journeys.

You can find these songs on Spotify on the "Holy Care for the Whole Self" playlist by laurasmithauthor, or I've listed the songs below so you can access them however you listen to music.

"Another in the Fire" by Hillsong UNITED
"Way Maker" by Leeland
"House on a Hill" by Amanda Cook
"Lean Back" by Capital City Music
"With You (Paradoxology)" by Elevation Worship
"Stand in Your Love" by Bethel Music and Josh Baldwin
"I'll Find You" (featuring Tori Kelly) by Lecrae
"Surrounded (Fight My Battles)" by UPPERROOM
"Thank You Song" by UPPERROOM
"Hills and Valleys" by Tauren Wells
"PEACE" by Hillsong Young & Free
"It Is Well" by Kristene DiMarco
"Came to My Rescue" by Hillsong Worship
"Never Alone" by Tori Kelly and Kirk Franklin

"Stained Glass" by Jon Guerra

"TESTIFY" by NEEDTOBREATHE

"Tremble" by Mosaic MSC

"Dancing with My Shadow" by Benjamin William Hastings

"I Am" by JUDAH

"By Your Side" by Tenth Avenue North

"Inhale" by MercyMe

"Joy of the Lord" by Maverick City Music

"Breathe/Rest (Spontaneous)" by Bethel Music and Cory Asbury

NOTES

Chapter 2—Allergies Are Real: *So Are Your Mental Health Issues*

1. Sherri Wilson Johnson, "God pointed me toward help," comment on Betsy St. Amant, "Anxiety attack," Facebook, December 16, 2021.

Chapter 3—A Tale of Two Grandmas: *You're Not Alone*

1. "About Mental Health," Centers for Disease Control and Prevention, updated June 28, 2021, https://www.cdc.gov/mentalhealth/learn/index.htm.

Chapter 4—The Beehive: *Community*

1. Starre Vartan, "Learn from These 5 Ways Bees Work Together," Treehugger, updated August 19, 2021, https://www.treehugger.com/learn-these-ways-bees-work-together-4868486.
2. "Friendships: Enrich Your Life and Improve Your Health," MayoClinic, January 12, 2022, https://www.mayoclinic.org/healthy-lifestyle/adult-health/in-depth/friendships/art-20044860.
3. Elena Renken, "Most Americans Are Lonely, and Our Workplace Culture May Not Be Helping," NPR,

January 23, 2020, https://www.npr.org/sections/health
-shots/2020/01/23/798676465/most-americans-are
-lonely-and-our-workplace-culture-may-not-be
-helping.

Chapter 5—What's in a Name?: *Naming Our Struggles*

1. "Understanding Your Diagnosis," National Alliance on
   Mental Illness, accessed April 5, 2023, https://www
   .nami.org/Your-Journey/Individuals-with-Mental
   -Illness/Understanding-Your-Diagnosis.
2. Timothy Keller, *Romans 1–7 for You* (Epsom, UK:
   Good Book Company, 2014), 22.

Chapter 6—Time for an Upgrade: *Replacing Old with New*

1. Bernard J. Luskin, "The Habit Replacement Loop,"
   Psychology Today, May 14, 2017, https://www
   .psychologytoday.com/us/blog/the-media-psychology
   -effect/201705/the-habit-replacement-loop.

Chapter 7—Skyline Dip and Brownies: *Memorizing Scripture*

1. "How to Stop a Panic Attack in Its Tracks," Cleveland
   Clinic, October 26, 2021, https://health
   .clevelandclinic.org/how-to-stop-a-panic-attack/.

Chapter 8—The Forgotten Moka Pot: *Rediscovering Lost Goodness*

1. Miriam Smolover, quoted in Wendy Maltz, *The Sexual
   Healing Journey: A Guide for Survivors of Sexual Abuse*,
   3rd ed. (New York: Harper Collins, 2012), 70.

Chapter 9—Pajama Pants and EpiPens: *Prayer*

1. Elizabeth Bernstein, "The Science of Prayer," *Wall Street Journal*, May 17, 2020, https://www.wsj.com /articles/the-science-of-prayer-11589720400.
2. Bernstein, "The Science of Prayer."

Chapter 11—Move and Groove: *Exercise*

1. Charlie Mackesy, *The Boy, the Mole, the Fox and the Horse* (San Francisco: HarperOne, 2019), n.p.
2. "Exercise: 7 Benefits of Regular Physical Activity," Mayo Clinic, October 8, 2021, https://www .mayoclinic.org/healthy-lifestyle/fitness/in-depth /exercise/art-20048389.
3. Ferris Jabr, "Let's Get Physical: The Psychology of Effective Workout Music," *Scientific American*, March 20, 2013, https://www.scientificamerican.com/article /psychology-workout-music/.

Chapter 13—The Boy on the Bridge: *Helping Others Helps Us*

1. Steve Siegle, "The Art of Kindness," Mayo Clinic Health System, May 29, 2020, https://www .mayoclinichealthsystem.org/hometown-health /speaking-of-health/the-art-of-kindness.

Chapter 14—Measuring, Stirring, and Tasting: *Creativity*

1. "Health Benefits of Vanilla," WebMD, updated November 23, 2022, https://www.webmd.com/diet /health-benefits-vanilla#1.
2. Ashley Stahl, "Here's How Creativity Actually

Improves Your Health," *Forbes*, July 25, 2018, https://www.forbes.com/sites/ashleystahl/2018/07/25/heres-how-creativity-actually-improves-your-health/?sh=634f872713a6.

3. Katie Trowbridge, "Don't Think You Are Creative? Think Again! A Different Look at the Meaning of Creativity," Curiosity2Create, updated January 4, 2022, https://www.curiosity2create.org/post/don-t-think-you-are-creative-think-again-a-different-look-at-the-meaning-of-creativity.

4. Makoto Fujimura, Rapt Interviews, Gather Ministries, accessed February 3, 2023, https://raptinterviews.com/features/makoto-fujimura.

Chapter 15—Field Trips, Fine Wine, and Fish: *When You Don't Feel Like Enough*

1. Shankar Vedantam, "How the 'Scarcity Mindset' Can Make Problems Worse," NPR, March 23, 2017, https://www.npr.org/2017/03/23/521195903/how-the-scarcity-mindset-can-make-problems-worse.

Chapter 16—Sunsets Are Free Therapy: *Getting Outside*

1. Laura Steffer (@lrsteffer), "Mount Hermon was beautiful. Loving being back in the field and working long hours and feeling like I earn my night of sleep," Instagram, March 7, 2022, https://www.instagram.com/p/Cazd38fKofP/.

2. "Mental Health Benefits of the Outdoors," Lifeworks Counseling, June 26, 2020, https://lifeworkscc.com/mental-health-benefits-outdoors/.

3. Elle Hunt, "Blue Spaces: Why Time Spent Near Water Is the Secret to Happiness," *Guardian*, November 3, 2019, https://www.theguardian.com /lifeandstyle/2019/nov/03/blue-space-living-near -water-good-secret-of-happiness.

4. Craig T. Lee, "Screen Zombies: The Average Person Will Spend 44 Years Looking at Digital Devices—and That's before COVID!," Study Finds, December 26, 2020, https://www.studyfinds.org/screen-zombies -average-person-spends-44-years-looking-at-devices/.

Chapter 19—Apple Suits, Robes, and Other Outfits: *Shame*

1. Brené Brown and Oprah Winfrey, "Dr. Brené Brown: 'Shame Is Lethal,' SuperSoul Sunday, Oprah Winfrey Network," OWN, March 24, 2013, video, 4:25, https://www.youtube.com/watch?v=GEBjNv5M784.

2. "5 Ways Shame Can Shape Your Life," Clearview Treatment Programs, accessed February 7, 2023, https://www.clearviewtreatment.com/resources /blog/5-ways-shame-can-shape-life/.

Chapter 20—Saint Bernards, Lasagna, and Border Control: *Boundaries*

1. Henry Cloud and John Townsend, *Boundaries: When to Say Yes, How to Say No* (Grand Rapids, MI: Zondervan, 2017), 107.

Chapter 21—Toppling Shelves and Cleaned-Out Drawers: *Creating Order*

1. Nadia Ghaffari, "The Mental Health Benefits of

Cleaning, Organizing and Decluttering Your Space," American Addiction Centers, updated November 21, 2022, https://recovery.org/pro/articles/the-mental -health-benefits-of-cleaning-organizing-decluttering -your-space/.

Chapter 22—Tadpoles, Trips, and Tears: *Grief*

1. "How to Overcome Grief's Health-Damaging Effects," Harvard Health Publishing, February 15, 2021, https://www.health.harvard.edu/mind-and-mood /how-to-overcome-griefs-health-damaging-effects.
2. David Kessler, "The Five Stages of Grief," Grief.com, accessed Feburary 9, 2023, https://grief.com/the-five -stages-of-grief/.

Chapter 23—When You're Run-Down: *Rest and Refuel*

1. Ernest Hemingway, *A Moveable Feast: The Restored Edition* (New York: Scribner, 2009), 102. First published 1964.
2. Eric Suni, "Mental Health and Sleep," Sleep Foundation, updated February 9, 2023, https://www .sleepfoundation.org/mental-health.
3. "How Much Water You Should Drink Every Day," Cleveland Clinic, October 14, 2022, https://health .clevelandclinic.org/how-much-water-do-you-need -daily/.

Chapter 24—Music Is All Around Us: *Gratitude*

1. *August Rush*, directed by Kirsten Sheridan (Burbank, CA: Warner Bros. Pictures, 2007).

2. Madhuleena Roy Chowdhury, "The Neuroscience of Gratitude and Effects on the Brain," Positive Psychology, April 9, 2019, https://positivepsychology.com /neuroscience-of-gratitude/.

3. Chowdhury, "The Neuroscience of Gratitude and Effects on the Brain."

4. Shauna Niequist, *I Guess I Haven't Learned That Yet: Discovering New Ways of Living When the Old Ways Stop Working* (Grand Rapids, MI: Zondervan, 2022), 58.

Chapter 25—What's Wrong with the Basement?: *Setbacks*

1. Pragya Agarwal, "How Does Lighting Affect Mental Health in the Workplace?," *Forbes*, December 31, 2018 https://www.forbes.com/sites/pragyaagarwaleurope /2018/12/31/how-does-lighting-affect-mental-health -in-the-workplace/?sh=311c63474ccd.

2. "Preventing Relapse and Managing Setbacks," Eisenberg Family Depression Center, University of Michigan, accessed March 29, 2023, https:// depressioncenter.org/outreach-education/community -education/depression-toolkit/want-stay-mentally -healthy/preventing.

Spread the Word
by Doing One Thing.

- Give a copy of this book as a gift.
- Share the QR code link via your social media.
- Write a review of this book on your blog, favorite bookseller's website, or at ODB.org/store.
- Recommend this book to your church, small group, or book club.

Connect with us. [f] [instagram] [twitter]

Our Daily Bread Publishing
PO Box 3566, Grand Rapids, MI 49501, USA
Email: books@odb.org

CW00672209

Pleasing Pets

Pleasing Pets

Phil Drabble

William Luscombe Publisher Limited
In association with Mitchell Beazley Ltd

First published in Great Britain by
William Luscombe Publisher Limited
Artists House
14, Manette Street
London W1V 5LB
1975

©1975 by Phil Drabble

All Rights Reserved. No part of this
publication may be reproduced, stored
in a retrieval system, or transmitted,
in any form or by any means, electronic,
mechanical, photocopying, recording
or otherwise, without the prior
permission of the Copyright owner.

ISBN 0 86002 050 9

Printed in Great Britain by
Alden & Mowbray Ltd
at the Alden Press, Oxford

Contents

Illustrations

1. Budgerigars are splendid pets which can be kept in a cage in a flat, an aviary in the garden or will fly free and return to feed and nest *facing page 32*
2. Tame rabbits are the ideal pets to start with. They are healthy, breed freely and are very easy to tame absolutely *facing page 33*
3. Peruvian guinea pigs are great fun but are not quite so easy to keep clean and healthy as normal short-coated cavies *facing page 48*
4. Cavies, or guinea pigs do well in hutches, moveable folds on the lawn or even quite free in the garden *facing page 49*
5. All tame gerbils were bred from an original stock of 22 imported into America from Mongolia in 1954! They are easy to feed, house and to breed *facing page 49*
6. A nylon net of shelled peanuts attracts gorgeous wild greenfinches as well as siskins and tits. They look so much lovelier free than in cages *facing page 96*
7. Greek tortoises do well in gardens during summer but need careful preparation for hibernation *facing page 97*
8. Sulphur-crested cockatoo. Cockatoos and parrots are long-lived, hardy and make excellent pets *facing page 112*
9. Bantams are among the few pets which pay for their keep! Half-a-dozen bantam hens in the garden or orchard will provide delicious free range eggs for the whole family *facing page 112*
10. Stick insects will eat common privet, breed freely and can be kept in the living-room of a flat *facing page 113*
11. Goats make friendly pets but it is necessary to make sure they don't do too much damage in the garden *facing page 144*
12. Fox cubs are not suitable as pets but this one, held by young Jane Springthorpe, was successfully released in isolated woodland where there was no hunting or shooting *facing page 144*

Both Author and Publisher would like to thank Mr S. C. Porter, F.R.P.S. for giving permission to use the photographs reproduced in this book.

Preface

Pleasing the pet you choose is quite as important as choosing a pleasing pet.

Some creatures are difficult to keep as members of an ordinary household and others are easy. They all have as much right to a dignified life as their owners but are too often neglected or discarded when their novelty wears off.

The object of this book is to suggest a range of pets which are suitable for owners with varying amounts of spare time and skill and space and money for food and cages. If I have erred, I have erred deliberately on the pet's side whether the question is space or food or necessary attention so that owners can have confidence that they are giving their pets a fair deal. Some creatures which are commonly sold are quite unsuited for captivity, and I have had no hesitation in advising readers not to swell the dealers' profits at their animals' expense.

I have only been concerned with those who wish to keep animals or birds or fish for pleasure and companionship, not for gain. Money often creeps in only on the edge of the slippery slope which leads to the extortion of the battery cage or the foetid air of intensive factory farming. Nor have I included advice about the treatment of disease because a little knowledge is often dangerous so that sick animals are usually better left to skilled veterinary surgeons than enthusiastic amateurs.

I have devoted part of the book to the rehabilitation of wild birds or creatures which have suffered accidents or been deserted when young. It is so easy to 'set them free' in the hopes that they will join their wild relatives and live happily ever after. The hard fact is that they will almost certainly starve or come to a bad end unless they have been skilfully taught to look after themselves.

This training for freedom is a fascinating business and the sight of one of 'my' wild birds or animals looking after itself successfully in complete liberty is one of the greatest thrills I know. It has only been rivalled in my experience by persuading wild birds or animals to come to feed or breed in my garden, where they grow as tame and confident as pets without having to sacrifice their independence. So I have devoted the last part of this book to ways of encouraging wild creatures, which are not pets at all, to take advantage of my hospitality without losing their freedom to come and go as they please.

This combines delightfully with having animals or birds, which have never been wild, but still have the liberty of my garden. Budgerigars can be trained to return to the safety of an aviary to feed and roost while retaining the freedom to fly where they like by day.

If the garden is fenced-in round the boundary, dogs and predatory cats will be kept harmlessly outside so that guinea-pigs or bantams or ornamental waterfowl have the next best thing to freedom while still being prevented from straying where they might not be welcome or fall into danger.

Keeping a captive in a cage bears no comparison with the pleasure of allowing the same creature to live almost as full a life as its relatives in the wild.

1 The Choice of a Pet

Take a good look at yourself before you choose a pet! The chances are that, however much you might enjoy the company of some creatures, your own personality or the place where you live would doom the relationship to failure before you had even started.

It is no use having spiders or snakes if you are allergic to creepy-crawlies. If you go away for weekends and have no friendly and reliable neighbour who will feed pets while you are away, you are obviously better equipped for keeping fish, which can live in an aquarium where they can fend for themselves for a day or so, than something which *has* to be fed three times a day.

It would be obviously stupid to covet something very large or very active, or possibly rather smelly, if you live in a flat with no garden. And it would be equally stupid to keep something which had to live outside and be fed and exercised seven days a week, in all weathers, if you are the sort of person who hates going out in the rain!

How far can you see into the future? One of the important things to consider is the normal lifespan of the pet you intend to keep. Mice, for example, are unlikely to survive for more than eighteen months, while a parrot could well go on for fifty years or more. Thus, a schoolboy, who has a cage of white mice, is unlikely to leave many problems for his parents when he goes on to university. But would they really want to be lumbered with his parrot when he marries a girl who cannot stand the sight of birds? If not, how do they make sure it will have a good home?

Neighbours should also be considered. I have vivid boyhood memories of a man about half a mile from home who kept peafowl. Their musical chorus drifted over on the wind whenever it blew in our direction. It was most attractive—at half a mile range, the lovely, wild melodious song being as sweet as church bells across quiet lazy fields

11

on summer evenings. But I should hate to live just on the other side of our churchyard where the jangle of Sunday bells must be loud enough to split my head, and close neighbours of the owner of the peafowl said the raucus row they made was more diabolical than heavenly. When they flew into the gardens around their owners' home, leaving choice flower beds stripped, as if visited by locusts, complaints mounted to such a torrent that they had to be banished to a stately home, too remote from neighbours for them to worry anyone but their owner's gardener.

Success with pets has nothing to do with the depth of their owners' pockets. Some of the commonest (and cheapest!) creatures are among the most delightful while exotic rarities often belie the dealer's promise and turn into expensive dead losses. Monkeys are a good example. They are dependent and appealing as babies, giving their owner the flattering illusion that he is indispensable, adored and all-powerful. However, when they grow up the males turn savage, give off an objectionable smell and have sexual habits which are unacceptable, even in our permissive society. In my opinion, they are quite unsuitable as pets and, when the family is finally forced to this conclusion, they are often presented to a zoo where they exchange the cossetting they have been brought up to expect for cruel bullying by their own kind.

When it does become impossible to continue to keep a pet, for any reason, it is far kinder to face the fact and to be practical rather than sentimental about it. It may be better to have it painlessly destroyed than to send it to strangers who are less sympathetic than its owner. Its whole sense of security and attachment to its home territory has been centred on the people and places it knows. Sudden removal to strange places and unsympathetic companions can be cruelly demoralizing and terrifying.

The best time to start keeping pets is as young as possible. Children should grow up on friendly terms with animals—and most animals are naturally good with children because they trust them. For example, a tame rabbit or guinea-pig soon becomes a very important part of a child's life. It supplies companionship and affection and often the first taste of pride of ownership. In later life, most people who are unsentimental but genuinely fond of animals

12

can trace the origin of such simple pleasures to joys of childhood pets.

All children are not so kind and gentle. Without firm discipline many of them will instinctively try to dominate and bully pets which are too weak and harmless to answer back or tell tales. Even the nicest children do not know their own strength so that they need careful training in how to handle small creatures without causing discomfort. They need to be told that animals would get as cold and hungry and thirsty and uncomfortable as they would without regular food and water and clean bedding. Most children need supervision and unobtrusive discipline to encourage them to put at least as much into their relationship with animals as they take out.

Nothing worthwhile is easy. The result of such early training is not just a lucky pet but a friendly, gentle child with a sense of responsibility all too often lacking in his elders.

One of the most important factors in the choice of a pet is where his owner lives. It is essential, for instance, to choose for a flat a pet which neither smells nor makes enough noise to annoy the neighbours. It must be something which is content with comparatively little space indoors and, as a bonus, it will help to be able to arrange a bulk supply of food and water so that the owner can go away for the weekend without a guilty conscience that he is causing hardship or discomfort. Creatures which will live in a vivarium or aquarium are obviously high on such priority lists, but cage birds or small mammals might also fit the bill. Stick insects and exotic foreign butterflies with limited lifespans are often ideal.

Do not overlook the fact that wild birds can often be attracted to bird tables or nest boxes near flat windows. I recently heard of a Londoner who had persuaded a kestrel hawk to nest in a box fixed outside the window of a flat seven storeys above the ground.

Watching a common starling rearing a brood of youngsters through the glass side of a nest box fixed to my window would give me more delight than the tropical splendour of some foreign rarity imprisoned in a cage.

A town house, with a small garden, offers surprising scope because it is then practicable to keep rabbits and

13

guinea pigs and bantams and pigeons which need more space and open air than creatures which will be content in the constricted space of flats. The fact that most town houses are likely to be at least a little more remote from neighbours adds the additional choice of mynahs and parrots which could well annoy the people in the flat upstairs.

Gardens in such town houses are often surrounded by high walls where rabbits and guinea-pigs can be kept more or less at liberty and there is often room for an aviary or pigeon even in a tiny garden. Just as it is easy to overlook the fact that wild birds will come to bird tables by windows of flats, it could well be possible to attract the most unlikely visitors to town gardens.

Foxes have settled with astonishing confidence in urban areas, where they are unlikely to do the harm that they wreak amongst game and poultry in the countryside. For example, I recently visited a friend who is a town vet and could hardly believe my eyes when I saw a large fox trot past the window and go down to a compost heap in broad daylight. I enquired whether it was a tame one belonging to a client, but was assured that it was quite wild and that it came regularly to the bird table in search of any scraps which fell to the ground below. It had dug a hole in the shubbery where it had reared litters of cubs which had provided constant entertainment for the last two years! The difference between that sleek fox, shining with health, coming and going as it pleased and shifty eyed 'tame' pet foxes, pining for their freedom had to be seen to be believed.

Those who live in the country with a large garden and, perhaps, a paddock and pool have riches which cannot be measured by the yardstick of £:s:d. They can enjoy fresh eggs, laid by bantams or attractive hens at liberty on free range, eating fresh grass and insects which impart superb natural flavour to their produce.

They can keep ferrets or goats or bottle-rear cade lambs and put up nest boxes to attract wild birds that are no more than romantic pictures in the books of townsfolk. Hedgehogs and even badgers can be enticed to feed beneath their windows, giving endless pleasure without sacrificing their freedom. Budgerigars can be kept in an aviary equipped with special entrances and exits which allow them to fly free as brilliant kingfishers by day but fasten them in, for their own safety, when owls are hunting at night.

I have derived immense pleasure from catching wild voles, insects or newts from which I have learned a lot more than I have ever found in books before setting them free again to continue their natural lives in the countryside, where I originally caught them. The wider one's experience in caring for such pets, the better the chances of success in coping with wild birds or animals which have been injured or deserted by their parents. When such foundlings are capable of looking after themselves, I know of no thrill as keen as setting them free in suitable habitat in the certainty that their chances of survival have increased because of the skilled care and attention they have had.

Try to resist the temptation of having too many pets at once. A great part of the pleasure of keeping animals is getting to know them as individuals, and it can be surprising to discover that all canaries and rabbits and guinea-pigs do not, in fact, behave alike. Their characters often differ as much as their owners'. Part of this difference stems from the way they are treated. The better they get to know their owner, the more friendly and affectionate they are likely to become. By keeping only a few pets at any one time, it is obviously possible to give each so much individual care and kindness that your time and effort will be repaid by mutual trust and affection.

It is also important to select pets which are likely to get on well with each other. Rabbits will live quite happily with guinea-pigs whereas a ferret, even kept securely in a nearby cage, will worry and unsettle them.

I find some pets, often expensive and exotic, less exciting than commoner creatures which may cost nothing at all. Fancy goldfish, which are sometimes difficult to keep healthy because their shape is so exaggerated that they suffer from chronic constipation, are far less fun than a bunch of lively sticklebacks which can be caught for nothing in most little pools in field corners. The goldfish seem to live for ever in spite of their infirmities and occupy valuable aquarium space where it would otherwise be possible to watch the butcher-red sticklebacks building their nests from pond weed and guarding their eggs against predators. When their bright breeding colours fade, all that

15

is necessary is to return them to their pond where they can continue life in the wild where they left off when they were captured.

For ten extremely happy years, at one house, we surrounded the whole garden with wire netting six feet high, stretched so tightly at the base that foxes could not squeeze under and our animals could not get out. It was quite an expensive exercise, but the result gave us far more lasting pleasure than the holidays we were prepared to forego to pay for it. It was a very pleasant house with a pool by the window, fed by a stream and waterfall, so that we could allow ornamental duck and pheasants the freedom to roam wherever they liked in the garden. Because everything had so much room, nothing was in constant fear of ambush with the result that even shy birds like lapwings grew delightfully tame and confiding.

In my view, a garden collection of birds and animals which are chosen because they will live in harmony, is the ideal way of keeping pets because it avoids the guilty feeling of getting pleasure at the expense of the pets one keeps.

2 General Management

Never choose a pet until you are quite certain that you know exactly how it should be treated and that you have the time to look after it properly for seven days a week.

There is more cruelty inflicted on pet animals and birds in sheer ignorance than wickedness. If you cannot provide the right food and conditions to give it a satisfactory life, with plenty of space and exercise, it is far better not to keep a pet at all. Luckily, some of the most satisfactory pets also happen to be cheap and easy to keep.

Warmth is often as vital to the welfare of young animals as food. A puppy will yap and keep you awake at night if he is cold, but many creatures simply suffer in silence.

Most animals and birds are never handled in the wild, so do not be surprised if your good intentions are greeted with suspicion or alarm. The golden rule is never to make a *sudden* or rough movement. Approach slowly and confidently, and do not try to pick your pet up until you are sure it will be happy to allow you to do so. A little patience at the start will produce the sort of relationship that gardeners with 'green fingers' achieve with plants.

Many young creatures which are reared by hand grow up with a 'fixation' for human beings. This really means that they regard human beings as they would their own mother. They sometimes rely on their owner so much that it may be as cruel to leave them as to inflict physical pain. Such creatures should be treated with great sympathy but, as they grow older, they will gradually become more independent, as they would of their own mother, and their need for constant human companionship should have eased by the time they are adult.

Meanwhile, if you have caused a young creature to acquire a human fixation, it is your responsibility to help it become independent. An animal's sense of security is often bound up with regularity. If you watch wild animals in their

17

natural surroundings, you will soon discover that they are far more punctual in what they do than you are. They will, for example, come to feed in the same place at almost exactly the same time every day, sun themselves to the same routine and use the same tracks from place to place so that they wear paths you can easily spot.

Even a tiger, pacing endlessly up and down his cage, is not so much looking for a way of escape as practising a routine exercise pattern.

So it is absolutely vital to feed and exercise and water your pets at times they will learn to expect and, when they fall into a comfortable routine you will be rewarded by seeing them grow daily more confident and relaxed.

It is also important to know why most young animals 'play'. It is not just for amusement, as it is with us but more often practice for the serious business of life.

Hunters, like dogs and foxes and stoats have more aggressive play than creatures whose chances of survival may well depend on their ability to run fast or dodge adroitly or know every possible line of escape so well that they can choose the best refuge by instinct instead of losing vital seconds thinking.

So, if a young ferret pretends to bite your finger, he is only practising for the day when he meets his first rat or rabbit in the earnest business of catching his dinner. His play will be as gentle as a kitten's because, at this stage, it is only make-believe and you can confidently join in the fun by cooperating, rolling him over and playing as you would with a kitten.

If a ferret bites you, it is nearly always your own fault. Almost certainly it is from fear, because you have not handled him enough to gain his confidence and, once he realizes that you are harmless, he will stop spitting and being defensive and become a playful pet instead.

Animals such as hares and deer, which are natural quarry instead of hunters, play by practising escape routines instead of attacking. They love to rush madly round dodging and weaving and there is a very thin line between such play and sheer blind panic. So be very careful about joining in such games in case your motives are misunderstood and the pace hots up beyond the safety line. It is safer to be content to be a passive spectator who simply enjoys the spectacle of such 'hare-brained' frolics.

Many animals have a definite toleration point for handling. They seem to enjoy a certain amount of gentle fuss and attention but soon get sullen and angry if liberties are taken beyond that point. Nor is it ever safe to generalize. Some animals, like some people, are quicker on the draw than others so that it is necessary to find out not only how different species react but different individuals too.

Some, such as male deer, are *never* safe if they become tame and lose their fear of Man. They are as savage as bulls, especially in the rut, or breeding season, and should never, on any account be kept as pets.

But very few animals are 'treacherous'. They do not grow savage for no apparent reason and turn upon their owners. They usually grow more intolerant gradually, as they become jealous of their territory and so possessive that they will allow nothing else to share it, or defensive if their mates or young are threatened.

This happens gradually and very little experience in managing pets will soon teach their owners to spot the signs in plenty of time to treat them with respect.

A few creatures, like mink, are openly aggressive and make no bones about it, but most animals will only bite through fear or nervousness, when they are in pain or being mauled beyond endurance. They give due warning that they will stand no more loss of dignity before doling out much needed discipline to their owners.

It is an immense pleasure to tame most animals and birds by gentling them. The easiest way to their hearts is often through their tummies and anyone who finds their favourite food, and has limitless patience to give the confidence that they will suffer no harm, will soon earn the reputation of 'having a way with animals'.

3 Simple Pets

A large number of animals and birds are particularly suited for life in a household because they are easy to feed and house in such conditions that they will probably be as happy as they would if living in the wild. A life of captivity shields them from dangers of predators and starvation and often disease as well.

A number of factors should influence their choice. It would be foolish to give tame mice to a child too young to realize how gentle he must be when handling them unless he had adequate supervision. He could probably get quite as much pleasure from watching the fish in an aquarium or canaries in a cage.

A town garden where rabbits can have a little liberty is ideal for introducing a youngster to the delights of pet keeping because he can sample the pleasures without the chores of cleaning out cages—and the rabbit can avoid his attentions when they get too pressing!

But when a child has reached a reasonably responsible age, tame mice are admirable pets to start with.

Mice

Among the cheapest and least exacting pets are tame mice. They can be kept in very small cages which are simple to make, are cheap to feed as well as to buy, become extremely tame, and breed very freely.

The old idea that the only tame mice are white mice has long since died. There is a large number of beautifully coloured varieties, and clubs have been formed which organize shows to popularize the more interesting or rare specimens. The varieties are divided according to colour and the two main classes are 'self'—which means the same colour all over—and 'marked'—which means that their coats are of more than one colour, often in a well-defined pattern. The black-and-white 'Dutch' mouse has an evenly marked black-and-white head (black sides and a white blaze) and a black rump with the rest of the body white. It is like a miniature Dutch rabbit.

At mouse shows, you will find almost every colour of 'selfs': reds, yellows, blues, blacks and whites and a bewildering combination of these colours in the classes for 'marked'. There are even mice with long and curly coats.

When you are choosing your pet mice, it is a good idea to go in for one of the less common colours, even if you have to pay a little extra for the original stock. They are all prolific breeders: unusual coloured mice are just as cheap to keep as the common varieties and the surplus is much easier to dispose of at a price which will cover the cost of their food.

Choice

Mice that are regularly handled are tame and docile; they bite only from fear and not from anger. So see your mice handled before you buy. If the seller has to pounce on his victim and holds it gingerly by the end of the tail, go somewhere else. It is quite safe to put your hand right in the middle of a group of mice that have been properly handled. The selected mouse should sit happily on the palm of one hand, whilst the forefinger and thumb of the other hand holds the base of its tail lightly, to prevent it taking any sudden suicidal leaps in mid air.

See that coats are glossy, eyes bright, and ears and feet clean. A healthy mouse should be plump without being fat, should move freely and well and not be in any way nervous. If you are buying from the breeder, look carefully at his cages to see that he keeps them clean. Mice kept in dirty conditions are always liable to ill health and should be avoided. Go to mouse shows and look at the mice that have not won an award as well as those that have. You may see some beautifully healthy creatures which are well-bred but have some very minor defect, such as a blemish in marking. If you can buy any of these at a sensible price (not more than ten per cent or so more than the price being asked in pet shops) you are sure of having stock that has been well looked after and may well breed you winners. On no account start with a lot of mice. They breed freely, and if you look after them well your stock will soon increase to larger numbers, perhaps more than you want. Instead, spend your money on one first-class pair, bred from pedigree stock, so that you have every chance of breeding youngsters which are first class and saleable too. Mice breed so rapidly that you may have difficulty in disposing of surplus stock unless it is of exhibition standard.

Housing

Before going to buy your first mice, you will, if you are wise, have already prepared their quarters.

Mice will live satisfactorily in anything from the most elaborate quarters to a simple wooden box with a perforated zinc top for ventiliation and a sheet of glass at the side for light. They need cosy sleeping quarters which must be dry and draught-free, and as much room for exercise as you can manage.

Pet shops get over the need for exercise, to some extent, by providing a relatively small cage from which the mice can emerge inside a mouse wheel. This simply consists of two circular disks, about four inches in diameter, connected by wire bars at intervals of about three-sixteenths of an inch, to form a cylinder. One disk has holes in it, mating with a hole in the cage, and the whole cylinder is mounted horizontally on a spindle, about which it revolves freely.

A mouse exploring the hole from his cage goes through to the inside of the cylindrical wheel, and, when he tries to climb, the wheel revolves while he runs to stay at the bottom. Mice appear to enjoy this form of exercise and will make their wheels spin like tiny treadmills, even when they are mounted inside the cage so that there is no question of their imagining they are escaping.

These cages with mouse wheels, sold by pet shops, are often made entirely of metal. They are excellent from the viewpoint of hygiene, but can be too hot or too cold, depending on their location; bad condensation in the mice's sleeping quarters is another possible snag. Nevertheless, if these cages are kept in a room with a reasonably steady temperature, and plenty of bedding is provided, they are quite satisfactory.

Medical research organizations, which keep an immense number of rats and mice, use extremely simple metal cages with no covered sleeping quarters. It is then possible to see nests of young as soon as they are born, although the mother will usually cover them with bedding, making it impossible for them to be counted. In these cages there is no detachable tray, and the mice have to be moved for the cage to be cleaned out. In every room of cages, there is one empty cage, which is kept clean. The attendant removes the mice from the next cage into this empty one and then cleans the cage they have just left; instead of returning them he puts mice from the next cage along the row into the one he has just cleaned and so on until all the mice have been moved to a clean cage. When the supervisor is on his rounds, he can see at a glance that the cages have been cleaned. And, because it is necessary to move the mice before cleaning their cage, he also knows that every mouse has been handled. This most important routine is to ensure that all the mice are tame and quiet.

So even if you do not adopt the clinical type of cage, at least make certain that you handle your mice as often as possible and never less than two or three times a week.

Mice can be kept very well in makeshift cages. Old aquariums are excellent, as they are ideal from the observation point of view, beautifully easy to keep clean, and virtually impossible to escape from if they are more than ten inches deep or fitted with a detachable (and ventilated) top. One of the advantages of an old aquarium is that, being watertight and having no wood to rot, it is possible to put an inch of soil and turf on the bottom, making the whole thing much more decorative than a clinical cage. The mice will play and burrow and amuse themselves enormously, and no pet does so well as a thoroughly happy one.

Perhaps the most amusing 'cage' of all for tame mice is a converted dolls' house. The windows need glass glued into them from the inside and all outside doors should have glass fixed behind them or really secure latches fitted. Ventilation can be arranged by cutting holes in the walls and fitting perforated zinc over them. Then hang pictures to obscure the ventilators from the front, leaving plenty of room for the air to circulate. Make sure that all communicating doors between rooms are open and that the stairs effectively join the two storeys. Make holes into the large wardrobes or

23

cupboards in the side away from the windows, and furnish with soft bedding material—and install the mice. They will be forever popping from room to room and floor to floor and will establish the 'fitted' wardrobes as headquarters. You will find that they are far more amusing when they have so much to explore than ever they are in unimaginative cages.

A final word of warning: make sure that the entire back or front is readily detachable for cleaning purposes.

Food

Mice are particularly easy to feed. They will eat grain in almost any form from bird-seed to whole maize. And they are particularly pretty to watch twirling a large grain of maize in their 'hands', while they nibble it exactly as a squirrel eats a nut. They like bread and cake and most household scraps, including a little meat in spite of the fact that they are rodents. Indeed, most rodents will not turn up their noses at an occasional carnivorous element in their diet. Chick rearing pellets, seeding grass, cheese and fat in the form of suet or bacon rinds or dripping, are also essential. Balance the diet by adding a little fresh fruit (apple will do very well), vegetables such as cubes of carrot, linseed for glossy coats, and cod-liver oil for extra vitamins. Mice also like something hard to gnaw, because their teeth (like those of all rodents) grow rapidly and can only be kept in check by constant work. A piece of bone is very good, but they also like very hard biscuits such as those sold for large dogs.

Do not give too much food at a time, because it will become wet and foul and pass any disease present in one mouse on the rest. Get hold of a number of small meat- or fish-paste jars, about as large in diameter as a 10p piece and as deep as they are wide. Put water in one and different food in each of the others. You will be able to see which food is liked best and give less of the others. Throw away surplus food each day and after washing the jar replace with fresh food. But each time, put a little less in the jar until the mice almost clean it up by next day. This is the ideal amount of food to give and can be discovered only with individual mice. Aim to give as much as they will clear up in a day with the minimum of waste.

Breeding

You may well have more difficulty in preventing your mice from multiplying than in encouraging them. They are exceptionally prolific and virile and will start to breed at about three months. The females come in season at extremely short intervals so any adult female left with a male will be pregnant in a few days, if they are both fit and well.

The fact that they are so prolific permits some interesting experiments in colour breeding. According to the Mendelian theory some colours are dominant over others (white being a recessive colour that is likely to be dominated by black, for example), and it is possible to predict, if you mate a black buck to a white doe, the proportion you will get pure black or pure white and the number which will show both colours. It is quite possible with coloured mice to test the theory experimentally; it will only work if you take a large enough number of matings to give a fair average, and you will find that the more mice you produce the nearer their colours will conform to the Mendelian pattern.

To make this experiment properly you must know which doe has been mated to which buck. The only certain way of doing this is to keep them apart for a month beforehand to make quite certain the doe was not pregnant before you started, and then put her in a cage with the selected buck. The doe will come into season within about five days and have her young between three and four weeks later. It is safer, although not always necessary, to move the buck before his doe has her young. Mice are naturally extremely gregarious and if conditions are right the buck should not harm the young. He should have the opportunity of separate sleeping quarters so that his doe will not have too much difficulty in ejecting him from the nest if his intentions do not conform to her ideas of a dutiful father. If, however, his diet is deficient in protein he may find a dish of succulent young mice quite irresistible. So it is safer, especially if you are doing experiments in colour breeding, to remove the buck well before the doe has her young.

For the last two weeks of pregnancy, try not to handle the doe at all. Mice are rather delicate at this time and it is easy to do them great damage.

If you are not selecting matings for show or colour

experiments, it is quite possible to breed mice in colonies without removing the bucks; if you are keeping them in a dolls' house for example. There may be a certain number of accidents—but there would be in the wild state, and mice are really so prolific that you are soon likely to have more than you want rather than less.

If you decide to allow a colony to breed as they will, the essential thing is to be quite sure that the does have plenty of snug boxes to choose from as nesting sites. The size cage for a colony of mice will be governed by the number to be kept. A very rough guide for a large cage, twenty-four inches by twelve inches, is that it will house two dozen mice. Large numbers like this are not, however, very satisfactory in a living-room because they will smell, no matter how hygienically they are kept. The golden rule is to have as large a cage as possible and only to keep a moderate number of mice, so that they have plenty of room for exercise.

When you have breeding mice in the colony, provide a small jar of fresh milk each day to help the does' own milk supply. But remember that there will soon be youngsters running about, so make sure the containers for milk and water are not deep enough for them to fall into and drown. At this time shallow ashtrays are perhaps safest.

Do not put bedding in the nest boxes. It is natural for the mice to do this for themselves, and if you put scraps of woodwool, thickly folded sheets of newspaper, or bits of sacking in the cage, you will see that the mice shred it up and carry it into their selected nest box, making a wonderfully warm and soft couch for their babies. If the doe is already pregnant when you introduce her to her quarters, there may not be time for her to make an adequate nest, in which case you should cover the bottom of the nest compartment with ten or twenty sheets of newspaper cut to size. She will shred these quite quickly without having to waste time carrying in each sheet.

I am very much in favour of supplying newspaper, not only as nesting material but as floor covering. It is extremely absorbent and does not harbour insect vermin. If you cover the cage floors, as well as nest boxes, with two or three sheets of newspaper, cut to size, it will absorb urine or spilt water or milk, and can be taken out wholesale and burnt, which greatly simplifies cage-cleaning operations.

The young mice are born naked and blind but develop very quickly. They should not be examined or handled until their mother brings them out of the nest. If they are interfered with too young, there is a grave danger that the doe may eat them. Even when they come into the open as prefect replicas of their parents, they are fragile mites and must be treated extremely gently.

Handling

It is as natural to pick up a mouse by his tail as a rabbit by his ears. Both methods are utterly wrong! Indeed, if you pick up a mouse by the tip of his tail, there is real danger of him struggling until the end skins and you are left holding the sheath, while he escapes in agony. Tame mice will climb into your hand as soon as you put it down to them. They become friendly enough to do this at an early age if removed from their cage every time it is cleaned. Mice kept in colonies usually have enough room to keep out of the way in one part of their quarters while another part is being cleaned. For this reason there is a temptation not to handle all of them equally but to spend most time with the favourite specimens.

A mouse that is not entirely tame should be gently lifted by the base of the tail, and put immediately on the palm of the other hand. Keep hold of the base of the tail to prevent him jumping off and damaging himself. When he is settled safely over a soft landing—a few inches above the carpet for example—let go his tail and put your free hand in front of him so that he can crawl on to it. Repeat with the other hand, allowing him to crawl from one to the other until he is used to your movement. Then he can crawl all over you.

Rats

Wild rats undoubtedlly spread an enormous amount of disease, largely because they run over all sorts of filth and then crawl over their own food supply. In addition they foul more food than they eat with droppings and urine. Most people have an instinctive and well founded aversion to rats.

In spite of this, one of the most engaging pets I ever kept was a wild buck rat, which I brought up from the time he was a naked, blind crawler. I shall refer to him again in Chapter 9, Advanced Animals.

Because of their instinctive aversion to rats, a great many people object to keeping tame domestic rats. It must be emphasized that it is quite essential to keep them under thoroughly hygienic conditions, as they are not naturally fastidious. It is also the responsibility of the owner to see that they do not escape, since they are a domesticated version of the brown rat, and will interbreed and go wild if they escape. But kept properly, they are intelligent and attractive pets. With the difference that they need more of the same kind of food and stronger cages, they may be kept quite satisfactorily on the same principles as described for tame mice.

Housing
Rats have such sharp teeth that a metal cage is a necessity. Failing an all-metal cage, keep them in a large wooden box, with a well fitting wire mesh front, which is made detachable for cleaning. The mesh used should be heavy gauge, half-inch wire netting and it should not only be used for the front: it should be fitted inside the other five sides of the box too, so that the inmates cannot gnaw holes in them. Whether wood or metal cages are used, newspaper, in multiple thicknesses, is ideal as floor covering.

Rabbits

Rabbits are ideal for people who want a pet that is harmless, friendly, hardy and easy to breed.

They can be kept either indoors or out, fed on processed food or largely on food the owner gathers himself, and are longer lived than some other pets, such as mice, which are unlikely to survive more than two years however well they are cared for.

Choice
Rabbits fall into three main categories: large breeds like New Zealand White and Beverans, which have been produced commercially by generations of selective breeding to make big carcasses for meat production; breeds like Chinchilla and the Rex breeds, which have soft coats with a

pile like velvet, have been produced mainly for the rabbit skin trade; and show rabbits, of which the Dutch is an old-fashioned example still popular after generations of changing fashion. The object with these breeds, as with other exhibition animals, is to produce specimens approaching the theoretical standard of perfection laid down by the specialist breed society.

It is assumed that readers of this book will want to keep rabbits purely as pets and will not be interested in slaughtering them for either their skins or the meat they provide. Nevertheless, it is preferable to buy good thoroughbred stock, rather than mongrels, because part of the enjoyment most good pet-keepers get is the pride of knowing their pets are not only tame and happy and friendly, but are good specimens of their kind as well. Go to a rabbit show and see which breeds appeal to you most. If you are entirely inexperienced, talk to the exhibitors, explaining that you want to take up rabbit fancying as a novice and ask about the good and bad points of the breed you like the look of. They will explain difficulties to you and help you choose a suitable breed. For example, few people would want to start with Angoras, which are produced for their wool combings, because it is a very specialist—and tedious—job to keep their coats in good condition. You will probably decide to start with one of the old-fashioned breeds, like Belgian Hares (which are not hares but rabbits which look like hares) or Dutch.

Buy the best stock, but not necessarily the best specimens, you can afford. It is better to buy a pair of rabbits with minor defects but coming from a long line of prize-winning stock, than wonderful specimens bred by chance mating. These are far less likely to reproduce their like than rabbits which are from a really good strain.

It may seem that too much stress is laid on obtaining the best and that a pet animal might just as well be a throw-out. My experience is that, until the novelty has worn off, any rabbit is as good as any other. But is also my experience that once an owner gets bitten by the bug of rabbit-keeping, he becomes interested in other people's rabbits too. And nobody likes his favourites to be compared unfavourably with other people's pets. The pride of owning the best, and learning to get it in as good a condition as is possible, ensures that the utmost pains are taken to keep your pet under the best possible conditions. And that means that proud owners tend to have the happiest pets.

Housing

Hutches. The simplest of all ways of keeping rabbits is in a traditional rabbit hutch. Basically, this is a box divided into two compartments, the larger of which has a wire-netting door. The smaller compartment, for sleeping, shelter, and producing young, has a solid wooden floor and a gap at the back wide enough for the rabbit to pass from one part of its quarters to the other. The roof of the hutch should slope, be covered with strong roofing felt, and have enough overhang to keep out the weather.

The smallest hutch size satisfactory for the smaller varieties, like Dutch, is three feet six inches long by two feet wide and high. The sleeping compartment should be one foot wide, leaving a space two feet by two feet six inches for the other part. It should be stressed that, although this is physically adequate for single rabbits on a commercial scale, in order to live happily as well as healthily, pet rabbits should whenever possible have larger hutches.

The netting used should be one-inch heavy gauge to exclude birds, which will eat food, and rats, which may eat the young rabbits.

I always make a point of looking at any housing units on sale to people keeping stock on a commercial basis. They have to economize on labour and still keep their stock healthy and well. It is often possible to incorporate their labour-saving devices into houses which provide more room and comfort than could be justified on a strictly commercial basis.

One of the greatest time-wasters in keeping rabbits in hutches is cleaning them out. To minimize this element, the commercial breeders use hutches with wire-mesh floors of sufficiently close gauge to avoid the risk of the rabbits getting their feet stuck. To avoid droppings falling on to rabbits in lower tiers a sheet of galvanized metal or asbestos is laid beneath each hutch, so sloped that all the droppings slide into a piece of spouting at the bottom edge of the dung tray. The hutch should be equipped with glazed earthenware feeding and drinking bowls and a miniature hay rack from which the animal can browse sweet hay that has not been on the floor and become fouled.

If more than one rabbit is to live in the hutch, the minimum dimensions must be increased to about five feet long by two feet wide, an area in which two adults or four young (until about half-grown) may be kept very happily. When a doe is due to have to have young, however, she is far better off by herself in a single unit.

Fold units. Rabbits may be kept very successfully in movable pens like poultry fold units. Each pen should be between four feet by two feet and six feet by ten feet, and should consist of a framework of two-inch-square or three-by-two-inch wood. It should have a covered weatherproof box in one corner (more if many does are kept) and the bottom should be covered by strong two-inch wire netting. The idea of this netted floor is to allow the rabbit to graze the natural herbage and to keep the supply sweet and fresh by moving the fold unit every day.

The covered box in the corner should have a solid floor if it is anticipated that the unit will be used for breeding, for the young creatures may well stampede and damage their legs unless the wire mesh bottom is half-inch gauge or less. The rest of the run can still have two-inch gauge base netting.

Further major advantages of this type of unit are that it does not have to be cleaned out if it is moved its own width every day; it is far cheaper to make than a conventional hutch; the rabbits have access to an unlimited amount of fresh green-food. While it cannot be used in exceptionally cold or wet weather, it is ideal for spring and summer.

The gauge of the netting on the walls and roof of a fold unit should certainly not be larger than one inch, and it is better still if half inch is used. This is because prowling cats have a nasty habit of putting a paw through the netting if the mesh is large enough, and 'fishing' for a catch. If the shelters are adequate, the rabbits will dive for cover and remain out of sight until the coast is clear. Even so, it is worth taking precautions against prowlers, either cats or rats.

If it desirable to use the fold for an extended period, a light frame can be made to fit on half the run over the wire netting. This frame should consist of roofing felt nailed to two-by-one-inch framing and it will act as shade from sun and shelter from rain.

Free Range. In suitable circumstances, rabbits may be kept loose in quite large areas enclosed by wire netting.

The netting should be six feet high, and the support posts should be sunk two to two and a half feet in the ground and five yards apart. A right-angle bracket should be fixed to each upright and a roll of eighteen-inch netting taken right round the enclosure horizontally, and laced to the top of the six-foot netting. This should project a foot outside and six inches inside, and it will effectively keep cats and dogs out and many other pets, which may be kept from time to time, from escaping.

The six-foot netting can either have the bottom six inches buried or a strip of eighteen-inch netting can be bent out and laid flat on the ground for a foot and overlapped with the guard fence for six inches. If small-mesh netting is used for this, it will keep rats out fairly effectively as well as larger vermin. The part that is laid flat on the ground should be covered with soil, which should be sown with grass seed. When this grows through the netting, it will be as effective as if the netting were buried, because nearly all animals wishing to tunnel under a barrier begin to dig right at its base and not a foot or so away. Another major advantage of using a narrow roll of netting to make good the base is that it nearly always corrodes first where it meets the ground. It can therefore be repaired more easily and cheaply than if the whole had to be replaced.

When an enclosure of this nature has been erected, put in several boxes, four-inch drain pipes, and corrugated sheets to make roofs for the rabbits to shelter under. If you do not do this, they will dig holes or warrens like their wild relatives and be very hard to catch.

The one snag in keeping rabbits on free range is that they do tend to revert to the wild. A good idea is to make a permanent corral, with a funnel shaped entrance against one side of the enclosure, and put some carrots, oats, or sweet hay there so that they get used to going to it to feed. It will then be quite simple to drive them into the corral when you want to catch them in order to keep them tame which should be done at least once a week. Handle them well and affectionately before you let them go back to their freedom.

1. Budgerigars are splendid pets which can be kept in a cage in a flat, an aviary in the garden or will fly free and return to feed and nest

2. Tame rabbits are the ideal pets to start with. They are healthy,
breed freely and are very easy to tame absolutely

It will work quite well for a while, if you put in one rabbit to every ten square feet. But if you intend to have rabbits on the same ground for several years—and it is a major operation to move so much permanent netting—the more space you allocate to each the longer it will take for the ground to get stale.

Some people put the does in hutches to produce their young, and there is something to be said for this, if only to rear the young ones tame. If they have the liberty of a large paddock all their lives, they are apt to grow up as timid as wild rabbits. If you do let them breed out on range, it is quite essential to provide plenty of alternative cover for nesting.

Food
Feeding rabbits is as easy or as difficult as you care to make it. Pet shops and corn merchants sell fully processed rabbit pellets which are made up to give a balanced diet. Practically all that is necessary is to tip these into a self-feed hopper, provide water and some green-stuff, and the rabbits will do the rest.

At the other end of the scale are people who spend hours a day searching for 'rabbit meat'—that is all the wild plants of the hedge-side and field that rabbits love. Together with a simple diet of crushed oats and bran, a selection of wild plants is all that rabbits require.

I steer my course between the two schools of thought. I give what roots are in season: carrots or parsnips or swedes. Rabbits also love hay, oats, bran, maize meal, barley, boiled potatoes, and fresh greens. These last are essential, and can consist of cow parsley, dandelion, clover, lettuce, kale, and cabbage. If your rabbit is tame or you have trained him to a lead (which is quite easy), let him out in the garden and hedgerow and make a list of the plants he chooses in the order of his preference, and repeat the experiment at different seasons to see how his tastes change. You will find that he likes his protein in the form of meat or fish if he gets the opportunity.

Be careful not to give him more than he will clear up at one time, and see that his droppings are firm and healthy. Frosted greens, too much sloppy food, too much young clover, sprouting corn, or unripe roots will bring about

33

serious stomach upsets from which he may die. Rabbits love variety and relish fresh green-stuff picked from the hedgerow. Take special care that the food you pick has not been sprayed with any of the new weedkillers or insecticides.

Handling

Never pick up a rabbit by his ears. They are delicate, sensitive and tender, so that it is very cruel to pinch or pull or squeeze them. The weight of the rabbit should be taken by putting one hand under his rump or belly and it is permissible then to steady him by holding his ears gently in the other hand. When he is thoroughly tame, it will probably be unnecessary to hold his ears at all, as he will learn to let you pick him up like a dog or cat, without scratching or struggling.

Moulting

Rabbits moult, as do most other fur-bearing animals and the state of moult is obviously of more importance to the fancier keeping rabbits for their pelts than to the owner of a pet. But it is important for the pet owner to know that his rabbit will change its coat throughout its life—the first complete change taking place between the ages of about six and sixteen weeks—and when moulting there is always a well-defined line of new hair. A little linseed in the food at this period, half a teaspoonful a day for each rabbit, will help the supply of natural oils which are essential to a new glossy coat.

If the coat is not glossy and shining between moults it is a sign that the animal is out of condition. Vary the diet and try to supply fresh tempting greens or succulent roots and add the same quantity of linseed as if the moult was just starting.

Breeding

The fertility of rabbits is proverbial. For this reason all young should be segregated into the sexes when they are six to eight weeks old so that they do not start breeding too early and sap their own strength.

Only allow your best to breed and put them to the very best buck you can get, specially chosen so that his good points will match the particular characteristics you are

34

hoping the young will possess. Before mating, make quite sure that both buck and doe are mature and in perfect health and condition. Their eyes should be bright and their coats shining, and they should be as agile and lively as athletes. See that their ears and eyes are clean and free from mucus.

If she is healthy, the doe will usually accept the buck's attentions at once and you will find it advisable to put her into the buck's quarters. Although buck rabbits have a dreadful reputation for eating the young, savaging the does and fighting each other, it is my belief that the females are at least as pugnacious. Remove her after she has been served, unless you are keeping your rabbits on the colony system, when you will notice that the bucks have not acquired their reputation without good cause.

When she has been mated, the doe will become pregnant and have her litter in just over four weeks. How many babies she will have depends on a number of factors, not least of which is the fitness of the doe and the adequacy of her food supply.

Rabbits have a marvellous means of birth control in reverse. If an insufficient number of ova have been fertilized, they are reabsorbed and the doe comes into season again quickly, without wasting time having a complete pregnancy to produce one or a couple of young. If, on the other hand, a large number—say nine or ten—ova have been ferilized and she is not in the pink of condition or the season does not coincide with maximum food supply, she will reabsorb the surplus when they are about as big as walnuts and produce what Nature suggests is the ideal number, usually four or five.

So if you want your rabbits to have large litters you can help by seeing that the parents shine with health and have access to a plentiful food supply.

The pregnant doe should have plenty of roots—mangolds, swedes, carrots—and fresh green-stuff; a moist mash of ground oats, bran and maize meal mixed to a crumbly consistency is helpful while the doe is in milk. She should have access to unlimited water, and fresh milk once a day if she will take it. If she gets too thirsty she may eat her own young.

A wooden box a little larger than a boot box with a basis of clean soft hay will be further furnished by the doe lining her nest with soft fur from her own belly. The box should have a low entrance, like the entry to a dog basket, so the young can get in and out easily when they start to run about. If they should topple out before they are strong enough to get back, the doe will carry them in herself as a cat would her kittens. The wisest plan if not to interfere with the young in any way until they come out of the nest. Certainly rabbits on free range, living nearer to their natural wild conditions, are likely to eat their babies if these are handled while naked and blind. On the other hand, a very tame pet doe may allow her owner to examine her litter almost as soon as it is born. Pick the doe up very gently and stroke her belly so that your hands smell of her and not of you. Put her in the outside run and give her a little carrot or bread or any titbit you know she is particularly fond of and wait until she is absorbed in eating it. Then just move the covering of the nest apart with your 'rabbity-smelling' fingers, count the young and replace the nesting material. If she has a very big litter, more than six or seven, and you happen to have another rabbit with a small litter born about the same time, it is possible to transfer the surplus from one to the other, evening up the numbers that each doe has to rear.

I would emphasize that there is some risk that either—or both—does may take offence and record their disapproval by devouring the lot. But if they are thoroughly tame and you are careful not to taint the nest or young with human scent, there is a good chance of success. This chance can be increased by shutting the does out of the nesting compartment for an hour so that they become so obsessed with the desire to get back to their young that they fail to notice the family has grown or shrunk a bit while they were away.

Another method of 'sharing' litters is to encourage two does to have young in the same nest. It is necessary to put them both with the buck at the same time, so that their litters are of the same age, and they must have lived in the same quarters without disagreement for some time. An added precaution is to include in their hutch a spare nest which is not so attractive as the extra large well-littered one you will have provided. The only snag in allowing two does to bring up two litters as a community is that, if there

36

should be some much weaker than others, they may well be pushed out by the strong, who will then thrive at the expense of the weaklings.

When the young leave the nest—at about three weeks—they will begin to feed themselves, although they should be allowed to suckle the doe for another fortnight, or three weeks if the weather is bad. Look them over carefully to be sure they are sound, healthy, and in no way deformed. It is far easier to harden your heart and dispose of any bad specimens as soon as they appear than a few days later when you have had time to get fond of them.

Weaning

Take the doe from the young at six or seven weeks, depending on their general condition and the weather, and keep the food rather dry: avoiding greens and roots for a few days, thus encouraging her milk supply to cease.

Leave the young in the surroundings they are used to, make certain that there are no draughts and that they are warm and dry, and feed them on clean fresh mash, roots, hay and whatever food you are giving to their parents. Be more particular than ever that the food is clean and fresh.

Two weeks later, separate the bucks of the litter from the does, and keep them segregated until you wish to breed from them again.

Identification

If you want to exhibit rabbits, or to breed them in any number, it will become important to you to be able to identify them so that you can mate selectively and be sure of pedigree. If it is not done there will be danger of too close inbreeding and you may mate brother with sister by mistake. It is not unknown for experienced breeders to mate brother to sister or mother to 'fix' some particular physical character, but inbreeding should not be practised except as a deliberate policy for genetic reasons.

To make certain of the pedigree of your rabbits they may be ringed with numbered rings as pigeons are. These rings are supplied by the British Rabbit Council, of Farnborough, Hampshire, and it is necessary to state the breed of your rabbit because the rings come in a number of sizes designed to fit any rabbit from the dwarf breeds to the giants.

The rings are fitted over the hock of a back leg at between

37

eight and ten weeks. By the time the rabbit is about three months old it will have grown too big for the ring ever to come off again, and after that, it will always be identifiable by its own number. It will be obvious that it is now necessary to keep careful written records to show which number doe has been mated to which buck, the date, and the number of litter produced. If these records are kept conscientiously, you will build up a fascinating history of both failure and success over the years. Should you buy or sell one of these numbered aristocrats it will be necessary to have the ring number transferred to the new owner. This means of identification is completely painless and reliable and much better than the old-fashioned tattoo—which was neither.

Ferrets

Since I was a small boy I have never been without ferrets. They are extremely useful to anyone keeping other animals which may attract the odd rat; and they also make very good pets.

Ferrets are a domesticated form of the wild polecat. A few years ago, scientists claimed that they could differentiate between a ferret and a polecat if they could examine the skulls. Then they found that if a 'polecat' was fed on soft food—bread and milk for instance—from the time it was weaned, and a 'ferret' was flesh fed in an open pen, with plenty of room for exercise, the differences would be reversed. One doctor of zoology who is doing research on the subject at the present time claims to be able to tell by the guard hairs of the coat.

My personal opinion is that there are no true polecats left in the British Isles, assuming that there ever was any real difference between ferrets and polecats. They interbreed so freely that any ferret lost on a day's rabbiting would cross with its wild cousins if it survived just long enough to learn to fend for itself in the wild. I think that ferrets are simply polecats made tame by centuries of domestication. And I am certain that, if ferrets are not 'handled' while they are still too young to do damage with their fangs, they will grow up to be quite wild and unmanageable.

38

Choice

There are various coloured ferrets. 'Whites' are really albinos with eyes as pink as a white rat. They are only white in their baby coat. When they moult into adult pelage their coat turns a pale yellow.

At the other extreme are 'fitchets' or 'polecats'. These have dark brown coats with a buff under-fur. The face is marked with cream between the eye and ear, on the lips, at the sides of the muzzle and the edges of the ears. The feet, tail, and chest are darker brown, almost approaching black. The eyes are dark brown. Ferrets thus marked have obviously descended from polecats, though there is some doubt about whether the Asiatic polecat was the original progenitor. Be that as it may, ferrets have been kept and have escaped in the British Isles certainly since Roman times and there has been plenty of time for them to mix blood with our native species.

White and fitchet ferrets have been crossed until there are ferrets about of almost every shade between the two, although, white being the recessive factor, all but the pure white (or yellow) ones have dark eyes. Most of the intermediate colours lose much of the shading of the fitchets and are more or less evenly coloured sandy.

Male ferrets are called hobs and females are jills. In some parts of the country they are called dogs and bitches, which are the terms used for wild polecats. But in either case, their young are called kittens. It is always best to obtain a young kitten, just as it has left the jill at about eight weeks.

Smell

Ferrets are members of the family called Mustilidae, all of which have a musk gland under the tail from which they can emit a powerful stench if hurt or frightened. The phrase 'stinks like a polecat' is self-explanatory, and the other members of the family are badger, otter, marten, stoat, weasel and polecat. There are also foreign members of the same group, of which the skunk is the best known.

Do not be put off by this characteristic, because the stink is only emitted under great strain and your pet ferret will not be offensive unless frightened or hurt, or, in the case of the hob, when excited by strange ferrets or in the breeding season. The hob ferret does smell stronger than his jill, so it is preferable to pick a jill for a pet. If kept clean, a jill does not smell and can be a most delightful and friendly creature. Mine are always tame enough to be carried about in my pocket.

There is great variation in sizes of ferrets—though the hobs are considerably bigger than their sisters. Large, strong strains are bred for rabbiting and small, lithe, so-called 'greyhound' ferrets are specially bred for evicting rats from their holes. My ideal for a pet is a small white jill.

Handling

Once tame, a ferret is as safe to handle as a domestic cat, though pet ferrets should always be handled and petted regularly to keep them tame. A ferret that has been allowed to grow up with no special care can be a very tricky customer to pick up. Always take precautions with strange ferrets until you are certain of the characters.

Clench your fist so that the skin is drawn right over the knuckles and slowly offer the back of your hand for the ferret to sniff. If it isn't at all used to being handled it will fluff out its tail, arch its back, and spit and chatter. In this case have nothing more to do with it, as ferrets that are allowed to develop to the adult stage without being handled are never satisfactory.

If it does grab at your hand, it should not be able to get a grip on the taut skin, and its teeth will close harmlessly. Had you presented a finger for it to smell, it could have bitten that and hung on like a bulldog. I have been bitten badly twice—once by a wild polecat caught in Radnor Forest—and the only way of making them release their grip is to apply pressure, with finger and thumb of the free hand, just where the base of the tongue meets the throat. This literally chokes them off.

I have dealt at length with vicious ferrets, because every ferret keeper should know what to do if he meets one. The majority of ferrets, however, are delightful and no more dangerous than any other pet with teeth for attack or defence. I would emphasize that they are not treacherous. A tame ferret does not suddenly go berserk, and a vicious ferret makes no secret of its viciousness.

Having presented the back of your hand for the ferret's approval, and found that it is tame, move your hand over its head towards the back until you can pick it up gently by the neck and shoulders. Its front feet should protrude between your first and second fingers, and it will lie contented in your hand. Once you get to know each other you can pick it up whichever way it happens to present and it will enjoy being handled and petted, cuddling down for warmth and comfort.

Housing

Many working ferrets are kept in simply appalling conditions, for there is a popular idea that any dark box is good enough for a ferret. Nothing could be farther from the truth. Ferrets, in good health, are lively and playful. They enjoy quarters as large as you can give them: at one time, I kept mine in an old turf-floored, wire-netting run, ten yards by five yards, which had been used for gamefowl. I buried two courses of bricks round the edge, below the netting, to prevent tunnelling out, and covered the top with one-inch gauge wire netting. I have never had better or fitter ferrets, although they only had a small weather-proof nesting box and were otherwise out in all weathers. They became as lively and agile as wild stoats.

It would obviously be quite uneconomic to provide such spacious quarters in the normal way, and ferrets will do very well in either a properly designed hutch or an open run and sleeping box.

Hutch

The ferret hutch should be a wire netting run about six feet long by eighteen inches wide, covered with strong wire netting half an inch in diameter. It should be raised from the ground on short legs. One end should consist of an entirely weather-proof sleeping box divided into two compartments each nine inches by a foot, with a sloping roof, hinged at the back and covered with roofing felt. The run should have a door for access and cleaning purposes and the bottom should be covered with heavy-gauge, half-inch wire netting. This will let all moisture drip through and save a great deal of cleaning out. Ferrets are particularly clean and leave all their droppings in a corner of the run, usually at the end away from the sleeping box. The netting in this corner corrodes fairly quickly, so that a refinement I always adopt is to nail thin steel bars of about quarter-inch diameter over the last six inches of the run a half inch apart. Most of the droppings fall between the bars, which last for years before they need replacing.

There should be a hole two inches in diameter leading from the base of the sleeping box to the run. If it is not put at the base, young ferrets may have difficulty in getting back to the nest from the run.

Nest Box and Run

Ferrets may be kept very well in a chicken coop covered entirely with half-inch wire netting (including the base), or in a wire netting aviary which is absolutely rat-proof. (What will keep rats out will keep ferrets in, though if it is netting turned up at the base, it must obviously be turned inwards.) Some people have a disused loose-box or pig-sty, either of which is ideal, provided it is rat-proof. Ferrets will climb vertical wire netting like squirrels. But they are unable to scale smooth brick walls or other smooth surfaces, they have little power in their back legs, and cannot jump over a two-foot-six barrier.

If they are kept in an open enclosure, all that is necessary is a warm sleeping box about twelve inches by nine by nine, furnished with soft dry straw. A bag partly filled with straw (enough to keep its mouth open) hung in a dry corner will become a favourite sleeping place: the ferrets will climb in through the open sack mouth. I always provide at least two sleeping sites and, when I notice the ferrets have changed from one to the other I take the hint and put fresh bedding in the one they have vacated.

Feeding

Ferrets are thirsty creatures and need a constant supply of fresh, clean water. They tend to spill water in open dishes, but soon learn to suck from a tube fitted in a rubber bung in an ordinary bottle, which is wired to the outside of the netting so that the bent glass tube protrudes into the run at the right height for the ferret to suck. To teach the ferret to use the bottle, fill it with milk for the first days. The ferret will smell the milk and quickly learn how to use the glass tube.

The old-fashioned diet of bread and milk produces weak

animals, chronically suffering from diarrhoea. One glance will indicate if slops is the staple diet, and, if it is, vast improvement will be noticed if a change is made.

Ferrets are carnivorous animals and raw meat and clean water is what they need most. Mine have any casualty birds, or poultry, rabbits and the raw heads and necks of any fowl we eat in the house. I find that most poulterers are only too pleased to provide fowl heads for the asking, and ferrets will do very well on them as a staple diet. If these are used, however, it is well to ask for heads from boiling fowl and specifically avoid heads from capons. (Cockerels were caponized—or castrated—by surgical means until a few years ago. The modern method is to implant a hormone pill under the skin of the neck, and if the ferrets eat this pill they, too, can become sterile.)

It is quite wrong to imagine that feeding ferrets on flesh will make them savage. Nothing keeps them tame but handling and human companionship. Without that, they may be unreliable whether fed on meat or milk. But, if they do get meat, their natural food, their droppings will be dark and firm, and there will be no complaints about smell.

Breeding

It is a positive necessity for most jill ferrets to breed, and the common belief that they will die if they don't is by no means groundless.

About April, the jill will come into season, a condition which will be at once obvious because the parts will swell to about the size of a thimble. If she is not mated, this swelling may persist for weeks, giving rise to female disorders which are often fatal. She should therefore be put with a hob ferret, who will seize her by the scruff of the neck and drag her, protesting volubly, round and round the pen until she appears exhausted. This cave-man courtship is perfectly normal and need give no cause for alarm; the love life of the whole stoat family is proverbial! Copulation also takes what appears to be an abnormal time (often several hours) and may be repeated at intervals in the next few days.

The jill retains her normal figure for a time before her pregnancy becomes obvious; then the hob must be removed lest he make a meal of the succulent young. The jill will give birth six weeks after she was served, and the kittens will

43

be naked, blind, and about the size of mice. If the jill is particularly tame, she may not object to their being examined or even handled, but it is really safer to wait until the young emerge on their own account.

Young ferrets are very slow to develop, and their eyes will not open properly till they are about five weeks old. During this time the jill will feed them and she should now be given as much fresh milk as she wants to help her own supply. She should also have plenty of fresh meat, some of which she will eat herself and some she will carry into the nest. I have seen young ferrets gnawing away at raw meat like old ones, long before they have ventured from the nest or even opened their eyes.

At four or five weeks, the young will venture into the run and, at first, the old jill will immediately haul them in again by the scruff of their necks. But they will gradually find their way round and should be encouraged to feed themselves on raw meat and milk as soon as possible.

At eight weeks they should be taken from the dam and put in quarters of their own, still feeding on mik and meat. By the time they are fourteen weeks old they should be on the same meat-and-water diet as their parents.

Training
You should start handling the young at four or five weeks, while they are still too small to have the strength to sink their teeth in. If they are fondled and made much of between the ages of five and eight weeks they will never be any trouble again, because they bite only in self-defence or because of pain. On the other hand, it is quite natural for them to bite and attempt to kill whatever furred (or feathered) creatures they meet, so you can keep them to be useful animals as well as pets.

When they are four or five months old they may be taken rabbiting, and this should not be too difficult, as small pockets of rabbits are becoming only too common now the initial waves of myxomatosis are spent. Choose a small bury of rabbits, with no more than six or eight holes, and put a purse net quietly over each. Then put two or three young ferrets at the entrance of a hole and encourage, but do not force, them to wander down into the bury. A good deal of patience may be needed at first, but it will be well worth taking things slowly.

When they get down the hole, Nature will do the rest. They will smell the rabbits and move down to attack. With luck, and if you have been quiet and worked up-wind to the bury, the rabbits will bolt from the danger and into your nets. Kill them at once and, when the ferrets follow them out, let them have a meal of fresh rabbit as their reward. Remember that the young ferrets will be very excited and in the heat of the moment might easily mistake your finger for another rabbit. Treat them as strangers, and proffer the tightly stretched back of your hand as a precaution.

If any of the rabbits do not bolt the ferrets will kill them underground and begin their feast unasked, leaving you to kick your heels and wait. In this case take an old ferret, attach a line to it by fitting a ferret collar round its neck, and put it down the hole by which the youngsters entered. It will join them at their feast and you may dig down to them by following the line, retrieving old and young ferrets and the rabbit as well.

When they are thoroughly used to rabbiting and will come out to be picked up without any trouble, they may be entered to rats. They should be at least six months old, and you will need a dog to catch the rats instead of nets. He must be thoroughly safe with ferrets, of course, as an untrained dog would be as likely to kill a ferret as a rat. If the rat bites the ferret, you must adopt the same precautions as you would for a strange ferret to avoid getting bitten yourself. When you get home, cut the fur close to the rat bite, to prevent it getting into the wound, and dress with a good antiseptic.

After ferrets have been worked for a while, they are as safe to pick up as when you are petting them. They are immensely courageous and, besides tackling rats and stoats, mine have even bolted foxes, if I have accidently put them in a drain which contained a fox instead of the expected rabbit.

Management

Hobs will nearly always fight strange male ferrets in the spring, and sometimes even those they have been brought up with. Apart from this, ferrets are friendly creatures and will live happily in quite large communities. It is always

45

necessary to segregate the hobs after the jills have been mated and it is better to give the jills a house each. This is not so much because they will eat one anothers' litters (though they will occasionally) as because the oldest or strongest kittens will push the weak to the outside and hog all the milk for themselves.

Cleanliness is absolutely essential and so is plenty of fresh water. If they have too much food, however, they will get fat and idle in an astonishingly short time, so always remove the surplus till next day as soon as they have eaten their fill.

Ferrets are quite long lived: I once had a very favourite old jill for eight years, and she bred me over fifty young.

Cavies or Guinea-Pigs

Cavies or guinea-pigs make beautifully tame and gentle pets, ideal as first pets for children, though their pleasant natures endear them to animal lovers of all ages. Indeed, they were kept as pets by the Incas of Peru before any had been brought over to Europe. Now the Incas have died out while their pets have waxed from strength to strength.

The Dutch are said to have brought them to this country about two centuries ago from their colony Guiana, in South America, from which they are supposed to have got their popular name of guinea-pigs. The first part is obvious enough, but they are not in any way like a pig, being cobby little rodents, with large blunt heads.

Their natural habitat was grassy plains, where they grazed, and they are highly gregarious. They are also extremely prolific, presumably because they are somewhat defenceless and need to replace high losses.

Choice

Cavies may be bought from most pet shops, but they are now bred in so many varieties that it is wise to go to a cavy show and see as many as possible in order to decide which type to keep.

Broadly speaking, cavies are divided into various coat colours and textures. There are three main coat textures: the smooth, which is commonest; the Peruvian, which is extraordinarily long; and the Abyssinian, in which the hair

46

curls into circular patterns, like rosettes, all over the body except for a crest of proud hair along the spine.

All three coat varieties may be obtained in a very wide range of colour, either 'self', which the whole animal is one colour, or 'marked', in which case the coat is required to be coloured in some specific pattern.

From the ordinary pet owner's viewpoint, the Peruvian is better left to experts. The hairs of the coat are frequently of excessive length, and the coat entirely obscures the creature's profile. The poor beast is a freak, produced by careful (though I think misguided) selective breeding, and it is very much a specialist's job to keep it in condition. There is nothing more pathetic than a Peruvian cavy with a tangled coat.

The Abyssinian, on the other hand, is something out of the ordinary without being grotesque, and the task of producing an animal with a coat of perfect texture looking as if miniature whirlwinds had caught it may well appeal.

So far as colour goes, there is an extremely wide choice in any of the three coat textures. Whites and chocolates and reds and blacks all have rich, shining coats that give a wonderful impression of luxury; and the patterns that are to be found among the 'marked' varieties range from black-and-white, like a Dutch rabbit, to the Himalayan, which is marked like a Siamese cat.

Housing

Cavies are easy to house. They can be kept indoors in boxes with wire-netting fronts, outside in weather-proof hutches or fold units, or even loose outside, if there is not too much danger from cats, dogs, or foxes. One friend of my childhood, a farmer's son, kept a whole colony of cavies loose near his father's mangel clamp and they were self-supporting source of constant pocket money. Since they were never properly handled, I cannot believe that the purchasers got very good value if they bought them for pets.

Hutches

A hutch three feet six by two feet, two feet high is adequate for a pair of cavies. It should have either one-inch or half-inch wire netting at the front (half-inch keeps mice out) and if it is to be kept outdoors, it should have a felted roof, be built of grooved and tongued boarding, and thoroughly weatherproof. Outside, it should have its back to the prevailing wind, good overhang from the roof, and be so sited as to catch the morning sun but supply shade in the heat of the day, and it should be mounted on short legs to be above any damp.

Indoors, it should be so sited as to get plenty of light and fresh air, and may rest directly on the floor, so that when the owner is present the pets can be given the run of the room.

Whether indoors or out, a box about ten inches square and six high, with an entrance hole, should be supplied for sleeping and breeding. This should be furnished with soft hay and the floor of the hutch proper should have a liberal covering of sawdust or peat, which must be cleaned out and replaced regularly to keep the whole thing sweet and clean.

Fold Units

In decent weather cavies may conveniently be kept in fold units like those for rabbits, with a weather-proof shelter and wire-netting bottom; it is useful to have half the unit covered. The whole unit should be about three feet by four, and can be kept on the lawn and moved over its width every day. The cavies will thoroughly enjoy grazing the green stuff through the wire netting and will contribute towards their keep by manuring the lawn and acting as 'selective weedkillers'. They will concentrate first on the clover and some other broad leafed plants which ought not to be there anyway. They will also act as unpaid lawn mowers, though it must be emphasized that they need other normal food besides grass.

At Large

Several of my friends keep their cavies in the garden, and they are most amusing, running about, with their queer little high-pitched whistling conversation. In every case the garden is relatively free of cats and quite free of foxes, and one is fortunate enough to have a walled garden in which a whole variety of birds and animals spend a very happy life.

Leave a few drainpipes of three-inch diameter about, or some old pieces of cast iron piping about the same size—pieces of flue pipe from greenhouses or any odd bits

3. Peruvian guinea pigs are great fun but are not quite so easy to keep clean and healthy as normal short-coated cavies

Above: 4. Cavies, or guinea pigs do well in hutches, moveable folds on the lawn or even quite free in the garden

Below: 5. All tame gerbils were bred from an original stock of 22 imported into America from Mongolia in 1954! They are easy to feed, house and to breed

that happen to be around. The cavies will play in and out of these pipes (which can be covered with soil and quite unobstrusive, provided their ends are open). Then, when danger threatens, there will be a mad scurry and in an instant every animal will be safely hidden.

Cavies at large need more than just pipes for shelter. They need a conventional hutch, with more secure, covered sleeping boxes than would normally be provided. They should be confined to this hutch for a week or so to become thoroughly used to it. Then it should be surrounded by a ring of temporary wire netting kept in place with stakes, and the door, which should be on ground level, held about three inches ajar by a wire hook obtainable from the iron-monger's. This is to allow cavies to run 'home' where it is impossible for a cat to follow them.

When the cavies run in and out of their hutch freely—and they should be fed there and shut there for the night—the wire-netting ring fences should be removed to allow them to have the freedom of the garden. They should not be fed in the morning for a while, but given a really adequate meal at night when they are shut up, to encourage them to re-gard the hutch as home. Then they will run freely in the garden and be shut up safely at night, when they should be handled and petted to keep them tame.

Wherever they are kept it must be rat-proof, at least at night, for a hungry rat will slaughter young cavies, and sometimes surprisingly big ones too.

Their hutch should be near the edge of the lawn and unless their numbers are allowed to increase excessively the amount they eat in the garden will not inconvenience any but exceptionally keen gardeners.

Food
Few pets are easier to feed than cavies because they will eat almost any cereal and almost any vegetable.

They need plenty of green food—the 'rabbit meat' that can be collected for nothing from the hedges. It can include clover and dandelion, groundsel, chickweed, vetch, seeding grass, etc., though cavies that are folded or at large will find a high proportion of their green fodder for themselves. They like plenty of roots, including mangolds, swedes, carrots, parsnips, also sugar beet tops, and garden plants like cabbage and lettuce.

Cavies are not as bad at gnawing their quarters as hamsters, for example, but they are rodents, and it is necessary for them to keep their teeth in trim. So they should always have a piece of sweet wood like apple, hazel, or willow to gnaw. This should be about an inch in diameter and six inches long.

The animals love bread, biscuits, apples, grain (including pigeon peas), cow-cake, almost any household vegetables or fruits, and sweet hay in winter fed in racks. They should have water available—though they sometimes get enough moisture from their food—and milk when they are suckling young.

The whole secret is to give variety so that the animals are able to pick and choose. Indeed, almost any animal that thrives on a number of different foods will do best when allowed to fill the need of the moment.

Hay and green fodder is best given in racks from which the cavies can pluck enough to browse without fouling the rest. Dry food is best offered in troughs, which can be scoured daily so that fouling will be kept to a minimum. Fresh green-stuff that can be grazed is best of all.

Breeding

Male cavies are called boars and females sows, from the common name guinea-pigs. The name is the only resemblance between the two species.

Two boars will sometimes fight so groups of one boar and four or five sows should be kept together unless there is plenty of room and cover. If there is ample room they are usually friendly enough to be kept in colonies to breed without fear of either the sows or the boars harming each other's young. It is commonsense, however, to provide plenty of nest boxes, so that any animals that crave solitude for themselves or their young can move to other quarters.

The adults do not always mate very readily, especially in cold weather. When they do, gestation is about nine weeks. Since they are reticent lovers, it is usually impossible to predict the exact period of pregnancy. The sow is so obviously in young at an early stage that it is easy to believe that she has been pregnant longer than she really has. She is also rather fragile at this time and should not be handled more than necessary, and then, even more gently than usual.

The young are born with their eyes open and their fur complete. They can run within an hour or so, and are enchanting but fragile creatures as infants. It is best not to handle them too much until they are sturdy. They will suckle their dams for a fortnight or so but begin to nibble and browse their parents' food almost from birth. Litters are usually small, two to four, and the female will often mate again almost as soon as her litter is born. The young, therefore, have to be self-supporting by the time they are about a month old in order to let their mother's milk dry off in preparation for the next lactation.

Hamsters

It seems very strange that one of the most commercially popular pets was virtually unknown in this country just before the last war except in scientific circles.

The first golden hamsters were found in Syria by some Jewish scientists on an expedition in the spring of 1930, and they took a nursing female and her litter back with them to Jerusalem. The hamsters proved very amenable to captivity and their descendants were exported for scientific work in other countries, a couple of pairs arriving in England the following year. The London Zoo obtained some and allowed the public to buy their surplus, from which most pet hamsters are descended. Since then, keeping hamsters has developed to the stage where a large number of clubs and societies have been formed, arranging shows and exhibitions and lectures.

Hamsters are bred in a variety of colours, though the true 'golden' hamster, a descendant of the 1930 Syrian specimen, is by far my favourite. It is smaller than the dowdy European hamster, which would become a plague if any breeding stock got free in this country. The golden hamster is comparatively safe, because it cannot stand the rigours of our climate except in warm captivity. At the same time, it is very prolific, and has given evidence of an ability to throw 'sports' or specimens that are non-typical as far as colour is concerned. These freaks or sports have quickly fixed the new characteristic of strange colour or coat so that their descendants will produce replicas consistently in a few generations. This is how the albinos, creams, piebalds, and others that appear at shows originated.

My opinion is that if it is possible to throw sports of this nature and fix the aberration, sooner or later a variety may appear that is as hardy in our climate as its European cousin would be. Hamsters are one of the varieties of pet that escape most frequently, because of their prowess at gnawing. If they could survive our climate in winter they might soon rival the grey squirrel as a pest.

Choice

Except for a number of colour varieties and a few coat mutations, there is not a very wide choice. Hamsters that are to be kept as pets can be any attractive colour, and should be healthy and lively, bold and friendly. They have been domesticated for relatively few generations and are still wild at heart. If it was not for their innate curiosity, most people would have little attraction for them.

Like ferrets, nervous hamsters will bite, not because they are aggressive so much as in defence. A tame hamster is curious, friendly, and affectionate. It is essential to purchase either an adult that is thoroughly tame or a youngster ready to be tamed. An adult of uncertain temper is very difficult to cure.

The best age to buy a youngster is about eight weeks, when it is just grown-up enough to have lost its baby shyness. Chivvying a nervous hamster round to pick it up is a sure way to frighten it into a permanently defensive frame of mind.

Handling

An inquiring finger poked into the nest of a sleeping youngster is most likely to receive a sharp nip. Try attracting one to the front of the run with a titbit: something small which the pet will relish and soon look for more. Few hamsters can resist whole maize, given a grain at a time, or sultanas, pigeon peas, or meal-worms. Rattle a tin, run your finger up the netting, or make any sound the animal will come to associate with food. The great thing is always to make the same sound before offering food, whether your pet is out of sight, asleep, or already waiting impatiently. As soon as it comes to your call, and is used to receiving some favourite morsel as reward, training can begin.

Hamsters do not sit and eat as much food as they want, they 'pouch' it. Their cheeks are extensible and, when they come across a supply of food, they stuff as much as they can into their pouches, go home, and store it to be eaten at leisure. So, in addition to the titbit, supply a quantity of food in a state that cannot be pouched too rapidly. Groats are very good and the hamster will like them.

While he is busy pouching his groats, run a finger gently down his back and increase the caresses until he will allow you to pick him up. This is the time to give him another meal-worm or raisin. He will quickly associate a titbit with your initial tattoo on his cage front and another with being picked up and fondled. Put out the stretched back of the hand for inspection, as you would to a ferret, and the chances of a shrewd nip are much diminished. Gradually your hamster will gain confidence in you, until you can pick it up, and fondle it, not only as you like, but as the hamster likes too. When you have reached this stage, you will really enjoy your pet. Like most worthwhile folk, his confidence takes a bit of gaining. But he is a pet with real character when you succeed.

Housing

I have referred to your hamster in the singular deliberately. Hamsters are a little aggressive with humans until they get to know them. They are always aggressive with their own kind, and they should be housed separately, even if of opposite sexes, to avoid fighting, though they obviously have to be brought together at mating time.

Not only are hamsters aggressive with each other, but they are also prodigious gnawers of wood. They will be out of a wooden cage quicker than any other pet I know. All the same, wooden boxes make wonderfully warm and cosy homes and they may be lined with heavy gauge quarter-inch wire netting, so that the box has the dual advantages of warmth and safety.

The cage for a hamster should be at least two feet by one foot by one foot; although they are often not particularly lively in the day, they may be very energetic in the hours of darkness, for they are, by nature, nocturnal. Many pet shops sell metal hamster cages, and these are rather liable to sweat from condensation. Several thicknesses of newspaper on the floor will help avoid this, besides providing your pet with an occupation—shredding it up. Newspaper is also useful because it is absorbent, and may be used with advantage as flooring for the cages of many other pets. A thick layer of sawdust may also be used.

Hamsters are naturally clean and, if a 1 lb jam jar is put on its side in the cage, many hamsters will use it as a latrine. If they take to it naturally, all that is necessary is to empty it each morning and wash it under the tap before replacing it. If they do not take to it naturally, they can sometimes, but not always, be persuaded to do so. Put a little soiled sawdust in it from the cage floor and then cover the rest of the newly cleaned cage with sawdust mixed with a little disinfectant to disguise all smell of hamster except in the jar.

The chances are that the hamsters will go into the jar when they want to empty themselves, after which they will do so regularly. It is a great advantage if you can persuade them to do this because the cage floor will keep so much drier and sweeter.

It is essential to empty the jar *every* morning because they will naturally refuse to use it if it is allowed to become unpleasant and your trouble will have been wasted.

It is especially important to provide hamsters with a piece of sweet wood—nut, apple, willow, or some other English tree—for them to gnaw on and use to amuse themselves. This will keep their teeth in condition and leave them less time to get up to mischief with the main structure of their house. A good way of supplying this sweet wood is to make 'perches' as you would for a bird cage, but fitted diagonally instead of horizontally so that your pet may amuse himself clambering as well as chewing it up.

If you supply a separate nesting compartment as you would for a ferret, you may see little or nothing of your pet, which will be on view mainly in the hours of darkness. Therefore, rather supply a shallow, open-topped box—a wooden cigar box will be good while it lasts—and he will make his nest inside this. Paper, hay, or soft oat straw that has been combined and not threshed is best for nesting. On no account give wool or any substance which is likely to be swallowed and may be very difficult to digest.

It will be remembered that the reason golden hamsters are not dangerous as pests, if they escape, is that they cannot tolerate the rigours of our climate. By the same token, they cannot tolerate extremes of cold and warmth indoors, which makes it important to keep the cage in a room of the house where there are no violent changes of temperature. A living-room which is warm by day and cold just when the hamster wants to wake up at night will be no good. If the cage is well ventilated it may be a good idea to have glass in the front rather than wire netting. The wire netting can form a panel in the back, made by removing a piece of the cage so as to expose the wire-netting cage lining.

Food

Hamsters are practically omnivorous. They will 'eat' almost everything, but it will only be pouched and then stored till wanted. It is therefore important to offer nothing that is perishable and would smell or go sour if stored. Bulk, in the form of maize, wheat, barley, oats, toast crust, or dog biscuit, will be greatly appreciated, give plenty of exercise in being gnawed, and come to no harm if stored for some time. Green food is essential and may be lettuce, cabbage, kale, or watercress; also important are roots, such as carrot, turnip, swede, plus apples, raisins, and any vegetation that would be given to rabbits or cavies.

In addition to this, hamsters are partly carnivorous. They will enjoy meal-worms and moist mash containing household scraps, such as cheese, lean chopped meat, or hard-boiled egg. But this should be supplied only in small quantities which will be eaten right away and not pouched and stored to go sour or bad. As a double check against rotting food, it is vital to keep the pen scrupulously clean.

Breeding

Hamsters are best kept alone, because, of all pets, they are surely the most prolific. They can breed at five or six weeks old, the gestation period is sixteen days, and the litter may well be eight. The female will mate again a month later! Astronomical possibilities may be visualized. Furthermore, the life of a breeding hamster is likely to be about two years, while, kept singly as a pet, it may live healthily for three. If, despite this, you wish to go in for breeding deliberately, a cage will still be needed for each hamster except for the very moment of mating.

The female comes on heat every four days and is likely to be extremely vicious with the male if she is not completely ready. She is more likely to be receptive at night than by day. Put her in the male's cage and he in hers, so that they can become acquainted at long range and accustomed to each other's scent. Then let them sniff each other through the netting of a cage, the female inside and the male outside.

If the female is receptive, she will probably go rigid, tail up, head held low. If she does, it is safe to put the male in with her. They will mate several times in quick succession, probably over a period of about a quarter of an hour. When the male begins to lose interest, they must be separated when coitus is complete. Should the female not be ready for mating, a fight is likely to develop which may go to the death if not stopped at once. This can be done either by handling both contestants with gloved hands, or by covering them with sawdust or soapy water to discourage them from biting. On no account use the naked hand, because fighting hamsters will bite hard on anything in sight.

Four days later, put the male outside the female's pen. If she is aggressive, she has almost certainly become pregnant; if she shows any affection she needs mating again.

When the female produces her litter, sixteen days after mating, she will become nervous and must not be frightened or she may well eat her young. She will make a wonderfully soft nest, which must not be disturbed until the litter leave it on their own, which will be when they are about a fortnight old.

In addition to normal food, the female must have fresh milk during the time she is in kindle with young. When the young emerge their growth rate is commensurate with the general reproductivity of their kind and they will consume an immense amount of food for their size. At four weeks old the males and females must be separated lest they breed amongst themselves, and shortly afterwards they must be put in separate pens to avoid fighting when they become adult.

Characteristic Habit
On each flank hamsters have a spot which is thought to be a

gland secreting minute quantities of fluid that has significance for recognition—as a badger uses its musk gland to place a possession mark on objects—or that is emitted as part of the sex cycle. Hamsters spend much of their idle time preening the fur round these glands, as a duck uses its oil-gland for preening the rest of its feathers. Grooming of this sort must be expected and is not a symptom that something has gone awry.

Hibernation

In their native country, hamsters hibernate. This occasionally happens to pet hamsters in autumn, the symptoms being extreme torpidity, their body temperature dropping almost to atmospheric temperature, and slowing of respiration to the point where it is easy to imagine the animal dead.

It is extremely dangerous to try to wake your pet, as death is most likely if you do. It should be kept cool, but well above freezing point, the chief thing to avoid being sudden changes of temperature. In autumn it is always advisable to be especially generous with bedding material so that a really adequate nest can be made. Then, if you happen to have a specimen that does enter partial hibernation, no great harm will be done.

Gerbils

Gerbils have only been commonly kept as pet in the last few years although they have many advantages.

Wild gerbils came from Mongolia and they are really animals of the desert, part way between a rat and a mouse in size. They have very large eyes and ears, not unlike our wild wood mice. Their tails are long and furry, more like dormice than wood mice, but their hind legs are longer in proportion than either so that they can leap almost like miniature kangaroos.

A major advantage as pets is that they are very fearless so that they do not bite from fear, as some creatures do, and can be handled with far more confidence than a strange hamster, for example.

Because of their desert origins, they can subsist for a long time without water and get most of the moisture they need from the green food they eat. A fringe benefit of this is that they pass very little moisture so that their cages remain odourless and free from urine. It is always wise to give creatures the opportunity of drinking, even when they are known to *need* little water, but a small container or a gravity feed bottle as sold for mice and hamsters in pet shops is all that they will need.

Because gerbils are desert-living animals, they are great tunnellers. They not only make tunnels to escape from their enemies but also as refuges from excessive heat and to avoid losing body moisture by evaporation.

So they can either be kept in cages, as rats or mice, but also in aquariums filled three quarters full of loamy soil instead of water. They will dig and tunnel in this and some of the tunnels will be along the edge of the glass so that is possible to watch what they are doing underground as well as on the surface.

They are diurnal, and active by day more than by night, so that it is possible to enjoy more of their activity in our waking hours than with many other species. It is amusing to put stones and small boughs on the surface of their sand so that it looks like a natural desert more than a cage and they can be allowed out when you are watching them because they are intensely curious and will enjoy exploring the room—but still return to their own cage which they will regard as 'their' territory.

The food they require is simple, and similar to rats or hamsters. They like grain and grass, fruit and seeds and hay. Wheat, sunflower seed, green vegetables will all suit them well and it is always interesting to offer a wide choice of different foods and then watch carefully to see the order in which they select it so that you can establish their list of priorities for yourself.

Gerbils pair and stay faithful to one mate far more than most other small animals. They will sometimes fight when first introduced so that it is best to put them in a cage divided by wire netting for a while so that they can get used to the smell of each other.

They should then be allowed to get together under strict supervision when they appear to *want* to get to know each other better, but they should not be left together until you are confident that they have accepted each other.

Once they have paired, they can be left together because the male will not eat his family as rats or mice might. Indeed, it is sometimes difficult to get a gerbil to accept another mate when once it has been paired successfully.

The gestation period is about 25 days and the litter may be anything up to a dozen young which do not open their eyes for 25 days. They are born naked as well as blind and mature at about 10 or 12 weeks.

When the young show signs of pairing off, they should be put into a cage for each pair where they can remain for life.

4 Cages and Aviaries

Wire Cages

The commonest type of cage sold for pet birds is also the least satisfactory. In every pet shop there is an array of ornamental cages with bars all round, to which are fitted perches, utensils for food and drink, a door (also of wire bars) for introducing and extracting the inmate, and a detachable tray to facilitate cleaning out the droppings and stale food. These cages are often brightly polished or coloured and may be designed to fit in with the decor of a living-room of contemporary style. From the pet bird's point of view, they are dwellings of the least desirable kind.

All birds like some choice of light and shade, of cover or exposure, of heat or cool. And all birds hate draught. In a cage where they are surrounded by wire bars, they have to put up with whatever conditions the position of the cage imposes. If it is in the sun, they can get no shade; if there is any draught they can get no shelter; and there is no protecting corner to give them security if something alarms them.

It is important to bear these limitations in mind if conditions in the house impose the necessity of having a cage of this type to harmonize with the rest of the furniture. If this is the case, be very careful how you site the cage in the room. If possible put it in a corner where there is no draught, and which is near enough to an eastern window to catch the morning sun before it gets too hot. Most birds love sunlight but skulk in the shade at midday. It is also just as important to shield your pet from direct firelight as from any other extreme condition.

Box Cages

If you are lucky enough to be able to decide on the type of cage which is most comfortable for the bird, instead of the prettiest type, you will probably choose a box cage, unless you want to keep one of the parrot-like birds. This family will chew wood and reduce any but all-metal cages to splinters; they are dealt with under the section Cages for Parrot-like Birds.

From the pet bird's point of view, a box cage has immense advantages over more elaborate and decorative all-wire cages. Most important of all are freedom from draught and certainty of shade even in direct sunlight. In a dark and dingy room it will therefore be necessary to go to as great lengths to pick a light spot as it is to pick a sheltered place for an all-wire cage.

One of the major functions of birds' wings is to enable them to escape from their enemies. At the first real sign of danger, a wild bird will either fly right away or into the nearest tree, bush, or other cover which will protect it. Therefore, one of the cruellest things that can happen to a caged bird is for it to be thoroughly frightened and yet unable to escape from the source of its terror. It is like being chased by a bull in a nightmare, when one's legs refuse to function. The danger of this sort of panic is obviously far greater in an all-wire cage than in a box cage where it is at least possible for the bird to cower in a corner.

Ready-made box cages can be purchased from all good pet shops, and the largest one which will fit comfortably into the room where the bird is to be kept should be chosen. If it is at all possible, a room should be selected where extreme variation between heat and cold can be avoided. Obviously, most people will want to keep their pet birds in the living-room where they can see and hear them, and, in this case, it is important not to put the cage too near the fire, so that the contrast at night, when the fire is out, will be reduced.

Construction of Box Cages
Box cages are perfectly simple for anyone who is reasonably handy at simple carpentry to make for himself.

Cage fronts may be purchased ready-made, complete with doors which slide up vertically, or are hinged. Some fronts have circular holes, so that feeding and drinking pots may be put on the outside of the cage and the bird may feed and drink by putting its head through the hole. The advantage of this is that it is not possible for the bird to foul the food and water with droppings.

61

Canaries and any of the British seed-eaters will usually feed and drink quite well by putting heads through a round hole in a cage front. But plenty of foreign birds are tiny enough to escape if the feed hole is left uncovered by its pot for a moment. Another major disadvantage of cage fronts with holes for feeding pots is that these covered pots hold quite a lot of grain, which is automatically taken from the top layers as the bird puts its head through the opening in the cage front to peck. Because the pot is covered, the bird cannot flick the husks away, and the top layer soon becomes a bed of husk, which buries the seed so effectively that the bird is unable to sort his grain from chaff. From outside, however, the seed pot looks full and it is fatally easy to think there is plenty of food when in fact the bird is extremely hungry.

The minimum size cage for pet birds is about twelve inches by ten, with a depth of seven inches from back to front. Standard cage fronts may be brought up to about forty by twenty inches or larger. Wires can be bought in straight lengths, with a perforated spacing bar to put them through, and this is a particularly convenient way of buying them, especially if you are going to make a suite of cages or want an odd-sized or shaped cage to to fit a specific space in your room. A cage front can be built in a matter of minutes to fit whatever size of box cage has been bought or made by simply cutting the spacer bar to length and threading the straight wires through.

It is always necessary to leave a gap between the cage bottom and the bottom of the bars deep enough to take the front of a detachable tray which should be an exact fit for the floor of the cage. This tray should be removed daily for cleaning and it should be covered with loose dry sand, which quickly sticks to the droppings, coating them and preventing them from contaminating the food. A modern alternative, which avoids the necessity of scrubbing and scraping sanded cage floors is a piece of paper, to which a permanent coating of sand adheres. Droppings stick to this rough sandpaper, which covers the floor of the cage as snugly as a fitted carpet. When these sheets of sandpaper are fouled they can be thrown away.

Some people use loose welded mesh bottoms so that the birds can walk on the dry and any excrement will fall straight through. This may be a fairly satisfactory solution for some of the fruit-eaters, which tend to be loose and sloppy in their motions, but for small seed-eaters the risk of injury through getting a foot stuck and panicking may well outweigh any advantage.

Making the wooden box, to which the front and perches are fitted, is neither more nor less difficult than making any wooden box.

It is obviously vital that all boards should be cut meticulously square. Before the top, bottom, and two ends are nailed or screwed together, they should be coated, on their ends, with one of the very powerful new adhesives. Before this has had time to set, the edges, which will mate with the back, should be coated and the back should be fitted and the whole cage checked for squareness.

The purpose of coating all mating edges with adhesive is so that when the box is finally assembled, all cracks where boards join shall be effectively sealed against entry by even the minutest form of parasite. Even under conditions of almost clinical cleanliness, cage birds will occasionally become infested by parasites. Most birds, given the opportunity, will either dust bathe or bathe in water, so the hosts themselves do not provide safe lodging in the day-time. Parasites, therefore, and red mite in particular, like to find a convenient crevice in which to lie up during the day-time, before sallying forth to clamber on to their host at nightfall, when he can do nothing to dislodge them but shuffle and scratch. At day break they migrate once more to the safety of their crevices, where they also hatch their young.

One further tip that an old fancier gave me as a lad, was to use hollow perches. He used to cut elderberry twigs of the right diameter to the correct length. He then hollowed them by burning out the pith with a red hot skewer. This hollow formed the perfect hiding place for red mite, or rather a trap. The perches would be burned every week or so and replaced by fresh ones. Nowadays, red mite are not the potential danger they were, because it is possible to deal with them effectively by coating the cages with modern insecticides. But take great care that the preparation you use is harmless to birds.

Painting

It is usual to paint box cages that are used as suites of breeding cages black on the outside and white in the inside. In bird-rooms or for collections of birds this looks neat, ensures light cages, and shows most coloured birds off very well. For a pet bird, likely to be kept in the living-room, it is practicable to paint the cage to harmonize with the surroundings. In general, it is well for the comfort of the bird to have the inside as light a shade as possible.

Sooner or later, most paints flake and begin to disintegrate, so that there is danger of the birds pecking at the particles and eating them. Indeed, some birds have strong enough bills to peck through sound paint when they are a little bored. It is therefore particularly important always to use non-poisonous paint. There is now a good variety on the market prepared specifically for aviaries and cages, and it is always safer to use this special paint. Always dilute it as thin as possible with thinners and apply several very thin coats, waiting for the last to be thoroughly dry and hard before applying the next. It is thus possible to get an extremely good finish, hard and bright, instead of a thick coat which never really hardens underneath and is a constant temptation to peck.

Perches

Perches may be round or rectangular, with bevelled corners; they may literally be tree branches of a diameter suitable to the span of the bird's foot and of overall size to suit the cage; they may be widely spaced or ranged at frequent intervals, depending entirely upon the species of bird to be kept.

The mechanism of a bird's leg is such that when it squats, as it does when it needs rest or sleep, its own weight pulls and tends to 'bunch' its toes, which close automatically to grasp the perch, and are held grasping it firmly even in sleep. If the diameter of the perch is too small, the toes will have to bunch so much to grasp it, that cramp will be induced. If the perch is too large in diameter the bird will be able to stand on it, but may well fall off in deep sleep simply because its span is not large enough to get a grip. It is necessary, therefore, to select the diameter of perch so that it is just a comfortable size for the bird to grasp.

Most birds will spend a great deal of their time on the highest perch. If two perches of different shape or diameter are placed symmetrically at the same height in the cage, it will soon become obvious by simple observation which an individual bird prefers.

Spacing of Perches

This also depends entirely upon the species to be kept. Canaries, finches, thrushes, and blackbirds will get a lot of exercise from two parallel perches, so spaced that they can just jump from one to another. It will be noticed that many birds adopt a rhythmic pattern of jumping from perch to perch and back for long periods without ceasing. It could easily be imagined that this 'dance' was a perpetual search for a large enough gap in the bars by which to escape. It is, in fact, a rhythmic reflex exercise pattern which many healthy birds adopt, probably almost unconsciously, as a means of working off energy and keeping fit.

Birds of the parrot family do not hop from perch to perch but more often fly or climb, and will spend hours climbing about rectangular section netting using both beak and claws. Many ground-loving birds, like Chinese painted quail, do not need perches. Tree-creepers like cloth or cork bark to clamber on, although they will use perches too.

It is impossible to generalize about size and spacing of perches, but it is vital to the birds' comfort to get them right. A knowledge of natural history is a good guide; it is often possible to get some help from whoever supplied the bird; trial and error and observation will usually provide the answers in any case, often more satisfactorily than slavishly following traditions that may be outdated.

Baths

Most cage birds love baths but will splash water about the room unless a bath with a plastic surround is used. This can be fitted in place of the normal cage door.

Allow birds to bathe in the morning, except in exceptionally cold weather, and then remove the bath and close the cage door. It is essential that the birds should have ample time to dry before settling down to roost for the night.

Cages

Show Cages

If you want to take up exhibiting, it will be desirable to join a cage-bird society. Many societies cater specially for the needs of one breed, and most breed societies have very strict specifications for cages used to exhibit birds competitively. It is only sensible that they should, as there can be less grounds for questioning the judge's impartiality if he has no means of knowing the owner of any particular bird.

Show cages vary a lot from breed to breed, and the specifications are subject to alteration, so before entering for a show it is wise to get relevant particulars from the show secretary.

Hospital Cages

Cage birds are difficult for amateurs to treat when seriously ill but the first necessity is to isolate the suspect, in order to avoid spreading unnecessary infection.

Generally speaking, the safest thing to do is to consult a veterinary surgeon with a small-animal practice. I have found ''oss and cow men' worse than useless for cage birds and most other pets.

The hospital cage should be a box cage of unpainted wood with a glass front and false bottom. It should be as small as possible consistent with the size of bird to use it. It should be unpainted so that it can be thoroughly scrubbed with disinfectant each time it is used and, if some particularly infectious 'patient' has been in residence, it is wise to sterilize the cage with a painter's blow lamp.

The purpose of the false floor is to allow a heating element to be put under the floor. A sixty-watt electric bulb is satisfactory, provided every precaution is taken against risk of fire. Instead of the usual wire, the front should be of glass, to keep the heat in and the cage warm when the heater is switched on below the floor. Ventilation holes covered by adjustable shutters should be provided in the back of the box to give some control of temperature.

To make a more elaborate heating apparatus, a jar of water may be put under the false bottom containing a one hundred-watt aquarium heater and thermostat. This can be set to maintain whatever steady temperature is required.

66

Most birds benefit enormously from heat when they are ill and a spell of twenty-four or forty-eight hours in a hospital cage at 90°F. or so will often work cures of apparently quite serious trouble. The heat must be constant, and it is amazing how often birds will come back on to their food when before being put in a hospital cage they seemed at death's door.

The one ailment that is common to most cage birds is coccidiosis. It is a dreadfully infectious complaint and a real killer, though young birds are more susceptible than old. It is usually contracted by taking water or food fouled by coccidiosis-infected droppings.

Look out for these watery droppings containing blood. Eyes will become dull accompanied by a rapid loss of weight. Of recent years a powerful drug has been evolved to put into the drinking water, usually for five consecutive days. It was developed for chickens, but is extremely effective with other birds and has saved thousands that would otherwise have been doomed. It should only be used on a Vet's advice.

Spare Cages

As time goes on, most birds fanciers accumulate a collection of assorted cages, ranging from boxes fronted by wire netting, to elaborate, highly decorative—but often useless—affairs which arrive as Christmas presents from well-meaning relatives. Keep them scoured and clean, out of the way, and it is surprising how often they will come in useful for a bird that is unwell or to separate a pair until the breeding season or confine an aggressive male to barracks. Like vases in the cupboard, they should never be discarded.

Cages for Parrot-like Birds

Parrots, macaws, and similar birds with immensely powerful beaks cannot be confined for long in cages containing much wood. They simply chew their way out.

Old-fashioned parrot cages were made entirely of metal and the only wooden furnishings were the perches. For parrots kept as pets in the house there is still nothing better than these, although the same precautions should be taken to avoid draught as with any other bird confined to an all-wire cage.

But these birds do love exercising their wonderful beaks and it is a pleasure and education to watch them. So give them some wood to 'work' on. Fresh fruit-tree branches about an inch in diameter are often available at pruning time, but the branch of any non-poisonous tree will be appreciated as a perch. As a demonstration of gratitude it will soon be shredded to pulp.

Some people keep these birds on a T-shaped perch on a stand. The bird is attached to the upright support by a chain to its leg, to which a ring is fixed which will slide up and down the upright. The upright must be so constructed that the bird can climb up or down by gripping its rough surface.

Should the bird get a sudden fright it may attempt to fly off but will be brought up short by the chain on its leg. The ring will slide down the upright and allow the captive to flutter to the ground from where it can climb back to the perch when it regains its composure. It will be an undignified performance—and therefore greatly to be deplored—but not actually dangerous.

No animal or bird likes to look stupid or be laughed at. (Some pets seem to have a sense of humour and enjoy people laughing with them though.) For this reason it is a bad thing to chain parrot-like birds to T-perches in any position where they are likely to panic or be frightened. But as an adjunct to a cage, a T-perch is often useful. In good weather, the parrot may be put out in the garden, under supervision, to avoid intrusion from cats or dogs. 'Good weather' need not be sunshine by any means. It will often be found that these birds love warm summer rain and will stand there, wings outstretched, revelling in every drop. When they have had enough, they can be returned to their cages and, if done with care, the very handling necessary to do this will make them tamer and tamer.

Because of their immensely powerful beaks, it is obvious that a bite from one of the larger parrot-like birds can be extremely dangerous. Until mutual confidence is established, always move them by putting a rod, about eighteen inches long and three-quarters of an inch in diameter into the cage and gently stroking the bird under the belly in front of its legs. If it is tame it will at once step on to this new perch which you hold for it. Carry it on this and, if it sidles towards the end you are holding you can change hands and hold the perch by the other end.

Before doing this, it is necessary to get on really friendly terms with the bird, which is usually easy, by stroking the back of his head, first with a pencil and eventually with fingertips. Only when it is tame enough to allow you to attach the chain to its leg is it wise to think about routine moves to the T-perch. But however tame it gets always move it on the wooden rod, because if it becomes scared for any reason at all it is liable to bite.

Some parrots and macaws become so tame and so fond of a T-perch that they are quite content not to stray if left with no chain attached to their legs. Personally, I hate the idea of chaining or caging any bird that it is possible to have free, and I think, where the risk of escape is relatively slight, it is well worth taking. Certainly a free bird in a conservatory or room is delightful. Outside, on a windless day, a tame bird will usually only fly to the nearest tree if frightened. But a stiff breeze geeting under it as it takes off can well carry it clean out of sight, and the new-found joy of flight may prove so intoxicating that it will escape permanently or, if it has been confined for a long time, the unaccustomed exertion may very easily bring on a heart attack.

Bird Rooms

Location

It often happens that the pleasure of keeping a pet bird provokes a longing for more. Soon, the collection becomes too large for the living-room and a decision has to be reached on where to house the expanding family.

In old houses it is sometimes possible to use a spare room, but with smaller modern houses it is usually necessary to build a room or shed in the garden.

In either case the principles to be adopted are the same.

Vermin

However carefully managed, birds scatter a certain amount of uneaten seed which will inevitably attract mice if they can gain entry. It is therefore most important, especially if the bird room is in the house, to take the most stringent precautions. Nail bevelled wood beading, three-quarters of an inch or one inch in width, right round the skirting where it joins the floor. This eliminates the sharp corners, facilitating sweeping-up operations, and making it more difficult for mice to enter. Check that the door fits tightly at the bottom, adding a draught excluder if it does not, and make good any other crevices in the room where mice could possibly enter. One place that is frequently overlooked is the back of the grate.

Security
If it is possible to do it without making the house unsightly from the outside, fit a wire-netting frame to the window so that it may be opened at will without any risk of a bird getting out of its cage and escaping. Safety doors are dealt with in the section on Entrance to Aviary and Flight later in this chapter.

Light
See that there is adequate light, both natural and artificial, and, if the business is to be taken seriously, have one of the modern 'dimmer' devices wired into part of the circuit. These devices, activated by a time-switch, cut off the light progressively, so that there is never full illumination one instant and utter darkness the nest. The lights gradually become dimmer simulating the approach of dusk, so that the birds have plenty of time to realize that the day is ending and go to roost before complete darkness falls.

Layout
Although the design of the bird room will be dictated by special needs and tastes, it is usual to have part divided into cages and part set aside for roomier flights.

The cages are most conveniently arranged in the form of shelves so constructed that divisions can be fitted at intervals of about eighteen inches. Thus, by keeping a number of sliding partitions, it is possible to use the space between two shelves, running the whole length of the room, as one long 'flight' cage, or a number of smaller cages of an intermediate size that is a multiple of eighteen. The sliding partitions may be solid or wire. When it is necessary to separate cocks from hens or two aggressive males, a solid partition produces the same effect as if they were yards apart, although only the thickness of the partition divides them.

When you want to introduce a new bird, or to 'pair' two up, a wire partition may be used, then slid out of the way—doubling the size of their cages—when the time is ripe for them to meet.

Building adjustable cages, in tiers of shelves, sometimes enables the existing wall of the room to be used as the back of the cages. Where this is possible, it is a great advantage, because the space between the back of a solid cage and the wall is just one more possible refuge for vermin.

The cheapest, and in many ways the most satisfactory, fronts, can be covered with wire netting instead of bars. A wooden frame should be made to clip between the shelves and be held in position by bolts or wing nuts. The design should be the same as for a box cage, with a sliding tray at the bottom to facilitate cleaning out. The bolts that hold the front in position should also secure the sliding partition, or a dummy piece of wood the same width, to maintain a complete cage front with no gaps when the partitions are removed.

If the wire netting is three-eighths of an inch mesh and the rest of the cages fit snugly to the wall, the whole unit will be mouse-proof. Immature mice can quite easily get through half-inch mesh, though this will just exclude adults. The fronts will have doors for servicing but, when the cage is empty, the whole front is detachable for thorough cleaning.

One side of the bird room, preferably the best lighted side, opposite the window, is now equipped with a suite of cages which are convenient to service and clean and can readily be converted to roomy flight cages.

It is difficult to emphasize sufficiently the importance of both flexibility and ease of cleaning.

Flight

The opposite side of the bird room may well be converted to a wire-netting aviary flight on the same principles.

Make a wire-netting front with three-eighths-of-an-inch mesh netting, the length of the room and about eight feet high. In exceptional cases it may be desirable to make the flight the full height of the room, but remember that when you want to catch a bird about eight feet is the maximum height you can reach without using a net. It is a bad thing to use a net except when absolutely necessary, as it terrifies the other inmates of the aviary. I prefer, whenever possible, to wait until it is dark and pick whichever birds I want from perches with the aid of an electric torch. If the room is higher than is convenient for the aviary flight, this will of course need to be roofed with wire netting.

The entrance door should either be so low that it is necessary to stoop to enter, which will deter birds trying to dodge past while the door is open, or a double door entrance should be made similar to the one described in the section on aviaries.

Movable partitions can be made a precise fit to divide the large flight into smaller ones, exactly as the partitions divided the shelves opposite into a suite of cages. Doors will have to be fitted to the front at intervals to suit the divisions that are made.

Sand is the best floor-covering for general use, as it is not only easy to clean up, but quickly coats the droppings so that they do not so readily contaminate food that falls to the ground.

Furnishing the Flight
The type of perches used will depend upon the species to be kept. If the birds are free-flying, do not clutter the place with too many perches. Put some perches at the corners, and a branch from a bush or tree of convenient size in the centre. But although perches of a size to suit the birds kept are a necessity, they should be so sited that they do not impede the flying space more than is necessary. Despite the need for care in siting, there should always be enough perches to go round. Many birds are innate bullies and there is nothing more unpleasant than a perpetual game of musical chairs, in which the weakest and most timid constantly have difficulty in finding an untenanted resting place, and are forever hounded from pillar to post.

There should be some cover at the back of the flight, and the most convenient and decorative method of supplying it is in the form of large pot plants of non-poisonous varieties. Obviously cheap and easily replaced plants should be used for destructive species, but for small insectivorous species it is often possible to provide cover and decoration in the form

72

of attractive flowering shrubs.

A shallow, wide, glazed earthenware dish can be placed in the centre of the flight to serve as a bath, care being taken that it is not immediately under a perch, where it would quickly become fouled by droppings.

Wooden seed boxes may be filled with good loam and sown with grass and weed seeds. When they are nicely grown the whole box may be placed in the flight, where it is likely to be appreciated both for the green food it supplies and also because it may harbour tasty insects. It is a wise precaution to stand both this box and the bath on a piece of linoleum to prevent the floor of the flight getting wet and rotten. A box of dry sand will be appreciated by many species, and, if they are seen to be using it regularly, sprinkle the sand with insecticide, and they will work it right into their feathers each time they have a dustbath.

Storage of Food and Utensils
With a suite of cages along one side of the room, and a flight along the other, there will be a passage left in the centre. At one end of this there should be a cupboard to contain spare fronts, cages, divisions, nest boxes or pans, eating and drinking utensils, and cleaning gear.

Food should be kept either in vermin-proof tins or a galvanized dustbin, depending on the amount to be stored. It is far easier to avoid vermin coming, by being scrupulous about not leaving food where they can get it, than it is to get rid of them when they do come. And, whilst on the subject, if by any chance you do get an influx of mice, and decide to poison them with one of the 'safe' cumulative poisons, it is doubly important to take precautions to avoid their contaminating food. Their urine, before they die, may pass on lethal doses to the bird-seed or meal, which may also become cumulatively poisonous.

For Visitors
The last requirement for the bird room is a comfortable chair, table, and electric fire.

It is pointless going to all the trouble of equipping a room for your birds if it is too uncomfortable to sit there and enjoy the fruits of your labours. So try and make it as pleasant for yourself as you have for your pets, so that it will be a pleasure and not a penance for your friends to join you.

Outdoor Aviaries

It is not always desirable to have a bird room in your house, and, in any case, it is often possible to have a larger flight outside than in. If you can manage to build this flight so that the window of your bird room opens into it you have the best of both worlds.

Failing this an aviary or garden shed may be equipped inside like an indoor bird room, but may have large outdoor flight connected to it.

There are a number of firms specializing in ready-made garden aviaries, often providing an outdoor flight as well. I suggest that you go to one of the major shows or garden exhibitions and examine a selection of these ready-made units closely. Because they are made by highly mechanized carpentry firms, you may well find you could not build one yourself either so well or so cheaply. In any case, you cannot fail to get some worthwhile ideas.

Site

The outdoor aviary should be sited to get sun and shade if possible. In any case, trees or quick growing evergreens like privet can be planted outside the flight to give shade. The whole structure should be sited to give shelter from the north-east winds.

Apart from the first essentials of shade and shelter, the aviary should be positioned to harmonize with the rest of the garden so that it is an amenity and not an eyesore.

If the garden is formal with rectangular lawns and beds in geometric patterns, it is usually appropriate to have a neat and carpenter-made flight and aviary to match the house or suit the surroundings. In an informal country garden, rustic larch poles and weather-boarded shelter will probably harmonize better. Or it may be possible to use some existing stable or outhouse for the indoor part and build a flight to blend with it. It is sometimes even possible to net in a stable yard, or use a garden wall as one side, so that a large enough flight can be constructed for you to sit inside with the birds, instead of watching them through the netting.

74

In this case, the floor of the flight should be lawned and planted to resemble the rest of the garden as nearly as possible. It is very hard to beat the sensation of sitting 'in' a garden amongst beautiful and exotic birds, which are flying about virtually at liberty.

Construction of a Flight

No more need be said about constructing the outdoor aviary than that it should be a shed, either purchased or built, on the same lines as the bird room described in the previous section. The one main difference will be that it will have an outdoor flight, either instead of or in addition to the one inside.

It must be realized, however, that apart from very hardy species most birds will need access to indoor quarters during the winter, while it will be necessary to confine some permanently from about the end of October till April. Even our own native birds like very sheltered cover such as holly, ivy, thick woodland, hollow trees, or buildings as a roost in winter; they will change their roost to suit the prevailing weather.

To cater to this need it is advisable to build a solid roof at both ends of the flight, over the top and extending two or three feet down the side. Perches can be arranged under these shelters and the birds can select whichever they want.

A trench should be dug right round the flight about a foot deep and eighteen inches wide. The bottom of this trench and the side nearest the flight should be covered by three-eighths-of-an-inch mesh wire netting which should be fastened to the bottom member of the frame and just overlap the external netting. The trench should be filled in. This should prevent rats burrowing under the floor, although a more permanent job is to use bricks instead of netting to bury round the sides. Rats will nearly always start to dig where the vertical netting meets the ground. They will not go two feet away and start what must seem to them an unnecessarily long tunnel.

Aviary Floor

The best floor for the flight is natural soil, turf, and plants. But water dripping from galvanized netting is good for none of these things. Furthermore, if the aviary is at all heavily stocked the birds themselves will sour the ground. There are several ways of overcoming this, but the best are either to change the soil completely or move the aviary flight.

In small flights it will not take many barrow-loads of soil to dig the whole floor out to a depth of about six inches. This can be exchanged for fresh soil from the garden to the benefit of both. Another method, and a very good one, is to build the flight in sections which bolt together and can be easily dismantled and moved. The aviary building should always have a window opposite the flight entrance, for birds hate flying from an open flight into a dark building; this will make it possible for the whole flight to be dismantled and re-erected on the opposite side of the aviary, giving the ground a complete rest.

If neither of these expedients is possible, it may be necessary to have a smooth, sloping concrete floor to the flight, which can be hosed clean regularly.

Shelter Construction

As has been mentioned already, the interior of the shelter will be very similar to the bird room in the house. Externally, it will probably be either of wood or asbestos sheeting and may well have a corrugated iron roof. Ideally, it will be constructed of one-inch tongued and grooved boarding nailed to three-by-two-inch framing. In practice this is unnecessarily expensive for most purposes and a satisfactory job can be made of five-eighths-of-an-inch matchboarding nailed to two-inch-square framing. This will meet the need, provided the inside is lined with wallboard (unless parrot-like birds are to be kept) or asbestos sheeting. This double thickness of wall will give good insulation in both hot and cold weather.

The shelter itself should be mounted on a foundation of bricks trenched deep enough into the ground to exclude vermin, and it is important that adequate air bricks are inserted to give proper under-floor ventilation. It is just as vital for the roof to be lined as the walls and there should be adjustable ventilators either in the roof or high in the walls.

The windows should be similar, opposite each other, and covered with wire-netting frames to prevent the birds flying into the glass, or escaping if a plane is broken. They should

76

open outwards, and any that are to be used as entrances to the flight should be entirely detachable.

Entrance to Aviary and Flight
Accidents are only too frequent when there is a single door giving access to birds flying freely. They become tame and fearless enough to dart towards, instead of away from, their owner and will very often dive through the space left the instant before the door closes. The one sure way of preventing this is to have double doors, so that you enter a porch, and close the door behind you before opening the door into the aviary proper. This is a minor refinement which can save many a valuable bird.

Equipment
The range of possible nesting boxes, nesting pans, and feeding utensils is almost as wide as the variety of birds that use them, so it is always best to find out what it has been used to when acquiring a bird. Birds hate enforced change and whilst the change of quarters is unavoidable, it is always wise to continue with the same food and feeding methods at least until it settles down.

If tropical birds are to kept, buy two heaters, wire them to a good thermostat in parallel, and check weekly that they both work. They are unlikely to give out at precisely the same time and the original duplication can mean saving valuable lives when heat would otherwise fail.

Perches
Screw-in stub fittings can be bought to mount perches by one end only. This avoids cluttering up valuable flying space and enables the owner to move about the aviary without emulating an Olympic hurdler. The diameter of the perch must be small enough for the bird to grip, but not so small that the foot does not grip as a reflex when the bird crouches in a roosting position. If in doubt, try a variety of perches and watch which are the favourites. Always scrub perches with hot disinfectant to clean them.

In open flights it will be necessary to feed on trays or in bowls covered by some form of shelter to prevent the food getting soaked by every shower.

Movable Folds

For large birds, such as ornamental pheasants, one-inch mesh netting can be used, and it is not necessary to have a bottom to the aviary except where foxes are present. It is better to have a light frame about ten feet by four, with an open shelter at one end. The roof should be of nylon net, to avoid injury if the birds fly up and hit their heads, and the whole should be made light enough to be moved by one person holding the handles at each end. It should be put on turf, or the kitchen garden when the crop has been gathered, and moved on its own width each day. The birds thus have fresh ground to work at and can amuse themselves by finding some of their own food.

Folds can be bought ready-made from the suppliers of game-rearing equipment, and the bottom eighteen inches is usually boarded with half-inch matchboard. This gives considerable protection against wind and a little against sun. The shelter at the one end provides protection from wind, rain, and sun.

These movable folds are an invaluable acquisition for any petkeepers as, with minor modifications, they are ideal for such birds as pheasants, partridge, and quail, and also for rabbits, guinea-pigs, and other animals that enjoy grazing.

Planning Permission

Before embarking upon any structural alteration to your house or erecting any permanent building outside, check with the local council if there is any need to obtain planning permission. Local by-laws vary, and so does the interpretation put on them by local officials. Most of them will give constructive advice about minor modifications that would bring your plans within the regularions—provided you ask first.

5 Budgerigars

The budgerigar is by far the most popular cage bird in Britain. It is hardy and friendly, breeds freely, and appears in a wonderful variety of colours.

Budgerigars are natives of Australia, where vast flocks, often tens of thousands in number, swarm on the plains. Their breeding haunts are in mallee scrub, which looks rather like silver birch scrub; several branches of a few inches in diameter spring from the same root. Moisture gets trapped where the branches meet, so there is usually an abundance of rotten wood, with holes and crevices, where whole colonies of budgerigars make nesting sites. These nests are usually in holes about six inches deep.

When the young hatch, they join the adult flocks which have no fixed territory but migrate as the food or water in the area diminishes, following the food supply rather than migrating at set times in traditional directions, as, for example, swallows do.

The wild birds are almost invariably light greens, but occasional mutations of yellow and mauves are seen in the wild flocks. One of the strongest characteristics of this, the smallest of the parrot family, is a tendency to breed mutations different from either parent. And by mating these sports back it is often possible to fix a new type which will breed true and be responsible for yet another colour or type to make the modern exhibition budgerigar so different from its wild ancestors.

Purchase

It is most important, before buying your first budgerigars, to decide exactly what it is you want from them. If you want colourful household pets, always providing gaiety and movement and cheerful chatter, there is absolutely no point in paying fancy exhibition prices. The important thing is to choose young birds of the colour that happens to appeal to you most.

I stress young birds because, if they are introduced to the house as soon as they leave the nest, they will soon become finger-tame and can be allowed out of their cage to fly about the room without fear of their being frightened when it is time to go back.

If you want a talking budgerigar, it is no use having more than one in the house, because he will not bother to learn to mimic you if there are others of his own species who can talk to him in his own language. If you want budgerigars for exhibition, it is always best to go to a reputable breeder, who is proving his ability by winning at important shows. Explain to him that you are a novice and would like to begin to show budgerigars. Do not expect him to give you a bargain but be prepared to pay a fair price, and the chances are that he will let you have excellent birds and help you with advice for as long afterwards as you require it.

House Birds

In many branches of the bird fancy it is customary to speak of 'house birds' with scorn. They are mismarked or too big or too small for exhibition. They are 'only' good for pets!

Long may it be so, because the owner who only wants a pet can often buy perfectly satisfactory birds in this way quite cheaply.

Feeding

Wild budgerigars roam over the Australian scrub and follow the seasonal harvest of the wild grass seeds they love. Their wanderings are also controlled by the availability of water, and besides the ripe grain they will eat a certain amount of greenstuff.

In captivity their feeding is extremely simple. Pet shops sell ready-mixed seed for them and it should be emphasized that there is no economy in buying cheap quality seed, because it may not be properly clean, containing husks and rubbish, apart from the fact that the grain itself is likely to be inferior.

If your budget is tight or you have a great many birds, you may find that it is cheaper to mix your own seed. A mixture of canary seed and millet will be found to be perfectly satisfactory, and the bulk may be further increased quite cheaply by the addition of a few groats, which are oats with the husk removed, or pin-head oatmeal, which is kibbled groats.

The real economy to be made in feeding budgerigars is in avoidance of waste. Like the manufacturers of mustard, birdseed merchants make their fortunes from what their customers throw away. Accordingly, buy a really good seed-hopper. It is absolutely vital that budgerigars have food in front of them at all times, for they will die in an extremely short time if it is not available. Seed must always be there, and it must not be covered by husks, so buy a hopper of the type which feeds the seed by gravity and allows the husks to fall into a tray below.

When using trays for seed, it is dangerously easy to think the tray is full, when in fact the seed has been eaten, leaving nothing but the husks. Furthermore, open trays become foul, whereas a good hopper always provides a small supply of perfectly clean seed.

Although canary seed and millet should form the bulk of the diet, budgerigars will enjoy a little of a wide variety of seeds as an addition or change. Barley, wheat, sunflower, linseed, hemp, and rape can all be added.

Seeding grass is not only the best—because it is the natural food, but one of the favourites too. It may be given either tied in bunches or, if the birds are in an aviary, a clod may be put in a flower-pot and replaced as often as necessary. In these modern scientific days, it is absolutely vital to be quite certain that any wild plants you introduce have not been sprayed with one of the dangerous chemical weedkillers or insecticides. They are decimating our wild birds and can be equally dangerous to pets.

A little linseed oil will add bloom to a bird's feathers and cod-liver oil is as good for birds as animals. The easiest way of administering either is to sprinkle a few drops on groats, which will absorb it. Use both in moderation as only a trace is necessary.

Lettuce, dandelion, spinach, peas in the pod, shepherd's purse, and plantain are all relished and beneficial. Do not let them wilt, but give a little fresh greenstuff regularly. Keep an eye on the droppings and, provided they are not loose, you are not giving too much.

Grit is absolutely essential. It can be bought in the correct grade from the pet shops, but be sure that it contains both lime in the form of crushed shell or limestone, and sharp insoluble grit. This is necessary to grind the grain in the gizzard, and the lime provides the calcium necessary for health and eggshell formation.

Food in the Breeding Season
For high fertility, it is necessary to supply vitamin E in some form. The simplest way to do this is to stretch a piece of damp flannel over a box in a dark, reasonably warm place. Sprinkle this with wheat, as you would grow mustard and cress, and when the wheat sprouts, feed a little to the birds. This will supply wheat-germ oil in its most natural and beneficial form. When the young hatch out, the old birds should be given about half an eggcupful of soft food a day. This can consist of chopped chickweed or lettuce or grated carrot mixed with crumpled soft brown bread. It will be found that the youngsters like this too when they are weaned. Always remove all stale food before giving more fresh.

Cages
If the site for the bird cage is to be in the living-room, you will want it to be as decorative and as in keeping with the general furnishings as possible. It may well be made entirely of wire.

No bird tolerates draught, and with an all-wire cage, the only way of avoiding draught is to site the cage in a part of the room which is itself draught-proof. Matters are sometimes eased by cages which have one side of glass.

Your birds will enjoy sunshine, but, when the sun gets hot, they will require shade, so if possible put the cage near a window which catches the early morning sun. If this is not possible it should be placed near some other window with a screen of some sort—simple cardboard or cloth will do—so arranged that by moving to one side of the cage a bird can always get shade if necessary.

Always err on the side of generosity, and see that your cage is bigger than necessary rather than too small. Budgerigars are such sprightly, active birds that it is very cruel not to give them enough freedom to stretch their wings and fly from one part of the cage to another. If your bird is alone, it is essential to provide him with as much to occupy his time as possible. Mirrors and balls, bells, ladders, and all sorts of toys specifically designed to amuse budgerigars are on sale at any pet shop. When you have examined and tried some, your own ingenuity may suggest variants that will amuse you as well as your bird.

Cock budgerigars are bolder and more easily tamed than hens. If you do not particularly want a talking bird (and like other members of the parrot family, budgerigars learn to talk well), it is possible to provide company in the shape of another budgerigar to share the cage. Even so, it is better to have two cocks than a true pair, because a pair will be so keen to breed that many of their delightful characteristics will never become apparent. Even if it is thought only right to allow them to live a full life, it is still not wise to keep a true pair in a cage all the year round. Two nests, or at the very most three, is all that they can comfortably rear without losing stamina and condition, so that they would have to be separated then in any case. On the other hand, two cocks will form an attachment for each other in the absence of a hen to distract them and can live happily together year in and year out with no disadvantage save that they cannot usually be taught to talk.

If it is not essential to have a particularly decorative cage, my preference is for the largest box cage that can be accommodated. This consists of a wooden box, say eighteen inches by twenty-four, nine inches deep, with a wire-barred front. It can be painted with white cellulose paint inside, to show the bird off to advantage, with any colour that will harmonize with the rest of the room on the outside.

The advantage of this cage is that it protects the bird from draughts, provides shade in almost any position, is cheap, and can easily be made up by any handyman, who has only to buy the wood and a loose cage front and sand tray for the bottom. It is not even necessary to scatter loose sand on the bottom of cages nowadays, provided they are made to fit one of the expendable sanded papers sold by pet shops for the purpose.

As with any other pet, of course, scrupulous cleanliness is essential, and cages and feeding utensils should be thoroughly clean at all times.

Having procured the cage, the next job is to select the

bird or birds and tame them.

Sexing

I have already said that cocks make the best pets; however, in young birds which have not moulted, it is often difficult to be certain which are the cockbirds. They usually have narrower, more lightly domed heads than the hens, whose heads tend to be lower browed and wider; hens' wattles are less rounded. Some people say that if you let the young bird nip your finger, the hen will give the sharper nip! But despite these clues, the fact remains that it is very difficult to be certain of birds when they are young enough to tame and train.

When they have moulted the cocks' wattles will be blue and the hens' brown.

Taming

The first stage in getting the young bird tame is to place his cage where he will see most movement and most people. Take no notice of him at all until familiarity has whittled away his shyness of you.

Then get a stick as thick as a pencil, push it gently and quietly through the bars of his cage and leave it there, as an extra perch, until he has forgotten it is something new. When he is quite used to it, touch him under the breast with it and gently push him backwards. He will either have to fall, flutter off his perch, or step upwards and perch on the stick you are holding, and he will soon learn that this is the easiest alternative. When he is quite used to your being near his cage and talking to him and persuading him to stand on a perch whilst you hold it, substitute your finger for the perch.

The secret of taming almost any bird or animal is limitless patience. It is important to learn your pet's reaction to the suspicion of danger. It will vary for different species, but, with a budgerigar, you will notice an almost imperceptible tightening of the feathers: he will shrink down ever so slightly, as if he had suddenly grown a little smaller, and his intelligent eyes will be watchful and wary. That is the signal for you to stop doing whatever excited him and stay completely motionless until the tension slackens. One minor fright before you have completely gained his confidence can undo weeks of patient work.

Gradually you will gain his trust, so that he will jump on to your finger as soon as you put it in the cage. If he will let you scratch the back of his neck with the tip of the other forefinger—and all birds of the parrot family adore having the napes of their necks scratched—you are beginning to make progress.

The next stage is to bring your finger just through the cage door while he is sitting on it. Whenever you open the cage door, for any reason at all, you should have checked that doors and windows are shut, that there is a guard over the fireplace, and that all cats have been banished from the room. Any dog allowed to stay must have your complete confidence.

Do not be in any hurry with this business of taming your pet. If he sits on your finger while you bring him just out of his cage, put him gently back. Gradually, day by day, you can bring him a little further, till be becomes as familiar with his new surroundings as he is with his cage. If he flies off and gets a bit panicky, leave him alone. Countless birds have been ruined by their owners chasing them about a room in a fruitless effort to catch them.

He will settle on a curtain or picture rail or some other high point of vantage. Let him have a good look round, and when all signs of uneasiness have vanished, go very gently and slowly up to him and hold out your finger. Touch him under the breast, and he will probably step on to your finger almost as a reflex action. If he does, return him slowly to the security of his cage; he will have done very well for the day.

On the other hand, if he eludes you and flies to another spot, on no account follow him round. He will forget your image as protector and friend and look on you as a hunter with himself as the quarry. Either draw the curtains, when you will probably be able to approach him quite easily, or wait till dusk falls. Then, before it is quite dark, move slowly—but steadily and not stealthily—towards him, speaking to him so that he knows who it is and does not imagine he is being stalked. I cannot emphasize too strongly that one mistake, in the form of a fright, will undo hours of patient work. After a time he will gain complete confidence in you and may be let out of his cage to fly about the closed room as often as you wish. When it is time to return, he will hop happily on your finger to be carried back to his cage or will learn to return for food and water of his own accord.

At this stage he can be taught a variety of amusing tricks. It is natural for budgerigars, which are curious and playful birds, to play with light cellulose balls, swinging ladders, and weighted dolls which spring upright again when knocked over. A little thought and experiment with an exceptionally tame specimen will stimulate his natural curiosity to persuade him to do a variety of tricks, not because he forced to, like some performing animal, but purely because it amuses him as much as his owner.

There is one snag in keeping budgerigars virtually loose about the house. Like all members of the parrot family, they have powerful and destructive beaks. In point of fact, these small birds have the least destructive beaks of their kind, but they can still do a certain amount of damage to soft wood, fabric, and wallpaper. Therefore, do not begin by liberating him in the best room of the house, and do not liberate him at all unless you are there to keep an eye on him. Like other birds and beasts of character, temperament and habits vary from individual to individual, and your choice may or may not be a lucky one in this respect. In any case, it is far more unusual to have a really tame, vivacious budgerigar than a smart room!

Breeding
It is possible to breed budgerigars either in a cage or aviary.

In either case, they are usually free breeders and it is more necessary to restrict the number of nests they have than to encourage them. If they are allowed to breed as much as they would like to, they use up so much energy in rearing their young that their own health suffers in consequence. The ideal number of broods they should be allowed to rear in a season is two and the most should be three.

There is only one method of restricting the number of broods they rear, and that is to keep the sexes apart except when you want them to go to nest. They will breed practically all the year round, if allowed, certainly from January to September.

St. Valentine's Day, 14 February, is the traditional time for birds to mate in this country, and it is as good a day as any to introduce your pair of budgerigars. It is best to bring the cock bird to the hen's cage rather than the reverse, because in strange surroundings he will be a little timid before he settles down. If you put the hen in to a cage that is already 'home' to a cock bird, he may begin to chivvy and chase her before she has settled, and make her nervous. Get them settled down before putting the nest box in or the hen may retreat to its safety and refuse to be mated.

Nest Box

When they seem perfectly happy together, the nest box should be put into the cage. It should provide the same conditions as a wild bird would look for in a hole in a tree. Since it will take up space in a cage that is already restricted in size, the breeding cage itself should obviously be as large as possible, preferably a box cage not less than twenty-four inches by eighteen, sixteen inches wide. It should be situated to get plenty of light and air, some sunshine (though there must always be shade), and, above all, no draughts.

The nest box should be hung up at the top corner of this cage farthest from the bars. There are a number of satisfactory nest boxes on sale in most pet shops. Wood is the commonest material, but carboard is satisfactory and can be discarded to avoid infection after each round. The essentials are that there should be a hole an inch and a half in diameter at the top of one side, which should be about six inches high, and the floor area should be about seven inches square. Obviously wild birds cannot specify the size of their nesting holes with exactitude, and a great deal of rubbish is talked about the necessity of having artificial nest boxes to exact dimensions. So long as the box is large enough inside for the hen to turn round without crumpling her tail and deep enough for privacy, she will be well satisfied. The lid of the box should be hinged for inspection and cleaning, but do not be tempted to open it unnecessarily, because you will only disturb the birds.

What is important is that the bottom should be concave like a small saucer. Budgerigars do not carry nesting material and in the wilds, the bottom of holes in trees are usually covered with chippings of rotten wood. If the bottom is uneven, flat, or convex, some of the eggs will be shuffled out of her reach and will not hatch. Wastage in the wild does not matter so much, because nature is naturally very wasteful indeed. To avoid this happening with your pet budgerigar, pet shops sell pieces of wood, cut to fit the bottom of nest boxes, in which a circular concave depression has been turned. When the hen lays her eggs in this depression they gravitate into a tight clutch which she can comfortably cover when she incubates.

There is some difference of opinion about how much of the floor of the box this depression should cover. Some people leave a considerable rim round the edge on which the bird may alight to avoid risk of her dropping straight on to the eggs and breaking them. If she does, my opinion is that either the box is too deep or the shells are too thin. The remedy for the first is obvious, and more limestone grit should cure thin-shelled eggs.

I believe that too small a depression for the eggs is more dangerous, because they are then more likely to be shuffled out to get chilled in a corner.

Incubation
The breeding pair should either be two young birds of last season or the season before, or one old bird and a young one. Do not breed from two old birds and, except in special circumstances, do not breed from any bird more than five years old. The young are less likely to be vigorous if you do.

If there is some special reason for getting a brood from a great favourite or outstanding bird that is getting older than five or six, try to breed in March or April when the spring weather should be the greatest help to youngsters which might otherwise be weakly.

When the pair you have introduced have settled down and explored the nest box you have put in, you will see that the hen will spend a great deal of her time going in and out of it. All animals and birds have to 'learn' their territory by repeatedly exploring every detail until they literally know it by heart.

If the hen is in good condition—and no budgerigar breeds satisfactorily if it is not—she should lay her first egg in about ten days, which, for the first 'round' will be about the end of February if you mated her on St. Valentine's Day. She will probably lay either four or five eggs in her first clutch, though more later on, and she will lay them on

88

alternate days.

Most birds will lay their full clutch before beginning to incubate them. If the nest is exposed they cover them carefully when they leave, but if the nest is hidden—and no nest is better hidden than the bottom of a hole in a tree—they just leave them until the clutch is complete. Budgerigars, however, are exceptions. They begin to sit sometimes as soon as the first egg is laid and sometimes when the second one is laid. Thus with a clutch of four eggs, the first egg to hatch will be eight days old when the last chips out. It is Nature's way to ensure the survival of the fittest, for if food is not plentiful enough to supply the complete brood, it will be the youngest and weakest which will succumb and the eldest will get more than its fair share of food and thrive. This is better than having a complete brood of equally weak and under-fed chicks. (An extreme example of this principle is the barn owl, which often has a brood of chicks several weeks apart in age. If food for them gets scarce, the older ones will actually feed on their weaker brethren.)

To avoid any disparity of size and strength with pet budgerigars—whose food supply shouldn't fail—some people remove the first and second eggs, returning them when the third is laid, so that the brood is of more even size. If this system is to be adopted, each egg must be replaced by a dummy egg, for the hen will desert if she realizes her nest has been plundered. It is important each day to change the position of the real eggs, which should be stored on bran or sawdust, or the first to be laid may not hatch. When left in the nest the hen 'shuffles' the eggs round as she goes to lay, preventing the yolk settling and sticking to one side.

Rearing

The staple bugerigar food of canary-seed and millet should be augmented as much as possible with seeding grasses, which would be eagerly sought after by birds in the wild state. Groats, to which a little cod-liver oil has been added, should be fed, also chickweed and dandelion in moderation. Most budgerigars love spinach and young carrots.

Breeding pairs may also have a little top-quality wheat; or brown bread baked solid in the oven and crumbled. Soft crumbly brown bread and grated vegetable, such as carrots, are also appreciated.

The parent birds will feed the young until—at about a month old—they are fully fledged; when they leave the nest they will quickly learn to accompany the older birds to the feed troughs.

By about six weeks they are self-supporting and can be transferred to separate cages. This is quite essential before the hen lays again, as the youngsters are likely to return again and again to the box where they were hatched, and they may cause the old bird to break her new clutch of eggs.

Before this next round of eggs is laid, it is most important to disinfect the nest. Take out the concave egg tray, scrub it with carbolic soap, and immerse in boiling water. Thoroughly scrub and scald the box itself because, even under conditions of clinical cleanliness, it is impossible to avoid parasites taking up their abode in the nest box.

I would emphasize that by 'parasites' I do not mean fleas or insects which would be objectionable to human beings. Birds are subject to red mite and various microscopic pests which can only be kept in check in the artificial conditions of captivity by the most scrupulous cleanliness. For this reason, there is a lot to be said for using cardboard nest boxes which are cheap enough to throw away after one round of youngsters have been reared in them.

When the youngsters are fledged and weaned from their parents, it is absolutely vital that they be encouraged to feed freely. Millet sprays should be hung up, food always supplied in the hoppers or fountains, and plenty of fresh water and grit should be available. It is worth repeating the warning that the greatest care should be taken to see that the grain hoppers are not covered with husk so that they look full, but in fact the grain is buried by husks.

One of the main pitfalls to be watched for in rearing budgerigars concerns this very question of cleanliness. Some parent birds get the nest boxes in far more mess than others. They litter the bottoms with surplus grain and husk which becomes fouled and sticky. This mess sticks to the youngsters' beaks, damaging the upper mandible—which is the weaker—more than the lower. The result, if not checked, is an ugly overgrown lower mandible, like the undershot mouth of a bulldog.

To avoid this once the eggs have hatched, inspect the box

every day and replace by an exactly similar clean one, or clean it out, as necessary. You will find that birds which were nervous at any interference before their eggs were hatched will not take any notice at all when they have chicks to occupy them. The advantage of cheap, expendable carboard nest boxes is never more evident than with parent birds which foul their nests.

Aviaries

It often happens that people who start with one budgerigar as a pet acquire a mate for it for company. And, by the time they have bred a round or two of fascinating youngsters, they find themselves enjoying the birds so much that they decide to start an aviary.

The details of construction of an aviary will be found in Chapter 4. It is, of course, absolutely essential that it be strong and vermin-proof, and desirable that it should be as large as possible. Always err on the side of generosity.

Half the attraction of possessing budgerigars is to watch a flock of them in motion. A large, well situated aviary flight on a sunny day, with a dozen or so birds of mixed colours scintillating like kingfishers as they flash about, is a sight that no one can forget.

The species is very hardy and can be kept out of doors all the year provided there is a warm indoor portion for shelter and sleeping, a windbreak against the prevailing wind, and some perches near the top which are dry and sheltered. The easiest way of achieving this is to have the aviary about six feet six inches high with the top twelve or eighteen inches consisting of vertical board or asbestos. Mated to this, in the form of a right-angle, can be another twelve or eighteen inches of horizontal shelter beneath which perches can be placed.

Budgerigars are singularly destructive to vegetation, so it is useless trying to get an elaborately planted aviary, for they will bark and destroy any bushes you put in. The aviary should, however, contain branches and shrubs and plants—for decoration, for perches, and for the birds to eat and gnaw. It is quite simple to get common shrubs or young self-seeded trees and transplant them to flower pots, which can be sunk level in the aviary floor. The, when the birds do mutilate them there is no problem about their replacement, and unsightly withered vegetation need not be left to clutter and disfigure the aviary.

Almost any young tree, tree branch, or bush may be used for perching, except laburnum or yew, which are poisonous. The birds will perch on the twigs and fly from bush to bush and gnaw a great deal of the bark, which they obviously find beneficial. A stump in the aviary floor can contain a succession of sods of turf which can be replaced as they wither or are eaten. If they are put back in some damp unfrequented part of the garden, they will regenerate quite quickly. If sods of seeding grass can be found, the birds will love it, and it can be given either in tied bunches or with its roots. The greenstuff they require as part of their diet should be supplied cut, in such quantities that they always finish wanting a little more, rather than being allowed to gorge.

Budgerigars are quarrelsome with other small birds, so it is cruel to try to persuade the smaller species to share their quarters.

Baths
Not all budgerigars will take advantage of a shallow bowl of water to bathe. Some people spray their budgerigars, but it is not really necessary. However, a clod of long grass on the aviary floor, thoroughly wetted, will often induce them to play in its dripping vegetation.

Breeding in Aviaries
There are both advantages and disadvantages in breeding in aviaries. There is no doubt at all about the pedigree of young birds produced in a cage which contains only two adult birds. But budgerigars are not noted for their fidelity, and one cock is likely to mate more than one hen and any hen may easily have been mated by more than one cock. Even if couples have been caged separately, and not introduced to the aviary until they have paired, they may easily decide to swap partners when a wider choice is offered.

To the pet-keeper, as opposed to the exhibitor, this may not matter, and it may be quite satisfactory to allow them to sort themselves out to their own satisfaction. Great care is necessary, even then, to avoid fighting. Hen budgerigars can be dreadfully pugnacious and will fight to the death for a nesting site on which they have set their hearts. The way to minimize this is to introduce all the pairs to aviary at the same time and to be careful to provide considerably more nest boxes than there are pairs of birds to use them. In this way, even if two pairs do both decide to use the same box, there will be considerable choice for the birds who have to give way. In addition, use exactly similar boxes, about three boxes to each pair of birds, and, if the boxes are in rows, have a vertical board between each pair of boxes so that, when a bird alights at the entrance hole, the boxes on either side are not visible to it. It is important that, so far as possible, the boxes should be at the same height, preferably in a row along the top of the aviary, shielded from the weather by the angle of eighteen-inch asbestos or board that will already be there.

The worst possible hens, from a fighting viewpoint, are just the ones the pet-keeper will have. They will be used to nesting in a cage, where there is no competition, and will have been spoiled by having complete freedom of choice. It is natural that they will resent competition from other females of their species, so, if you do want to introduce pet budgerigars to aviary life, do not do it, if you can help it, during the breeding season. The best time is at the end of the season, when you separate cocks and hens. Strange hens, slightly out of condition after rearing their young, in strange surroundings, would have plenty of time to get used to each other before being confronted by the incentive to fight which competition for nesting sites provides. If you do get an incurable fighter, give her away or make a pet of her in a cage. There is no room for her in a community.

Having got your breeding stock established in the aviary, treat them as you would caged birds, removing the young in the same way. If the hen lays again before they are properly weaned, the cock will look after them quite well until they are ready to be moved.

The major advantage of aviary breeding, apart from the obvious one that the young birds have much more room to use their wings, is that you will probably have several nests of young at the same time. Now budgerigars, apart from their intense competition for nesting sites, have a very strong community spirit. So, if one pair has six or seven young and another four or five, neither will object if you transfer one or two from the larger brood to the smaller and even things up. Similarly it is very sensible to put the large (and older) from one brood together and all the small ones from the two broods in the other nest. By these means you will take some of the burden from birds, which would have had very large broods to deal with, and remove the necessity for the weaker and younger members of both broods to compete for food with their older and stronger brothers.

From the owner's point of view, although budgerigars in an aviary are unlikely to be as tame as the spoiled darling of the living room, their wonderful colours and agility do show off to best advantage on the wing in a large flight.

After Breeding
At the end of the breeding season, when two or, at the very most three, rounds of youngsters have been taken, the sexes must be parted. If you leave them together they will go on trying to breed and take so much out of their constitutions that they will not be so good next season. Furthermore, late youngsters that don't have 'the sun on their backs' never do as well as their elders. In the wild, shortage of food at the end of the season, and the need to migrate away from their breeding territory will put them out of condition to breed. Each pair, under good conditions, would rear two or three broods of four or five. The wild budgerigar population does not increase over the years, so all but two out of every twelve or fourteen must die from disease, starvation, predators, or least likely, from old age. No bird-keeper could tolerate losses on this scale, so artificial limitations to activity are as necessary as artificial food and shelter.

The question of keeping budgerigars at liberty will be dealt with in the chapter on The Garden Collection.

6 Simple Birds

A great many birds, even when they have not been bred in captivity, take extremely well to life in a cage or aviary, are simple to feed, and do not need artificial heat except as a protection against frost. Even very hardy wild birds take precautions in very cold weather so that, when they are confined and deprived of the opportunity of strenuous exercise and seeking the type of cover and shelter they need, it is always wise to see that the temperature in their quarters does not fall below about 40° F. Neither should they be exposed to too wide a variation of temperature between day and night.

British birds are excluded from this section because it is illegal to keep most of them in captivity unless they have been bred in captivity. They are treated separately in Chapter 8.

The birds that are covered here can be purchased from good pet shops or livestock dealers, kept in non-specialist cages or aviaries and fed upon food which can mostly be bought in package form.

Choice of Bird

Before deciding what breed of bird you would like to keep, it is necessary to be quite clear if it is to live in the house with the family, outside in an aviary or bird room, or in the garden or paddock (as, for example, one would keep pigeons or domestic poultry).

When you have decided broadly what it is you would like, buy the trade paper dealing with that type of bird for a week or so and study the advertisements both of birds for sale and forthcoming shows. Visit anyone in your area who keeps or has what you want for sale. Most fanciers will be so glad to help a budding enthusiast that they will not only show you what to look for, but what to guard against. At shows and exhibitions you will be able to find whole groups of enthusiasts and to compare what each tells you. The more people you get to know, who keep pets similar to yours, the greater the enjoyment. The enthusiasm of fellow addicts is an infectious and enjoyable emotion.

Having made certain what you want, be quite clear in your own mind whether you want it purely as a pet or whether you would like to exhibit or breed for sale. If the latter, expect to get no better than you pay for. If you can possibly afford it, buy birds that have proved themselves by winning in stiff competition. If these are beyond your purse, buy birds of the best possible breeding, as they are more likely to produce good young, than flashy-looking birds which happen to be exceptionally good results from inferior stock. This book, however, is designed for people who require pets as opposed to a source of income.

All exhibitors breed stock that does not come up to show standard and most are only too glad to sell it at a very reasonable price to someone with no ambitions for show awards. Find out exactly what is wrong before you buy. If it is the markings or feather texture or some purely superficial defect, the bird will be absolutely no liability as a pet. If it is some physical defect, do not buy it. Rubbish, in the form of deformity, is dear at any price.

Bantams

Bantams are diminutive specimens of the large breeds of poultry, and there is a bantam variety of most recognized breeds.

The advantage of bantams is that they need less space, and are usually very tame, confiding, and decorative. The hens will lay eggs, much smaller than normal hen eggs, but none the less tasty. I would far rather have one fresh bantam egg, from a bird that had been allowed a fair degree of liberty, than a dozen big 'shop' eggs, from battery-kept birds, producing insipid eggs which have been kept some time in transit.

Bantams may not be found for sale at every pet shop, but will be advertised in the trade papers produced for poultry farmers, smallholders, etc.

Accommodation

Some bantams, the Old English Game variety, for example,

6. A nylon net of shelled peanuts attracts gorgeous wild greenfinches as well as siskins and tits. They look so much lovelier free than in cages

7. Greek tortoises do well in gardens during summer but need
careful preparation for hibernation

are hardy, and need only a warm house to roost in and as large a run as you can give them. They are very small and you may even be able to give them the freedom of the garden, if only in winter. The colour and movement they will provide may well compensate for the little damage they do. Other bantams, the more exotic show specimens with feathered feet and very soft feathers, are better confined in an entirely covered pen in bad and muddy weather.

Any normal poultry pen is suitable for bantams, provided smaller-diameter perches are fitted. Movable poultry arks, with a shelter at one end, are admirable, and so are the movable fold units advertised in sporting and country papers for rearing pheasants and partridge. If part of the garden is lawn and shrubs, it may be possible to net it off unobtrusively to confine the bantams, in which case they will need only a small wooden shelter sufficient to lay and sleep in.

Bantams are very hardy (except the soft-feathered exhibition varieties) and will roost out in evergreen trees such as yew, dense holly, or rhododendron very happily, provided the plantation is dense enough to give good cover from wind. Should you wish to prevent their flying over into an adjacent garden, it is only necessary to clip the outside eight large flight feathers of one wing. This throws the bird out of balance so that he cannot fly in a straight line, and it is perfectly painless. It is not so effective to clip both wings.

If an old shed is available or a stable, or one end of a garage, bantams can be kept there very easily simply by running a length of wire netting partition with a door in it. A board about eighteen inches wide should be placed under the perch to prevent droppings falling to the ground and fouling food. A nest box, or suite of nest boxes, about as large as full-sized biscuit tins or orange boxes can be put under the dropping board.

Remember that foxes and big cats will take bantams, so it is vital that they are shut up or roosting high enough to be out of harm's way.

The floor of the indoor shelter should be covered to a depth of four to ten inches with broken straw, peat, or husks from threshing. Grain can be thrown into this and the birds will take excellent exercise scratching for it, especially in cold wet weather when they would be miserable outside.

97

Food

Feed bantams as you would ordinary domestic poultry. They should have one feed a day—the evening meal—of whole grain. Either wheat or mixtures of wheat, clipped oats, barley, and kibbled maize can be used. It takes longer to digest solid grain than soft mash, so if they are fed in the evening they will not be famished by daybreak.

The other feed may consist of wet or dry mash. Corn merchants sell specially blended poultry meal which may be fed dry in troughs or hoppers. The advantage of feeding meal from hoppers is that it is not quite so demanding on one's time. More than one day's supply can be put in the hopper and the birds can then help themselves as they want, so that it is quite possible to stock them up over the week-end.

Bantams also need fresh green food. If they have free range in a garden or paddock, they will get all they need. If they have only a small run, which can't be moved as a fold unit (which gives the advantages of free range), it is better to divide the run in half so that they can change about and have fresh ground every month or so. The other half should have lime forked in and be left to lie fallow till wanted again. Every six months the top spit of soil should be removed entirely and replaced by fresh soil from the garden.

The birds need an adequate supply of fresh clean water at all times, preferably in a self-priming fountain, which should also be large enough to last over a week-end, if it is ever necessary to leave them for as long as that.

Grit

Bantams need hard grit—preferably flint chippings, to help them digest their food. Like other granivorous birds, they grind the hard corn in their gizzards and need stones of some sort to help in the process. Wild birds, pigeons, and partridge, can be seen along the verges of country roads in the early morning searching for grit. To keep grouse on grouse moors it is vital to ensure a supply of hard stone chippings, and it is equally vital to keeping domestic poultry or cage birds in condition.

Bantams also need grit containing lime. This can be bought in the form of limestone chippings or crushed shell—sold as 'oyster shell grit'. Without it, your birds will lay soft-shelled eggs.

Many corn merchants sell mixed grit that is supposed to supply both needs. I prefer to buy separately and feed separately. The birds crave the type of grit they are short of and will quickly sort all the flint or all the lime from mixed grit, and it will be obvious which supply needs replenishing.

Breeding

If you wish to breed from your bantams, have a young cock with up to eight old hens or a two- or three-year-old cock with yearling hens.

Collect the eggs and store them vertically by standing them on end in a bowl of sawdust or poultry meal. Turn the eggs nightly so that they stand on the other end. This is to stop the yolk sticking to one end.

When a hen goes broody she will cluck and fluff out her feathers, remaining in the nest except to feed, water, and evacuate.

A nest of soft straw should be put in a quiet spot and enclosed in a wire-netting run about six feet by four feet, two feet high. Dummy eggs should be put in this nest and the broody placed on them late in the evening. The hen should be settled by next day, when the eggs you want her to hatch can be substituted for the dummies. Place food and fresh water regularly in the run, so that she can leave the eggs to go and feed when she wants to.

In twenty-one days the chicks should hatch and should not be interfered with for twenty-four hours, by which time they should be strong and dry. Remove the whole run to the lawn or paddock with short grass, provide a thoroughly weather-proof coop inside the run, and put your hen and chickens in the coop first thing in the morning.

Provide a shallow drinking bowl and feed them on chick-crumbs obtained from a dealer in poultry requisites; give the hen wheat and grit. Move the run daily to fresh ground (it does not matter if the coop returns to ground already used after a week) and the chicks will be ready to leave the hen in six weeks.

Precautions against Insect Vermin

Bantams will keep themselves scrupulously clean if given the opportunity, but are just as susceptible as other birds to fleas and lice if their conditions are not satisfactory. They keep free of these pests by taking a dust bath. For this they need dry sand or soil. Ashes, though sometimes provided, are not satisfactory.

Supply a box about eighteen inches square and ten inches deep, half filled with dry sand or fine soil. The birds will lie in this and shuffle it through their feathers, removing any insect pests as they do so. If insect powder is scattered over the dust bath from time to time, so much the better. If they have an outside run and their sleeping pen is raised about a foot from the ground, as it should be to avoid rats, the soil under it will be sheltered and dry, and the birds will dust bathe underneath it.

Red mite are small nocturnal creatures which live in crevices between boards in the pen, where perches meet the walls, or similar places. They sally forth at night, creeping along the perches to gain access to their hosts and returning to safety before dawn. They are white at night and red, from the blood they have sucked, in the morning. They are completely harmless to human beings and are simple to control.

Paint any likely crevices with paraffin. Lime-wash the pen regularly on the inside and, if it is wooden, creosote the outside. In the case of severe infection with mite, the underside of the perches may be painted with nicotine sulphate. The warmth from the roosting birds will cause fumes to be given off which are deadly to insects. Nicotine sulphate is highly poisonous, and can be absorbed through the skin, so great care must be taken in handling it.

Pigeons

Pigeons are particularly satisfactory pets to keep because they can live extremely happily in very little space. They may be kept in one of three ways, depending upon the variety chosen and place where the owner lives. Some (normally only rare, exotic, and very valuable varieties) need aviaries, some may well be kept at liberty, and others may be set free for exercise only. The worst enemies of pigeons are cats and, where cats abound, it is necessary to keep pigeons in enclosed aviaries and pigeon pens, letting them out only for exercise. When they have had enough exercise, they must be shut up safely in their pens.

There is an enormous number of fancy varieties, as well as the performing pigeons dealt with in detail in the following pages. Some, like exhibition fantails, would be easy meat for the first cat that prowled and need to be kept in an aviary if there is any danger from cats. If you are lucky, as I am, in having a cat-proof garden, nothing looks better than free-flying fancy pigeons. They are colourful and provide bright splashes of interesting movement throughout the winter months, when the garden would otherwise be colourless. They can be kept either in a dovecote on a pole or the wall of the house, or in some disused loft or shed.

Pigeons are very hardy and simple to keep. They will normally live for many years, become extremely tame, and in suitable surroundings they can be given their liberty. They are particularly prolific breeders and it is fairly easy to 'fix' new types. There is, therefore, the choice of breeding for performance, with competitive varieties, or of producing even more beautiful examples of the ornamental varieties.

Performing Varieties

For the purpose of this book, performing pigeons will be taken to include racing pigeons, which are usually treated separately, tumblers or rollers, and tipplers. These varieties are dealt with individually below.

Racing Pigeons or Homers. Racing pigeons are the best-known variety, because baskets of pigeons going on races can be seen at railway stations every week-end.

For competitions, each owner's loft is marked on a large scale map so that the exact distance can be calculated to the race point where the birds are to be liberated.

All birds are taken to the club where each is fitted with a numbered rubber ring on its leg. They are then taken to the point where they are to be liberated, which may be anything from fifty to five or six hindred miles away. They are liberated simultaneously by an official of the club, who telegraphs the exact time of liberation back to the club.

Meanwhile each owner has been issued with a sealed clock with a cardboard dial. To prove that his birds have arrived, he has to get them into his loft and remove the rubber rings on their legs. Each ring (one for each bird) is put into a special small box which is inserted into the clock, where it punches a hole in the cardboard dial at the precise moment of clocking in.

When the clocks are returned to the club they are opened and a list made of the times of arrival of all birds. The total time taken is calculated and the exact distance each bird has flown is taken from the map, because some members of the club will live nearer to the race point than others. The bird that has flown home fastest wins the race.

Pigeon racing can be a very exciting sport, and it is not enough just to have very good pigeons: the skill of the owner in getting them fit and training them counts as well. They must be fed on the very best quality pigeon corn, in which peas will predominate, but which also contains rape, hemp, linseed, tares, and a little maize. Corn chandlers sell ready-mixed pigeon corn and it is quite good to start with. As you gain more experience and meet other fanciers, you will probably buy corn separately and experiment with special mixtures of your own.

The birds must be given enough to keep them fit and strong but not enough to make them fat and lazy. A good guide is to give them as much as they will clear up in ten minutes, twice a day and to remove the surplus.

They should be let out to fly twice a day before they are fed. They will fly round in circles for anything from twenty minutes to a couple of hours, and should be encouraged to take maximum exercise by flying as long as they will. As soon as they come down they must go straight into the pen and never be allowed to loll about on adjacent rooftops and buildings. If they do, you will never win a race because you can only prove his time of arrival when he comes down for you to remove his rubber ring and put it in the clock.

Besides training in the athletic sense of getting fit, racing pigeons are trained to return home. They are put in a basket and taken two or three miles and released. From that distance they will see familiar landmarks and should fly straight home any time after they are ten or twelve weeks old.

The distances they are taken, gradually increase to ten, twenty-five, fifty, and one hundred miles or more in the general direction from which they will later be expected to race. So far they can obviously learn to 'home' from memory. But as they become proficient they can be sent across the sea to France or Spain, too far away to see the landmarks they know, and they will still fly home. Nobody really understands how they do it.

Tumblers or *Rolling Pigeons*. There are several varieties of rolling pigeons, but they all behave in much the same way. When they are flying they turn one or more backward somersaults in mid air. Some of them are 'individual rollers' and others are 'kit rollers'. Competitions are held with 'kit' rollers, usually Birmingham rollers, and a judge goes round to the loft of each competitor to judge the performance of a 'kit' of stipulated size (say eleven, thirteen, or fifteen birds).

These birds are let out of the loft and must fly freely for a minimum period, usually twenty minutes. During this time the judge watches them and awards points for the quality of their rolling. Ideally the whole kit should roll at the same time and marks are deducted if any fail to roll. The somersault should be so 'tight' that the bird appears to be revolving on a florin.

The training of rolling pigeons is similar to that of racing pigeons as regards fitness and exercise, but they are not taken away from their loft for a flight and would be unlikely to return if they were. Care should be taken in allowing them to fly when they are moulting because, when they are sore, they sometimes start to roll and go on rolling till they crash on to the ground, often with fatal results, presumably because it puts too much strain on their tender new feathers to 'brake' hard enough to stop rolling.

There are as many theories why rollers roll as how racing pigeons find their way home, but nobody really knows the answer to either. Some people say rollers suffer from a form of epilepsy and can't help rolling, others that they roll because they like it. To perform properly they need to be as fit as racing pigeons, and they, too, should be exercised before feeding. Some will fly safely with a full crop, but a very fast roller, liberated with a crop full after feeding, may well spin out of control to crash to the ground.

The individual rollers, like Oriental rollers, will sometimes fly higher and roll deeper than kit flyers, but there are no competitive events to prove their skill, so fewer people keep them.

Tipplers. The other variety of performing pigeon is the

tippler. Tippler flying tests the skill of the trainer more, perhaps, than any other form of competitive bird fancying.

The competition consists of liberating a 'kit', of specified size (say three or five birds) in the presence of the judge. They will go straight up to a good altitude where they will fly in circles for the sheer joy of flying. They must be seen at least once every half hour until they descend to the loft and nobody is allowed to do anything to frighten or otherwise discourage them from landing. The kit which stays in the air longest, entirely of its own accord, is the winner.

The skill, therefore, in tippler flying is to get the birds so fit and exuberant that they will fly from choice. When it is realized that in midsummer a good kit will often fly continuously from 4 a.m. to 10 or 11 p.m., sometimes having to be brought down by artificial light, it will be clear that training tipplers is the very pinnacle of the art of producing fit and vigorous livestock.

Reaching that degree of perfection is an art which only advanced pet owners will master. In principle, however, aim to feed them on the most nutritious food possible, producing strength without fat, and to give as much exercise as the birds will take until two or three days before the competition. Then they must be closely confined so that, on the great day, they will be like children escaping from school to holiday.

Accommodation

Tipplers, tumblers, and racing pigeons are best kept in a pigeon loft and only allowed out for exercise, to ge them fit and to show off their prowess.

The loft should be divided into three compartments, two of which should have breeding boxes in the form of divided shelves fronted with wooden bars at inch-and-a-half intervals. In the front of each breeding box should be a door five inches high and four inches wide, hinged at the base, so that it can be shut to imprison a pair of birds in the box, or opened into the horizontal position to form a perch for them to alight on before entering. There should be one nest box for each pair of breeding pigeons, and each nest box should be equipped with two earthenware nesting pans.

In addition to the nesting boxes, which will not be used out of the breeding season, there must be a perch for each bird. These perches can be in the form of a honeycomb of boxes, open at the back and front, mounted on brackets about two inches from the wall. The size of these boxes will vary with the breed of pigeon, but each box should be about three inches from back to front and just large enough to allow the pigeon to stand comfortably. The purpose of mounting them clear of the wall is to avoid a great deal of cleaning and scraping, because most of the dung will fall, at the back or front, directly to the floor.

If the loft is large enough to accommodate all the pigeons roosting at one level, the perches may alternatively be circular wooden discs about three inches in diameter, mounted on wire brackets. They must be so spaced that a pigeon standing on one cannot reach to peck his neighbour, since they are inveterately quarrelsome creatures.

The third common type of perch consists of rows of pegs about five inches long and one inch wide. Sloping boards are nailed to these perches so as to form a porch roof above the lower perch to protect the occupant from droppings.

The height of the loft should be six feet six inches at the front and five feet six inches at the rear; it should be about eight feet wide. The length will depend on the number of birds to be kept, but the whole loft should be mounted on wood or brick piers a clear two feet six inches or three feet from the ground, to give no harbourage to rats.

The most important part of the loft is its front. It should be boarded solid half way up and the top should be barred at one-inch intervals or covered in wire netting of one-inch or inch-and-a-half mesh. For most birds the extra expense of one-inch mesh wire netting is warranted, because it keeps the sparrows and rats out.

There should be a door into each of the three compartments. These compartments should be divided by bar or wire netting partitions and should be connected by communicating doors.

Along the front edge of the roof of the loft there should be a vertical board at least one foot high. The purpose of this is to discourage the birds returning to the loft from alighting on the roof. They must be trained to land on the staging at the front or to go straight into the loft itself. If one is there oneself, they can re-enter through the open door of the compartment in which they are normally confined. But for times when one is not present when the birds return the loft should be provided with a trap. The simplest form of trap consists of an opening along the top of the door about six inches deep. This opening will normally be kept closed by a hinged board the size of the opening. The hinges will be on the lower edge of this board so that it can be dropped into a horizontal position, forming a platform.

Pieces of galvanized fencing wire, three-sixteenths of an inch gauge, will be bent in the form of large staples an inch-and-a-half wide and seven inches long. These will be hung loosely on wire-netting staples so that they hang in a row all along the inside of the opening at the top of the door. Since they are seven inches long and the opening only six inches deep, it is obvious that they will overlap on the inside and, being loosely hung, they will open inwards but not outwards. A bird landing on the platform will soon learn to put his head through the bars, which hinge inwards with his weight and allow him to drop down on to the floor of the loft. As they will not open outwards, and there is no platform near them on the inside, the pigeons will be unable to escape the same way.

Exercising Performing Varieties
To get the performing varieties fit, they must have regular and vigorous exercise.

They will normally be allowed out twice a day, before their morning meal and before their evening meal. If they are fit, they will be keen to get into the air and, when they have had their exercise, they will be hungry and go straight through the trap back in to the loft where their food will be waiting. They should normally be given just as much food as they will clear up in ten or fifteen minutes.

If performing pigeons are allowed full liberty they tend to sit about on the rooftops and take far less exercise than if only liberated specifically to fly.

Their chief advantage, from their owners' viewpoint, is that it is possible to keep them in a cat-ridden area, have the pleasure of seeing them fly free and the satisfaction of getting them into good enough condition and training to do well in competition, and still have them shut safely in their loft when nobody is available to guard them from danger.

Fancy Pigeons

One major advantage of 'performing' over other 'fancy' pigeons is that the performing varieties need only a relatively small loft, and yet the thrill of their prowess can be enjoyed without nuisance to others or danger to themselves, since they will be either in the air or safely shut up in their pen.

There are, in addition, an almost infinite variety of fancy pigeons of every imaginable shape and size and colour.

Some of these, show fantails, the feather-legged varieties like fairy swallows, and any of the very valuable exhibition birds are really safe only in an aviary.

Pigeon Aviary

The aviary should consist of a loft as described for performing pigeons. But, instead of having a trap to imprison the birds when they land, the loft should open on to a wire-netting flight also divided into two compartments. Thus two of the loft compartments will open into separate flights, and there will be a third loft compartment which is not attached to an aviary flight. The purpose of this is to be able to separate cocks from hens or young from old, as will be explained in the following section.

The flights should be at least six feet high and as long and wide as possible. The floor should be concrete, which can be hosed, or loose gravel, which the rain will keep fairly clean, but can, in any case, be changed as necessary to avoid the ground becoming stale. If possible, a small patch of turf should be laid in a position with no perches above it, and also replaced as necessary. Flat perches should be supplied similar to the ones in the loft.

Establishing Fresh Pigeons

If you already own pigeons which are accustomed to your loft, it is fairly easy to persuade newcomers to settle down.

Keep the fresh birds confined to the loft for a week if they are young birds, and two to three weeks if they are adults. Make sure that the perches are so fixed that the birds can see out of the loft and get to know by sight as much of their new surroundings as possible. Provided the existing birds come in through a trap and cannot get out again, it will only be necessary to catch the newcomers while the others are let out for exercise. (There will, of course, be no problem of establishing birds to be kept in an aviary.)

When the newcomers are thoroughly used to their new quarters withhold their food for one complete day, so that they will be very hungry by next morning. Let them out with the others while their appetite is keen, and there should be no difficulty at all about getting them in. See that they are fairly hungry when liberated for the next few days and, after that, they should give no further trouble. Let them strut around the pen. Avoid frightening them into flight, but allow them to explore further afield gradually.

Racing pigeons have an exceptionally strong homing instinct and are often extremely difficult to establish in a new loft. If they are kept in until the breeding season, allowed to hatch eggs and feed young, it should be perfectly safe to let them out and, by the time they finish feeding one pair of young, they will be incubating the next pair of eggs and be most unlikely to try to find their way to their old home.

If you do not own pigeons already with which newcomers will soon learn to stay, either start with young birds which have not been let out of their own loft, or old birds which must, if at all possible, be kept in until they are feeding young.

Management in Loft
Since pigeons are so prolific, they will breed almost all the year round, if allowed, and become very debilitated in the process.

To control this, the loft is divided into three sections. One has no nest boxes, and young birds are put here as soon as they learn to pick up food for themselves, to prevent them from importuning their parents.

The other two sections contain nest boxes and roosting perches. Out of breeding season, from September to February, the cocks are all put in one section, the hens in the other, and the nest boxes are shut up.

Breeding
The traditional day for 'pairing up' is 14 February, St. Valentine's Day.

Choose the matings you want very carefully, and shut the

108

cock and hen of your choice in a nest box for a week or ten days. Feed and water regularly and be certain the box is light enough for them to see to feed. The earthenware nest bowl should have been scrubbed out and half filled with sawdust.

When the pairs have settled down, they may be given the freedom of the loft again and it will be found that they will stick to their own nest boxes and be faithful to their own mates.

Pigeons lay two eggs and take it in turns to incubate. The cock sits most of the day-time and the hen at night. If, as is advisable, you have arranged all your pigeons as mated pairs, you will find all the cocks sitting for part of the twenty-four hours and all the hens the remainder. There will thus be little opportunity for either to philander while their mates are busy sitting on a clutch of eggs.

When the young hatch, they are naked, weak, and blind, and both their parents feed them by regurgitating predigested food, called 'pigeon's milk', directly into the mouth of the young. Before the young have fledged, their parents will be sitting on another pair of eggs in the spare nest pan, with which the nest box should be furnished. The original pair of young will be 'weaned' and able to pick up food for themselves before the next pair hatches. (The incubation period is eighteen days.) As soon as they are weaned, they should be put in the third compartment of the loft reserved for young birds, and given as much food and water as they want instead of two ten-minute periods to cram in a day's supply.

Feeding

During the breeding season, the old birds also need feeding with as much best-quality pigeon corn as they want. There must always be fresh water in a special pigeon fountain, which prevents them fouling it or bathing in it, and a plentiful supply both of lime and flint grit. Some grit manufacturers also supply a pack of mixed minerals, of which the birds are very fond, and though not a necessity, it is a luxury they appreciate. Another item of food which pigeons love is rock-salt. If a good lump is put on a saucer in the pen, it will be greatly appreciated.

If the birds have no access to green-stuff, a little fodder

beet, lettuce, or similar green food should be provided. This will be taken more as a tonic than a serious contribution to diet.

Baths
Pigeons delight in bathing and should have a bath at least twice a week. An old earthenware sink about four inches deep does very well, or any shallow bowl with a flat bottom. It is best to put the bath outside the loft and allow the birds to bathe after they have had their exercise, before shutting them in the loft to feed. If, as sometimes happens, the birds become infected with red mite, an infusion of boiled quassia chips put in the bath will quickly cure them. Quassia chips are extremely bitter, and the mites appear to find them quite intolerable.

Pigeons at Liberty
The main reason why most of the ornamental varieties cannot be kept at liberty is because of the danger from predatory cats and dogs and, in wooded country, sparrow hawks. In residential areas where neighbours are keen gardeners, some trouble may be experienced if one's birds occasionally plunder the local gardens.

If you are lucky enough to have a relatively cat-free garden and no very keen gardeners too near, it may be possible to keep your pets in a dovecote. You will have to forego the advantages of keeping cocks and hens separately to prevent them breeding, but the same end may be achieved by removing the eggs as fast as they lay them, or puncturing them with a needle as soon as laid, so that the birds incubate, but never hatch them. Cross-breeding can be prevented by keeping pairs shut together until they mate and only introducing mated pairs to the dovecote.

It will be wise to feed mainly pigeon peas and beans (which are too large to be taken by sparrows) and to feed plentifully. Fat and replete pigeons will do very little damage in the garden.

The Dovecote
A great many ornamental dovecotes harmonize well with a flower garden. The dovecote itself is really nothing more than the suite of breeding boxes from the pigeon loft. Since

the birds get all the exercise they want, the dovecote should be as small as is convenient. For country gardens, a large barrel may be divided into three or four tiers. Each tier may be further divided with vertical partitions into two or three nest boxes, and each nest box must have an entrance hole about four inches square with a ledge on the outside for the birds to alight on. A metal roof formed into a cone like a dunce's cap will keep the weather out, or thatch may be fixed to a conical 'roof' made of heavy-gauge wire netting. Doors must be so fixed that the dovecote is easy to clean out, though this should only be necessary at comparatively infrequent intervals, and each nesting compartment should be furnished with earthenware nest pans, as for the loft.

For a more formal garden, a carpenter-made dovecote, either purely functional or in the likeness of a human habitation, may be thought more suitable.

The normal position for the dovecote, certainly the barrel-shaped type, will be at the top of a pole. The pole will need to be sunk in the ground for about one-third of its length, and the bottom of the cote should be eight feet from the ground, to give protection from cats. Other types of dovecote are fixed to walls of houses and outbuildings, or it may be possible to fit a suite of nest boxes inside a loft or barn and allow entry through holes cut in the brickwork.

I have had trouble with a barrel-type unit because jackdaws used to raid the eggs and quite large young. I found the only cure was to move the cote within gunshot range of my bedroom window, after which the surviving jackdaw found less perilous plunder elsewhere.

Canaries

The first cage bird I ever owned was a Roller canary, which lived for eleven years in a large box cage at right angles to the window, where he could get plenty of fresh air, exercise, and a choice of light and shade, since the corner nearest the window never caught the sun. He was so tame that we used to let him loose in the room for hours at a time, but he was always ready to jump on an outstretched finger and be returned to his cage with no fuss at all.

There is a very large variety of canary breeds including Belgian, Border, Crested Norwich, Dutch Frill, Gloster,

Lancashire Coppy, Lizard, Norwich, Plainhead, Roller, and Yorkshire. All will do well in either cage or aviary and, since they are not aggressive, they can be kept in a mixed collection of small seedeaters or in a colony of canaries.

Some of the show varieties rely for their success in exhibitions upon their colour. Special 'colour food' can be bought which contains tasteless pepper, but it should be used only under the guidance of an expert.

The main singing breed is the Roller, which has perhaps the sweetest song of any cage bird. It is soft and subdued, but covers an immense repertoire. Roller canaries are specifically trained to sing the correct song by letting them hear only a 'schoolmaster' when they are young. This schoolmaster is a mature bird which has a song as near perfect as possible. Attempts have been made to get the perfect song by making tape recordings of a number of prize-winning birds and then joining only the best passages of each. But Nature can still out-do science and the arts. The very best tape recording will not train young birds so well as a mediocre schoolmaster.

Roller canaries are such good mimics that they will copy other aviary birds and spoil their own song, so, if you want them to sing, they are the only breed of canary not suitable for life in a mixed aviary.

Feeding

Out of the breeding season, canaries should be fed on canary seed, rape, hemp, and pin-head oatmeal, with a little bread and milk. They should also have apples, groundsel, carrot, and dandelion. They can eat as much pin-head oatmeal and rape as they will, but only about a teaspoonful of canary seed a day.

To keep really fit, canaries should have egg food in addition to a diet of seeds. Hard boil an egg and remove the white. Crush and crumble the yolk with six arrowroot biscuits, and allow a half a teaspoonful for each bird on alternate days.

If the birds are a little out of condition, increase the egg, plus a little fat in the shape of suet, and notice the quality of the motions. If they are constipated, increase green-stuff, adding shepherd's purse and groundsel; if loose, more canary seed and rape in their food will help.

Top: 8. Sulphur-crested cockatoo. Cockatoos and parrots are long-lived, hardy and make excellent pets

Bottom: 9. Bantams are among the few pets which pay for their keep! Half-a-dozen bantam hens in the garden or orchard will provide delicious free range eggs for the whole family

10. Stick insects will eat common privet, breed freely and can be kept in the living-room of a flat

Never allow stale food to accumulate. Try to feed in amounts the birds will just clear up. Any surplus should be put on the bird table in the garden, where it will be greatly appreciated.

Breeding

The birds may be paired up on St. Valentine's Day in the south and two or three weeks later up north. There will be plenty of time to take three nests from birds paired in mid March, and it is unwise to take more than three clutches, so there is no real point in subjecting the young birds to cold weather by hatching too early. Late-bred youngsters are never as robust as their older brothers, while the extra brood takes far more out of the old birds than the brood is worth.

Canaries will breed as a pair, or one cock will mate two or three hens. A double breeding cage should be used for the introductions. This is simply a box cage, twice normal length, with a wire partition which can be slid out when the birds have obviously taken a fancy to each other.

Introduce a nest pan when they have settled down and fasten it to the back of the cage adjacent to a perch so that, in due course, the old birds can stand on the perch and feed the young in the nest. The first egg will appear in about two weeks and subsequent eggs will be laid on alternate days. Some fanciers replace the first eggs by dummies until the clutch is complete, in the belief that all the young will then hatch together. Wild birds do not do this, yet rear their young successfully.

The earthenware nest pan will be fitted with a felt liner, but the birds stimulate each other more effectively if allowed cow-hair or similar non-absorbent nesting material. If not absorbent, the nest should be well ventilated or it will be easily fouled.

If the weather is very dry, the membrane beneath the shell may become so hard and tough that the young bird cannot chip out. To prevent this, the eggs should be sprinkled with tepid water for a few days before they are due to hatch.

Rearing Young

In fourteen days, the eggs will hatch. The hen should, by now, be accustomed to the egg food and milksop she will

113

feed to the young, but, for the first few days, she is likely to kill them by kindness and overfeed a little. A mid-day feed of milksop will take the edge off the rich egg food and the seed should be restricted to canary seed and rape. Conversely, some hens are slow to learn to feed, and the young will need some supplementary hand-feeding to get them going. A sort of glass syringe is specially made for hand-rearing small birds and it is most effective; it will be found in good pet shops. But do not begin hand-feeding, even as a supplement, unless absolutely necessary.

Many nursing hens love flowering chickweed and almost all take soaked seed avidly. Teazle and rape should be soaked for twenty-four hours, rinsed under a running tap, and dried off in a cloth. This is as nutritious and easily digested as any food you can give.

If the hen feeds too much hard seed for the young to digest, they will sometimes contract diarrhoea, which will coat the hen and themselves. (Normal excreta comes away in a sac, and the old bird carries it away from the nest.) To avoid diarrhoea, do not feed over-rich food at first, grind egg food to a fine paste and see that soaked seed really is soaked and then dried off.

Seed merchants sell ready-mixed (and ground) rearing foods and these are by far the safest for the novice to use. Every fancier has his own recipe and, with experience, most pet owners experiment until they eventually devise a mixture which they firmly believe to be better than all the rest. But the merchants make their living by selling a simple mixture which really works.

Weaning
At twenty-one days the young will leave the nest, and should be confined to the other half of the breeding cage by replacing the division. The old birds will feed them between the bars, while the young can be encouraged to begin foraging for themselves. As soon as they are self-sufficient they can be removed from this cage entirely, but it is most important to be sure that they are feeding themselves properly when away from the old birds. If they are not, they should be put back into their half of the divided cage for a day or two longer.

Some old canaries will feather their own young if left in

the same cage after they leave the nest, so the device of separating them by bars is necessary and practical.

Young birds need nutritious food, consisting of egg and breadcrumbs or biscuit, dried milk or milksop, green food, and soaked seed. It is impossible to be too scrupulous about cleanliness, as sour food will produce loose motions.

While they are growing, they should have as large a flight as possible and maximum fresh air and sunshine. They can be gradually weaned on to their adult diet by the time they go into their autumn moult.

Young and old need grit and will appreciate a piece of cuttlefish bone gripped between the bars of the cage.

Other Simple Foreign Birds

Acclimatization

Most commonly kept foreign birds come from warmer climates than ours, and it is wise to deal only with reputable dealers or breeders and to ask, quite definitely, whether the prospective purchase is acclimatized. You will have to pay a bit more if it is, but at least your new pet will be less likely to die of pneumonia. On no account buy an unacclimatized bird to start with.

When you have more experience, there is no great difficulty in acclimatizing most foreign birds. If they come from warmer climates, as they mainly do, they should be kept initially at a temperature of not less than 65°–70°F., controlled by a thermostat. This means using some well-lighted but small draughtproof room. The temperature can be reduced gradually, about 5°F. per week, down to room temperature. It should never be allowed to fall below 45°F. Obviously, it is wise to buy birds from abroad in spring so that they have the summer to get used to our climate. The worst possible time to buy would be the month or so before Christmas. A bird feeling the cold fluffs out its feathers. If your birds are sleek and tight-feathered they are all right.

During acclimatization, a wide range of food should be offered, including small cubes of bread and milk, replaced daily.

General Management

Many birds are bullies, so try to keep any collection as

much of a size as possible and remove any birds that show aggressive traits to a cage on their own.

Some species, like weavers, will live most happily in a colony, but others need a separate territory for each pair and will fight, often to the death, with others of their own species. On the other hand, they will be quite amicable with birds of other species which do not compete for food or nesting sites.

Some birds pair for life; some experience just a passing fancy which does not even last until the arrival of the family; others pair for the season and spend the rest of the year with birds of their own sex. There are literally hundreds of foreign birds available so that is is quite impossible to generalize.

As a guide, a sample list with treatment of the commoner ones follows:

Sample List of Foreign Birds

Doves. Only one pair of doves (Diamond doves, Senegal, Barbary, Tambourine, etc.) should be put into a collection. They need coarse sand, oyster-shell grit, millet (white and yellow), and canary seed. They mix well with other birds but fight amongst themselves—whoever described doves as being gentle had not tried keeping a number. They are particularly fond of bathing.

Finches and Sparrows. A wide variety of finches are imported and they can be kept together satisfactorily provided they are grouped according to size and their aviary is as large as possible, with plenty of cover and alternative nesting sites. The common varieties include cut-throats, firefinches, Gouldian, grassfinches, singing finches, Java sparrows, and diamond sparrows. These are good mixers. They need canary seed, the millet prescribed for doves, and, in addition, live food to rear young. Meal-worms, pricked gentles (gentles are very indigestible if the skin is not punctured), and ant cocoons are also necessary.

Waxbills. These are beautiful birds, and some sing sweetly. They need the same food as the finches and sparrows above, but like, in addition to seed, as much live food as possible.

Weavers. Some of the most attractive and interesting of all foreign birds, these are very hardy and will spend much

116

of their time weaving elaborate nests, although they rarely use them for breeding purposes in this country. Some weavers are rather quarrelsome, so beware their behaviour with other birds. In addition to canary seed and Indian millet, they should be fed spray millet.

Whydahs. Some of the whydahs are very beautiful. They are active birds, at their best in a large aviary. Treat them in the same was as weavers.

Cardinals. These are big flamboyant birds. They are not good for group collections which contain any of the foregoing smaller species except, perhaps, the larger doves and some of the weavers and whydahs. Any of the latter proving quarrelsome with smaller birds can be tried with cardinals, though a careful watch must be kept. They need canary seed, millet, and hemp, and are passionately fond of any live food that comes their way, as well as having a taste for green-stuff.

Quails. My favourite quail is the Chinese painted quail, a tiny bird like a miniature partridge. The quails are all ground birds, living and nesting on the ground. They breed quite freely and the young are active at once, running about like bumble-bees in search of food. They eat white and Indian millet, canary seed, and seeding grasses, which they love. Clumps of seeding grass should be put in the aviary and replaced as necessary. They need a pan of dry sand to dust bath and a plentiful supply of grit.

7 Advanced Birds

Advanced Birds

There are two main factors which make it more difficult to keep some species of bird in captivity than others. For example, I am including in this chapter those birds whose food is more difficult to obtain, or less easy to store than the commercially packeted grain which suffices for the simpler birds. Some birds need a constant supply of fresh fruit or live insects or even nectar, and it would be quite disastrous if their supply failed for a day. Then too, a great many birds which are commonly kept as pets will not stand our climate and require a temperature which never drops below their safe minimum, even in the hardest winter.

In addition there are some of the smaller insectivorous and nectar-feeding birds which have but a short life span at best, and even for that brief spell are as delicate as butterflies.

The variety of species obtainable from pet shops and livestock dealers runs into many hundreds, so that it is obviously not possible to deal with them individually, especially as any one species may only be available at irregular intervals. Before embarking on any of the more exotic and difficult birds, it is wise to get as much experience as possible with the commoner, cheaper varieties.

Foreign Softbills

For general notes on feeding softbills see pp. **128–9**.

Temperature

There are so many softbills, from such diverse parts of the world that it is not possible to generalize. Really delicate birds, like humming birds—which also require nectar in special containers—will only do well kept at tropical temperature, preferably at liberty in a tropical greenhouse kept to a temperature of 70°F. to 75°F. Under these conditions they look magnificent as they flit about and hover before their nectar pots like exotic tropical butterflies. But the fact that a bird comes from the tropics does not necessarily mean that it need be kept at a thermostatically controlled high temperature. Although tropical days may be hot, the nights are often extremely cold, and some birds sink to a state of torpidity, something like a short hibernation. In any case nature has provided in birds' feathers a most effective means of dealing with wide temperature variation. When it is hot they are compressed and sleek, reflecting much of the sun's direct rays. When it is cold, feathers are fluffed up like layer upon layer of super-efficient string vests.

Whatever bird you keep, tropical or temperate, it is always a safe rule to see that their sleeping quarters are above freezing point to avoid any chance of frostbite or feet frozen to perches.

Mynahs
The one snag with softbills, especially birds of fair size, like the mynahs, is that their diet produces loose motions and they are rather messy to keep in the living-room. It is a great pity because the hill mynah is perhaps the best mimic of all and often out-talks the best parrots. They are also active birds; the hill mynah needs a cage at least four feet long.

Shamas
Amongst the loveliest songsters in the world are the shamas from the Malay Peninsula and India. They are striking-looking birds with very long tails, white rumps, chesnut breasts, and glossy backs.

They are not particularly fond of fruit but will do well on insectile food, scraped carrot and minced lettuce, and live meal-worms and gentles.

They must have facilities for a daily bath and must not be kept in a temperature of less than about 55°F. Being quarrelsome they should be kept alone or with birds of their own size in a large aviary.

Fruitsuckers
These birds will live either on fresh ripe fruit (grapes, oranges, etc.) and insectile food, or a mixed diet containing

119

nectar.

The preparation of this liquid diet is as follows: Mix equal quantities of baby food, condensed milk, and honey to a smooth paste. Dilute with hot water to a smooth thin syrup, and feed, when cool, in deep narrow glazed vessels, large enough for the birds to get at the nectar but small enough, in diameter, to minimize the chances of getting their feathers sticky.

Bulbuls

These sturdy birds live well on a normal softbill diet. See that they do not fight and bully other birds—including their own species. It seems that individual birds vary immensely in aggressive habits and one good, quiet bulbul is worth a cageful of quarrelsome ones.

Parrots and Parrot-like Birds

Parrots

One of my first memories as a child is an ageless little woman, with a grey complexion, grey hair and eyes—and a grey parrot. The only touches of colour were in the bird's scarlet tail, white face, and wise yellow eyes. They seemed a perfect match for they were quite inseparable. The bird spent most of the day perched on his mistress's shoulder, where he would sit by the hour lovingly preening her hair. I confidently believed that they were both one hundred years old.

Looking back, I can see that I over-estimated. But parrots do live to a great age, and forty or fifty years is not uncommon.

Properly tamed and trained, they make delightful pets. They crave company more than freedom and it is kinder to have a parrot in a small cage in the bar parlour of a busy pub than in a huge aviary where it never sees people.

The best of all talking parrots is the African grey, the one that was constant companion to the old lady of my childhood. It comes from equatorial Africa and is a naturally friendly and docile bird. There are a large number of other breeds of parrot, some like Amazons, extremely beautiful. Generally speaking, the grey is the best talker of all, but odd specimens of the more exotically coloured can make most attractive pets as well.

At one time parrots were freely imported, until it was discovered that some birds carried a disease which is transmissible—and sometimes fatal—to man. It is said that many young wild parrots contract this disease, overcome it, and are subsequently immune. Those which were caught and exported at the critical stage were highly dangerous, and so a ban has been put upon the import of parrots. For this reason it is no longer normally possible to buy young untrained parrots. (A young bird may be distinguished by the different colour of its eyes. In the grey, for example, the eyes of young birds are dark but they turn a lovely clear yellow in the adults.)

Before the ban, it was reasonable to buy a young bird fairly cheaply with the intention of teaching it to talk. By the same token, an old bird that would not talk was not a very encouraging investment. Now that there are virtually no young birds for sale, it is sensible to hear the prospective pet's abilities demonstrated before you part with your money. If the parrot will not talk, it may still prove good value for money, though obviously the purchaser will have some initiative in deciding the price.

Talking

Nothing will make a parrot talk. But a parrot which has remained obstinately silent for a couple of years—so far as intelligible sound is concerned—may quite easily begin talking for no apparent reason.

Certain conditions are necessary, however, before success is likely. The bird must be thoroughly settled and tame and comfortable. It must have reasonable sympathy with the people about the house and see as much of them as possible. Nothing is more miserable than a lonely parrot.

Having said that, the rest is largely a matter of patience. Every time you come into the room repeat a simple phrase like 'Good morning, Polly'. Every time you feed the parrot use a set phrase. When leaving it for the night, always use a phrase that becomes a habit.

If there is no success from this, try letting the bird hear as wide a variety of sounds as possible in the hope that one will fire its instinct to mimic. One bird I knew could do a perfect imitation of a lavatory flushing, another imitated the fantail pigeons on the lawn, and a favourite sound for most parrots is a cork exploding from a bottle. Once the urge to imitate has been aroused, there is every chance that the bird will go on and widen its vocabulary to include human words. Indeed, some of the very best parrots do not learn phrases and then repeat them for the rest of their lives; they pick up a constantly changing vocabulary, each new acquisition appearing to blot out a previous one. If you get a bird like this you are lucky indeed. He will be an ever-changing source of amusement for years, instead of a rather boring repetitive old man.

But however long it takes to persuade a parrot to talk (and adult-caught birds hardly ever do talk) there is nothing for it but patience.

Sexing
I have referred to the talking parrot as 'he', whereas, in fact, most captive grey parrots are hens. They are, in any case, difficult to sex, though when a pair are together, it can usually be seen that the male is a little more heavily boned, and his head is just slightly more flat-topped and square, as with pigeons.

Breeding
True pairs have bred successfully in aviaries (having a minimum of wood to be pared and heavy-gauge netting). They need a large hollow pillar, like a pillar-box or grandfather clock, with a hole at the top for entry, and chippings of wood at the base inside on which the eggs can be laid. When they are paired, their display of affection takes the rather unusual form of regurgitation of food for their partner's delight. A very tame bird who has no mate sometimes lavishes this affection on its owner who may well be disconcerted, but should not be worried. It is a token of affection, not a symptom of illness!

Cockatoos
There is a wide variety of cockatoos from the continent of Australia, some of which will talk, though very rarely as well as an even moderately good parrot.

They are beautiful crested birds, extremely amenable to aviary life, where they breed freely, though they must not be mixed with smaller birds except after closely supervised experimentation.

The snag with cockatoos is that they tend to be frightfully noisy and will screech and scream incessantly when in the mood, so that they cannot normally be kept in the house and will annoy the neighbours outside unless you live in an unusually isolated position.

Macaws

The largest of the parrot family, some macaws attain a length of as much as thirty-six inches. They are brilliantly coloured, immensely powerful birds which, like parrots, live to a great age in captivity. Like cockatoos, they are excessively noisy and therefore unsuitable pets for a great many people.

If they are to be kept, they should either be housed in a large aviary constructed of heavy-gauge netting fixed to metal posts, or kept on a stand with a chain. Many macaws become so fond of their stand, after a time regarding it as their own territory, that the chain may be dispensed with without much risk of their straying.

The one thing to guard against, in this case, is sudden fright. Should anything really startle the bird into taking to the wing as a reflex action, it is likely to land in the top of the nearest tall tree where persuading it to leave may well be very difficult. Macaws in aviaries become very powerful on the wing and there is nothing more beautiful than these great gaudy birds in flight.

Feeding Parrots, Cockatoos and Macaws

Ready-mixed parrot food can be bought in packets, and the reputable firms put out a good balanced diet that will keep the bird in perfectly sound health. At the same time, your bird will probably enjoy variety, especially additions of sunflower and canary seed. Peanuts and hemp and millet may also be offered as additions, or it is a good plan to watch which seeds the bird tackles first in his mixture, and increase the proportion of these.

In addition to packeted food, fresh fruit is essential. Nearly all the parrot tribe love bananas and dates; most like apples and oranges; and quite a lot are fond of lettuce and watercress, fresh garden peas, beans or sprouts.

123

Fresh branches—or stout twigs—of apple or other non-poisonous trees such as beech, ash, willow, sycamore, or nut are very important indeed. They prevent boredom by providing something to be whittled away, and the sap and young wood seem beneficial to the birds as well. In addition to this, grit and cuttlefish bone are very helpful to general health. If the bird is off colour, soft food, consisting of boiled pearl barley or maize, may be greatly appreciated.

Give fresh drinking water at all times.

Baths

Unlike most birds a parrot will not normally avail himself of either a dust bath or a bowl of water.

In his native climate there is enough tropical rain to answer the purpose, and most parrot-like birds love to be out in a summer shower. They will spread their wings to catch every drop and often hang upside down to let the water trickle down between the feathers.

In captivity the same effect can be secured either by putting the cage or stand out in warm rain or by spraying the bird with a syringe, which most of them will revel in.

Many parrots will only preen themselves when their feathers are thoroughly wetted. Preening stimulates a supply of oil, from the oil gland, which is necessary to keep the feathers in good condition. A lot of miserable, bald, feather-plucked parrots, whose remaining quills are dry and shabby, could have remained in excellent condition if only their instinct to preen had been stimulated by spraying with slightly tepid water.

Under normal circumstances it is important to house parrots out of draught. When wet from their spray, it is vital.

Cockatiels, Parrakeets and Lovebirds

These are the smaller members of the parrot family and really all do better in aviaries than in cages. They are noisy but beautiful, especially in flight, and breed well in aviaries. They tend to be quarrelsome, and two males should not be kept in one aviary if any females are present, though bachelor parties of males do all right. Indeed, it is unwise to keep two male parrakeets in adjacent aviaries as they will often bite each others toes off through the netting.

Cockatiels are far gentler and are such free breeders that

it is necessary to remove the nest boxes out of season to give them a rest and prevent them debilitating themselves. They are not usually aggressive with birds other than their own species.

This group should be fed on canary seed, millet, hemp, sunflower seed, millet spray, seeding grass, and green food.

8 British Birds

There is a great deal to be said for keeping many of our British birds. Their song is as sweet as any in the world; some are as beautiful as the most exotic foreigners; many are particularly confiding and easy to tame; and they naturally accept our climate. Finally, many of them settle to cage life as easily, it seems, as they do to an aviary.

British birds are physically easy to keep in good health, but many of them are, rightly, protected by law, so that it is illegal to possess most species unless they are 'close-rung'.

In theory, this means that they must have been bred in captivity and have had placed on their legs a numbered metal ring which will not pass over their feet after they are a few days old. Certainly it would be practically impossible to 'ring' an adult-caught bird in this fashion. But when I was a boy it was common practice to place a wire-mesh riddle over a brood of larks just before they fledged, and the parents would loyally continue to feed them through the wire mesh until they were properly weaned. So close-ringing gives only partial protection, since it would obviously be possible to ring a brood of wild birds at the correct age and catch them a little later.

The real protection that British birds have acquired is fashion (because it is now considered despicable to capture them) and availability. So many are genuinely bred in captivity that it is less trouble to obtain one legitimately than to go to all the trouble of finding and ringing and catching a wild brood.

So before you keep a native bird in captivity make certain it is close-rung or that it is not covered by the protected list. The exceptions to this list are mainly birds which can be proved to be harmful, birds such as carrion crows or house sparrows. As the exceptions are varied from time to time it is wise to check with the police before keeping a bird which is not close-rung.

Hardbills

Chaffinch, greenfinch, goldfinch, linnet, brambling (or bramble-finch, a winter visitor), redpoll, twite (or mountain linnet), bullfinch, siskin, and hawfinch.

As with foreign birds, the simplest British birds to keep are those feeding on seed, which is easily obtained and stored.

The British finches take very readily to cage life and will breed in either a cage or an aviary so long as their diet is satisfactory and they are undisturbed by other birds or by people. Give as generous a sized cage as possible with plenty of light and air but no draught.

It is essential that all British finches have plenty of water available for bathing as well as drinking, though in hot dry weather they will sometimes take dust baths as well.

Diet

The main ingredient of the seed mixture should be canary seed, which should form half the bulk of the mixture. To this should be added almost as wide a variety of other seed as is obtainable. Rape, teazle, linseed, sunflower seed, groats, dari, hemp, and maw are all easy to get commercially and should be mixed in about equal parts to form the other half of the mixture. Appetites and preferences of individual birds vary, and you will notice when you clean the seed pots which varieties of seed tend to be left untouched. Omit these from the mixture for a while, but do not jump to the conclusion that other birds of the same species will necessarily follow the same pattern of likes and dislikes. Indeed, your own birds may well develop other tastes in a few weeks' time.

In addition to bought seed, British hardbills are passionately fond of fresh wild seed. Shepherd's purse, dandelion, groundsel, chickweed, dock and various ripe fruits and berries will be taken avidly by most. Goldfinches, the loveliest of all the finches, feed in the wild state on ripe thistle seeds, and a pet goldfinch on a thistle in an aviary is as lovely as a 'charm' of his wild brothers and sisters in the fields. Many of our native birds like watercress and lettuce or dandelion leaves as well. Perhaps the best free food of all is the weed seed thrown out as waste on every farm when they are threshing the corn. A pile of all kinds of seeds grows under the threshing drum, and many fanciers kept their birds in quite good shape on these seeds during the war, when it was impossible to buy foreign seed for domestic pets. There is just one word of warning though. Make certain from the farmer—who will usually be only too glad to give the stuff away—that the weed seeds have not been subjected to any poisonous spray. It is not very likely that they have, since the same spray might have contaminated the corn as well, but it *always* worth checking. Nearly all British finches enjoy a little live food—gentles or meal-worms or flies—all the year round. When they are rearing young, it is essential that they have access to the sort of diet that a softbill would need. Buntings—of which the yellow bunting or yellow-hammer is the commonest—do well on finch diet with the addition of rather more insectile food.

Softbills

Birds which are insectivorous or fruit-eaters do not need powerful nutcracker bills like seed-eaters (which have to crack off the husk to reach the kernel), and are therefore referred to as softbills. Indeed, many of them, like tits and wrens, have weak sharp-pointed little beaks, specially evolved for pulling insects from crevices, or, like thrushes and blackbirds, worms from their holes. In general, softbills are more difficult to breed than seed-eating species, largely because of the enormous quantity of small food the young require.

Feeding

The keeping of softbills has been greatly simplified by the sale of ready-mixed insectile foods by all good pet shops. This food consists of a high-protein mixture containing a proportion of prepared insects and, although not sufficient in itself, it does form a very good basis which has brought this class of bird within the scope of pet-keepers as opposed to highly specialist bird-fanciers, who were prepared to catch or breed food for their pets. In additon to the insectile food from the packet, insectivorous birds will need some

128

live food as well. Meal-worms can be bought by the pound and stored in tins of bran. The tins must have perforated tops, to allow breathing, but I would emphasize the necessity of keeping the holes very small, as the meal-worms can escape through an astonishingly tiny hole. I cut quite large holes in my tin lids (about 3 in. square) and solder on fine wire gauze as supplied to garages for petrol filters. Nearly all birds are passionately fond of meal-worms, but they are very rich and should only be used as an adjunct to the proprietory food. About six live meal-worms a day will be enough for a bird the size of a robin. Excess meal-worms will give rise to liver complaints. Gentles, the larvae of bluebottles, are obtainable from shops dealing in fishing tackle. They are stored chilled, as they pupate and hatch into bluebottles in warmth, so it is wise to buy small quantities as often as possible. For delicate or young birds, I find it better to puncture the gentles before feeding to the birds, as their skin is very tough and indigestible. Common house-flies are admirable food, if you have patience to catch them, but it is *most* important to be certain they have not been contaminated by insecticide sprays, some of which are almost as dangerous to birds and man as they are to insects. Ant cocoons are excellent. They can be purchased from pet shops, where they are usually described as ants' 'eggs' and are sold dried. These are not so nutritious as cocoons taken fresh from the nest and, if you are in country which has a lot of anthills or wood-ant nests, it is well worth collecting a bucketful occasionally and keeping the soil, cocoons, and live ants until required in a large tin ventilated with metal gauze, as described for keeping meal-worms. The live ants will be eaten as greedily as the cocoons.

One point that is most important with all softbills and the thrush family in particular: because of their diet, their motions are rather free. It is vital to have a generous layer of sand on the floor of their cage and to keep all perches scrupulously clean. Otherwise, their feet will first of all get sticky, and then unbearably sore. Partly for the same reason, adequate bathing facilities are quite indispensable.

Thrushes
The Song Thrush. When I was a boy, there was scarcely a miner's house in the village where we lived that did not have

a cage on the wall containing a thrush. The birds cost nothing, for they were caught as fledgelings. When they grew up they were, if hens, liberated and probably died of starvation before they learned to fend for themselves; if they were cocks, they had no trouble about food for the rest of their lives, and enriched the murky air, in exchange, with lilting song that dispelled the gloom. Nobody bothers to catch thrushes nowadays (throstles we called them). They are too easy to breed in captivity. When reared, they are easy to feed too. Good insectile food should be the basis, with the addition of scalded biscuit meal, fed crumbly dry, to which meat meal has been added, plenty of live food, not only gentles and meal-worms, but also snails, worms, and caterpillars, and fresh fruit in season. Every long-suffering gardener will surely know to his cost how much thrushes and blackbirds love currants and raspberries and strawberries. And although gardeners grumble at the depredations, I for would much rather have no strawberries in my garden than no song of blackbirds and thrushes.

The Mistle-Thrush. The mistle-thrush is the largest of the thrush family in this country and it also sings the loudest, if not the sweetest. In my part of the Midlands it is often called the thrice-cock or storm-cock, from the rhythm and timing of its song, and it is one of the earliest birds to nest in my garden, rearing three broods nearly every year in a tree by the pool beside the house. A friend of mine had a mistle-thrush for years which he had reared by hand from a fledgeling, and it was one of the most attractive pets I ever saw. Completely fearless—it suffered under the delusion that his outstretched hand was an amorous hen mistle-thrush—it acquired such a fixation on its master that other birds were of no more importance to it than inanimate objects. It sang by his window from morning till night and became so tame that a cage was no longer necessary and it wandered at liberty in the garden, coming 'home' to its cage only when it was hungry.

For food and conditions it was only necessary to treat it as a song thrush with a larger appetite and a need for slightly more living space.

Blackbird

The blackbird should be treated in the same way as the thrush. It song is even sweeter and more mellow, and it has a large appetite for snails and fresh fruit. When it has its adult plumage, the male is easily distinguished by a denser black colour and yellow beak.

Fieldfare and Redwing

Both these birds are migrants of the thrush family. They do well with similar treatment to the song thrush except that they relish even more fresh fruit and live food in their diet. The fruit may include a lot of wild berries such as mountain ash and yew.

Ring Ouzel

A bird of mountain and moorland, migrant to our shores, which does well with the same treatment as described for the thrush. Loving mountain country, they are particularly fond of bilberries, holly, mountain ash, and elderberries. Fresh bathing facilities are essential.

Smaller Softbills

Nightingale

Perhaps the most glamorous of all British birds is the nightingale, not in any exotic visual sense, but because its song is always supposed to be quite incomparable. As a matter of fact, I prefer a good mellow blackbird to the best nightingale, but the fact remains that the nightingale song is wonderfully limpid and mellow. Perhaps another factor that influences my judgement is that my part of the Midlands (central Staffordshire) is just north of nightingale territory. Twenty miles to the south the bird is quite common; to the north, it is practically unknown.

The food required is insectile, augmented with a little hard-boiled egg and biscuit meal (steamed and crumbly) and as much live food as possible; but bear in mind that a surfeit of meal-worms is bad for the liver.

Nightingales are migratory birds and will become restless and fidgety as the time approaches for them to leave for other shores. You must be particularly careful not to frighten them and do everything possible to make their forced stay more attractive, for example, by offering the most tempting food possible. The instinct to migrate is far stronger than any innate desire for freedom. I have no doubt that most captive birds can be supremely happy in a cage where food and drink are easily available, temperature is always kind, and bullying or predatory birds are unknown. I am far less happy about the idea of keeping migratory birds in captivity in spite of the fact that they appear to survive in first-rate physical condition.

Wheatear, Whinchat and Redstart
These are all insectivorous migratory birds. All can be kept in captivity but the same reservations apply about our right to confine birds with migratory instincts perhaps too strong for sublimation.

Whitethroats, Blackcaps and Warblers
These birds can all be kept in captivity, and should be fed on insectile food supplemented with plenty of small live food, such as young meal-worms, immature (home-reared) gentles, small caterpillars, and flies. They look well, sing well, and live a comparatively long time. Despite this seeming evidence of their suitability for a life of captivity, I hate the idea of confining migratory birds to this country, let alone a cage.

Tits
It is fairly easy to keep blue tits, great tits, and cole tits in captivity, though they are not often found as cage birds because most people prefer to keep something less likely to be seen in their own gardens.

The song of tits is not particularly attractive and the long-tailed tit, the most beautiful of the family, is not easy either to keep or to breed in captivity. They are all protected, so that it is illegal to keep a specimen caught wild.

In any case, tits in general become so tame in the wild that they can be observed by most people as easily through the dining-room window as through the bars of a cage.

If they are to be kept in a cage at all, remember that, as with other insectivorous birds, they spend a great proportion of their time hunting for their prey and do not normally come across great mountains of food on which

132

they can gorge. Nothing is worse for any pet than boredom, so it is essential to find your insectivorous birds plenty to do by furnishing the cage with bark from trees, stones with crevices, and any natural hiding place where the birds would be likely to find live food in their wild state. They will spend hours searching about in this 'cover' and you can prevent them becoming disillusioned and frustrated by liberating a few small spiders, wood lice, or other small non-flying insects so that they can creep into the shelter provided in the cage. The birds will then spend hours hunting or waiting for them to emerge, exactly as they would in the wild state.

As generous a ration as possible of natural live food in the shape of small meal-worms or gentles should be provided and added to a basis of insectile food and a little hard-boiled egg dried off in biscuit meal. Put the food in wide shallow vessels large enough for the birds to get in and 'pick over', but it is essential to put down only as much food as will be cleared up quickly, as it will otherwise be fouled. Scald the utensils before refilling.

As for other softbills, fresh bathing water is as essential as grit.

Wagtails
The wagtails can be kept in captivity fed on insectile food with ample addition of live food, but they are such active, vivacious birds, covering immense areas of ground every day in their characteristic dashes, that they are not recommended for a life of captivity.

Wrens
Wrens may also be kept, though the live food will have to be chopped up immediately before it is offered, as a meal-worm or gentle may be too large for them to manage whole.

They are essentially such hunters, though, that any chopped meal-worms should be offered before the reflex wriggling has ceased. Wrens are not really recommended as pets.

Larks
About thirty years ago, the most popular British bird of all was the skylark and, despite its natural soaring flight, it

commonly lived for years in a small cage, even before the days of prepacked insectile food. Years ago it was fed on biscuit meal and egg, finely chopped meat, grated vegetable, a little bird seed, and a constant supply of fresh turf. It ate some greenstuff from this and caught some of its own live food too.

Larks are rarely kept nowadays because they are difficult to breed in captivity and it is illegal to capture them. They are also becoming scarcer in the wild state as they fall victims to the new methods of scientific agriculture, which so frequently covers the land with the poisonous sprays which kill insect pests and the lovely birds that prey on them alike.

Jackdaws, Jays, Magpies, Crows and Ravens
These are among the most rewarding British birds to keep. They are unprotected, so it is legal to take them from the nest as fledgelings, and indeed you will be doing a good turn to the rest of the birds in the neighbourhood if you destroy any you do not intend to keep.

By the same token, none of these predators must ever be kept in an aviary with other, smaller birds. If they do not kill them, they will harry and pester them and steal their food for fun. In their wild state they make their living by plunder. They steal eggs, murder nestlings and chicks, and attack ill and weaker birds and animals.

But I repeat that, in captivity, they can be quite charming, if rather mischievous.

Having found an occupied nest, examine the young and try to assess their age and state of feathering. The main flight feathers, which are to be found at the outside of each wing, will be soft and pulpy at the base until the young bird is almost fully fledged. When it is nearly ready to fly, these feathers will be firm and dry, and the rest of the feathering will appear almost complete. The ideal time to take the birds for hand-rearing is within twenty-four or forty-eight hours on leaving the nest. After that, they will be too strong on the wing to be caught, and before that they are always a little more difficult to rear.

Hand-rearing. Place the young bird in a deepish box similar in size to its nest, but deep enough to prevent its jumping out. Cover this with a soft piece of wool or cloth, partly to keep the bird warm and partly to keep it in a subdued light. When this cloth is removed the bird will 'gape', first as a threatening defence mechanism, but later as a reflex to the proximity of food. This is the time to pop food into the gaping maw from a small spoon (the wooden spoons given away with ice cream cups are excellent), a pair of blunt tweezers, or a special food dispenser. These dispensers can now be bought for hand-rearing smaller birds and are basically small syringes through which soft food can be squeezed into young beaks.

It may well be that the young bird will not gape obligingly at first, in which case it will be necessary to force-feed the first night. Hold the bird gently in the left hand, so that the thumb and first finger can hold the base of the beak, with the back of the head at the juncture of thumb and finger. Gently, but firmly open the beak with the other hand and slip the left thumb and finger between the mandibles to wedge it open. Only a raven would be strong enough to damage you at this stage, and gloves should be worn for him.

With the right thumb and finger take a piece of mixed soft food (for mixture see below) and put right at the back of the beak. Push it down the maw with the forefinger. Repeat, to give what would be judged to be about half a cropful. Then leave till next morning. Most wild creatures are afraid at first and are slow to feed the first time. This applies as much to bottle-reared mammals as to hand-reared birds. But hunger is a good sauce and they will usually begin to feed long before they come to harm from starvation, provided suitable food is offered either by bottle or as described for birds. So force-feed only as much as is strictly necessary to preserve health. They will become tame and confiding much more quickly if taking their food from you is a pleasure and not an ordeal.

By next morning, your fledgeling will be very hungry and, when you remove the warm cover from his box, he will probably gape instinctively and you should have a tasty morsel ready to pop in before he has time to change his mind and shut his beak again. If you are successful in getting it *well down*, so that he can't shake it out again, he may refuse to gape again. In this case cover him and leave him for about an hour and try again. He will in all probability let you get a couple of beakfuls in this time and, by the end of the second day he will be screaming to have his gaping beak crammed every time he hears your approach. More force-feeding than strictly necessary at the start simply delays the time when he regards you confidently as his foster parent and may well instil in him a fear of you he will never overcome. So the skill in rearing fledgelings lies in judging how necessary for survival it is to force-feed and in persuading—or allowing his hunger to persuade—the young bird to regard you as his natural giver of food.

For birds in the jay-raven group, I believe in feeding on a moist, crumbly insectile mixture to which is added hard-boiled egg, *finely* chopped raw meat and bread and milk. In my school-days I reared magpies and jackdaws almost exclusively on hard-boiled egg and bread and milk with success that might surprise a great many of this generation who have been brought up at a time when insectile food is readily available.

As soon as the young bird is gaping freely when you approach, remove him from his 'nest' and keep him in a larger cage.

Here he will get exercise and should be so situated that he can see as many people as possible coming and going close by him. He will soon lose all fear of people and, associating them with the arrival of food, he will gape and squeal to be fed as soon as you come in sight.

This is the time to leave him out of his cage a good deal. He will not go far away from his source of food and will follow his owner about wherever he can.

As he grows older, he will learn to find food for himself in the garden, and you must decide whether to allow him to revert to the wild or whether to confine him more closely to his cage. As a naturalist, I usually allow the birds I have reared to return gradually to the wild because I feel I have the best of both worlds that way, learning a great deal about my pets that is not in books without greatly inconveniencing them. Readers of this book, however, will probably want to retain their young birds as pets.

Ravens are too big for a cage and should be kept in an aviary with an open-sided shelter against the weather. It is essential that they should have no other birds smaller than

136

themselves confined with them. The rest of the group may be kept in either a large cage—at least four feet by two feet six by one foot six—or, better still, an aviary.

I have always found jackdaws preferable to magpies as pets, for jackdaws seem insatiably curious whereas the 'pies are naturally nervous and suspicious. Jays are quite delightful.

Food for the group consists of a basis of soaked dog biscuit with almost anything else to supplement it and give variety, ranging from a whole dead rabbit to addled eggs or meal-worms.

In the wild, the whole group will eat carrion, nothing being too dead or too high for them. They will eat mice, frogs, beetles, worms, insects, eggs, small birds, and fruit. They are good mimics, and I know one raven, at a local zoo, that has as good a Black Country accent as any of the visitors who pay to see him.

Mules and Hybrids

Many fanciers of British birds have persuaded them to interbreed. In the fancy, a bird bred from a canary and some other species is a mule, and a bird bred from two species other than a canary is a hybrid. As with progeny of a horse and a donkey, a mule can have sexual intercourse but will not prove fertile.

Apart from scientific curiosity as to what species will intermingle, if only for a generation, there are various reasons for producing mules and hybrids. Crosses between canaries and other finches often have very sweet songs as well as being very beautiful. Furthermore, the combination of colours which will result by mating, for example, a clear yellow canary with a goldfinch (or a seven-coloured linnet) cannot be forecast exactly, and no two progeny may be exactly alike. Similarly a roller canary mated to a linnet may produce immense variations of song.

Technically, the first part of the mule's name derives from its father and the second part from its dam. So a mule produced by crossing a cock canary with a hen goldfinch would be a canary-golfinch mule. The more common way of getting the cross would be to mate a cock goldfinch with a hen canary, to produce a goldfinch-canary mule. Similarly a linnet-twite hybrid would be the result of crossing a cock linnet with a hen twite.

The production of most mules and hybrids is quite simple, as they will usually pair quite freely if caged together in April out of sight and earshot of a member of the opposite sex of their own species. In that case they will often ignore the foreigner in their own cage to get to one of their own sort across the room.

Feeding and treatment is as for the young of the hen bird.

9 Advanced Animals

Hedgehogs

Some of my most successful pets have been British animals which virtually never come on the market in pet shops—and never should. They can only be obtained more or less by accident.

Best of all are animals such as hedgehogs, which may be caught, tamed and released to become semi-wild, but bolder than their truly wild fellows which will not tolerate close observation or interference.

Even adult hedgehogs are easy to tame. Sharp prickles are their defence mechanism, so that they have no natural need to be cunning and wary. It is quite possible to catch an adult and to have it very tame within a week or so.

There are two main snags: fleas, and the animal's ability to escape. All wild hedgehogs have a great many fleas, largely because they find it impossible to scratch their own skin or back and sides because of their prickles. If you watch a hedgehog closely, you will see fleas crawling about among the spines. Don't be put off. For one thing, these fleas seem peculiar to hedgehogs and will not bite people, though they are uncomfortable enough when they crawl up the back of one's neck. With modern insecticide dusts, they are easy enough to exterminate, but do be careful to use an insecticide that is guaranteed harmless to animals.

The hedgehog's extraordinary ability to escape is a far more serious obstacle. He can scale a wall you would think impossible, and a wire-netting fence seems to be no deterrent at all. He is very strong and can root with his little pig-like snout under anything within his power that is physically movable.

I was once asked to collect a dozen live hedgehogs by a bacteriologist, and I put them in the saddle-room annexe to the stable until I was ready to take them to him. The room had a tiled floor and close fitting windows and door, and there seemed no possibility of escape, but my dozen hedgehogs had shrunk to eleven by morning. I examined every nook and cranny, and there was only one exit to the outside world. In theory that was quite impossible and I shall never be certain how my hedgehog escaped: the only faint possibility I could see was the chimney.

Obtaining a Hedgehog

I once knew an old gypsy who was fond of hedgehog to eat. He would walk around the hedge-banks of a field, looking for the tell-tale 'runs' or paths that hedgehogs use to get to the nest in which they spend most of the daylight hours (they are like the runs partridges make to their nest). He had an uncanny knack, and would stop and reach a hand into the hedge bottom, and, three times out of five, it would hold a hedgehog when he withdrew it.

It is a knack I have never acquired. When I want a hedgehog, I wait till summer. (They hibernate from about the end of October till March although they will emerge for a brief spell if it is really warm, especially in late January or February, when they will be very hungry and must have food available.) It is a bad thing to get them very early in the season, because they are thin and out of condition after hibernating and need more and better food than it is easy to provide in captivity. Besides in the summer they are much easier to find out hunting, at dawn or sunset.

When the dew is heavy on the ground, hedgehogs make little paths through it as plainly as if they had been wandering through snow. It is possible to follow these tracks, by skirting the edge of a field from where the feeding hedgehog has left a criss-cross maze to where he lies snug and hidden in thick cover. And just before darkness falls or just after dawn it is quite common to find hedgehogs foraging on short turf for the worms which come out in the dew to mate.

When you do find a hedgehog, it is important to be certain that it is not a sow suckling young which would starve if you took their mother.

The easiest—and most humane—way to make a hedgehog uncurl is to sprinkle it with a fine rose of a watering can. Watch very carefully and you will notice that the ball of spines relaxes long before it uncurls. In extreme danger the animal literally screws himself into the tightest possible ball with nose pressed right into his fleshy posterior. This tightens the skin which makes the bristles stand stiffly erect, but it is an uncomfortable posture to maintain. The first stage in uncurling him is to relax the skin tension and to wait quietly for any signs of danger. A gentle spray from a watering can at this time produces the illusion that it is raining. Now, slugs and snails and some insects come out into the open during showers, which are therefore favourite hunting times for hedgehogs. A gentle watering will usually make him forget you are there and he will wander off as if nothing had happened.

This is the time to thrust your fingers gently underneath him. He won't bite and there are not prickles underneath, but soft, rather coarse, brown hair. The most likely reaction will be muscular tension, ready to roll tight into a ball at the first sign of danger. Keep perfectly still until the tension relaxes again, and, with luck, your hedgehog will have taken the first steps to tameness by wandering freely over your hands. This is the time to look underneath, when you will see—and feel—the teats freely exposed if you have picked a nursing sow. In this case, release her again where you found her and follow patiently, when she will lead you to her nest of young. If they are old enough to look like miniature hedgehogs, it is quite reasonable to take the whole litter, sow, nest and all, and the sow will rear them. But never take young hedgehogs till they're running about and their prickles are hard.

I cannot emphasize too strongly that, in this case, it is absolutely vital to keep them in a safe place, because, if the sow does escape, you will be left with the problem of hand-rearing them.

Food

If you look at a hedgehog's teeth, it will be obvious at once that he is carnivorous and makes his meals of living prey—worms, beetles, etc.—or what dead flesh he can find. So the basis of his diet is animal: meal-worms, dor-beetles, earthworms, slugs, snails, and almost any largish insect. He will also eat raw egg—if you crack it—dead mice, and sparrows, and almost anything else he comes across, including raw butcher's meat, especially liver. Meal-worms and bread and milk are particular favourites, and our

141

hedgehogs learn extraordinarily rapidly to uncurl and come out for food. As soon as yours does this, the battle is won.

The next step is to put his cage in the garden, surround it with temporary wire netting, and only let him out while you are there. When he has had sufficient exercise, feed him in his pen so that he becomes accustomed to feeding and sleeping there. After a few days, remove the temporary wire netting, and with luck you will have a hedgehog perfectly free to come and go as he pleases, but who will actually choose to live in the home you have provided. Failing that, he should return each evening for an easy meal.

Give him his bread and milk, scraps of cooked and raw meat and vegetables as you would give them to a cat, his live food in dishes, and his eggs with their shells cracked. To get your hedgehog tame, feed him at dusk and stay with him for half an hour each evening, offering food piecemal as he will take it. He will be shy, at first, and it will be necessary to leave a supply for the night to avoid any risk of hunger due to his reticence. But very soon he will become quite fearless and friendly.

If you are lucky enough to get a young hedgehog that has just been weaned and can look after himself, he will need extra bread and milk and succulent live food, but will quickly repay the trouble you may take by becoming exceptionally tame and confiding. When very young, the spines are soft, like coarse hair. At this age rearing is difficult, and warmth as well as food is necessary. But within a few weeks the youngsters will be perfect replicas of their elders.

Hibernation

Hedgehogs go into complete or partial hibernation, depending on the weather. In normal winters, they make a thoroughly warm nest, usually in leaves, sometimes in holes—rabbit holes are common—but always well insulated (a number of ex-pets winter deep in the debris of our old holly hedge). Pet hedgehogs will usually sink into a state of torpidity about the beginning of November and this will last until the spring.

During this hibernation their body temperature drops to about atmospheric temperature and respiration becomes slow.

In order to survive, it is necessary for them to put on a good layer of flesh in the autumn, so that they can literally live on their fat. The most satisfactory way of preparing for this is to liberate the hedgehogs in the garden during the middle of September, by increasing the size of their run, as described, until they are not confined at all. They will find a great deal of their own food and become so active that they seem to be 'working' all night and often by day as well. The result will be an increase of weight, difficult to attain in captivity, which will carry them safely through the winter.

Next year, your pets may live free but should regain much of their tameness if you put food out for them in the evenings. And these semi-wild pets combine the best of both states. They are bold and friendly enough for you to study what wild animals do, and they are living full and natural lives, as happy as if they had never seen you.

Mice, Shrews and Voles

In almost every thick hedgerow, in every 'tussocky' field, in bramble bushes, and in the garden there is a wild population of small mammals, all of which many people think are mice. Most of them may be caught in various 'catch-'em-alive' traps on the market, the best of which is the Longworth trap supplied for Natural History research and obtainable through the British Mammal Society.

Wild Mice
Some of them are mice, the two commonest being the wood mouse—or long-tailed field mouse—and the yellow-necked mouse. Few but naturalists would know the difference, for both are a brilliant russety colour, with white bellies, large ears and eyes, and very long tails. The yellow-necked, which is not quite so common, has, in fact, a yellow cross or spot where throat and chest meet.

Neither of these mice make very good pets, in the sense that they are not easily handled, because they bite very shrewdly, and are always shy unless captured when exceptionally young. Worse from the point of view of suitability as pets, they are nocturnal and will be little in evidence by day.

Housing. They can be kept in a large, glass-fronted

143

wooden box, with plenty of ventilation holes covered by perforated zinc, and are most attractive animals to observe, though it must be repeated that they are unlikely to become tame enough to handle, and will probably escape if you try handling. Many countrymen, not appreciating how many subspecies of field mice there are (about seventeen varieties are claimed by scientists), call them greyhound mice. They have large eyes, long legs and tails, and are indeed well named, as anyone who has tried to recapture one that has escaped will agree.

For the best effect, the floor of the box should be covered with the same sort of debris as you would find in the wild habitat, to make their cage as far as possible a replica of their own domain. A freshly cut turf is a very effective alternative flooring. There should be a branch for the mice to climb, and a jam jar on its side filled with dry grass for a bed.

Feeding. They will eat grain, fruit, nuts, acorns, bread, cubes cut from root crops such as carrot, turnip, swede, and they are fond of a little meat.

No anxiety need be experienced if they escape: they will fend for themselves without difficulty. To catch them while the cage is being cleaned, drive them into their jam-jar bed and cover the mouth.

Shrews

Nobody should attempt to keep a live shrew unless he is prepared to take a very considerable amount of trouble. But, for those who are really keen, this will be a rewarding pet. Shrews are not mice, but small carnivorous mammals which live entirely on insects, spiders, worms, and any small live food they can capture. They are exceedingly pugnacious and not in the least averse to feeding on vanquished shrew. Two species are commonly found on land and one in water, and all can easily be distinguished from mice or voles by their exceptionally long and pointed snouts. They quickly become bold enough to feed from the hand and are active by day.

Housing. Shrews do not jump or climb as well as mice and may be kept in open-topped cages, provided the sides are slippery. Empty aquariums are very satisfactory for this purpose, provided there is about an inch and a half of dry

144

Top: 11. Goats make friendly pets but it is necessary to make sure
they don't do too much damage in the garden

Bottom: 12. Fox cubs are not suitable as pets but this one, held
by young Jane Springthorpe, was successfully released in
isolated woodland where there was no hunting or shooting

13. Swallow tail butterfly. Many butterflies can be bred in captivity and later be released where there is plenty of natural food for their caterpillars to re-populate the countryside

earth covering the bottom to insulate the inmates from the cold glass. Open-topped biscuit tins will do at a pinch. A cover is only necessary in the interest of the animal's own safety, should there be a cat or other predator in the household.

Since shrews are so pugnacious, solitary confinement is the only satisfactory method of keeping them, unless an exceptionally large cage is provided, furnished with plants and rocks and other 'natural' cover. In this case a pair may be housed together. Do not expect them to be tame. They have hearts like lions and will do battle with your finger as readily as with a spider or another shrew.

In spite of this, shrews are exceptionally interesting creatures to keep for a short time for observation, and may be released in natural surroundings without a qualm when the effort to maintain their food supply becomes onerous.

Feeding. The only really satisfactory diet for shrews is a constant supply of live food. Spiders, beetles, centipedes, small worms will all suffer the same fate, probably much more quickly than it is convenient to replace them. Meal-worms and gentles should be used as standbys, but there is nothing like a variety of freshly caught insects. The shrew will eat about half his own weight every day. In emergency, he will eat fresh meat. A glass squarium, used as a cage, will confine his live food while the shrew hunts and devours it.

Shrews' digestion is such that they cannot survive even relatively short periods without food and should never be left for more than two hours without a meal. They need fresh water and access to fresh greenstuff and bran or oatmeal. Meal-worms should be sprinkled with a spot of cold-liver oil.

Voles

Unlike mice and shrews, voles make charming and easily tamed pets. My experience is that among wild animals only the hedgehog is more easily tamed than the field vole. He is like a short-tailed mouse from the rear, though his coat is russet on the back and cream below, but his head is most unmouselike: far blunter, with eyes nearer the nose than the ears.

The habitat he likes is tussocky grass and rushes with

dense cover. He makes a network of 'runs' through the grass and also in the roots. When caught, he can be handled at once if treated gently, and becomes as tame as a domestic white mouse within a few days.

His near relative the bank vole, is slightly larger and stronger, and inhabits hedgebanks where the bramble or ivy or other cover is dense. He is very like the field vole, the major physical difference being in dentition. But he is more aggresive, will often kill and eat a field vole if he meets one, and is not so easy to tame, nor so pleasant, owing to a more powerful and frequent bite.

Housing. Although bank and field voles are not great jumpers, they should be kept in a glass-fronted cage—an aquarium will do—with the top covered.

They are very active by day, and it will be found that they do not expect danger very much from their own level, and can be examined through the side of their cage without taking offence. Their great enemies are hawks and owls and other predatory birds which descend on them from the sky; if you examine them from the top of their cage, they will panic at once.

They get so very tame that dense cover to hide in is not essential, and they will take quite readily to a jam jar on its side furnished with bedding of bracken fronds or hay. A pair of either species will usually live well in the same cage, but there should be a nest box or two for each animal.

Food. These voles will do well on a diet of corn—wheat, oats, maize, barley, etc.—acorns, nuts, and fruit, ranging from apple cubes to hips and haws. It will be found that bank voles in particular love fruit, and relish blackberries, raspberries, and small pieces of apple. The field vole needs a large volume of fibrous vegetation as well, and should be given a tussock of coarse grass, which should be replaced frequently. Both varieties like fresh greenstuff such as peas, beans, clover and lettuce. And both like a certain amount of animal food in the form of beetles and other insects or even dead birds or mice.

Both varieties of vole are particularly well suited to cage life and will often survive considerably longer than they would in the wild which, even barring accidents, would be less than two years.

Wild Rats

One of the most engaging pets I ever had was a common brown rat called Haw Haw. I had found the nest, killed the old doe, and put the five naked and blind young in my pocket to give to the ferrets.

Then I decided to try the experiment of rearing them, although they were so very young.

A fifteen-watt pigmy bulb inside a flat tin supplied the vital warmth necessary. A sock stretched over the tin diffused the heat and was absorbent enough to soak up the excreta and urine which the doe would have cleaned up when she licked the coats of her offspring.

Feeding

I was completely unsuccessful in getting the young rats to suck either through bicycle valve rubber tubing, normally so useful for animals too small to use normal teats, or even wool soaked in milk. As a last resort, I filled a shallow tin lid with soppy bread and milk and placed it immediately over the fifteen-watt pigmy bulb, which maintained it at about blood heat. Nature did the rest and the young rats were feeding well by sucking the milk from the bread long before their eyes were open. After that there was no check in their growth: they soon began to eat the bread as well as sup the milk, and their diet was then extended until it was exactly the same as that described earlier in the section on tame rats.

Taming

The main difference between young wild and domesticated rats is that the wild ones are far more subject to groundless panic. The important thing with wild animals is to get them thoroughly accustomed to being handled because far more bite through fear than through anger. Once they associate handling with food and become bold, the first battle is won.

The trouble with my young rats was that, when one panicked the fear was immediately communicated to the others. There appeared only one answer to this. The young rats were isolated and it was found that careful handling of each separately was very successful.

One young buck was reared and handled every time he

was fed, until he began to associate his owner directly with food. This is a most important principle in taming young wild animals. Instead of leaving more food than they require in the cage, so that they take a little every time they want it, they should be hand-fed as often as they need food. (This is not possible with animals like shrews—moles are even worse—because almost the whole of their waking hours are spent feeding.) Even with creatures as hardy as rats, food must always be left in excess of their need overnight or when the owner will be away for a period longer than the normal interval between meals. Immediately on return, however, all surplus food should be removed and as much time spent hand-feeding as possible.

Movements should never be sudden or jerky, nor should they be so slow as to give the impression that the young animal is being stalked by stealth. A slow, uniform approach will soon be acceptable, and it will help if you always make the same sound, which will also come to be associated with food.

Once tame does not mean always tame. It is quite useless to spend hours taming your rat and then to think all you have to do to retain his affection is to feed him and clean him out regularly but only handle him now and then. Most animal memory for unnatural discipline is short. If left to their own devices they will soon revert to their instinctive mistrust. Some people make a habit of handling and petting, even if only for a few minutes, every day.

A good idea is to find by experiment a favourite food and always offer a titbit, so that you may leave adequate normal food as you would for an adult domesticated rat.

As your rat grows to maturity he may well try out his strength a little and, if he senses he has mastered you at all, and that you are in any way afraid, there is a possibility that he will gradually become savage. He is most unlikely to become savage suddenly, however, so that you may have a protracted period of trial of strength. My experience is that with a little persistence it is fairly easy to win the trial and, once we knew where we stood, my tame rat settled down into an altogether delightful and affectionate pet.

His cage and food were similar to the normal house and diet of a domesticated rat.

To keep a wild rat you must have a Ministry of

Agriculture permit and if you let it escape you will be committing an offence.

Squirrels

Red squirrels are becoming rare and should on no account be kept as pets. Grey squirrels are very variable, and I have known bucks become so aggressively savage that they will fly at the face of anyone entering the pen and attack in a most dangerous manner. In any case, they are classified as pests by the Ministry of Agriculture and may not be kept without an official permit.

Housing

If you can get a permit to keep grey squirrels for scientific study you will find them so agile and active that it is positively cruel to keep them except in quarters large enough for vigorous exercise. No ordinary portable cage, even fitted with an exercise wheel, is big enough. A disused attic or loft with wire netting fitted to the window will be excellent, provided it is well lit. Failing that, the largest aviary that can be obtained will do.

There should be branches and poles and shelves for the squirrels to climb and leap and chase each other in play. At least one nest box, about one foot square and eighteen inches deep, must be provided for each squirrel. Entrance should be made through a hole three inches in diameter under the eaves of the box, which should have a hinged lid.

If the squirrels are in an outdoor aviary, the portion of it where the nest boxes are placed must be covered and thoroughly proof against wind as well as rain. It is better to have a lean-to aviary with holes through the walls of a building, so that the nest boxes may be thoroughly insulated from frost and extreme cold.

The bottom of the boxes should be covered with peat or wood shavings and sacking, and hay should be provided as alternative bedding. The principle of having at least one box for each squirrel, preferably with a surplus box or two, will give opportunities for experiment with various bedding, ranging from wool to just shavings or peat, and for you to observe preferences. It also gives opportunities for alternative choice when the weather changes.

Generally speaking, the nest boxes should be hung as high as possible, access being arranged by a convenient branch or pole.

It will usually be discovered that a pair of squirrels will live amicably together, but that more than one buck in an enclosure is liable to lead to fighting. Whether or not this happens will depend partly on the individual squirrel and partly on the size of the enclosure. A large enclosure, kept quiet and undisturbed, will sometimes encourage squirrels to breed in captivity.

It will be necessary to clean out the bedding periodically and disinfect, for squirrels, like most other animals, are subject to fleas. These fleas are so specific that there is a separate species for red and for grey squirrels.

It is possible that these fleas have some connection with the disappearance of red squirrels when grey appear in the wild. Whole colonies of red squirrels die off from a disease rather like rabbit myxomatosis, and another fatal complaint known as squirrel mange has been recorded occasionally amongst red squirrels for many years. It is not yet clear if the two diseases are the same or similar, but a modern theory suggests that grey squirrels are carriers of a disease not fatal to them which kills red squirrels if they are bitten by a flea which has been feeding on grey. This presents no danger to human beings.

When thoroughly tame, your squirrels may be let loose in the house while you are there to see they come to no harm.

Food
Captive squirrels need a very varied diet with nuts of almost any kind as a basis. Hazelnuts, walnuts, and almonds are devoured with relish. Rosehip syrup is very good and so are apples and similar fruit. They will eat maize and other corn, and dry bread; they love freshly cut boughs of apple, hazel, willow, etc., to bite.

Water for drinking should always be available, and a little fresh milk is often appreciated.

Stoats and Weasels

I have had great success with both stoats and weasels. The difficulty is to obtain them at an age when they are old enough to rear but young enough to tame. About eight weeks is the best age, when their eyes are open and they are crawling but not actively running about.

Gamekeepers, woodmen, rabbit-catchers, and threshing machine operators are the most likely people to catch them. My best weasel, which I was able to let loose in the drawing room every night, was found as a kitten in a wheat rick when it was being threshed. Weasels are implacable enemies of rats and mice and frequently take up their abode in rickyards where their food is immediately available. It is interesting to notice that, although they are such bloodthirsty hunters, they commonly store what prey they cannot eat in large numbers, and presumably return to eat the dead rats or sparrows or mice when fresh food becomes scarce. Although it is an established fact that they store their surplus kills, my own belief is that if their game supply gets thin they are more likely to move on to better stocked preserves than eat carrion.

To distinguish a stoat from a weasel is quite simple. The stoat has a black tip—the tippit of ermine—on his tail, which is much longer than a weasel's. Apart from this he is bigger, up to about seventeen inches long—as against ten inches or so for a weasel—and altogether stronger. His favourite natural diet is rabbit, though he will eat almost anything he can kill, including mice and birds. Since number of rabbits have decreased there are also fewer stoats. Weasels kill rats, mice, moles, birds, and also love birds' eggs. Both stoats and weasels have white bellies, and general colouring of varying shades of brown, ranging from khaki yellow to chocolate.

Nobody is quite certain that stoats will not interbreed with ferrets, though the chances are against it. I once succeeded in persuading a very tame buck stoat and jill ferret to share the same aviary, though they never became friendly enough to mate. For many weeks I divided not only the aviary but the actual sleeping box by stout half-inch wire netting, till they both became thoroughly accustomed to each other's smell. Then I removed the partition. For days they lay at opposite ends of the nest box which had an escape hole at each end to prevent either getting cornered. Gradually they learnt to tolerate each other and live together, first in a state of armed neutrality, and later of complete indifference. I should like to repeat the experiment, introducing the participants at a much earlier age.

Housing
Ideally stoats or weasels should be housed in a large aviary—half-inch netting must be used—with a concrete floor and a double door to prevent escape. Always keep a few bits of drain pipe in the aviary for the inmates to play in. If an animal does accidentally slip past you and escape, never chase it. Watch the direction it takes, which will probably be into the nearest thick flower bed, and slip round putting drainpipes at strategic points where it is likely to emerge. Then walk quietly through the cover and the chances are very good that it will dive for 'safety' into the first familiar pipe it comes to. Be very gentle and quiet in popping a brick at each end, and then you can return pipe and escapee to the aviary without its ever becoming scared. If you chase and chivvy it, you will undo in minutes the weeks of work you have spent taming it.

The aviary should contain thoroughly weather-proof nest boxes, which should be fitted with sliding doors over the entrance holes. When you want to move an animal, he can then be persuaded into his nest box, which can be shut and moved in safety to some other place from which he cannot escape when he emerges.

When I am taming stoats or weasels I have an ordinary box birdcage about two feet by eighteen inches by one foot, covered with wire netting instead of bird-cage bars. I keep the stoat in this box in the house where he can see people at close quarters all day, and return him to the aviary at night, using the aviary nest box as travelling box. During the day he loses his fear of people, and at night he leaves his rather cramped quarters for a spacious aviary where he can get all the exercise he needs.

Food
Stoats and weasels need as much fresh meat as possible. Freshly killed sparrows, mice, fowl heads, rabbits, or rats are ideal. But it is not always easy to get as much of this type of food as they need. Raw egg is a very effective substitute. If you give whole eggs, the animals will shove them round their pen with their noses like circus dogs

playing 'football'. Rats move eggs the same way and I do not believe that it is a conscious method of moving the egg so much as an attempt to bite something which is too large and too smooth for them to get their teeth into. The result, inevitably, is that sooner or later they smack the egg into something hard and crack it. The rest is easy. They eat as much as they can of the contents, though some usually gets lost in the litter. To avoid this waste, it is wiser to break the egg into a dish, from which they can lap it, instead of wasting so much. But the 'whole-egg' trick is always an interesting demonstration as a party piece.

Fresh clean water is a necessity, and the floor of the aviary should be covered with peat or wood-shavings. It will be noticed that both stoats and weasels use one corner of the enclosure as a latrine.

To avoid shavings and peat dust in the house, I always cover the floor of the cage with several thicknesses of folded newspaper. This is clean and absorbent and can easily be burnt and replaced daily, avoiding any unpleasant smell in the house.

Feigning Death
If stoats or weasels are thoroughly terrified they sometimes appear to die. The attack commences when they roll on their sides, legs twitching, eyes unseeing. They soon go quite rigid and appear to be dead. Within a few seconds they seem as lively as usual, and many people who have seen this in the wild have said that the animal 'shammed death' and then ran off as soon as its enemies' attention was distracted.

My conviction is that animals, including foxes, have a fit when badly frightened, which lasts ten or fifteen seconds before they recover. This is often long enough for the attention of their enemies to wander, so that there is an opportunity to escape the moment they regain consciousness.

It is most important not to handle your pet for a little while after it has come out of one of these fits. The tamest stoat or weasel is likely to bite instinctively and viciously until its nerves have completely recovered.

Both the tame weasels that I have owned became subject to fits, which seemed to come on after violent exercise. The first used to spend every evening dancing all over the

153

furniture (and its occupants) in the drawing-room. He would hide under cushions and stalk one's finger with all the stealth of a tiger. But he was as gentle as a kitten when captured and loved nothing better than to be rolled on his back and 'attacked' by my fingers in retaliation. After a while, however, the exertion began to result in momentary fits which increased in duration, despite restriction of his exercise, until at last he died. His successor succumbed to the same complaint.

It is a condition well known to scientists and is caused by a nematode worm which starts in the nostril and works its way up the nasal passage into the skull which it eventually perforates.

This produces fits which eventually prove fatal and the percentage of skulls of wild stoats and weasels which show these perforations indicate that Nature is capable of controlling the population growth of wild animals which do not have many predators.

Mongoose and Mink

Both these animals are obtainable commercially, but are difficult to get young enough to tame. Indeed, mink are difficult to tame even when handled young, though I intend to try rearing one with an exceptionally docile ferret I have as a foster mother.

The housing and feeding of both animals should be as described for stoats and weasels, but a Ministry of Agriculture permit is necessary to keep mink.

Foxes

Fox cubs are probably the most easily obtainable of our larger British mammals, and also the least satisfactory.

If obtained young (and a great many litters are dug out and destroyed every spring), they are easily reared and become very tame with their owner, but somehow they never really lose that faraway look. They are always restless and shifty and I have never owned or seen a tame fox that hasn't given me the impression that he would rather return to the wild.

Therein lies the real snag. So many tame foxes do return

154

to the wild either because they escape, often under the compulsive urge to mate, or because their owners tire of them or take compassion and turn them free.

It is mistaken kindness. If it becomes impossible, for any reason, to continue to keep a tame fox, it is far kinder to destroy it than to free it. It will have lost its respect for—and some of its fear of—man, and will have had no experience in catching its own food. Poultry will be the easiest and most obvious 'game' and it is likely to end its days in a trap, struggling for breath at the end of a gas-filled tunnel, or lingering in pain from shotgun wounds. So, if you want a fox, make up your mind quite definitely to keep it as comfortably as possible to the end of its days. And, if you change your mind, have it destroyed humanely.

Housing

Foxes can jump, dig, and climb anything that gives a reasonable foothold, like wire netting. It is wise—and rather difficult—to train them to a collar and lead from earliest cubhood. Put a collar on each time before you feed the cub and attach a cord or very light lead. Hold the food in front of the cub and just let it feel the pressure of the lead, so that it comes to associate walking forward and just being restrained on collar and lead, with food. When the cub tries to move off in other directions, try to go with it so that, as far as possible, the lead slows him in the direction he wants to go instead of actually stopping him. On no account drag him in the direction you want. Never do more than anchor him until he chooses to go your way. Then give him a titbit. No amount of patience will be wasted on this training because an adult fox well trained to a lead can spend quite a full and happy life. If it becomes unmanageable on collar and lead, it will have to spend its days fretting in a cage.

Having trained it to collar and lead, do not, on any account keep it chained to a kennel. It is cruel to do this to a dog but diabolical to a wild creature.

A fox needs the largest open wire-netting run that is available but, in any case, never less than thirty feet by six feet. It will be found that in captivity most active animals will develop the habit of pacing up and down the boundary of their enclosure for long periods. This is not necessarily, as is commonly thought, evidence that the creature is 'trying to escape'. Indeed once it has established itself comfortably, it will regard its cage as 'home', its natural territory, and would probably be very frightened if it did escape to strange surroundings. The usual explanation for continual pacing up and down a boundary is that a subconscious exercise pattern has been evolved, by which the animal keeps itself as fit as if it had to hunt for its food.

Accordingly, it is usually better to make the wire-netting enclosure long and narrow rather than short and square, for by this means a greater area will be actively used as exercise space.

A thoroughly weather-proof shelter is necessary, either inside the wire-netting run or abutting on to it. Ideally, a brick stable or pigsty should be connected, by a hole with a trapdoor which can be bolted, to an outside wire-netting enclosure. This should be wire-netted on the top as well as sides, and the netting (of heavy gauge) must either be buried at least eighteen inches in the ground, or, better the whole should be floored with concrete, laid so as to give adequate drainage.

The purpose of having a large indoor portion is to give not only a warm bed, but a feeling of security, should the fox be frightened by something strange approaching the outdoor run.

One tame fox that I knew, a vixen, lived quite free as an indoor pet. She was as clean as a dog in the house, went out with wild foxes in the winter, and had several litters in the shrubbery. But this was not only very exceptional, it would not have been possible at all if her master had not owned a large estate on which he could prevent her being shot or hunted.

Food
Foxes will live quite well on the same food that you would give to a dog, except that they require a rather higher proportion of meat. They also need vegetables, and like bread and broth or dog biscuits soaked in broth as well. They like as much raw meat as they can get and, since they are natural scavengers, birds or animals that have died do not appear to harm them. In the wild, they will dig up and eat animals after they have been buried and had time to go rotten.

156

Poultry heads can usually be had from the fishmonger's for the asking, and so can fowls, which have died, from most poultry farmers. In the latter case avoid exceptionally light birds—which may have died from tuberculosis—or yellow birds, which are likely to carry jaundice. Foxes are very susceptible to jaundice, and it might well pay to have them inoculated in exactly the same way as puppies are now commonly treated.

They love rabbit, healthy rat and any dead birds that are available. The food can then be made up in bulk with scraps, soaked dog biscuit, and vegetables. It is a good plan to pour a little fat on bread and then bake it absolutely hard in the oven. Crunching it will help keep their teeth scaled and white long after they would otherwise have decayed.

Hares

Although charming books are written from time to time by people who have kept pet hares in captivity, they do not, in my experience, make good pets. They are fairly easy to find in country that suits them, for the doe hare has her young or leverets fully furred, with eyes open and able to run within a few hours of birth. She hides each in a 'form'—or hollow where she squats—at times fully exposed and at others partly hidden by a light patch of nettles or reeds.

She leaves each of the litter, which usually numbers three or four, in a separate form, to spread the risk of some predator finding and killing the whole lot. Then she goes only at intervals to suckle them. By watching quietly at dawn or dusk, it sometimes possible to discover where the doe hare goes to suckle her young.

They are then easy enough to pick up because they rely entirely on their protective colouring for camouflage, and until they are relatively strong on their feet they will squat motionless to be captured rather than try to escape.

Capturing your leveret is but half the battle. If they are very young it is often difficult to persuade them to take to the bottle. They do well on ordinary human babies' food mixed with a little lime water and, though they sit out alone in the open, they do better with a little heat for a few days. But is depressingly easy to get them too young to rear or too old to tame.

Housing

Housing hares is very difficult. They are exceptionally unintelligent, panicky creatures which take fright at all manner of unexpected things and dash frantically round in sheer terror, banging into anything that gets in their way. From that point of view, a relatively small run, about three feet square, with wire-netting top and solid boarded sides, is best. It should have a wire-netting bottom, too and an adequate shelter for the hare to hide in and take cover from the weather or from prying eyes.

The point of the solid boarded sides is that the run can be moved where you wish, without the hare realizing he is in fresh surroundings and flying into a panic. To him, inside, his home looks more or less the same whether on the lawn, where he can graze through the netting bottom, or in the sitting-room where he is best on a sheet of brown paper or tray of peat, to avoid him soiling or eating the carpet. Although hares seem to keep well, physically, in such a small pen, it is always a poor life for so active and wild a creature, and I am never very happy to see captive hares.

Even under the best condtions, such as a walled garden (where they will prove very bad gardeners!), they either seem to become shy skulkers or savage unaffectionate brutes which will attack a placating hand with flailing sharp-clawed forefeet.

Food

Feed as you would tame rabbits.

Bush Babies

Bush babies have recently become popular as domestic pets and may be purchased at animal dealers and pet stores. Their main snags are that they are nocturnal, they tend to smell, and they leave wet footprints where these are least wanted.

They breed fairly freely in captivity, though the males have to be segregated from each other when they are adult as they are bullies and enjoy fighting. Their price is such, however, that few private households would want to keep more than a single pair.

There are various varieties, the commonest being the

maholic galago, which is like a very small monkey about a hand's breadth high.

The temperament of bush babies varies with individuals, and they can inflict a nasty bite if so inclined. A really tame and confiding specimen will only come as a reward for any amount of patience and disappointment.

They are very susceptible to cold and draught, so it is unwise to buy from dealers in the early part of the year unless there is good reason for believing they are not likely to have caught a cold. Evidence should be sought that the specimen you are thinking of buying is reasonably young. Some people seem to have great difficulty in keeping bush babies in captivity for more than a couple of years, but I believe draught and sudden changes of temperature to be the commonest causes of failure, as others have little difficulty in keeping them happy and healthy for several years longer than normal.

Housing

Bush babies are notable for their immensely agile and long leaps. A tame one in the room in the evening, when he is really wakening up, has all the agility of and far more grace than a grasshopper. So, before letting him out of his cage, make sure there is an adequate guard in front of the fire and that there is no delicate china in vulnerable positions.

This agility governs the minimum size for the cage: if it is less than eight or nine feet high, there is every chance of damage through over-exuberance tempting leaps longer than the space available. The ideal is sole use of a spare attic or box-room, which should be fitted with a suitably guarded tubular heater and thermostat to prevent the temperature dropping below about 50°F. Failing that, a large, aviary-type enclosure will do quite well.

In either case there should be plenty of branches, shelves, and sloping planks about, to give adequate opportunity for climbing and the aerobatics for which these wonderful athletes are famous.

At least one nest box should be provided for every inhabitant, preferably with some surplus to give the opportunity to pick and choose sleeping quarters. These boxes should all be placed high up, with a branch or board leading to a three-inch hole for entry. Each should be furnished with a different amount and quality of bedding, ranging from soft straw and hay to wool, in order to establish individual preference by direct observation.

Food

The staple diet of bush babies is sound fresh fruit and vegetables. Once again tastes are very individual, and it is wise to give as great a variety as possible and remove the surplus before it gets stale. Grapes, bananas, apples, oranges, carrots, berried fruit, and soft fruit in season will all be accepted. Occasionally cod-liver oil should be put on whatever food appears to be favourite or on bread if it is eaten. Water must always be available and fresh milk must be offered every day.

In addition to this basic diet, it is essential to supply live food. The easiest—and one of the favourites—is meal-worms, for they can be bought from pet shops almost the whole year through. At least a dozen a day should be given, though it is unwise to allow the pet to gorge because they are rather rich. Furthermore, meal-worms are so much enjoyed that they form the ideal means for taming a shy or strange bush baby. Keep them in a tin which you can rattle, so that the sound of the tin becomes associated with food. Once you have broken the ice and your pet has learned what it is you are offering, never give a meal-worm for nothing. The price must be that he comes and takes it from your fingers.

After a time, you will find that if you rattle your tin, even in daylight, your pet will emerge, yawning and grumbling a bit, to taste the delicacy you have brought.

You may open the cage and he will come fearlessly in search of the coveted food, and, when it time to curtail his carefree gambols, he will return happily to his aviary or room on promise of the rest of the ration. This is much more satisfactory than wild chases that destroy any mutual confidence you have established, and you can shut him up knowing he is quite happy to be back.

Deer

People with a paddock or field adjoining the garden may consider keeping a deer. Red deer are too big for pets, and

160

Top: 14. The author fitted a glass-sided nest box against his study window so that he could watch this blue tit feeding her young at close quarters without disturbing her

Bottom: 15. Canaries are delightful songsters, do well in a cage and breed freely in an aviary

16. Great tit at nest box. It is more fun to watch wild birds nesting free than to keep them in the most elaborate cages

both red deer and roe deer are, in any case, very difficult to get hold of.

There is not much difficulty in getting a fallow deer, however, because they breed freely, and people who keep a herd of fallow in their parks have to keep the numbers down by disposing of the surplus.

On no account have a buck. All tame male deer become dangerous and a tame buck will inevitably have to be destroyed, because he will become so dangerous that he might easily kill someone. It will not even be possible to turn him loose with the herd he was born into, because once he has lost his fear of man, he will attack on sight during the rut or mating season, if not at other times of the year as well. On the other hand, a pet doe or female fallow deer is quite delightful.

The time of year to obtain her is June. Fallow deer have their fawns in June and drop them in a clump of bracken, nettles, or rushes, where they lie like leverets, alone and immobile, for three or four days. The does only visit them at intervals, to suckle them until they are strong enough on their legs to run with their mothers if danger threatens.

During these early days of the fawn's life it is possible, if you are observant, to wander across reedbeds—the reeds that grow on sour land, not in water of course—or patches of nettles or bracken and spot a fawn lying in its couch. If it is still very young, it is not difficult then to pick it up in one swift sure pounce.

Rearing

She will squeal like a hare when you catch her, a horrible sound. (If you catch a buck, let him go again!) But within twenty-four hours she will be suckling from an ordinary bottle fitted with a baby's teat; I have had good success with ordinary baby food. The thing to watch is that the fawn's motions are not loose. A tablespoonful of lime-water with each feed should avoid this. If constipated, add a little sugar.

But young deer have another peculiarity. For some time they do not appear to have the instinct to void their faeces without stimulus. It is probable that the doe licks her fawn under the tail while she is suckling it, and eats any droppings that are made. This could account for the fact that fawns do not appear to foul the form the lie in, and it could

161

also explain the extraordinary absence of scent to give a fawn's location away to its enemies. The result is that a fawn being reared on the bottle needs artificial stimulus to open her bowels or she becomes seriously constipated.

The easiest way is to stroke her under the tail with a piece of soft rag, while she is suckling. Her response will be immediate. After a week or so, they very act of suckling will be stimulus enough and she will empty herself automatically every time she is fed. By this time she will be stronger on the legs, and if she were still in her wild state she would presumably be moving with the does and the need to guard against betraying her hiding place by scent would no longer arise.

When you first get a fawn she will panic every time you approach. It is therefore advisable to keep her in a large, deep box for a few days. She does not need exercise at this stage, and the more room she has, the harder she will bang herself if she does begin to rush about. The very worst possible place to confine her is in any enclosure with wire-netting sides. Her focus is not yet good, and she will try to dash to safety straight through the wire-netting, cutting her nose and face in the process.

Within days, she will associate you with her feed, and that is the time to transfer her to more spacious quarters. Some sort of paddock—even a movable fold—should now be used, because fawns begin to graze a little very early. They are highly selective, and ours loved the short, sweet, clover for which our lawn is notable!

Food
The seeding heads of grasses are favourite food at this stage and so are the most broad-leaved plants, including ivy. The fawn will follow like a lamb, and cannot be with you too much, especially as she will do no real damage in the garden. By the time she is weaned, most keen gardeners will not welcome her, decorative though she may be.

By seven or eight weeks, the bottle-feeds can be dropped from four to three a day and she can have as much freedom as you can manage. Ordinary sheep-netting fixed close to any decent hedge will confine her for some time, as, oddly, deer are slow to learn to jump unless frightened.

Always feed in whatever shelter has been provided and

you will find that fawns do not like bad weather and soon go home to shelter. Full weaning should be complete by the end of September, though I am a great believer in providing a bottle once a day for as long as possible because this helps in getting the animal thoroughly tame and fearless. (After the first two weeks or so, it will have been necessary to change from a baby's teat to a lamb teat, sold by all agricultural chemists.) It is also a good plan to allow—no encouragement is generally needed—your friends to give your fawn a bottle so that she grows up to regard the entire human race with trust and affection.

When the fawn is weaned, feed a couple of handfuls of calf-rearing pellets night and morning, and provide plenty of good sweet hay in a covered hay rick and ample grazing. Deer are fond of eating leaves of tree and shrubs as well as normal herbage, and seem particularly fond of some broad-leafed species such as ivy, blackberry, rose, and lime. They are said to be among the very few animals which can eat yew without harmful effects. My deer always comes when I feed the domestic poultry, and is inordinately fond of a handful of wheat or fowl meal. Wheat is not good for most farmyard animals but does not appear to have any ill effects on deer at all.

Housing
Ideally, a paddock of about an acre should be divided, so that the deer can be confined to half for a few weeks while the other half is rested. But a deer will do quite well on half an acre if fed additional hay, oats, and greens when the grass is very close cropped. Two does may be kept, but a single doe will usually become tamer and more affectionate.

Breeding
It is not possible to breed pet deer in captivity because of the difficulty of keeping a tame buck.

If a local park has a herd of fallow deer it might be possible to turn a pet fallow doe out with the herd during the month of October when the rut takes place, in which case she is likely to be mated by one of the park bucks. She can then be caught, if thoroughly tame, by being offered sweet biscuit or bread or whatever titbit has been found to be irresistible. She should be two or three years old before mating, and will have her fawn the following June. (Wild does mate at 18 months.)

Roe deer rut in July, but will not normally be found in enclosed parks, so that the only practicable means of breeding roe is to find a zoo which keeps a buck.

10 The Garden Collection

Method of Enclosure

A minimum height of six feet is necessary for the netting employed and, if there are many foxes or cats in the neighbourhood, it will be necessary to have a one-foot overhang outwards at the top, as either will run up and over if there is not a horizontal overhang to prevent them. While you are at it, it pays to have overhang inside the enclosure as well as outside. So many creatures that you may keep are as likely to run up and over as cats are to come in. The simplest way to accomplish both is to stretch taut lengths of sixteenth-of-an-inch gauge plain wire, also galvanized and blacked, level with the top of the posts, but kept one foot on each side by horizontal braces of one-inch-square oak.

Each upright wire-netting support post should have a T-piece bound to it with thin wire. The overlap support wires are then fixed to the extremities of the horizontal projections of this T. An inverted L will suffice for overhang on one side only. A third plain wire should be stretched tightly along the top of the posts.

It is vital that all three wires should be so taut that they give out quite a musical note when strummed, or the netting itself will always be flaccid and unprofessional in appearance. The secret of obtaining the required tautness is to have a really firm anchorage at each end. If the corner posts are on the boundary of your property, it will be necessary to stay them diagonally, with solid stays in compression. The ground must be firm and solid, and a large piece of flat stone—paving slabs are excellent—must be sunk into the ground at an angle of about forty-five degrees. The foot of the stay should be bedded against it so as to absorb its thrust at right angles. The other end of the stay should then be fixed solidly to the upright corner post, which should be sunk at least two feet six inches below ground for six feet above. It should be rammed absolutely solid, and, if the soil is light, it will be better to set it in three feet. If this corner post is not on the boundary, it may well be possible to arrange the strainers in tension instead of compression. This is done by fixing a wire from the top of the corner post down to a peg driven into the ground three or four yards away. The wire must be in the same direction as the horizontal it is desired to strain, and the peg must be driven in at an angle, like a tent peg, at least three feet into the ground. In order to apply tension, fit double-ended straining bolts into the run of the wire, which can then be tensioned almost to breaking point, simply by adjusting the straining bolts with a spanner or tommy-bar. Having erected posts and top straining wires round the perimeter of the garden or enclosure, all is now ready to put up the wire netting. Three-inch mesh will be adequate for the top portion, though one- or two-inch mesh will be better at the bottom. One-inch is the largest size that is rat-proof, so, if you are going to liberate small animals or birds that are likely to suffer from attacks by rats, it is worth going the whole hog and putting one-inch-mesh netting round the bottom.

In any case, it is worth putting a separate band of netting at the bottom, since it nearly always rusts or perishes first just above ground level, and it is economical to be able to replace a narrow strip instead of having to scrap sound netting simply because a few inches have gone at the bottom. The cheapest thing, therefore, is to have heavy-gauge three-inch-mesh netting from two feet above ground to the top. This will require four-feet rolls. A three-foot roll of one-inch-mesh netting should be put below this, laced to it, the bottom foot being either buried or bent outwards. The final result will then be a band of one-inch-mesh, rat-proof netting two feet high all round, and this will keep chickens and small animals in and vermin out. The top four feet will last for years and will be protection against foxes, dogs, and cats.

There are two schools of thought about burying or turning out at the base of the netting. If the netting is to be round your boundary, you may have no option but to dig a trench one foot deep, bury the bottom of the netting, and fill in the trench. In any case, this is really the soundest practice, because it prevents practically everything, including rats tunnelling either in or out. The disadvantage is that it means a lot of very hard work and there may be hazards like tree roots to contend with. The other method is to dig a very shallow trench—three inches deep will do—and lay the netting horizontally along this, the turn-out being outside. Then cover this shallowly with earth and seed with grass seed to consolidate. Where there is already turf, it is enough to mow it very short, lay the foot of netting on it and allow the grass to grow through. Within a few weeks, there is a solid mat and it is impossible ever to get the turn-out of netting up again. The reason it is enough to lay netting along the surface rather than bury it is that most animals that will dig under netting, including rats and foxes, always start to dig at the base of the upright netting, and are, of course, stopped at once by the horizontal piece lying along the surface of the ground. It does not occur to them to go back one foot *away* from the fence and start digging there. To get the netting taut, *hang* the four-foot heavy-gauge piece on the central wire strainer. By putting a three-inch nail through the top mesh and twisting round the straining wire two or three turns, like a tourniquet, it is possible to lace the netting to the strainer so that nothing will shift it. Similarly, lace the top of the one-inch mesh to the bottom of the three-inch mesh, and bend the bottom foot outwards or sink in the trench, depending which method you propose to use. To obtain tension, and also discourage too vigorous digging, put a single row of barbed wire round at ground level and peg firmly down. The only remaining thing is to roll a two-foot strip of two- or three-inch-mesh netting horizontally round the top, lacing to the three strainer wires. This prevents anything climbing over and is really as effective as a complete covering of netting except for full-winged birds. The enclosure is now complete and, though it is a lot of trouble to erect originally, it is not nearly so costly as it would appear. In my opinion it is worth it simply for the pleasure of being able to turn the dogs out, night or day, in the knowledge that they cannot wander off and get into mischief or be run over. When one further considers the pleasure of having all sorts of pets around one under conditions of almost complete liberty, I know of few ways I'd rather spend a little money.

Vermin

Food which is attractive to domestic birds and animals is certain to appeal to vermin as well. Where there are poultry or rabbits or guinea-pigs, there will be wild rats and mice, if they are not disturbed. I have found it far easier to go to some initial trouble to keep them out than to be forced to take violent action to cure an invasion.

One inch wire netting round the enclosure will help, but, if rats can find no way through it, they will climb over. The simple thing to do, therefore, is to leave one or two tunnels through the netting, with the mouth of the tunnel flush with the outside. Every exploring rat will find the tunnel, which must have a diameter of about three inches. It must, however, be a very special tunnel, from which there is no escape. In the days before gin traps were banned, it was common to have a few tunnel entrances, each guarded by a gin. Now there are various approved traps sold for setting in tunnels, and the only modification required is that the tunnels must be constructed of a size to suit the particular trap chosen.

The approved traps kill outright and should be examined regularly and reset when they have caught a rat. If this simple precaution is taken, you will never be seriously troubled by vermin. I usually catch from seventy to one hundred rats a year in a trap-line of four traps, and never reckon to have more than the odd rat on the ground.

As an additional precaution, I rest a paving slab on four bricks, so arranged that there is about an inch space below the slab. In the cover thus provided, I put a couple of handfuls of corn, and any rats that come, tunnel in to get it. When it is being taken regularly by rats or mice, I simply replace the corn by one of the anticoagulant rat poisons. It must be understood that rats need to eat this about five nights running, after which their blood ceases to clot and they die. The advantage is that one dose of it is unlikely to harm domestic pets, but it is important to take precautions to prevent stock having regular access to it. This is usually made clear on the instructions. It is also important to make sure vermin that has been feeding on this type of poison does not have access to animal feeding stuffs. A case was reported recently of dogs showing symptoms of poisoning after they had fed several times on meal on which rats suffering from anticoagulant poisoning had urinated.

The third method that I use to prevent vermin joining my pets, is to leave old pipes, about three inches in diameter and six feet long, outside my rat-proof netting. When I let the dogs out at night, they love to hunt round the perimeter, and any wandering rat that is exploring the area takes cover in the pipes. The dogs then mount guard till I come with flash light and stick to poke the rat out. And that is one less.

Stock for the Garden

A very wide range of animals and birds will do well at liberty in the garden, but great care must be exercised as to how they are mixed. Some, like tortoises and guinea-pigs, are harmless to other stock. Others, like peafowl, are very bad mixers, and would kill many smaller pets that shared their quarters. So far as damage to the garden itself is concerned a great deal will depend upon the extent and type of garden.

Bedding out plants tend to be very vulnerable to a wide variety of pets. Those that don't eat them tend to trample them or scratch them up. Plants like primulas, which offer attractive greenstuff early in the season, are also potential victims.

Most of our garden consists of shrubs, lawn, and pool. It is therefore, fairly labour-saving, and most of our creatures spend a lot of time on the lawn—where they usually look their best and many relish the fresh young grass—while they get among dense shrubs or under or in the holly hedge in hard weather. They do extremely little damage to the plants—my wife is a keen gardener, and she agrees that the movement and colour they provide more than compensate for what little harm they do.

The choice of stock is so wide that it is not possible to be specific about what will or won't mix. Obviously it is unwise to include any predator, like fox or badger, amongst a collection which may include many of his prey. Hedgehogs are notorious thieves of eggs and must be excluded if you hope for success with ground-nesting birds like partridges or pheasants. Most cock pheasants are pugnacious, and it will be one miserable vendetta for them if your garden is not large with enough cover to give a territory and sanctuary for

169

more than one cock, though several hens will agree very well and mate with a single male bird.

The more birds you keep under conditions of partial liberty, the better naturalist you will become. It is possible to observe them thus so much more accurately than under the artificial conditions of cage life, and, even if you do lose one or two creatures through battles and dramas, you have the consolation that it was probably a very natural way for them to perish.

Pinioning

Is is essential to pinion or brail most birds which are to be kept free to roam in a garden. Full-winged birds, which can fly freely, will fly out and often try to walk back. When they reach the netting from the outside, they will pace endlessly up and down and not think of going a few paces back to fly over. When night falls, they squat at the foot of the netting, as near to home as they are able to get, and all the first cat or fox leaves is a pathetic bundle of feathers to bear witness, in the morning, that your pet at least tried to get home.

I firmly believe that is kinder to take steps to prevent birds flying over your netting, but give them the whole area of the garden in which to wander, than to coop them full-winged in a relatively small pen. In the wild, birds like ducks, pheasants, and partridges fly mainly as a means of escape or to get to new feeding grounds in different seasons. You do not see ducks or pheasants or partridges wheeling and gambolling in the air, as will jackdaws or performing pigeons, for the sheer love of aerobatics. They fly with a set purpose, and, if the need for that flight is absent, I do not believe they notice the hardship of being grounded. Indeed, at shooting parties, it is often very difficult to persuade hand-reared birds to take to the wing, as they would much rather run to safety.

So I have my pheasants and ornamental water fowl pinioned. This means that the tip of one wing is removed. It is a small joint which carries the last, or outside, seven or eight flight feathers, and when they are gone flight is so lopsided that the bird cannot rise from the ground.

The proper time to carry out this operation is when the bird is less than seven days old. The wing tip, at that stage, is soft gristle, and, when it is snipped off with a sharp pair of scissors, it does not appear to cause the young birds any serious inconvenience. It is, of course, vital to know exactly where to snip, and the operation should always be performed by a veterinary surgeon.

The most dangerous time to perform the operation is when the bird is almost full grown but not fully feathered. The worst combination of all will be encountered at this time. The cartilage of the wing tip will have hardened to bone, but the feathers will not be mature and will still have a copious blood supply to them. There is grave danger of the bird bleeding to death if operated on now, and few veterinary surgeons will attempt it. This does not mean that adult birds cannot be pinioned. Provided that the feathers are quite hard and the bird is not in a process of moulting, pinioning does not appear to cause the trouble one might imagine. Birds that are pinioned one day will be feeding boldly and freely within forty-eight hours.

There are two alternatives to pinioning, both of which can be done by an amateur. The services of a veterinary surgeon will not be required.

Brailing consists of fitting a specially made clip or strap to the outside of one wing, and it has exactly the same effect as pinioning except that surgery is not necessary. It is commonly used for wild pheasants that are caught up for laying. When enough eggs have been collected, the brail is removed and the bird returned to the woods, where she will probably lay again and rear a brood of her own. Brails can be obtained from gamekeepers' suppliers.

The other method that can be used to 'ground' birds in an enclosure is wing clipping. The outside eight feathers—the large flights—should be cut off short with a sharp pair of scissors. It is probably neater to leave the end two feathers and clip the next eight or nine, as it is then not obvious, when the wing is closed, that the bird is clipped. This is entirely painless, no worse than cutting your nails, and it is just as effective as pinioning until the bird grows new feathers. In theory, it should last until the time for the bird to moult, when it will be necessary to catch it and repeat the operation. In practice, few birds drop all their flight feathers at the same time, or they would be grounded by nature as effectively as if they had been pinioned. So the stumps you leave when clipping will gradually drop out and be replaced and the first you know will be when you see a bird you fondly imagine to be safe sailing merrily over your garden fence. So do not place complete reliance on wing-clipping with birds that are very precious.

There is a fourth, and again purely temporary means of grounding birds, which may be particularly useful when you want to get hand-reared wild birds self-supporting prior to liberation. If a hand-reared bird is simply turned loose, it may starve before it has learned to look after itself unless food is exceptionally plentiful. So what is required is some method of keeping the bird about while it is fed less and less and encouraged and taught to find its own food.

If the last six flight feathers are plucked from one wing, the same effect will be produced as if it had been pinioned or clipped. But clipped feathers will not be replaced until the cut stumps have moulted out. If the feathers (or the stumps) are plucked, they will be replaced by new feathers in about six or eight weeks. What is more, the feathers will obviously grow comparatively slowly so that he will not be able to fly suddenly, the whole transition being gradual enough to give him every chance of learning to fend for himself by the time he is independent.

I often use this method when introducing new adult birds to the garden or if birds have to be separated temporarily. For instance, some drakes have to be kept from molesting the ducks or other species during the breeding season, while they can be left full-winged for the rest of the year. I catch them in the spring and clip them, keeping them to the part of the garden I have reserved for them till their ducks have finished laying. Then I remove the stumps and they are fully airborne again in a couple of months. Ducks are one of the few birds which sometimes do moult so quickly and extensively that they deprive themselves of the power of flight for a short time, usually in July. Then they take to large pools, with plenty of reeds for cover, and skulk on the water until their new feathers are through.

Pheasants
Almost any garden is improved by the addition of a pair of pheasants, at any rate initially. The larger pheasants, silver and Chinese, are a little too robust for delicate flower borders and may not delight the heart of the dedicated

172

gardener. A garden comprising mainly shrubs and lawns is not likely to take much harm, and the added beauty will more than compensate most people for what bit of damage they do. Pheasants will get all the shelter they need from a good shrubbery. Do not make an aviary.

There are a number of very different varieties of pheasant from which to choose. Few are lovelier than the varieties commonly found wild in Britain, the Chinese ringneck and the Mongolian. But they are rather large and rather aggressive. In the comparatively small space of a garden they often fight, not only with other cock pheasants, but with bantams as well. The same, to some extent applies to the silver pheasant, although I have found great differences between individual silvers. Some are very bad bullies and others will live peacefully with their fellows even in relatively small areas of confinement.

My favourite pheasant is the golden. His colours are flamboyant reds and golds and yellows, so that he looks like a graceful macaw as he struts and prances on the lawn. His movements are staccato and he has a thin, pleasant whistling call which never sounds loud—but can be heard at a surprising distance. He is small and very peace-loving for a pheasant, and we have no complaints about any damage mine do in the garden.

Most extraordinary of all, my golden pheasants get very much tamer free in the garden than ever they would in an aviary. They seem to know I could not corner and catch them if I wanted to, and develop vastly more confidence in the knowledge of this secuirty.

Partridges

Partridges are perfectly delightful birds to have in the garden, and they do practically no damage whatsoever. It should be remembered however, that they are birds with a very strong sense of territory, and their natural territory is larger than any normal garden, so that it will not be practicable to keep more than one pair after they have mated at the end of January or the beginning of February. So I cut the feathers of the wings of chicks, to get them established. I live in the country, and when they moult and grow adult plumage, they gradually extend their range away from the garden until only one couple is left by next spring.

I always take a nest of partridge eggs and hatch them under a broody bantam. Indeed, so many nests get exposed when the hay is being cut, that there is never any difficulty about getting a clutch of eggs. Partridge hens are so brave and such wonderful mothers that, if the eggs are nearly due to hatch, the hen often sits on her nest until she is killed by the mowing machine.

Rearing

It is now possible to buy 'crumbs' specially produced for rearing young partridge. They are a balanced food and extremely effective. Most dealers in gamekeepers' equipment sell them, and some game farmers advertise them. They are well worth bearing in mind.

In the wild state, young partridges live very largely on flies and insects, and it is a great help if the coop with the broody is placed on the lawn at the edge of a thickly planted flower bed or close—within a couple of yards—to a row of peas or other fairly thick cover in the kitchen garden. It is absolutely essential that there are no crows, magpies, or jays about, as young partridges are particularly vulnerable to them. They are also a great favourite of domestic cats, which will kill the adults too.

If you live in good anthill country, the top taken off an anthill, placed in a bucket and tipped out a bit at a time to the chicks will be greatly appreciated. They will not only eat the white 'eggs'—which are really cocoons—but the adult ants as well. When they get older they are also very fond of gentles and I usually make a 'maggotorium' at the bottom of the garden. This consists of a framework about ten inches off the ground, across which is stretched half-inch-mesh wire netting. I buy a pound or two of lights from the butcher and put it on the wire netting, covering it with a piece of sacking. When I first put it up, I put a few gentles (the maggots of meatflies, sold at fishing-tackle shops) on the lights. After that wild flies will lay their eggs on the lights. As the maggots hatch, a lot of them fall through the netting and the young partridges will spend much of their time searching for booty below their 'maggotorium'. It is quite astonishing how quick they are at picking off adult flies too, which are attracted by the smell. If the bottom of your garden happens to be near a neighbour's house, I

174

should buy gentles rather than trying to breed your own.

As the young partridges grow, they will enjoy groats and then wheat, and they will run to you in a covey for food whenever you appear. Ours often come into the kitchen for food. They make the most attractive little confidential crooning sounds and are altogether delightful. Pheasants can be reared on exactly the same lines but partridges must be guarded against stoats, cats and foxes.

Ornamental Waterfowl

One does not need much water in the garden to be able to keep a few ornamental water fowl, and no birds are more beautiful or more tame.

An ordinary garden pool about ten feet by six feet will do, provided you arrange a platform at water level so that the bird may walk up the last few inches to the top of the surround, which is usually a few inches above water level.

If you are making a small pond especially for ducks, be certain that the surround is either stone or concrete, from four or five inches below water level to a couple of inches above. Ducks love to 'dibble' at wet soil and they will quickly erode the bank where it meets the water unless you prevent them. Another way of doing this is to make a sloping bank and lay on it a strip of half-inch-mesh wire netting eighteen inches wide, with nine inches below water and nine above. Before filling with water, sow this patch with grass-seed and do not allow the ducks in until the grass has formed a dense enough mat to conceal the netting completely. When the ducks work at this they will immediately come up against a firm barrier of wire netting which will work as effectively as concrete (but not so permanently) to prevent them from eroding the bank. The snag in this method is that the netting eventually perishes and breaks into fragments of rusty wire which can be dangerous to the ducks if they swallow it. It is a method I have used for many years without accident, but is not one you should try without assessing the hazards.

If you are lucky enough to own a garden with a stream, as I do, no power should deter you from keeping water fowl. Even if the garden has only a stream and no pool, it is usually simple enough to dam the stream to form a pool, in which case there will be none of the worries of making it water-tight as is necessary when the water is not free. The one thing to watch is that you don't raise the water level above the foundations of house or buildings, unless the soil is an impervious clay.

Immediately round the pool should be a lawn of fine grass which can be mown. If, for any reason, this is not practicable, put a sloping surround of washed gravel, otherwise it is only too easy, with ducks paddling in and out of the water, to have a sour mudpatch. If there is no stream to run through the pool, it is best to arrange drainage facilities so that you can empty it and refill with fresh water when necessary. At one side of the pool, preferably the opposite side to the house, there should be a good screen of evergreens, rhododendrons, holly, azaleas, etc., where the birds can shelter from the weather. They do not need any building or shelter, and probably would not use it if you offered it, but they do need somewhere well out of the wind where they can also get shade if they need it.

Always feed the birds on the lawn between the pool and the house. They will come right up to the windows when they settle down to the place, and spend half an hour or so picking up the widely scattered corn on the lawn. They will discover all sorts of worms and wireworms and insects and spend a good deal of their time keeping the lawn free of pests. Some of them, like shelduck and widgeon, will also get a good deal of their living by grazing, and we find that selective grazing and constant fertilizing by our ducks keeps the grass in wonderful condition.

One word of warning. Be extremely careful what weed-killers or lawn-dressings you use lest you poison your birds. Some of the fungicides, weedkillers, and insecticides are dreadfully dangerous. We never use any poison on our land at all because, however careful we may be to shut our stock up, it is impossible to give protection to the wild birds.

Stocking the Pool

There is an extremely wide variety of lovely water fowl from which to choose. Some are very gregarious and others are arrant bullies. If your pool is very small, have only one or two pairs of birds on it, carefully chosen so that they do not interfere with each other.

As with so many other pets, some of the most beautiful

176

water fowl are also the cheapest because they happen to breed very freely.

Carolinas and mandarins are brilliantly coloured, seeming to be made from gaudy cardboard, yet neither cost as much as many less attractive, though rarer ducks. Pochard and tufted are among the lovely native ducks, both are diving birds and their legs are set so far back that they are out of their element on dry land. Teal—tiny, friendly, harmless, and very beautiful native duck—always do well with us, and it is quite possible to keep more than one pair on the pool, though generally speaking, it is wise to have only one pair of a given species, as they are prone to fall out with their own kind more frequently than with other ducks. Some species of ducks, common mallard and ruddy shelducks, for instance, and Egyptian and Magellan geese, are particularly aggressive and unsuitable for a mixed collection. The geese are dreadful bullies and will inflict actual harm, apart from the fact that they will make the whole collection so jumpy that they will spend their time skulking in cover instead of looking beautiful on the pool or lawn. Ducks, on the other hand, have a different method of being unpleasant. The drakes don't fight, but they harass ducks other than their own mates to such an extent that they become completely demoralized, and leave if full-winged, or lie up until dusk in cover if unable to escape.

So do not over-stock, and check that any species that attracts you does not happen to be one of the more aggressive varieties.

Some of the geese, red breasted and maned geese in particular, are very gentle and mix well with other water fowl provided they are not in too small an enclosure. The diving ducks are amenable, but Chiloe widgeon, some of the shelduck, and most geese simply make life a misery for the other occupants of the garden.

Feeding
Ornamental water fowl like mixed corn with a high proportion of wheat and barley. It is a sensible precaution to sink a number of shallow troughs or to make the pond in the form of a relatively deep centre with the last eighteen inches to the bank having a hard bottom at a depth of about six inches. This is often done with ornamental ponds so that

177

plants liking shallow water can grow round the edge.

It is then possible to give one feed on the lawn in the morning, to keep the birds used to coming into the garden and to enjoy their company. The evening feed should be thrown into the pool so that it falls in the shallows at the edge. The ducks have no difficulty finding it under water but rats and sparrows are denied access just when the garden is most likely to be undisturbed at dawn and dusk. If you have diving ducks throw a small handful for each into the deep water and watch them put mermaids to shame by their grace as they dive for it.

When the breeding season approaches, about March, some people give a few ordinary poultry laying pellets to encourage the birds to lay. This is sound enough practice, but do be careful not to overdo it. It is fatally easy to produce dropped ovaries if ducks are forced too much with these specialized diets, and I rarely give mine anything but corn. I prefer keeping them a bit longer to breeding a few extra young I only have to part with when they grow up.

Breeding
Some species, like mandarins and carolinas, normally nest in holes, and they require nesting boxes. Others, like teal, widgeon and tufted, like thick cover to make a nest, and I provide clumps of reed, pampas grass, coarse grass, and shrubs. It is often difficult to get enough dense cover early in the season, and some of my birds love the shelter at the base of a thick holly hedge.

Geese usually make a scrape, often with practically no shelter, on a flower bed or gravel path. The gander will stand by it and chivvy every intruder for days, so that it is usually obvious where they will nest. The thing to do is to watch for the goose to lay and steal the egg the moment she leaves the nest, replacing it with a common duck egg, so that it is no great disaster if a crow finds the nest and steals the eggs. When she has laid her clutch, the goose will start to incubate, despite the fact that there are only duck eggs in the nest. The first night she sits, move her and take all the eggs. She will then desert and, with luck, come into lay again in about a couple of weeks and lay a second clutch. If you once let her go properly broody, the chances of her coming into lay again that season are not nearly so good.

178

The eggs you have taken should be stored in a cool place until the clutch is complete and then hatched and reared by bantams.

The same technique applies to the eggs of ornamental ducks. The duck will usually lay in the morning and will be the last one coming to feed or the first away, depending on whether she is laying before or after you feed. While you are there she will probably be very coy and refuse to go to nest. So make a great show of going away, hide at a distance, and use a pair of good glasses to watch where she goes. I usually find it takes two or three mornings to discover the nest. The first morning I see the general direction and decide where to stand the next day to get a clearer picture. The second I decide more or less exactly where the nest is, and the third I get the exact spot and count the eggs while the duck is safely feeding. With valuable species or exposed nests or in late frosty weather, I exchange the real eggs for some that do not matter. And I always mark the eggs I put in with indelible pencil so that there is never any doubt which is the new-laid egg.

Incubation

On the whole, ornamental water fowl are not the best of mothers. It is quite essential that the young ducks should start life in a coop and wire-netting run, for if they get on the pool, the other ducks will drown them unless there is quite exceptional space and cover. Ornamental ducks are likely to panic and trample their young if they suddenly find themselves shut in a rat-proof coop at night or a six-by-four-feet run by day. Also, there is no chance of a second brood from birds already rearing one.

I therefore use silkie bantams to incubate and rear my ducks and geese. To be precise, my bantams are not pure silkie but are from a silkie hen mated to a silkie×game bantam cock. This gives a little more fire, in defence of her chicks—or ducklings—and a little less chance of the young being entangled in the pure silkie feathering.

I keep a number of corrugated-iron hen coops that can be shut and made completely rat-proof at night, and I put a comfortable nest box of soft straw in each. These are put about in the paddock where the silkies live, so that they take to them and lay there. I collect no silkie eggs when the ducks begin to lay so that, with luck, there is a broody silkie in each coop when the ducks are laying.

When I have a complete clutch of duck eggs I remove the silkies' own eggs and replace by the ones I want to hatch. If at all possible, I sit several different clutches of duck eggs at precisely the same time. When they all hatch I put as many as possible under one hen so that two hens will rear the ducks hatched from three sittings or one will rear two sittings. This allows the spare broody to lay again and be ready for a late clutch of eggs, and it also means I need fewer coops and runs.

Rearing
When the ducklings hatch, leave them a full twenty-four hours under the hen. They begin life absorbing the residue of the yolk and are much better left alone to get thoroughly dry and strong. More chicks and ducklings are lost by impatience to see them on their feet too soon than almost any other cause.

When they do go out, try to get the run on to either clean turf or well drained gravel. The hen in the coop must be quite dry, so that she can warm the ducklings coming off the water, and it is best to put her either on about four inches of peat or a bottom of half-inch-mesh wire netting. I prefer the peat.

The ducklings need water to dibble in and swim in. Ideally it should be running water and, if it is possible to net in a small portion of slowly running brook, this will be ideal. Remember the ducklings can dive, so net the water to the bottom.

Failing this I use a dustbin lid inverted and let-in flush with the turf. Put a couple of slates or tiles in the first day as, if the water does get slopped over the edge, young duck cannot always climb out.

The water will need changing two or three times a day because it will get covered by a very thin layer of oil from the ducks' glands above their tails. This will lower the surface tension and, if they are in too long, they will get bedraggled and wet, when they are likely to get pneumonia.

The great thing with young ducks is to get them feeding at once. A great many people hold up their hands in horror at the very mention of bread and milk. I have never found it does mine any harm and it seems the best thing of all on which to start young goslings.

But ducks need fresh green food and live food above all else. The easiest way to provide this is to collect quantities of duck-weed and put it in shallow dishes of water near the coop. Do not put it in the dustbin lid, which should be left for swimming. The duckweed will contain an immense amount of fresh water shrimps, mosquito larvae, daphnia, and other minute animal food which will do the young ducks more good than any prepared food.

For bulk I use biscuit meal specially prepared for ducklings by dealers in gamekeepers' supplies. This is put in a saucer as far from the water as the run will allow. The reason for this is that each time the ducklings eat the biscuit meal they run and dibble at the water and then back to the biscuit, which quickly gets paddled into a foul porridge if it is too near the water. For this reason, I feed it little and often and always throw away the soggy surplus.

The ducklings should be pinioned when they are seven days old and allowed into a netted-off portion of the main pool at three weeks. They will be grown and feathered and independent at eight or ten weeks, after which they can be treated as adult ducks.

They will not come into colour until their first autumn and it should be noted that most species of ducks moult into eclipse after the breeding season. That is to say the brilliant drakes become as dowdy as their ducks when the need for courtship is over. It then becomes important that they should be inconspicuous so that they do not attract the attention of predators either to their young or to themselves when they are moulting. They usually come back into colour between September and November. Some species, like chiloe widgeon and ruddy shelduck do not go into eclipse.

Rearing Geese
The same procedure is adopted as with ducks up to the stage where the goslings are hatched. The geese themselves are better, quieter parents than duck, and the chief purpose in rearing under silkies is to allow the goose to lay a second and sometimes a third clutch. It is quite satisfactory to allow her to rear the last clutch, however.

Feed as ducks except that goslings need quantities of fresh, tender short grass, and the bulk of their food is grazed. They like the vegetable content of duckweed better than the animal food it contains, though both are good for them.

Move the run every day to start with then twice a day, and by the time the goslings are a week old a six-by-four-feet area of grass will not be enough for them. They should then have access to as much of the lawn as is practicable and the amount of grass they will consume in their first eight weeks is truly prodigious. Once they are adult, their appetite for grass becomes more normal. Continue with biscuit meal and grain till their appetite wanes. Then feed as for ducks. It is most important that both ducks and geese have access to flint and limestone grit at all ages.

Pigeons at Liberty
In a protected garden it is possible to keep many breeds of pigeon loose that could nomally survive only in an aviary.

Exhibition fantails, for example, carry their heads so far back that is is impossible for them to see directly ahead when they are displaying. Unprotected, they would fall victims to the first cat or ill-trained dog they met. On the other hand, kept in an aviary they get so fat and lazy that not only do they take practically no exercise, but it is often impossible for them to mate without having their lovely tail feathers cut. At liberty, as I have kept and bred them for years, I have not found it necessary to trim them in any way, and the birds are active enough to look after themselves in storm and high winds.

Other breeds that are satisfactory and decorative at liberty are all the 'blowers', breeds which inflate their crops with air when they are displaying. The best known, perhaps, are pouters and pigmy pouters, but I am very fond of Norwich croppers, and my favourites are Bohemian brunners which are strong fliers and in flight look as if they have swallowed a large apple.

There is an almost infinite variety of other fancy pigeons which look well in a garden, but the ones to avoid are the performing varieties and those with heavy feathering on their feet, such as fairy swallows, because they get caked in mud. To do well with tipplers, rollers, and racing pigeons you must regulate their exercise and watch their diet. They often lose the will to perform when they are at liberty all the time.

Housing
A major advantage of having pigeons at liberty is that they do not require as much room as they would in an aviary, nor does their pen need cleaning so often. All that is really required is a pen the size of the breeding boxes in a pigeon loft. Each pair will need a box large enough to take a couple of nest pans and a couple of roosting perches.

The dovecote itself should be soundly made and quite weather-proof. It should be divided into horizontal storeys by movable shelves, and the shelves should be subdivided into boxes by sliding partitions. All that is necessary then to clean the quarters thoroughly is to take shelves and partitions out of the dovecote, scrape, scrub, and replace them.

If it is possible to make holes into the inside of a fowl pen, the nest boxes may be fixed to the wall over the droppings board and the boxes themselves floored with one and a half by half an inch welded mesh netting. The pigeon droppings will then fall straight through on to the fowls' droppings board and the pigeons will need very little cleaning out indeed.

Feeding
Garden pigeons should be particularly well fed to prevent them raiding your own or your neighbours' gardens. If they are fed on mixed corn and particularly if they are given rather more than they will clear up, you will at once be plagued by a horde of sparrows which will be far more difficult to get rid of than rats. Pigeon peas and beans are slightly more expensive than mixed corn but are too big to be stolen much by small birds, so that the additional cost is easily recouped.

It is essential to be sure that there is an adequate supply of fresh grit and clean water available at all times. Feed the birds regularly, move slowly and deliberately, give the same whistle or call each time you go out, and you will soon have a flock of beautiful birds only too anxious to display their affection by eating from your hand.

183

Barbary Doves

Very few people keep Barbary doves at liberty because it is not realized how much more attractive they are on the wing than flitting about in an aviary. The one snag is that it is absolutely essential that they roost under cover. This is not because they are not hardy but because their lovely creamy colouring makes them very conspicuous to owls, and tawny owls appear to find them irresistible.

It is best either to produce a breeding pair at the beginning of the breeding season or a young pair just weaned. My preference is for a breeding pair, and I like a fairly large shed or building to house them: a potting shed or other outhouse is ideal. It will be necessary to keep it shut for a couple of weeks, until they are acclimatized, and to have a trap door or opening window so that they can be allowed or denied access as you see fit, after that. Once they are used to their quarters, there will be no further trouble.

I find the easiest thing to do is to make a rough, temporary wire-netting door with a perch or two fixed to it at right angles. The doves can spend their days sitting just inside the door, surveying the world outside.

Nail a small box in the form of a shelf with a shallow lip, within about six inches of the top of the wall under the roof. An old cigar box is admirable or the sort of shallow box used by gardeners for transplanting seedlings will do. With luck, your doves should use this as a nesting box, and a couple of perches should be nailed fairly close to it for roosting. A spare perch should be provided right on the other side of the shed because the cock is apt to be over-enthusiastic in driving his hen, though when she is just in breeding condition she likes it.

Having confined them to their shed, always feed as near to the door as possible so that they begin to associate food with the view immediately outside.

After they have been restrained for two or three weeks, do not feed them for one whole day. During their confinement you should have spent as much time as possible with them, but certainly never less than a few minutes every time you feed them. So, by now, they should be completely tame and have the utmost confidence in you.

The morning after their day without food, they will

therefore be even more delighted to see you than usual. Walk very quietly up to their wire-netting door talking or whistling to them as usual. Open the door very gently and throw a few grains of corn on the ground outside. I cannot emphasize too strongly that you must only give them a very few grains as it is vital not to satisfy their appetites at this stage.

Let them have a little corn, and then give them time to take stock of their surroundings. Unlike pigeons, which usually fly on to buildings, your doves are likely to fly to the nearest tree. When they have been there for a little while try to call them back and offer a little more grain. If they come, throw some into their shed and then give them as much as they will clear up, but do not feed them again that day. If they do not come, leave them till evening. They are unlikely to go far away and, by then, they will be really hungry and are likely to go in quite easily. Repeat the routine next day and, if they are not difficult, leave them loose after that and only shut them in at night. From then on, given a very light feed in the morning, near the door, when you let them out and their main feed when they come in to roost. Once they start to nest indoors, they are likely to give little trouble.

Even when they are settled, it is always necessary to watch for signs of the urge to roost or nest outside in trees and bushes. If they are difficult to get in one night, shut them in next day and omit the last feed unless they are feeding young. They are worth any trouble this may be, and will delight you by their tameness, their lovely gliding display flight, and their constant musical calls. Furthermore, since they will interbreed with turtle doves, they may attract wild ones in summer. These did not nest in my garden until I kept Barbaries.

Do not be led to believe from this that doves are really peaceful birds. That is one of the myths peddled by politicians and romanticists. Cocks will fight until one gets mastery, so you are unlikely to persuade more than one pair to occupy any one outhouse. They will usually drive off even their own young when they are old enough to be weaned, and you will find it necessary to establish them in other quarters if you want to keep more than the odd pair safe from owls. In point of fact, they will usually do all right in summer if the garden is well wooded, and it certainly is nothing to be unduly worried about if they stay out the odd night. But when the leaves are off the trees and there is not much dense cover, they will not last very long,

Food
Barbaries will eat small mixed corn, wheat, barley, etc., but when they are rearing young they need canary seed and millet.

Peafowl
Peafowl are not birds to keep in a small garden nor if you have close neighbours. They kick up a tremendous row, which I personally find attractive, but I have every sympathy with folk who have to endure it not from their own choice but from their neighbour's. The birds are also dreadfully destructive in the garden, being strong enough to scratch up mature plants and large enough to lay waste vast patches in satisfaction of their appetites. Apart from that, they are quite delightful in their proper place, which is gracing the lawns and formal clipped yew gardens of stately homes.

After obtaining your peafowl, the first difficulty is to get them to settle down. They are great wanderers and are quite likely to begin quietly walking along the nearest hedgerow or to the nearest wood—and keep on walking. So rig up a temporary enclosure to start with and feed and keep them there for a couple of weeks. Then omit to feed them for a day and let them out next morning. Every time they think of wandering off, attract them back with a few grains of corn. Before they have had as much as they want, entice them back into their enclosure and finish feeding them there. Repeat the performance for a day or two and then leave them out without feeding them. When you call them in to roost they will be ready for a big meal.

Continue feeding once a day in the evening until they have established a safe roost, which they will probably choose high up in a fir tree, or other tall evergreen.

If they fly down outside your garden enclosure—and I would not pinion or wing-clip peafowl—they are unlikely to be worried by foxes in daylight unless the hen lays away. The sitting hen is very vulnerable, so it is important to provide good cover for nesting sites in the area you want her to choose. Among ivy on battlements of old ruins is attractive to them, so in ordinary gardens, provide cover like rushes, shrubs, or St. John's wort.

You must keep the hen and chicks confined in a smallish enclosure until they are strong, otherwise she will walk them off their legs while they are very young. Once they are virile enough to keep with her, she will prove a most wonderful mother. She will stay with them—or they will stay with her—for months, and it is always amusing to watch an old peahen fly up to roost with a brood of young almost as big as herself. She spreads her wings out over them all and acts as a giant umbrella long after they seem quite grown-up enough to look after themselves.

The young are rather susceptible to coccidiosis, and this can be largely prevented by a meal specially prepared to include a particular drug. Veterinary chemists also supply a preparation which has to be put in drinking water. This last is to cure the complaint and it is remarkably successful although the birds dislike it so intensely that they must have no opportunity to get at untreated drinking water for five days. The drug is so powerful that it must not be continued longer than that. It is most unusual for birds which have been cured to get the complaint again.

Liberty Budgerigars

Budgerigars, full-winged and at full liberty are among the most striking pets you can have in your garden. Their chatter is ceaseless, their colours are kaleidoscopic, and their flight powerful and swift. You do not need a large garden to house them, nor even a large aviary, and they will fly to millet sprays outside your windows as readily as blue tits to suet.

The late Duke of Bedford pioneered the methods of persuading budgerigars to stay around when not confined, and a great many people have modified his methods since, some even dispensing with an aviary during the summer, and persuading their birds to nest in boxes put on trees, like tit boxes. As it is necessary to have an aviary in the winter, it is better to begin by operating a flock of birds which have an aviary as base, even though you try them completely at liberty later, to breed.

187

The basic principle in keeping liberty budgerigars is that they will be unwilling to go far away when they have young and the young will stay around if freed as soon as they leave the nest. Out of breeding season, the hens are confined in a flight in full view of the cocks, which stay around to be near the hens. That is the basic theory, but not all the birds will subscribe to it. Some will inevitably stray and be lost, and it is quite essential to realize this before a start is made.

Birds from proved homing strains, that is strains where several generations have been at liberty, are likely to suffer smaller losses than birds bred by parents whose ancestors have spent years in cage or aviary. But birds from a homing strain will be more expensive to buy and you should consider buying throw-outs from a breeder of show birds. By throw-outs I mean birds which have colour blemishes but are completely sound physically. Birds with incorrect spots or that are too pale or too dark for exhibition purposes will look just as delightful flying in your garden as winners from the shows. You will be able to buy these birds very cheaply if you look at the advertisements in the trade papers catering for breeders of small livestock, and they will be every bit as lovely as their more expensive cousins sold as 'liberty bred'.

Do not expect to have one hundred per cent success with either. You will be likely to get some losses even with birds whose ancestors have spent generations at liberty. Birds which were bred in cages or aviaries may well have considerably less innate sense of location.

Nevertheless, with ordinary luck and good management, you should end your first season with about the number you started with. That is, if you start with half-a-dozen pairs, you are likely to lose about as many as you breed the first season, but the ones that are left will mostly be young ones staunch to their home.

The Aviary
You will, in effect require two aviaries and two flights. One will contain the birds which are not, at the moment, free, and the other will house birds free to come and go as they like during most of the day.

The structure should be located in a clearing close to trees and evergreen shrubs. It is important that birds coming in should have somewhere congenial to alight and those leaving the flight should just flit on to a tall bush or small tree to get their bearings before flying any great distance.

In point of fact, it is surprising what a small range free budgerigars have when once they are settled. Usually they do not go more than about a couple of hundred yards from their aviary.

The aviaries themselves should be similar and can, in fact, be one fairly large flight divided down the centre by a wire-netting partition. The top eighteeen inches should be covered by vertical asbestos sheets, to give complete protection from wind, and all but the centre of the roof should be covered, to give complete weather-proofing. The general effect is of a Dutch barn with the vertical sides netted. All round the top should be a row of exactly similar nest boxes—as described earlier in the chapter on budgerigars—with at least two and preferably three boxes for each pair to choose from. There should be vertical screens between them to prevent the hens seeing each other when they are perched at the entrance to their nests. In general, management should be similar to that you would give a stud of budgerigars in an aviary. Since they will be free to come and go as they like and, more important, where they like, it is essential to make their quarters as attractive as you possibly can.

There should be plenty of perches, so that there is no need for any competition amongst the birds. They will like them placed as high as possible, which will have the added advantage that they will be out of the wind and rain, shielded by the roof and vertical sheeting round the top of the flight. In addition, put the same sort of branching twigs you would in a normal aviary, which the birds can amuse themselves by shredding. The casual perches should be stuck in heavy untippable flowerpots, fairly low down, so that the birds can see all round the aviary flight when using them.

The most important parts of a liberty aviary are the entrances and exits. There should be two of these, one in the wire-netting portion of the aviary roof and the other half way up the aviary side, also in the wire netting.

These entrances should be six inches square and they should be intersected by a strong cross made of stout, plain, galvanized wire. The purpose of this is to make quite certain that the resultant hole will not admit anything much larger than a budgerigar. The worst thing which might enter through a six-inch hole would be a cat. At the same time, fairly large entrance holes are desirable, chiefly so that the birds may learn their way in and out quickly and easily. And remember, when you are successful, there will be a constant stream of home-reared youngsters to learn the ropes all summer.

Immediately beneath the entrance hole in the roof there must be a feeding tray. This should be about a foot square and three or four inches deep with drainage holes in the base, since it will be exposed to the wet. A wooden box with a perforated wood—base is good.

There should be a ladder fixed rigidly upwards from this tray towards the hole in the roof, but so arranged that it does not protrude through it. The Duke of Bedford found that he did best when the top rung was three and a half inches below the exit hole, and anyone starting liberty budgerigars for the first time is advised to read his booklet *Homing Budgerigars*, published by *Cage Birds*.

In the feeding tray there should be millet and oats and canary seed, and it is most important to be sure there really is seed there and that the birds have not eaten the seed and left a heap of unattractive husks.

A second entrance hole, also six inches in diameter with a baffle bar in the form of a cross, should be put in one side of the aviary near to the bush where the birds are likely to alight.

Close to this entrance hole there should be another feeding tray of food, though this one may be placed under the solid portion of the aviary roof, so that the food does not get so soggy in wet weather. Thus, the birds have two holes, where they can enter or leave at will.

When you want them confined to the aviary completely, in bad or foggy weather, all that is necessary is to fit a cover over each hole.

But, even when they are at liberty, you will not want them out at night. It is found, in practice, that they come back to the aviary for food or to visit their nests or young every couple of hours or so.

Accordingly, a wire-net funnel, four inches in diameter at

the top, and one and five-eighths inches at the tip, and about four inches long must be fitted to each entrance hole at least three hours before sunset. The ladders from the feeding boxes will have to be moved, as the tunnels will, of course, point inwards like the entrance to a sparrow trap. When the birds next call home they will enter by the funnel and will not be able to find their way out again. They will thus be confined safe from owls and prowling cats at night.

Liberating

Pairs of budgerigars can be kept at liberty during the breeding season from late February or March until October. If it is decided to keep them breeding as late as this, it is important to limit the number of young they rear by taking some of the eggs, or they will become weak from the prolonged strain. The alternative to this is to have twice as many pairs as you would normally use, allow the first lot to rear a brood—they can start in February—then swap them with the other pairs which have been kept in the resting aviary with no nest boxes. All the young bred will be left in the liberty aviary, whilst their parents take alternate spells in confinement, with no nests, and at liberty both to fly where they will and to breed.

When the breeding season is over, all the hens must be kept in the resting aviary while their mates can spend the winter at liberty. The hens in full view next door will act as a powerful attraction to keep their mates happily anchored nearby.

The best time to start up a liberty aviary is the spring. Get pairs of adults, and mate them in the liberty aviary—which will have its exits temporarily sealed—exactly as if you were breeding in an ordinary aviary.

Do not let any of them out until the first round of youngsters are just about to leave the nest. There will be a few losses at first, but there should soon be a good kit of brilliant, active birds to delight you every time you look through the window or go into the garden.

Complete Liberty

Advanced aviculturists have found it possible to go one stage further. They feed the birds in the aviary, allowing them to come and go exactly as with a liberty aviary, except

191

that the netting funnels are not put in place to ensure the whole flock roosting inside.

Then a number of nest boxes are placed round the garden, of the type normally used to attract tits. If they are well spaced out there should not be serious fighting over them. The budgerigars take well to these and, under good conditions, will rear young completely at liberty, but go to the aviary to feed.

The success of this method depends almost entirely on freedom from predators. Cats or owls about at night will bring certain doom to the plan.

Wild Birds in the Aviary

One of the major troubles with liberty budgerigars is that their food is very attractive to wild birds too. Great care should be taken to lay no temptation in their way by spilling food outside the aviary. Even so, sparrows, hedge sparrows, etc., will get in, and the only thing to do is to trap them in with the funnels and catch them at night (so as not to frighten your own birds, as thrashing around with a net in the day-time will). If you take them far enough away before letting them go, they will bother somebody else.

Tortoises

One of the commonest, least understood, and most misused pets in many gardens is the humble tortoise.

There has been a great deal of publicity about the cruelty involved in importing tortoises in recent years. The ones that do best in our climate are the spur-thighed, and Hermann's or Greek tortoise, which have more and smaller shell plates than the spur-thighed. Both come from the Mediterranean region and both need similar treatment. The male spur-thighed has a longer and more pointed tail than the female, which has a flatter shield covering the tail. In the male Greek tortoise, the tail marginal plate is divided into two giving twenty-four marginals to the female's twenty-three.

It is always best to keep a true pair because, apart from the fact that they may be bred, they appear to enjoy each other's company.

The selection of a specimen you want should take into account the fact that it is probably some time since they were caught and properly fed. Apart from pressure due to

192

the weight of others in the consignment, they have probably been subjected to undesirable fluctuations in temperature.

First of all, therefore, weed out any with damaged shells. Then examine legs to see that they are sound and unchafed by the string which their captors sometimes use to tether them. Then choose a specimen with bright eyes and make sure there is no trace of yellow fungus round his mouth, as this is a common and deadly complaint. Pick one that seems heavy for his size, as he is less likely to be half-starved, and finally get a good lively one.

These precautions are necessary because of the dreadful conditions some tortoises have to endure between capture and sale. But, if they are observed carefully and you succeed in buying a healthy specimen, he should live happily with you for many years.

The best time to buy is from May to July when the tortoise is likely to have been out of hibernation long enough to feed well, and will find plenty of suitable food in most gardens.

Tortoises are not carnivorous and they do not eat worms, slugs, and beetles as is widely believed. They are vegetarian, and most fond of plants with succulent leaves. They love clover and lettuce and most tender seedlings, including weeds like dandelion, and do not need artificial food, like bread or bread and milk, though some will eat it avidly.

They do not like wide variation in temperature. They need access to shade in the heat of the day and the protection of a house or shelter at night. If your garden is small enough for the damage a couple of tortoises do to show, put them in a shelter at night and take the edge off their appetites by feeding them on juicy succulents, like lettuce and dandelions, before turning them loose the next day. Some love sliced banana and similar fruit.

Always provide water in a sunken shallow dish that will not tip if the tortoise treads in it with his front legs, for that is the natural attitude of drinking. In the autumn your tortoises will get very sluggish because the time for their winter hibernation will be approaching. This will usually occur during October. Put them in a large wooden box on a thick bed of leaf-mould. Cover to the top, so that they are buried in leaf-mould, and store the box in a cool dark place. If the temperature gets too warm, they will wake prematurely and be unable to feed. If it gets too cold they will die. A cellar is ideal, failing which an unheated outhouse, thoroughly insulated against frost, will do.

When the tortoises wake from their winter sleep, they should have access to fresh green food and water, but it is most important to bring them indoors at night until the danger of frosts has passed. Put them in the warmest, sunniest corner of the garden in the morning so that they get thoroughly awakened and start to feed as soon as possible.

Breeding
Tortoises mate before, sometimes a considerable time before, eggs are laid. The female excavates a hole by urinating and bringing the wet soil out stuck to her back leg. The eggs are laid in this hole, which is then covered over and, in their native land, they would incubate by the power of the sun.

If they are incubated about 80°F. they will hatch if fertile in a variable period, apparently dependent on conditions. One fairly satisfactory method is to suspend a glass container, holding dry sand covering the eggs by half an inch, in a tropical aquarium maintained at the temperature required for breeding tropical fish. The humid atmosphere above the water in a tropical aquarium will benefit the eggs. About three months is likely to elapse before they hatch; the eggs will usually appear at the surface of the sand before the tortoises hatch.

The young tortoises should be kept in a vivarium at 75°F.–80°F., and fed on fruit pulp at first. Soft fruit like tomato or grape is best, but let them graduate to tender lettuce and clover as soon as possible. 'Little and often' is the golden rule in feeding at this stage, because the food will go flaccid so quickly in the heated vivarium.

They should get as much sun as possible when they are young, subject to the proviso that there is always shade available if they want it and they should not be allowed to hibernate their first season. To avoid this, it will be necessary to keep them in their heated vivarium, and their food for the winter will have to be mainly fruit pulp, owing to the difficulty of getting fresh succulent greens in winter.

11 Goats and Cade Lambs

A lot of people who dislike the hard labour of mowing lawns think that, if they buy a goat or lamb, their troubles will be over and their grass will be kept as neat as a bowling green.

They will find that the snag is that both goats and sheep will find plants that they like far better than grass—usually the choicest and most expensive plants in the garden!

Whatever their failures as lawn mowers, goats make delightful pets. They are browsing animals as opposed to grazers. That is to say they wander while they are feeding, taking a succulent mouthful wherever they fancy instead of cropping the grass methodically to leave it as a mown lawn.

Cottagers, who kept goats for their milk in the countryside got over this snag by fitting a collar and chain so that they could tether their goat where they wanted it to graze instead of allowing it to pick and choose where it liked.

This is still a good idea for two reasons and it works as well with a tame lamb as it does with a goat. By tethering it on a comparatively short chain, which is moved every day, you will prevent if from eating plants you don't want it to touch either because they are precious or poisonous. (Both goats and sheep are rather stupid about eating leaves like yew, which are very poisonous, and rhododendron, which is poisonous if taken in quantity.)

The other reason for tethering them is to make sure that they are put on fresh ground every day and that they do not return to land where they have previously grazed for as long as possible, but a minimum of two weeks.

This is because goats and sheep are both very susceptible to infestation by internal parasites which spend part of their life cycle on the ground. A healthy goat or sheep can pick up worms or liver fluke by grazing on pasture where another animal has passed the infection on in its droppings.

If the ground is allowed to lie fallow for longer than the

195

critical part of the life cycle of the parasite, it will be safe for grazing again.

So long as the grazing of goats is controlled, they are delightful pets, both friendly and affectionate.

They need fresh water, a weatherproof shelter for nights and a few processed 'goats nuts' to eke out their ration of grass. In summer, when there is a good flush of grass, they will not need any artificial feeding at all, but in winter or when they are producing a good quantity of milk they will need a ration of one of the proprietary brands of goat nuts (or sheep nuts) and clean hay to pick at in winter.

They are wasteful feeders and the hay should be offered in a hay net to prevent them pulling out more than they need and trampling it instead of eating it.

Goat kids or young 'cade' lambs are easy to rear on the bottle, with ordinary cow's milk or one of the dried milks especially prepared for the purpose. Youngsters that have been reared in this way are far tamer and more affectionate than animals which have been reared naturally and only come into contact with human beings after they are weaned.

12 The Aquarium and Vivarium

An aquarium or vivarium is ideal for those people who live in flats and are frequently away for a weekend or even longer.

Fish will often live in an aquarium for a very considerable time without attention provided it has been well stocked with 'live food' before being left.

The live food itself will often multiply and breed under the very conditions which suit the fish, so that it is usually easy to find suitable accommodation or kind friends when holidays come round if your pets live in an aquarium or vivarium.

Although the most avid fish fancier would not claim that his pets showed much intelligence or affection, they are usually interesting and often very beautiful. And even awkward neighbours cannot claim that the inhabitants of an aquarium make too much noise or smell!

In many ways fish and reptiles are satisfying pets because it is often possible to observe their whole life cycle, there is an almost infinite variety from which to choose and nothing is more beautiful than some of the more exotic species of tropical fish.

Furthermore, less specialized knowledge is necessary to keep them in good health than is needed for many apparently more simple animals and birds.

Seeting up a Tank
Pet shops sell a wide variety of aquaria, ranging from the old-fashioned goldfish bowl to large and costly welded frames, fitted with plate glass and all sorts of trimmings, from thermostatically controlled heaters to water reconditioning plant.

The worst possible aquarium, which is still commonly offered, is the old-fashioned spherical goldfish bowl. It offends all the basic principles of good fish keeping. The aim should always be to get the maximum area so that the water can absorb as much air as possible; but a goldfish bowl is smaller at the top than half way down. Lighting should always be from the top, a goldfish bowl receives light on every side. Temperature should never fluctuate; but a goldfish bowl is susceptible to every draught, hot or cold, that eddies the air. Never buy a goldfish bowl.

The best tanks are the angle-iron frames fitted with glass on sides and bottom, except the very large ones which should have a slate base to withstand the great weight of water they may be required to hold. The most usual of these tanks have an angle-iron frame with both webs of the angle equal, usually one inch. These look rather clumsy and it is better to try and obtain one made from an angle either one inch by three-quarters or half an inch. Having a smaller web towards the front makes the whole appearance much neater, and there is still plenty of overlap to secure water-tightness at the ends which are not seen so much.

Since fish 'breathe' air through their gills, and water absorbs air through its surface, you should, as just mentioned, choose a tank with as large a surface area as possible. A tank of a given volume which is shallow in relation to its size can hold more fish than a tall deep one.

There are various ways of minimizing this difficulty, so, if you happen to have a space in the house where a tall tank would look 'right', don't be put off. At worst you will not be able to keep quite so many fish as the volume of water would theoretically sustain. But in any case, overstocking is no virtue. A high density of plants will compensate to a large degree and there are on the market mechanical and electrical aerators, which bubble fresh air through the water. Not much of it will have time to dissolve on its way to the surface, but the passage of air bubbles through the water will have the effect of keeping it moving so that a patch of stale water will not settle at the bottom of the tank.

Always choose the biggest tank you can afford or can house. The more space your pets have to swim, and the more patches of plant that are available for shelter, the happier they will be, because their lives will be less different from the wild state.

Having brought the tank, make quite certain that the spot where you want to mount it is absolutely firm and solid.

198

Tanks of even quite moderate size hold a deceptively large amount of water, and if the stand is not flat and firm the strains set up will be so great that even a high-quality tank may spring a leak.

If you have bought a new tank, it is a sound plan to leave it all night under a gently running cold tap in case there are any traces of water-soluble paint, adhesive that seals the glass, or any other substance which damage the fish or harm the plants.

Furnishing the Tank

Nothing looks worse than a good aquarium tank full of nothing but water and fish. To get full value it must be planted, and here there is immense scope for miniature landscape—or waterscape—gardening.

Before the plants will grow it is necessary to cover the base of the aquarium with well washed aquarium sand. This, in fact, is very fine gravel, and ordinary sand should not be used because it packs so tightly that everything below the surface goes black and, after a time, will smell sour. Nor should coarse gravel be used, because food particles fed to the inhabitants of the aquarium will fall beyond their reach into crevices in the gravel, where they will decay and foul the water.

Before introducing the water, cover the floor of the tank with this correct grade 'sand' sold specially for the purpose. Do not apply a uniform covering, but have about two inches depth at the back sloping to about half an inch at the front. Make various humps and hillocks, uneven as the bottom of a natural pond would be.

Now add some rocks. Choose natural rock, preferably water-washed. The easiest way is to stop every time you happen to pass a rapid flowing brook and choose an old stone with an interesting shape. Experiment by first of all almost covering it with the sand at the bottom and then progressively raising it until an interesting vista is produced when examined from the front. As a general rule the rock on an aquarium bottom should be near the back and ends, leaving a fairly large open space in the centre.

Planting

Whether you intend to have a cold water or a tropical

aquarium it will need to be planted, and the principles are exactly the same. The main difference will be that you can get a lot of the plants you want for a cold-water aquarium for nothing from the nearest pond, whereas you will have to buy tropical plants from the aquarist's.

Put plenty of plants in the tank. First cut some strips of thin lead sheet so that you can clip a strip very gently to the root, just below the crown of rooted plants. Some species, like elodea, for example, will propagate quite easily from cuttings, and in these cases it is merely necessary to clip the lead to the base of the cutting to be planted. The purpose of the lead is simply to prevent the plants floating to the surface if they are disturbed before they have thrown down adequate roots into the sand. It will be obvious that any plants, which naturally float, like duckweed, should not be weighted with lead. In any case, floating plants are not ideal for an aquarium because they block out too much top light.

Having weighted your plants, place them in groups about the tank so that you can visualize the effect when water is added. Some people advise putting loamy soil under the aquarium sand, but my experience is that it tends to go sour and that plants do very well without it provided that they have plenty of top light.

It must be emphasized that the plants will look very much more natural in groups than planted evenly over the floor of the tank. In general the tall ones should be planted at the back, with short ones in front, as they would be in a flower border, and usually it will look better if species are grouped together.

One of the charms of keeping an aquarium, however, is that it is possible to uproot the whole lot at intervals and replant to give an entirely fresh effect, in the knowledge that you won't even retard the plants' growth perceptibly. The rocks, plant groups, even species can be made to look as if the whole aquarium has changed radically.

The one main principle, which should not be overlooked, is that plants should always be so arranged as to give dense patches of cover and large open spaces for the fish or other inhabitants to swim and exhibit themselves. Young fish and small, vulnerable livestock will be able to hide and shelter in the cover and larger pets will be seen to their best advantage with natural plant-life as a background.

It will be found, in summer with cold-water plants, and all the year round with tropicals, that growth is so rapid that it is necessary to be quite ruthless in pruning, or the whole aquarium will get a tangled mass of overgrown vegetation. On the other hand, do allow your patches of cover to grow really dense to contrast as effectively as possible with the open patches of water you leave.

When you have decided exactly how you are going to plant the aquarium, cover the roots, and lead that anchors them, up to the crown of the plant, exactly as you would do on dry land. Elodea and other plants that are being propagated from cuttings can be covered in sand to the depth of about one inch. Put a saucer in the middle of an open patch and siphon water gently on to it. The saucer will so diffuse the flow of water that the contours you have made in the sand will not be disturbed and the saucer can be retrieved just before the tank is full.

Fill the tank to within a quarter of an inch of the top, so that there is no chink of light between the top member of the frame and the surface of the water. When lit from the top, this will give a delightfully solid effect, greatly preferable to a partially filled tank.

Lighting
After the aquarium has been planted and filled, it is necessary to light it. Top light is vital. If the aquarium is placed in a window, the side towards the light should be blanked off, as this would be too much. This can be done either by painting the glass on the outside, or by sticking paper or cardboard on the outside. In either case, black or dark green will be most effective. Some people have a piece of cheap mirror cut to fit the back glass exactly, and this looks very effective as the tank not only looks twice as wide as it is, but the apparent increase in size gives a real impression of distance. Furthermore, the stock of inmates immediately doubles!

Before top lighting is fitted, the top of the tank should be covered with a sheet of plain glass, to prevent undue evaporation caused by the heat of the lights, and to keep the inmates from escaping. Tropical fish in particular have a nasty habit of jumping out of uncovered aquaria.

Do not put the sheet of glass so that it fits the top exactly.

Try glueing matchsticks at intervals round the edge, where the glass will rest on the frame of the tank. This will allow a circulation of fresh air to the water surface to the benefit of both plant and animal life in the water, and the fact that there is only a space the thickness of a match between the cover and the tank will prevent any but the smallest creatures escaping.

An opaque shade is necessary for the lights, the usual ones on sale being metal troughs with solid ends to fit the top of the tank precisely. Light shines down into the water, which it illuminates as a solid block, but no light is directly visible from any other direction.

It is not possible to be specific about the exact intensity of illumination required. It is better to err on the bright side, and most tanks about two feet by one will take two sixty-watt bulbs quite satisfactorily. The cost of this illumination twelve hours a day will be just under two pence per day, so that it is not a serious consideration.

Minute particles of vegetation called algae will grow and stick on the glass, and this algae is the best guide by which to assess if the illumination is correct. It will be green if there is plenty of light and brown if there is not enough. It is better to err on the side of too much rather than too little light, so all is well as long as the algae is green. The same applies to some extent to the plants. They will look green and healthy if they have plenty of light—provided other conditions are correct—but brown and dowdy when they are starved of light.

Maturing Water
If you have access to a supply of clear soft rain water, use this for the aquarium. Failing that, tap water will do.

In either case, when the water has been in your aquarium for a few days, the chances are that it will go cloudy. On no account change it for fresh, or the same thing will happen again. The cause of this cloudiness is the production of myriads of algae and diatoms; these often increase until the water will tolerate no more and then die off as suddenly as they came, leaving water with a wonderful sparkling clarity, far clearer than when it came from the tap. It is known to aquarists as 'mature' water and is guarded most jealously, often lasting for years with no attention but topping up, to

202

compensate for evaporation. The better the plants become rooted and flourish the more likely the water is to become mature, because the plants themselves will absorb a great deal of the impurities.

Cloudy Water

Although it is common for the water in a newly set-up aquarium to become cloudy and clear again of its own accord, it sometimes happens that an established tank becomes opaque. The most likely cause is over-feeding, the surplus food having decomposed. Failing that, a fish or animal may have died. In either case, the water should be removed by a siphon, filtered and returned, the main cause of the trouble being eradicated in the process.

Acidity and Alkalinity

Precise definitions of acidity and alkalinity of water are recorded in terms of pH values, which indicate the hydrogen concentration. The pH value of water is a scientific measure of the potential hydrogen which is necessary to fishes' health. It is not necessary to understand the scientific implications, as pet shops sell papers which change colour when dipped in the water so that the correct value can be established by rule of thumb. The universal indicator paper is red between the values of pH1 to pH3, brown for pH4, and paper number 5267 goes from pink to mauve, from pH5·2 to pH6·7. Paper 6883 changes from yellow to carmine from values 6·8 to 8·3. This particular paper range covers neutrality, for neutral water, neither acid nor alkaline, has a pH value of 6·7. Most plants likely to be found in an aquarium do best with slight alkalinity which suits fish and animal life too.

When animal life becomes too thick on the ground it is likely to give off excess carbon dioxide, which will be converted to carbonic acid if not absorbed, and change the neutral pH value to acid, which will be bad for both fish and plants.

Animal and Plant Balance

All animals, land or water, absorb oxygen. In the case of fish the water is passed through the gills and the oxygen absorbed rather as our lungs abstract oxygen from the air. Just as too many people in a small room would suffocate because they would use all the oxygen and give off too much carbon dioxide, so fish will die if an aquarium is too thickly populated. It is, therefore, important never to overstock.

The fish abstract the oxygen they breathe from the water and it is replaced by the oxygen that dissolves from the air into the water at the surface. The process can be accelerated by installing a mechanical aerator which passes air bubbles through the water. Some air is dissolved as the bubble rises, but the physical passage of the bubble is too rapid to give time for much absorption. The physical movement of the air, however, causes eddies in the water which is constantly in circulation, presenting a continually changing sample to absorb fresh oxygen as it reaches the surface.

Quite as important as the acquisition of fresh oxygen is the disposal of stale carbon dioxide and carbonic acid. Fortunately, plants need carbon dioxide just as animals need oxygen, and their function in a properly balanced tank is to absorb the carbon dioxide and to feed on the excreta and physical waste products of the animal life. It will therefore be appreciated how important it is to have an adequate supply of growing plants in every satisfactory aquarium.

Cleaning

A properly balanced aquarium, either cold-water or tropical, will accumulate a certain amount of debris, or mulm, on the sand around the plants. In time, most of this will rot and be absorbed by the root system, provided you do not overfeed and the tank is not overstocked with animal life. But this brownish scum, only slightly heavier than water, is rather unsightly, because a fish swimming near the bottom tends to disturb it. The easiest thing to do is to siphon it off through a fine gauze or charcoal filter and return the clear water to the tank. This takes no more than a few minutes once a fortnight or so.

The inside of the glass will become caked with algae which has to be cleaned off from time to time. It accumulates so slowly that it is difficult to appreciate how much it does impede the view until it is cleaned. The easiest way to move it is with an ordinary safety razor blade mounted at right angles to a handle slightly longer than the depth of the tank. This can then be scraped up and down as if you were cleaning the dropping board of a fowl pen with a dutch hoe, except that the glass you are scraping is the vertical side of the tank. Although this is very effective, I find that a two-inch diameter rubber sucker, such as is used to hold an ashtray to a car windscreen, is even more effective if mounted to a flexible handle—an old hacksaw blade is ideal.

For heavily stocked tanks, it is now possible to buy filters operated by the air bubbles from a mechanical aerator, which trap drops of water between each pair of bubbles, carry them up a glass tube, and drop them into a container which filters the water and returns it to the tank.

A great many fish and other inhabitants of the aquarium are particularly fond of the minute animal life—daphnia, cyclops, etc.—which breeds in the well-stocked tank. The snag about continuous filtration is that it not only clears the water of unwanted debris but it does tend to kill off beneficial minute animal life as well. It is therefore inadvisable to use continuous filtration unless you have an unusually heavily stocked aquarium or there are other special reasons.

Looking after Plants

Whether you have a cold-water or tropical aquarium, the plants will need periodic attention. In tropical tanks, vegetation grows profusely and it will probably need pruning nearly every time the glass is cleaned. If the plants are simply growing in the sand, it will not matter if they are uprooted, pruned, and replaced. But some people put loam under the sand, or even in small pots and if this gets mixed with the top surface of sand, the whole tank will become turgid. On the whole it is better to snip off what is not wanted with sharp scissors and not to disturb the root system more than is necessary.

In cold-water tanks the plants will not grow so profusely, but it will be necessary to thin out long shoots of elodea and vallisneria because they will grow long enough to reach the top of the tank, lie along the surface, and obscure the light.

Species of Plants

There are literally scores of plant species suitable for furnishing the aquarium, not all of which will be available at the same time.

I have found it an advantage to be able to keep either cold-water or tropical fish in the same tank, being able to change the temperature by the touch of a heater switch; in this case the aim is to have as many plants as possible which will thrive at room temperature or in a tropical tank. A further advantage is that, as one thins out and prunes the tropical tank, it is possible to furnish additional tanks with the surplus. It should be remembered that plants will not stand a sudden change from tropical to temperate heat, even if they belong to a species which will thrive in either. The simplest thing is to place them in a spare heated tank and reduce the temperature progressively by daily adjustment of the thermostat.

Some of the plants which are suitable for either tropical or cold-water tank are:

Acorus gramineus varigatus: Green and white foliage.

Acorus pusilla: A dwarf rush.

Cabomba: Of varying species. *C. aquatica* is a brilliant green and *C. rosaefolia* is red. The cabombas are of a feathery habit, they need light, love warmth—doing better in tropical tanks—and like a peaty subsoil or pure peat if possible. They can be propagated from cuttings weighted with lead.

Ceratophyllum demersurum: An attractive hornwort.

Elodea crispa: A good oxygenator which prefers a cold aquarium to a tropical one. Propagated by cuttings.

Elodea grandiflora: Does well in either tank.

Eriocaulon spetangulare: Attractive, with fine hair-like leaves.

Fontinalis antipyretica: Like a dense elodea, very good for spawning.

Heliocharis acicularis: Hairgrass. Very attractive but sometimes difficult to start. Should be planted in a small pot of good loam, just covered with sand. Propagate from runners.

Ludwigia mulertii, and other varieties: Really a bog plant, with pale green leaves, red on underside. It will grow quite satisfactorily submerged. Should be propagated by cuttings.

Myriophyllum: Various species. It has feathery leaves

related to the milfoils; needs plenty of light. Should be
propagated by cuttings.

Sagittaria: Various species, very good oxygenators.
Propagate by runners.

Vallisneria: Several species, especially suitable for growing
clumps and masses at the back of the aquarium. With a
grass-like leaf, it is a good oxygenator. Propagated by
runners.

All the above plants grow submerged and rooted. There
are an infinite variety which have not been mentioned, but
the above are all hardy and will grow in either cold or
tropical tanks.

There is also a wide variety of floating plants. In a
decorative tank filled to the top frame their value is ques-
tionable as they block out a lot of light and, anyway, only
their roots are visible. In tanks where fish, especially live
bearers, are breeding, floating plants will provide very good
cover for the young fry, as well as a certain amount of food
in the shape of the minute animal life and algae that live
there. I suggest:

Ceratopteris cornula: A floating fern, this is admirable
for a tropical tank, while

Riccia (Crystalwort), *Salvinia* and Frogbit, will grow in
either cold or tropical tanks.

Other Equipment

If you want to breed, or keep varieties of animal life which
will not agree, you will want spare capacity. You can either
obtain a number of smaller tanks, or you may decide to use
other types of container which may be bought
comparatively cheaply. Old earthenware sinks are a good
example of this, and are quite satisfactory for keeping a
number of small cold-water fish, or even breeding small
tropicals in a heated fish house.

You will require a small catching-net for transferring the
inmates of one tank to another, and this should be as large
as can easily be manipulated in the tank in which it is to be
used: about six inches across for a tank two feet by one foot
by one foot. For square tanks, it is best to choose a square
or triangular net, to avoid small fish dodging away in a
corner, as they surely will with a round net.

A feeding ring, consisting of a perforated plastic hemisphere, fixed to a ring of cork for buoyancy, is the ideal means of feeding small live food, like enchytrae, which wriggle through the perforations singly, and are caught by the fish before they have a chance to hide in the cover at the bottom of the tank.

The siphon used in clearing the mulm, or debris, can be a simple rubber tube. All that is necessary is to fill it with water, put a finger firmly over each end, put one end in the tank and the other over the side, lower than the water to be siphoned off. Take the finger off the end under water first, and when the other end is freed the water will flow from it. On no account suck to start the flow, as aquarium water can hold bacteria which could be very dangerous. Pet shops now sell siphons which start automatically when used according to instructions.

Aeration

A salt-water aquarium always needs aeration. Unless a tropical aquarium is heavily stocked, it will not need mechanical aeration. Cold-water aquaria are more likely to require it, partly because some fish commonly kept, like goldfish, are gross feeders, expelling a good volume of excreta. But even so, a well-balanced tank, with ample light and plants, should be perfectly satisfactory as it is.

If the fish spend a great deal of time at the surface with their mouths open, do not believe it is because you have managed to get them very tame. The more likely explanations are that you have been over-feeding then and the surplus food has gone sour or that there is not enough oxygen in the water.

The remedy is to siphon off the water and return it though a filter—and then to feed less in future. If this does not cure the condition and the fish still gasp at the surface, buy an aerator.

There are several types available, all more or less efficient. The main difference is that the original type is a piston and cylinder worked from a small electric motor and eccentric and a later type has no motor but is worked by a vibrating diaphragm.

The cylinder and pump delivers the greater volume of air and is suitable for aerating a number of tanks. It should also

17. Long-tailed field mice can be caught in the wild, kept for a
while in an aquarium containing logs and grass and then set
free in the wild again

18. Don't keep your tame mice in any old box for a cage. Give them plenty of room—an old doll's house is excellent—and the mice and you will both enjoy a better life!

be silent. The vibrator is usually cheaper and, mechanically, perfectly adequate for one or two tanks. The thing to watch is that it should be silent. Plenty of aerators which seem admirable in the noise and bustle of a pet shop can make just enough noise to be fraying to the nerves in the quiet of one's own sitting-room.

Diffusers
It may be desirable to have either large or small bubbles of air. For aeration it is usually better to have small bubbles, since a large number of small bubbles present a greater area of air surface to the water than a smaller number of larger bubbles.

But aeration bubbles may also be required to provide circulation of water, so that all the water in the tank comes in contact with the surface air. This is more necessary in a cold-water tank than a tropical one, because the convection currents produced by the submerged heater are usually sufficient to ensure adequate water circulation. This is one of the main reasons aeration is not so vital in tropical aquaria.

If small bubbles are required, an air-diffuser, which is usually an unglazed block of porcelain, is fitted to the tube leading from the aerator, and the air emerges as a myriad of tiny bubbles. Fewer larger bubbles agitate the water more.

Constant Filtration
One use for strong bubbles is to provide constant filtration. Air bubbles are injected through a T piece almost at the foot of a vertical tube, the top of which is bent over so that it ejects into a filter. The air bubbles trap tiny columns of water which they carry up the vertical tube and spill over into the filter, through which the water returns, purified, to the tank.

This is a refinement which will not be required except for overstocked or over-fed tanks.

Stocking the Tank

Pond Life
Some of the most fascinating creatures which do well in an aquarium cost nothing but the trouble of catching them. For

that reason, they are rarely to be found in pet shops. They are not commonly kept, except by young children in the miserable sterility of a jam jar, and yet they are extremely rewarding. This sort of aquarium should be set up with the same care as you would take for more exotic and expensive inhabitants. It should contain as wide a variety of cold-water plants as you can obtain, preferably collecting them yourself from the pool you intend to raid for captives.

One of the charms of this type of aquarium-keeping is that it is possible to have a complete change of animal life at no cost to yourself and no inconvenience to the creatures concerned. All that is necessary is to empty your pets back into the pool where you caught them and to catch some more.

Experience will show that some creatures are immediately eaten by others, so that it is necessary to choose a team that will tolerate each other and then to have a complete change when you want to study another group. By this means the more squeamish can safely study both hunters and hunted without the necessity of witnessing conflicts that occur so constantly in the wild. Return the aggressive creatures, like the great diving beetle, to their natural surroundings when they are in need of food, and replace them by freshly caught specimens.

Equipment

Since you will have to capture most of the creatures from a pond yourself, you will need a net and some carrying jars. The net should consist of a strong handle, about the thickness of, and the same length as, a broom handle. A strong wire frame should be fastened to this by a couple of worm-drive clips such as are supplied for fixing the fittings to hoses.

It is wise to have two nets on frames which can be interchanged on the same handle simply by slacking off the hose clips. One net, for catching fish and newts and large water beetles, should have a mesh of about one sixteenth of an inch and can be made of muslin or, better still, nylon gauze. The other net, for dredging in mud and for capturing minute insects, should be of finer material, and I find that the small cloth bags which pigeon grit arrives are admirable. Some people make a hole in the base of the fine net and bind a large-diameter test tube in it, but conditions in mud are so turgid that I have never found much advantage from this refinement.

You will also need jam jars with metal tops and water-tight tin boxes for transporting your captives home.

Methods of Capture

Choose small weedy ponds. It is useless trying to keep creatures which inhabit fast-flowing streams, like trout and crayfish, in an ordinary aquarium, as they need cooler conditions than you are likely to be able to provide and they like constantly changing water.

If you choose a large pool, well stocked with fish, there will be less chance of catching the small life that you want because you will be in direct competition with the fish.

Quite small, shallow pools, no more than a few yards across or a couple of feet deep, are often richest in the sort of life that is best suited to captivity in an aquarium. But it is necessary to make sure that there is ample vegetation.

There are really three methods of catching the creatures you will want.

Some of them, like newts and some water beetles, rise periodically to the surface to take in a supply of fresh air for use while they are submerged. Keep very still on the bank for a quarter or half an hour and watch what is coming to the surface in various parts of the pond. Submerge your net with the large mesh and wait until a victim surfaces. In the case of a newt, you will have to see it on the way up, because it merely gulps a bubble of air in its mouth and returns to cover without a pause. But if you see the newt coming up, it is usually possible, with a steady sweep, to scoop it up in the net.

With water beetles, there is usually more time, because they rest with the base of their bodies just protruding above the water surface for some seconds while they take on air, which is stored under the hard wing cases or as a bubble on their body.

Another fruitful method is to dredge the net firmly through the water plants, or even to scoop out large bunches of plant on to the bank. An enormous variety of life spends most of its time hidden in vegetation, and it is necessary to examine each plant closely before discarding and to sort out with great care the debris which will accumulate in the net. Newts, fish, beetles, snails, water scorpions, spiders, tadpoles, skaters, larvae of various insects, caddis worms, will all turn up in time. They should be sorted and put either into the jars of water or tins of wet plants. Fish, of course, should be put in water and so should anything with delicate limbs or appendages, though care must be taken that each community are of approximately the same size and that any known aggressors, like *Dytiscus* larvae, the dragon-like grubs which turn into great carnivorous beetles, are put where they can do no harm. Many of the more robust creatures will travel best in wet water plants, which will also restrict their movements.

Another fruitful source of capture is to dredge up scoops of the black foetid mud from the floor of the pool. Larvae of all sorts of insects live here, and so do various worms, like tubifex. When a dollop of mud has been decanted on the bank, sit quietly and watch for movement. Presently a portion of it will be seen heaving, as if the seat of a miniature earthquake. An old tea-spoon will lift the victim clear, when he should be dropped in a small container of water to swill off the mud, so that his identity becomes more obvious. Then transfer him to the appropriate container, which should hold only creatures of comparable size.

Although microscopic creatures could hardly be classified as 'pets', the fact remains that with the aid of a low-powered microscope a great deal of enjoyment and interest is to be had by anyone keeping a fresh-water aquarium. The water itself, plant life, and even the mud are teeming with simple life which only becomes properly visible under a microscope. Every tiny moving speck turns into a writhing monster as soon as the drops of water containing it appear on the microscope slide. I would emphasize that, to enjoy this aspect of aquarium keeping, all that is necessary is a quite cheap low-powered instrument.

Newts
There are three species of British newt, all of which are excellent as inmates for the cold-water aquarium. The largest is the crested or warty newt. The male develops a striking crest from head to base of tail and another from base to tip of tail in the spring, which is the breeding season.

212

The male smooth newt also develops a crest which is unbroken from head to tail, though this newt is slightly smaller. The third species is the palmate, which is more local than the other two, though quite common in parts of south and west England. All three species have less exotic females, but their habits are fascinating.

They are amphibian and need access to dry land, though their habits will be almost entirely aquatic during the breeding season. They should have a platform arranged in one corner of the aquarium sloping down to the water surface so that they can climb out if they so desire. It is best to use a small saucer or dish which can be wired into position about half an inch under the water. A small piece of turf can be put into this so that it rises like a green island from the surface of the tank.

Newts also require a fairly heavily planted tank if they are to breed successfully in captivity.

Hibernation
They hibernate in winter under stones, in crevices, and even, quite commonly, in cellars.

If you want to keep newts over winter, the best practice is to put them in a box containing a shallow bowl of water and some rocks resting on, but not imbedded in, mud. Place the whole box—which must have a secure cover because newts can climb—in a cellar or other room where the temperature will be steady and cool without freezing.

The newts will emerge from hibernation about February and can be transferred to a cold-water aquarium, which must also be securely covered.

Feeding
They are carnivorous and will eat scraps of finely chopped meat, but do far better on live food. Water shrimps, enchytrae, tubifex, and small earthworms will suit them admirably. The will also catch small water insects, such as water-boatmen and caddis larvae, and will worry quite large snails like terriers, till they sap their powers of resistance and drag them from their shells.

Newts are quite suitable for keeping in a community with sticklebacks, and other fish about their own size, the great silver water beetle (but *not* the great diving beetle, which will attack them), and any smaller cold-water insects which can be regarded as potential live food. They should not be kept in a tank with fancy goldfish, like veiltails or shubunkins, as they may damage their fins.

It will be noticed that the newts will feed heavily, put on weight, and then suddenly lose their appetites. This is because they are about to change their skins, and it is a fascinating process to watch in the aquarium. The whole skin splits and the creature emerges from it, sometimes with so little damage that the whole skin floats in the water like a perfect ghostly newt, complete to the tiniest detail such as the 'fingers' of the 'hands', pulled off like ladies' gauntlets. It is common for the newt, which emerges shining and resplendent in his new suit, to eat his cast-off clothing.

Breeding

Newts breed well in captivity and the process is among the most interesting of any that takes place in either a cold-water or a tropical aquarium.

The female is heavy with spawn by about March and will lie languidly among such plants as elodea or cabomba, or any mass of vegetation. The male, resplendent in his breeding colours, will display himself in front of her, curving his body and tail and cavorting in his weird dance of love.

When the female is ready, the male liberates a spermatophore which consists of a gelatinous case containing hundreds of spermatozoa and it is usually oval and about two millimetres long.

The female has a cloaca, through which she will lay her eggs, but first she picks up the spermatophore with this cloaca. The case ruptures, freeing the spermatozoa inside the female, who subsequently produces a chain of fertile eggs like a string of sausages. She detaches each egg with her delicate front feet, which she uses like hands, and makes each into a separate parcel by placing it in the leaf of a water plant.

The eggs hatch into tadpoles, which grow their front legs first, instead of hind legs appearing before front as is the case with frogs. The tadpoles have external gills, which are gradually absorbed until the youngsters become perfect miniature newts.

214

It takes three to five months for the tadpoles to develop into newts, and those which hatch late in the season will not complete their metamorphosis till the following year and will spend their first winter entirely in the water, as aquatic creatures.

When they become perfect newts, however, they crave dry land and must not be forced to remain in an aquarium, even one with an island in the corner, which may be adequate for fully adult newts in the breeding season. They take to a life on land for two or three years until they are completely mature and come into breeding condition for the first time.

This may seem an extraordinarily long time before so small a reptile is ripe to reproduce itself. But newts are exceptionally long lived—they will live from fifteen to twenty years in an aquarium that suits them. This makes them additionally attractive as pets.

Sticklebacks

Sticklebacks are the small fish—Jack Bannocks—that most children begin by keeping in jam jars. They do not keep them for long because the oxygen supply is not sufficient to sustain them and they usually die a miserable death by suffocation.

Kept properly, they are as attractive in an aquarium as newts and can easily compete for attraction and interest with the more exotic and expensive items on the pet-shop lists.

There are two species of stickleback found in this country, the common three-spined variety and the less common ten-spined. The three-spined has three spines on its back and one on its belly. The ten-spined has from seven to twelve spines. Both species are pugnacious and use the spines for defence and offence. The three-spined is found in almost every small pond and can be caught in a net of fairly large mesh, either by singling out an individual and stalking him in open water or by trailing the net through fairly dense plants.

The ideal time to keep sticklebacks is in early summer when they are breeding, as their habits are at least as interesting as the most sought-after tropical fish.

Use as large a tank as possible, which must be well

215

planted, and keep no more than one male, though several females will mate with him.

When in breeding condition, there will be no doubt about the sexes. The females are a dowdy brown while the males blush a glorious bluey pink all over their bellies. We used to call them 'butchers' as children.

Breeding
The male will begin by making a nest in the plants. This will be an oblong structure with only one entrance large enough to contain his mate. It will be neatly suspended among vertical plants like *Elodea densa* or cabomba.

When it is complete, he will search out a gravid female who is ready to spawn and drive her into the nest, where she will deposit her ova and then make good her escape by breaking out, often through the walls of her mate's barrel-shaped nest. The cock-fish then enters and fertilizes the eggs by ejecting his milt into the water. Then he seeks out another mate and repeats the process until there are enough eggs in his nest.

Now he stands guard over it and keeps a current of fresh water flowing over the eggs by 'fanning' it in from the outside. This is because even at the ova stage fish need oxygenated water to breathe. When the young hatch out, the male still stands guard and drives them back into the nest should they try to escape before they can swim strongly.

At this stage the young fish need infusoria, as described in the section on Live Foods.

When they are ready to become self-supporting, the father lets them escape from the nest. There must be plenty of dense vegetation then for them to skulk in, or he will forget the good work he has put in and eat them.

Feeding
Sticklebacks need plenty of live food to get them in breeding condition; they will eat daphnia, cyclops, enchytrae, tubifex, chopped earthworm, small snails, etc. It is also a good thing not to scrape all the green algae off the tank (which must be well lighted), as the fry will pick at it when they get past the infusoria stage. When the females have spawned, move them to another tank, and remove the male when he ceases to guard his young.

216

Aquatic Insects

In every pond that is well stocked with plant life, there is a wealth of insect life as well.

The beetles are especially interesting because in many cases their larvae live in water too, often preying, like dragons, on almost anything that moves, even though it may be considerably bigger than themselves.

The two largest beetles are the great silver water beetle, which is harmless and vegetarian, quite excellent for a community tank, and the great diving beetle, *Dytiscus marginalis*, which is slightly smaller. This must never be kept with any other creature, up to the size of a newt, unless this companion has been put in as live food. *Dytiscus* in both larval and adult form is an implacable hunter. It has pincer-like jaws which dig deep into the fleshy part of its prey. A substance is then injected down the hollow fangs which dissolves the prey, and it is sucked up like living soup.

There is a whole host of smaller beetles which swim strongly with legs adapted as oars, and most of them have wings under their horny wing cases, and will fly if they are allowed to climb out of the tank and escape. The whirligig beetles, small oval black beetles about a quarter of an inch long, swim in schools on the surface playing an eternal game of tick. When alarmed they dive for the sanctuary of the plants, but are soon irrepressibly back at their games.

Most of the beetles come up periodically for air, which they collect under their wings as they protrude their tails above the water surface. They can easily be caught whilst thus refuelling. Their larvae can be dredged from the pond when one is scooping for plants and other life.

Dragonflies cannot be kept in an aquarium or vivarium because they feed by 'hawking' other insects in flight. Their larvae are very like the larvae of the great diving beetle both in appearance and temperament, and do well subject to the limitation that they will devour almost anything weaker than themselves.

Water Bugs

Do not be put off by the term 'bug'. Although some of the water bugs belong to the same family as the human bed bug, they are completely harmless to human beings and are amongst the most intriguing occupants of a cold-water aquarium.

Perhaps the best-known are the water boatmen, boat-shaped creatures which propel themselves through the water by means of specialized legs which are long, covered with 'feathering' at the end so that they look exactly like a pair of oars. But water-boatmen can propel themselves with as much facility under water as normal boatmen who skim along the surface.

There are a number of species, some vegetarian and some carnivorous. A good rule is to avoid the sort which swim on their backs—they will damage other inmates—and choose the ones that swim with their backs—and wing cases—uppermost.

The group of bugs includes a large number of other attractive species, including pond skaters, which are equipped to take advantage of the surface tension of the water, and can literally run on it. It also includes the water scorpion, an interesting creature with a long projection sticking from its belly. This is not a sting, as many people believe, but a tube through which they take in a supply of air, by projecting it through the water surface. Water scorpions, despite their name, are completely harmless to people.

Water spiders

There are several species of aquatic spider which are of the utmost interest as some of them make a bubble nest of air which they take below surface in the form of a bubble attached to their bodies. Their habits are similar to those of land spiders. They look extremely beautiful as they hunt among the plants encased in their silvery bubble.

Caddis Flies

A number of insects have larvae which are soft and vulnerable, but protect themselves by building around them most wonderfully camouflaged houses of tiny pebbles, pieces of plant stalk, leaves, or whatever is available. They carry this case with them wherever they go, retiring into its comparative safety when attacked. Caddis fly larvae are vegetarian.

218

Other Pond Life

In addition to the above, there is an almost infinite variety of aquatic flies and their larvae, ichneumons, which prey on other insects, water snails and mussels, leeches (which are most effective and swim like miniature versions of the Loch Ness Monster), and all the minute life which can best be studied with a microscope.

Broadly speaking, there are two ways of accommodating such a great variety of creatures. One can either keep small communities of similar-sized creatures and change them frequently, so that there is no need to feed them on other creatures whilst in one's care, or one can put everything one catches into one large community tank and watch for oneself the drama that is played every day by wild creatures in their natural surroundings. I prefer the latter way, though I do avoid overstocking with the really voracious creatures like the great diving beetle.

Cold-Water Fish

Apart from catching your own pets for the cold-water aquarium, it is quite possible to obtain from dealers stock which you would be unlikely to catch for yourself.

British fish such as roach, tench, carp, and rudd are beautiful to look at and very satisfactory to keep. Pike and perch prey on their fellows and must be treated as rogues like the great diving beetle.

These fish will eat proprietary dried food, such as ants 'eggs'—which are really cocoons—dried daphnia, Bemax and also gentles, small meal-worms, small earthworms, tubifex, enchytrae, etc. Except for perch and pike, most do quite well in a community tank.

Bitterling Minnow

This fish deserves individual treatment because of its exceptionally interesting breeding habits.

It is a pretty, silvery little fish with rosy fins, and in the breeding season the male is a lovely flushed golden colour.

To breed succesfully, the bitterling minnows need a swan mussel in the tank. This mussel is a bi-valve which lies partly submerged in the mud and, like other mussels, it feeds by siphoning water through its body—the shells are slightly open and two siphons project except when danger threatens.

219

The water thus siphoned is filtered and ejected, the mussel retaining what edible matter was in suspension.

When the female bitterling minnow is ready to lay her eggs, she produces a long tube, hanging from her body, which passes her eggs, fertilized by the male, into the shell cavity of the mussel. They are safe here from predation, and the flow of water through the mussel's siphons keeps the eggs fed with oxygen.

There is, however, a snag. When the fish deposits her ova into the mussel she stimulates it to reciprocate by ejecting its own embryos into the water. Each is provided with a tiny hook, and may get attached to any fish, including the bitterling minnow, in the area. The tiny mussels bore through the fish's skin and feed on its tissue for several months, so that it is wise to have only one swan mussel and to remove any fish from the tank the moment the minnows have spawned.

Except for this experiment, it is not wise to keep mussels in aquaria as it is not easy to tell when they die, and their fleshy bulk may cause serious pollution.

Goldfish

Goldfish are probably the cheapest and commonest commercially obtainable aquarium fish. There is a large number of varieties apart from the common golden carp of goldfish bowls. Some, shubunkins, veiltails, and comets, have been specially bred for their long and exotic fins. They are mostly short-bodied fish and should be mixed with nothing but the most inoffensive tank-mates lest their beautiful fins should be nibbled.

It is essential to give some fresh live food. Chopped earthworms are excellent, though bright manure worms should never be used. This fresh food is necessary because their short bodies and sluggish movements make them specially liable to constipation. This, in turn, will exert pressure on the delicate swim bladder, by which fish maintain their balance, and if this becomes deranged, the fish will be noticed upside down or at all sorts of peculiar angles. In this case feed nothing but chopped worm for a few days, after which the condition is likely to be cured. But if this happens often or for long, the swim bladder will be irreparably damaged and there will be no alternative but to destroy the fish. My favourite among goldfish is the golden orfe, a sleek, long, active fish which may be put in the garden pool when it grows too big for the aquarium. A school of these, darting and weaving like tropical zebra fish, is very hard to beat.

The Bass Family
Sun, moon, diamond, and peacock-eyed bass are colourful, tame, attractive fish for aquarium or garden pool. But they are rather aggressive and do not do well in mixed collections, especially those containing fancy-finned fish.

Loach and Catfish
These fish feed on the bed of their habitat and are thus satisfactory only in an aquarium: If they are put in a pool they are hardly ever seen.

The Tropical Aquarium

Tropical fish are even easier to keep than creatures whose natural habitat is water in temperate climates.

All that is needed, in addition to the tank, plants, and food already described, are an efficient heater, thermostat, and thermometer. There are various types of heater on the market (including gas and paraffin, neither of which I like owing to the difficulty of thermostatic control, the risk from gas fumes, and the messiness of the continual recharging that is necessary with paraffin). There are a number of cheap electric heaters on the market which are highly efficient. Some, usually the more expensive ones, are specially designed as 'bottom' heaters and there is no doubt that heat applied at the base of the tank is ideal because it produces constant convection currents, which continually present fresh water to dissolve air at the surface.

My own experience is that the normal cylindrical heaters, mounted in a test tube, are perfectly satisfactory when covered with a thin layer of aquarium gravel. This keeps them entirely submerged and the thermostat can be mounted in a back corner, concealed from view by a dense clump of vallisneria or elodea.

It takes about two and a half watts to raise a gallon of water 1°F. above room temperature, and it must be noted that it costs no more to have heating capacity double the

221

expected requirements than it does to have only just enough, apart from the initial cost. All that happens, if you have twice as much heat available as you need is that the thermostat only allows it to work half as long as a heater half the size. The total watts consumed will be exactly the same. So I always have two heaters wired in parallel, so that if one should fail the tank will not go cold.

Assume that you have got a ten-gallon tank in a room which may under extreme circumstances—when you are away for a week-end in winter, for example—get as cold as 32°F., or freezing point. You tank must not fall below 72°F., so that it will be necessary to heat the water 40°F. This will take $(10 \times 2 \cdot 5 \times 40)/(1_{10})$ 100 W. You can therefore be quite safe in allowing a one-hundred-watt heater for a ten-gallon tank, though I should prefer two sixty-watt heaters wired in parallel. It is so rare for a heater to fail that I should take the chance it would not go wrong under such extreme conditions; and one sixty-watt heater would be enough to maintain minimum temperature for a room temperature of 52°F., which is colder than most people like their rooms to get. It must also be remembered that the heat from the top lighting takes a considerable load off the heater.

It is wise to get an electrician to wire the two heaters in parallel and the thermostat in series. Then screw the thermostat adjustment well over to allow a theoretical heat considerably more than you want and watch the temperature rise on your submerged thermometer.

The correct heat for a community tank is from 74°F. to 78°F. (72°F. is a minimum), and when the temperature reaches 78°F. adjust the thermostat so that it just flicks off. The temperature will then fall until the thermostat comes into operation again, the temperature drop being less for the more sensitive and expensive thermostats.

Never introduce any fish until the tank has been effectively maintained at the correct steady temperature for several days.

It should be noted that the temperature will affect the fishes' activity and lifespan. If they are kept relatively cool—say 72°F.—they will be comparatively sluggish, but tend to live longer. Most of them require a temperature of at least 80°F. for breeding, at which temperature they are very active but tend to 'burn themselves out' comparatively

222

quickly. It is advisable to allow winter temperature to be a few degrees lower than in summer.

Stocking the Tropical Aquarium

Like a great many creatures kept as pets, some of the most beautiful and interesting tropical fish are also the cheapest. This is simply because they happen to be so very easy to breed that the supply is at least equal to demand. But I often think that the newcomer to tropical fish-keeping has an advantage over the old hand. He can enter a dealer's with a perfectly open mind and examine the fish for sale, without being prejudiced by the prior knowledge that this is rare or that is hard to breed. There is nothing more beautiful in nature than, for example, a really good male Siamese 'fighting fish', or more fascinating to watch than swordtails, which bring forth perfectly formed live young, instead of the more usual ova from which most fish hatch. Yet neither cost more than a few old shillings. So do not be unduly influenced by the dealer's salesmanship. Choose what appeals to you, and only take advice to the extent of avoiding aggressive or voracious fish if you intend to keep a community tank.

There are literally hundreds of different fish which will live well in a tropical aquarium, but only a few of the main groups will be dealt with here, since the general principles of keeping any of them are broadly similar.

Live Bearers

Besides being exceptionally interesting, most of the live bearers happen to be beautiful, hardy, and cheap. So they are ideal for beginners.

Lebistes retuculatus, the guppy or millions fish, is the most humble of the group. The female, which is larger than the male, is a rather dowdy, deep-bodied fish, tapering away at the tail, and she is about two and a half inches long. The male is about half her size, multi-coloured with exotic patterning. These fish produce so many live young that 'sports' or unusual specimens are quite common. By separating these into another tank and breeding back to the parent, it is often possible to fix an entirely new strain, providing a fascinating experiment in genetics.

By this means some most beautiful strains of guppy have

223

been evolved over the past few years, and clubs have been formed to foster this specialist variety alone. It should be noted, however, that it is necessary to be ruthlessly selective in the specimens kept for breeding. If guppies are left to interbreed promiscuously, the progeny will revert quickly to the inconspicuous wild coloration.

All live bearers—and a great many other tropical and cold-water fish besides—are fond of browsing on lush algae, so it is important when cleaning the aquarium only to scrape it off the front, but to leave algae on the back and ends as additional food. Not only vegetarian fish will appreciate this, but snails as well.

When the young have been produced, make quite certain that there is plenty of massed vegetation, in which they can take shelter from larger fish who may fancy them for a meal. In a community tank, as in nature, it will be found that a high proportion of losses will occur in this way. With fish that breed as readily as guppies, this does not usually matter as the full number of fry would otherwise be difficult to dispose of and would overstock the tank. So it may be as well to allow the same sort of natural wastage as would have occurred in the wild, and supply welcome live food to the other fish at the same time.

If you are trying breeding experiments or fixing a strain, or if there is some specific reason to preserve the fry, on no account try to move the young fish from one tank to another. Move the old fish and leave the youngsters the tank to themselves. They are so fragile when young that serious damage and deformity are almost inevitable if they are handled.

Other live bearers are equally attractive and easy to deal with. The Mexican swordtail is a handsome chap up to three inches long, in a variety of colours, including a striking red.

In the male lower rays of the tail are so elongated that he looks like a swordfish in reverse. The species hybridizes readily with the platy, or moonfish, which is rather similar except that it has no sword on its tail.

There are a considerable number of other live bearers but my favourite is the black mollie, which is a graceful fish of an intense and velvety black. It makes a beautiful foil for some of the more exotic inmates of the aquarium.

While live bearers are breeding they should be kept in

Top: 19. "Garden" fantail pigeons are easy to keep (except where there are destructive cats!) and look delightful in the the garden

Bottom: 20. Muscovy drakes are huge birds up to 12 lbs but their ducks are only half that size. They are fine in gardens where there is a pond

Top: 21. Male great-crested newt. Newts are happy in an aquarium
in the breeding season and can be returned to the wild at the end
of the summer when they normally leave the water

Bottom: 22. A shoal of sword tails and mollies in a tropical
aquarium. Tropical fish are easy to keep, even in the smallest flat,
and can safely be left without harm or cruelty if you go away for
a weekend

relatively shallow water as the young need access to the surface soon after birth to ensure the proper functioning of the swim bladder. They are often too weak to swim up the full height of a deep tank.

There are various other means by which the young of live bearers may be protected. When first born they tend to sink so a sheet of glass may be placed in the tank so as to leave a space between the glass and the sides too small for adults to pass but wide enough for newly born young. The glass should be larger than the surface area, so that it has to be sloped, or two pieces may be used in the form of a V. The young will then gravitate to safety and the female and glass may then be removed. There are various changes which may be rung on this principle, but none, I think, as good as natural dense plants in which to skulk.

Labyrinths

Labyrinths are among the most fascinating fish kept in either hot- or cold-water tanks. Although they have gills, they gulp down bubbles of air from the surface, like newts, and they have the ability to survive very considerable periods out of water, because there is a labyrinth in their mouth capable of functioning like a lung and absorbing oxygen from the air.

Gouramis are commonly kept; paradise fish look nice but are too aggressive for any normal community tank; but my favourite labyrinth is *Betta splendeus*, the Siamese fighting fish. He is not particularly aggressive except to males of his own kind. In the East, these fish are kept separate, like fighting cocks, and matched to fight for money. When two males are put into a tank they spread their glorious tail and fins, and then dart into the attack. Each tries to bite his opponent's fins or tail and they continue the attack until one or other cannot swim any more.

In this country, they have been selectively bred for glorious colour, and few are aggressive enough to fight to the death, though it is impossible to keep more than one male in a tank because they would otherwise damage their glorious fins. But the breeding habits of the labyrinths in general, and Siamese fighters in particular, are as intriguing as the stickleback.

The male first selects a place for the nest and proceeds to

225

blow bubbles of air covered by tenacious mucus. These bubbles stick together in a raft-like honeycomb, about an inch-and-a-half round and half-an-inch thick. Next he displays himself to the female by raising his flamboyant fins and tail and bending and twisting his body to display every possible angle. The female, if she is ready to spawn, is passive, and he gradually guides and shepherds her till she is under his nest. Now he encircles her body with his, clasping her till the eggs fall out and sink to the bottom of the tank. He releases her to pick up the eggs, one by one, in his mouth and blow them up into his bubble nest, where they remain suspended, each in a tiny bubble. He retrieves his mate and repeats the performance till she is spent. Then she had better look out for, having laid her eggs, she holds no more attraction for him and he will sometimes attack her so savagely that she dies. It is therefore necessary to provide dense cover to hide and protect her.

When the eggs are safely in the nest, the male guards them until they hatch and then shepherds his precious brood to keep it from harm till it is self-supporting.

Siamese fighters are carnivorous and need as much live food as possible. Enchytrae are excellent, chopped earthworm is adequate, and daphnia and fresh water shrimps much appreciated. The fry usually need infusoria to start with, soon followed by daphnia and cyclops. If the earthworms are small enough to be swallowed whole, do not chop them up. It is better for carnivorous fish to gorge at intervals than to eat a little and often. One really good meal a day will keep them in first-class trim.

Chiclids

The breeding habits of the chiclids are somewhat similar to the Siamese fighting fish, though the most interesting is probably the Egyptian mouthbreeder. The female has a disaproportionately large mouth where she not only incubates the eggs but shelters the fry.

The best known is the angel fish, which is quite satisfactory for community tanks while young and looks delightful amongst a shoal of other angels when adult. But on the whole, chiclids are better avoided because of their unusually aggressive habits and voracious appetites.

226

Killifishes

This group contains a large number of fish, many beautifully coloured, but like chiclids, they are aggressive, and better avoided since there are plenty of attractive fish which are more peaceful from which to choose.

Catfishes

A queer, whiskered, scale-less group which creep about the bottom of the tank and are frequently used as scavengers. They are interesting, but have one disadvantage; if there is much mulm on the bottom of the tank they are apt to stir it up, making the water cloudy in their efforts to sift out the edible matter amongst it. They are omnivorous and will eat what the other fish in the tank leave, but like prepared dried food.

Carps

A very large family of beautiful fish which mostly do well in a community tank. Zebras, pearl danios, and white cloud mountain minnows are long, graceful, fast-moving fish, forever showing fresh colours as different angles of light strike them.

To get in breeding condition, they need plenty of live food, enchytrae, daphnia, tubifex, and finely chopped earth-worms, though they do quite well on prepared dried aquarium foods which can be bought ready-mixed from an aquarist's.

For successful spawning these fish need a temperature around 80°F. and an abundance of thick cover like *Myriophyllum* which is dense but pliant enough for relatively weak fish to drive through. The eggs remain sticking to the leaves like goldfish eggs. Indeed, the whole method of breeding is similar.

When the gravid females are seen to be heavy with spawn, the process can often be accelerated by removing about an inch of water from the tank and replacing with well aerated cold water which would be enough to lower the temperature from 80°F. to about 75°F. The heater and thermostat will, of course, return the temperature to 80°F. more slowly than it fell with the addition of fresh, aerated water.

This group also contains many of the barbs, which are

also delightful aquarium fishes though the larger of them should not be mixed with very small fish.

Characins

A large group of beautiful community fish, such as flame fish, beacon fish, and neon tetras. Although they are lovely and, in the main, harmless fish, they are not easy to breed and have to be imported from Africa and Central America, where they are common and still relatively cheap to buy.

Live Foods

Most aquarium fish do better if part of their diet consists of live food.

Ants' Eggs

Ants' 'eggs'—which are the pupae, and not eggs at all—can be collected by anyone lucky enough to live in country where ant-hills abound. All that is necessary is to dig over and riddle ant-hills, picking out the white 'eggs' and taking them home for the fish—and birds if you keep an aviary. But first ask permission of the owner of the land.

Infusoria

Infusoria is the 'green water' produced by making an infusion of hay, chopped lettuce, or other similar vegetable. Properly matured it contains a very high proportion of both animal and vegetable life, which is normally visible only under the microscope. Once a culture has been produced, it reproduces so rapidly that if conditions are good it will quickly become so thick that it kills itself off. An easy way to avoid this is to make it in a jam jar, and then put a drop of the culture in another jar of fresh water where it will multiply. It is thus possible to have a range of jars with the culture at varying stages of concentration from practically pure water to turgid masses on the verge of extinction.

To prepare infusoria, scald hay or green vegetables and allow to cool. Take a little of the water at the edge of a pond (if it is muddy it does not matter) and add this to the infusion. Place on a sunny window sill and nature will do the rest.

This holds a slight risk of raising things that you did

not want from the pond, along with those you did. The best way to avoid this is to buy the initial culture from a dealer and have a look at it under a low-power microscope. You will thus see the creatures you want. It is then quite simple to collect your own cultures from a pond and sort out the animal life you want under your microscope. As most of this low form of life is unicellular and breeds simply by dividing, you need very little fresh culture to infect a jar of infusoria.

This infusoria is absolutely essential to newly hatched fish, which feed on it until their mouths are large enough to cope with daphnia, cyclops, etc.

Daphnia

Take a large shallow bowl—an old wash-stand hand basin is excellent—and put in some infusoria and a few live daphnia, which can either be caught or bought. In a sunny position, the daphnia will feed on the infusoria and breed very rapidly.

If you have an unstocked garden pond, this is wonderful for breeding daphnia on a scale enough to cope with broods of young fish.

Most aquarists working on a commercial scale find pools in the country which grow wonderful cultures of daphnia and they will travel miles to collect them. By no means all small pools hold it—large ones have fish which keep it down—but very often pools used as watering places for cows, quite small pitholes in the corners of fields, which dry up in hot weather, hold abundant cultures whenever there is water in them. The eggs survive long periods in mud and hatch when the pool fills again.

Enchytrae

Enchytrae are small white worms which many books say live under dustbins. I have often looked under mine with no success whatever! They are rather expensive to buy, and, if you do buy them, insist on buying by weight after checking up on the price per ounce in the trade papers. Some dealers are in the habit of selling enchytrae other than by weight, and there never seems as much for one's money. Once you have got a few enchytrae they are easy to breed, though it takes several weeks before the stock seems to increase.

229

When you have a thriving culture, it is possible to breed them as fast as you use them up.

Take a wooden box about two feet by one foot, six inches deep, and fill it with moist loamy soil. The soil scratched to the surface by moles is very good for this or well rotted turf. Wet it thoroughly and allow to drain through drainage holes in the bottom of the box. Ideally, you should be able to flood the surface from the fine rose of a watering can, and the water should drain straight out of the bottom, leaving the soil thoroughly moist but not soggy, in the process.

Make rows of depressions about one inch in diameter and half an inch deep, three inches apart, all over the surface of the box. This will give about four rows of eight depressions.

Put a few enchytrae in each depression and cover them with soppy bread and milk, level with the surface of the soil. Cover the whole surface with a sheet of glass, which must lie flat on the soil to prevent evaporation, and keep in a dark cupboard.

The enchytrae will feed on the bread and milk and multiply. The purpose of putting dollops at intervals is to encourage the worms to concentrate where they can be collected instead of diffusing all over the box.

When the cultures are vigorous, a few worms can be lifted from each pile on the end of a matchstick without disturbing the rest. The culture should be kept fed on milk sop and will prove invaluable for feeding fish and, at a pinch, carnivorous birds, shrews, and all kinds of pets that need live food.

The Vivarium

The vivarium is normally used for keeping snakes and reptiles, which are sometimes combined with aquarium live-stock by incorporating a small pool in the arrangement.

In principle the vivarium can be treated as a dry aquarium. Except for keeping large snakes, it can be about the same size as an aquarium and, provided it has a closely fitting lid, a standard aquarium makes a perfectly satisfactory vivarium. The lid must have adequate ventilation holes covered by perforated zinc.

It is immaterial whether you use the same tank in turns as a cold-water and tropical aquarium and then a vivarium, or whether you buy a specially constructed vivarium from a dealer. In the latter case it will probably consist of a metal box having a glass front and ventilated top, with top lighting and provision for a small pool somewhere in the centre.

Cover the base with aquarium sand, as you would a normal aquarium, but so arranged that the vessel to hold water is sunk to the lip, to give the effect of a natural pond. Add rocks and plants in small pots—potted meat jars are very good—and sink the jars so that the vegetation appears to be growing from the sand. Take as much trouble landscaping it as you would a cleverly planted aquarium, and also provide branches for the many inmates which love to climb.

Many of the creatures you may want to keep will feed on flies, so it is particularly important that everything is well made and tight fitting. Cover the bottom with deep leaf-mould for hibernation in cool temperatures, but not freezing ones, during the winter.

Terrapins

Common European pond tortoise and terrapins will do quite well in many garden ponds or in a pool in the vivarium, where it can climb out of the water.

Ideally, the pond should have steep sides, from which the terrapin cannot escape, and an island in the centre where it can climb to sun itself and rest on dry land.

Terrapins eat their food under water and are largely carnivorous. If the pond is large enough, and sufficiently well planted to support much insect—and water—life, the terrapin will catch a good deal of its food. Indeed, it will catch some of your fish if they share the same home, so do not introduce it to your goldfish pool. Terrapins will love tadpoles, small newts, frogs, and water beetles, but can also be fed on earth-worms, meal-worms, gentles, or even raw meat. The one point to watch if terrapins are fed on other than live food is that any they don't eat will pollute the water. One method of avoiding this is to fill a large flat bowl about six inches deep with water and put the food in this. Any that is not eaten can be disposed of by lifting the bowl out at frequent intervals and emptying it.

In their natural state, pond tortoises hibernate in the mud

at the bottom of their ponds, and this is sometimes successful in suitable ponds. Otherwise they must be removed and hibernated as a land tortoise, though it will be found necessary to get them in a cool place quickly as they are so very much more lively than their terrestrial cousins. If they don't become inactive right away, they tend to use up their food reserves so that they will not survive the winter when they do settle. Some terrapins are hardy; they will live out of doors in summer but must be hibernated in winter. European pond tortoises are the commonest hardy variety, and they will do well in any garden pool or large vivarium where the land slopes right to the water's edge. The pond must be surrounded by netting or fence with overhang to prevent escape.

They will eat live food, preferring earthworms or gentles, and soon become tame and come to the surface to be fed.

They must be hibernated in leaf-mould in a cool, but never frosty, room and, if they wake in the spring before the danger of frost is past, they must be kept in an indoor vivarium until it is safe to put them out.

Some of the most beautiful half-hardy terrapins come from America and need a pool kept at about 70°F. to do well. They should be fed as the hardy varieties. Avoid young specimens, which tend to be very delicate.

Newts

Outside the breeding season, when they show an urge to leave the water, newts may be kept in the vivarium. They will need water in which to swim, rocks set so that there is space under them where they can creep for refuge on dry land, and a humid atmosphere. To achieve this, see that the glass cover fits tightly and all lighting is on the outside of the cover. Any evaporation from the pool should then hang about as moist air.

Newts will feed in the vivarium as they would in the aquarium, and usually prefer to take their food from water.

Frogs and Toads

British frogs and toads may be kept under the same conditions as would suit newts. They will enjoy flies to feed on and also small meal-worms and small earthworms and gentles. But it is essential that frogs, toads, and lizards see their food move, or very often they would rather starve than bother with it.

Other Frogs

There is a wide variety of other frogs available to choose from, including edible frogs, which are about three inches long, the male often being a bright green.

The tadpoles need infusoria to begin with, but will soon feed on raw meat suspended in the water or very fine fish food put in a bag like a tea infuser and shaken gently in the water at meal-times, to give a finely suspended cloud of food.

Perhaps the most popular and attractive frog is the active little tree frog. It is bright green—though remarkably able to blend with its surroundings—and about an inch and a half long.

It has adhesive pads on its toes and can climb almost anywhere, including straight up the vertical glass side of the vivarium. There must be shade available, but it will be found that tree frogs are sun-worshippers and love to bask for hours in hot sun.

Their food is flies, in size anything from greenfly upwards, which they catch by rolling their sticky tongues out with extreme speed.

There is one snag. Tree frogs have extremely powerful croaks and a most monotonous note. You will not want many males in the house. In a greenhouse they are both attractive and beneficial.

Toads

There is a wide variety of toads which may be kept under the same conditions as frogs.

The most interesting species is probably the midwife toad, the male of which carries the eggs round with him during their incubation, stuck to his body like a girdle.

Axolotls

Perhaps the most curious reptile which is kept as a pet is the axolotl or salamander. There are a number of varieties which can be bought from dealers and the axolotl is, in fact, the immature form of the salamander.

It is a newt-like reptile, breathing through gills, being entirely aquatic, and living for years, often its whole life, in this form. It will feed on worms, gentles, and raw meat and must be kept in an aquarium.

It is, however, possible to induce metamorphosis so that it changes from what corresponds to the tadpole stage in newts to the adult salamander. To do this it is first necessary to get the axolotl in first-class condition by feeding very plentifully on live food. At this stage it should be kept in a shallow tank in the vivarium, rather than in an aquarium.

The next stage is to evaporate the water from its tank slowly so that first the axolotl has difficulty submerging and then cannot submerge at all. It will be forced to forsake its gills and begin to use its lungs and within a week or so it will turn into a salamander. During this period it will need an extremely humid atmosphere or to be sprayed regularly.

Salamanders do not spawn but give birth to live tadpoles which turn into axolotls, most of which leave the water as salamanders. Those whose development is arrested may remain as axolotls for years unless the change is forced as I have described.

Snakes

The commonest snake kept as a pet is undoubtedly the grass snake. A great many species sold under this name are not, in fact, grass snakes at all, but a similar snake is imported in large numbers from Italy.

They need a vivarium with a pond and a humid atmosphere. The snag is that they are difficult to feed. Small live frogs are the diet which grass snakes require, but it is often very difficult to persuade them to eat even these in captivity. They need good conditions and bright light, but if they will not eat within a couple of weeks, it is kind to set them free in dense vegetation near water.

It should, of course, be realized that many reptiles are erratic feeders and prefer gorging and banting for long intervals to regular feedng.

There is quite a variety of other snakes, but on no account be persuaded to have a poisonous variety.

The constrictors and pythons are all right if you want something that size, but take specific advice from your dealer before buying any snake. Always see him handle it without gloves or tongs, for what a professional won't do would indeed be foolish for an amateur; and make sure that it is a species which will accept food in captivity, or you are wasting your money.

Lizards

Many lizards are ideal for keeping in a vivarium. They are colourful, active and, for the most part, harmless.

Beware how you pick them up, for many, including our native brown lizard, have the facility of shedding their tail if held by it. It can be most disconcerting to be left holding a still-writhing tail while your pet runs away. He will probably grow another in time, but a stump-tailed lizard in your vivarium will tell every knowledgeable visitor how clumsy you have been.

The brown lizard and the green lizard are two of the most attractive to keep as pets. They need somewhere to climb and somewhere to sun. For food they need live flies which can be introduced in quantity to the vivarium, in confidence that they will be snapped up when in reach of a lizard's tongue. The common lizard has live young and breeds quite well in captivity. It is a major item of diet for adders—which should on no account be kept—and lizards and snakes should not be kept in the same enclosure.

The slow-worm is not a snake as many suppose, but a lizard which has only vestigial legs. It does well on small worms, slugs, wood lice, etc.

Chameleon. This is perhaps the most interesting of the lizards. It catches its prey by stealth not speed, being quite incredibly slow and deliberate in every movement save that of its tongue which unfurls, catches a fly on its sticky pad, and returns too fast to be followed by the naked eye. They need bright sun to do well, and will eat caterpillars and almost any insect small enough to swallow.

Large Lizards, etc.

There are many monitors, skinks, and large lizards available, most of which in my opinion are more suitable for zoos than as pets. In any case, see the dealer handle them before buying.

Alligators

Some people, though I do not number myself among them, seem to have a strong desire to keep an alligator. They are now quite readily available and, though they do not really coincide with my idea of a pet, they are quite simple to keep.

They need a vivarium with a built-in tank, or an aquarium into which a landing stage has been built. They need to live at the temperature of a tropical breeding tank of about 80°F. Alligators will not eat unless they are thoroughly warm, and by no means always then. Their diet should consist of pieces of meat, live frogs, gentles, worms, small fish, etc. If he won't eat, turn the heat up to 85°F.; but there will be a lot of evaporation at this heat, so keep the tank topped. The more successful you are the more he will eat. The more he eats the faster he'll grow and the shorter the time before you get badly bitten.

13 Waifs and Strays

I have enjoyed as much pleasure by restoring waifs and strays to liberty as from any of the pets I have kept in captivity.

A fringe benefit of my job as a naturalist is that complete strangers often bring me young animals or birds they have 'rescued' or 'found abandoned' or 'lost'.

Before describing how to deal with them I should like to make it crystal clear that it is often no kindness to a young animal or bird to pick it up and 'rescue' it. Birds are the commonest victims of such do-gooders who see a lonely fledgling, obviously lost and hungry, so they pick it up and take it home.

If they had left it where it was the odds are that its parents, who were probably busy feeding the rest of the brood, would eventually have heard its cries, and come to collect and feed it. It would then have been reared naturally and suffered none of the perils which befall so many victims of too much kindness.

Once you do 'rescue' it, however, it is your responsibility to care for it until it is able to look after itself. But it is a responsibility which often turns out to be immensely satisfying so long as you are successful.

The commonest animal waifs which arrive on my doorstep are young fox cubs—and the chances are that they really are in trouble. But think about it *very* carefully before you prove to be a soft touch.

Vixens are often shot or dug out at lambing time and their cubs, which look exceptionally attractive and appealing, are rescued and given to someone as pets.

They are easy to rear as most young animals and need warmth at least as much as food. I use an ordinary infra red lamp, as sold by agricultural dealers for lambs and chickens, and I hang it in an outhouse where the floor has been covered by clean dry straw. Use wheat or oat straw and avoid barley straw because it is an irritant.

I hang the lamp about 15 inches above the straw nest and leave it for half an hour to arrive at a steady temperature, making sure that it is well shielded from draughts.

It is simple to confirm it is the right height by putting your hand in the nest for a few moments to check that it feels about body temperature without being uncomfortably hot or cold. The height should be adjusted if it is.

Put the cub in the nest under the lamp and leave it alone for a while. It will probably crawl away and explore the whole shed but, when it feels cold, it will find its way back and settle down just near enough to the light to feel exactly the amount of heat it requires.

If the shed is so large that there is any real danger of the cub getting lost and unable to find its way back to comfort, or if the cub is so young that it is not properly mobile, make a sensible sized kennel area by surrounding it with simple barriers.

The important thing is to be quite sure that, if the cub does get too hot, there is plenty of room for it to crawl out of the immediate area covered by the infra red bulb.

Comforting heat is vital for young foxes, badgers, otters, stoats, hedgehogs and other animals which are normally reared in a nest or den and suckled by their dam.

Young deer and leverets (the young of hares) are born with their eyes open and can run within a few hours of their birth.

They do not need artificial heat but should be kept dry and sheltered and reared on the bottle. Undiluted cow's milk does not suit many youngsters and I have found that Lactol, made for rearing puppies and kittens, or ordinary dried baby food are far more suitable than cow's milk. Human baby food which has remained unsold until after the date marked on the tin can often be bought cheaply from chemists and is perfectly satisfactory for rearing young animals. But whether this or Lactol is used, it should be mixed strictly according to the instructions on the tin.

Do not be worried if a young animal will not feed for the first twelve hours. It is accustomed to finding the teat on its mother by scent and will fight against sucking a strange rubber teat until its hunger overcomes its shyness. If you force feed it at this stage you may make it permanently bottle shy. It is far better to leave it to get very hungry, which it will do in twelve hours or so.

I try to use plastic bottles because I can squeeze them enough to force a few drops of milk through the orifice of the teat even when the animal is not sucking. A spot of warm appetising milk put on a young animal's nose will make it lick itself clean by instinct and a little patience at this stage will usually encourage it to suck when once it has tasted it.

It is often necessary to experiment with different sizes of orifice and I deliberately err on the large side until the youngster is feeding freely. If the milk is too difficult to suck out, a cub will often stop trying as soon as the edge is taken off its appetite so that it will not get enough nourishment to thrive and grow.

When once it is feeding greedily, it is better to reduce the size of teat orifice because if the milk flows too fast, it will plaster the cub as well as giving it indigestion.

The young of animals are reared naturally in a nest or den are often unable to empty themselves without physical stimulation by their mother. If they did empty their bowels whenever they felt so inclined, the nest would quickly become foul and their fur matted and sticky.

Nature copes with this by including a substance in their droppings which is deficient in the mother's diet. She develops a craving for this deficient substance and she eats the droppings of her own young to get it.

The result is that the nest is kept sweet and free from droppings while the mother, who is Nature's vacuum cleaner, obtains the elements in her diet to keep her healthy.

This natural hygiene routine goes even further than that. Many mammals, while very young, *cannot* empty their bowels without physical stimulus even if they need to. So their dam, craving for the shortage from their droppings, licks their hind parts, as a cat will wash her kittens, and the physical contact causes the young to evacuate as a reflex action.

It is vital to know this when bottle rearing very young mammals, ranging from creatures as small as stoats to animals as large as deer. If the youngster's anus is stroked with a soft damp cloth, its instinctive reflex is to empty itself. If this is neglected it may suffer, sometimes fatally, from constipation.

It is equally important to watch out for symptoms of unsuitable milk, which may cause either diarrhoea or constipation. If the motions are too loose and the animal is scoured, it will become dehydrated and die. The remedy is simple. Put a little lime water, obtained from the chemist (*not* lime juice!), in the milk and the motions will dry up. About half a teaspoonful to a feed is usually enough.

If the motions are hard and constipated, a little sugar added to the milk will usually do the trick.

In either case it is important to remember that the sugar or the lime are not effective at once so do not be impatient because an overdose of the cure is as bad as the complaint.

Common sense and a reasonable knowledge of natural history will indicate when to offer solid food and wean away from milk, but the sooner an animal gets onto its natural diet, as alike as possible to its wild relatives, the better. The one exception is for animals which it is intended to keep permanently as pets instead of returning to the wild. The longer these will stay on the bottle, the tamer and more affectionate they are likely to become.

It is not always a kindness to 'return' creatures to the wild. Foxes, for example are natural hunters but they spend a long time, as cubs, learning to hunt with their parents and learning how and where to escape when danger threatens.

Foxhunters do not start cubbing until August or September, when the cubs are almost full grown. The main purpose, apart from training young hounds what quarry they may hunt, is to split up the litters of cubs and disperse them.

Where foxes are not hunted, they will often stay together as family parties for well over six months. Hand reared cubs which are set free, with no experience of hunting for themselves, run the real danger of starving because of sheer inability to catch their own food.

An additional hazard is that a hand reared fox cub will not be afraid of Man. His most likely hunting grounds are therefore poultry pens, game reserves and pet rabbit hutches which are likely to bring him to a bad end and get wild foxes a bad reputation they do not really deserve.

So, however forlorn and pathetic it may look, harden your heart and do not rear a fox cub at all unless you know precisely where you can set it free.

Foxes are not suited to a life in permanent captivity and it is often kinder to destroy orphaned cubs humanely at the start than to rear them in a loving home but to be forced, in the end, to turn them loose in hostile country where they will be persecuted.

Although badgers are even easier to rear on the bottle than foxes they are far more difficult to establish in the wild successfully. This is because badgers are so intensely territorial that a resident badger will not tolerate a stranger on his domain. He will attack an interloper so viciously that he may kill it.

The Badger Act of 1973 makes it illegal to kill them, dig them out, cruelly illtreat them, buy them, sell them or keep them as pets. Despite this there are still louts who kill them deliberately and incompetent game keepers who damage them accidentally. The result is that there are orphaned cubs in need of help each year and people who know how fond of badgers I am often bring them to me.

Mustilidae 'scent' their territory with a tiny drop of musk from their anal gland. They even 'scent' each other to prevent fighting amongst badgers of the same colony who treat badgers which smell of the 'colony' scent with respect. Any badger not tainted with this scent is liable to be attacked.

It is easy enough to rear cubs on the bottle, as described for fox cubs. They should be weaned onto a varied diet ranging from bread-and-treacle (badgers love sweet things!) to raw meat and eggs. Give them the same sort of food a puppy of the same age would have.

When they are about half grown, about September or October, they would normally be able to fend for themselves and, if they can be put in a large wood where there are no wild badgers or game keepers they have a reasonable chance of survival. But if you do not know a landowner who is fond of badgers but does not have a colony on his estate, you should contact your County Naturalists Trust (address at your local library) and ask to be put in touch with one of the naturalists who specialize in rehabilitating badgers.

Young hares, or leverets, are far more difficult to rear by hand than either foxes or badgers, but they are easier to set free successfully when they grow up.

241

Hares usually have four leverets which are put in separate forms, or open nests above ground and only visited when it is time to suckle them. This limits the risk of a whole litter being wiped out by a predator—as he is only likely to find one at a time!

If the doe hare is shot or caught by a predator, the leverets must be reared by hand or they will die. It is often difficult to *start* them sucking a strange teat and they are prone to fade from weakness and die before there is much chance of rescuing them.

Once they start they are easy enough, and it is sometimes possible to persuade a she-cat to rear them with her kittens. The way to do this is to take the cat away from her kittens for an hour and pick them up and handle them. Rub the kittens on the leveret's fur so that, when the cat is allowed to return she will be so keen on washing the scent of humans off her precious litter that she won't notice there is an extra one with long ears!

I have used exactly the same trick to persuade a ferret to rear a young weasel about the same size as her own kittens.

Leverets do not make particularly good pets when they are reared because they are so subject to fits of blind panic, for no apparent reason, that they bang into things and injure themselves. This is the time to let them go in the largest corn field you can find. It will give them cover and protection from their enemies and all the natural food they need. Their own mother would have another litter within a few weeks of their birth and leave them to their own devices, so the problem of getting them established is much less difficult to solve than it is with predators which have to learn to hunt or establish a territory for themselves.

Most other British animals are fairly simple to rear and the important thing to remember is that warmth is as vital as food when they are tiny.

Read the best natural history book you can get about their habits so that you know the exact diet they will require when weaned and the sort of habitat they would choose in the wild, so that you will know where to release them when the time comes. Successful pet keepers are good naturalists who use plenty of common sense.

Birds are usually easier to rear and often easier to establish in the wild as well. But never pick up a fledgeling

242

simply because you *think* it has been deserted. The chances are that its parents will soon hear its hunger cries and come back to feed it if you wait awhile.

If you do know that one or both parents has been injured or killed, you may have to rear the youngster or leave it to starve. You are most likely to get saddled with one of three main groups. Seed eaters, ranging from pheasants or partridges to sparrows; birds of prey, which need meat; or soft bills, such as thrushes and blackbirds which need insects or worms or other live food. There are hundreds of possible species you might try so that it is necessary to consult your natural history book about the diet and habits of the particular one that you find.

Birds which open their bill, or 'gape' for their parents to cram food in are easy. Small pieces of bread and milk or hard boiled eggs make a good basis for their needs.

Birds of prey, hawks and owls, need raw meat in small chunks but it is vital to know that they also need feathers or fur because they cannot digest meat unless they have something to form 'pellets' of indigestible food which they eject, or 'cast', after they have had their meal. They cannot survive without this.

Poultry breeders usually destroy all their day old cock chicks and keep the pullets for laying. It is often possible to get these surplus chickens cheaply but, if it is only possible to get fresh butcher's meat, it is essential to wrap the small chunks in feathers or fur or even cotton wool to supply the roughage hawks and owls need to make their pellets.

Even seed eating birds sometimes need soft food while still in the nest. (House sparrows collect caterpillars to feed their brood for example.)

Special mixtures can be bought from pet shops for rearing soft bills and old bird fanciers used a crumbly 'cake' which had a high proportion of hard boiled egg.

Pheasants, partridge and wild duck will eat hard grain from the start though duck also love bread and milk. Corn merchants sell 'chick crumbs' which are greatly improved by an addition of hardboiled egg, crushed up with the shell on to provide grit.

It is important to get young birds feeding on natural food as soon as possible. Seed eating birds will normally feed themselves almost from the start and will look after themselves in the correct habitat when they can fly and are past the need of artificial heat.

At the other end of the scale, birds of prey can be very difficult. They will starve if released until they have learned to catch healthy wild prey. I have overcome this to some extent by accustoming them to a large outside aviary and allowing them out for a few minutes when they were hungry just before feeding time. I then entice them into the aviary for their food—and leave them shut in.

They gradually learn to fly further but come back to feed, at which stage I leave the aviary open all day, with food available inside when they want it.

As they become more independent they come back less and less frequently until they eventually take to the wild. Even after that, they sometimes hang around for weeks and I had one kestrel which roosted in our eaves all winter and nested in the wood, with a wild mate, next spring. It made all the trouble of getting her in a fit state to look after herself well worthwhile.

14 Bird Tables and Nest Boxes

However fond I am of pets, it gives me even greater pleasure to persuade wild animals and birds to share my garden of their own free will.

It is not even necessary to have a garden because I heard recently of someone who had persuaded a pair of kestrel hawks to nest in a box fixed to the window sill of her seventh storey flat!

Most nice people put out a few crumbs for the birds. If they just throw them out of the window, the chances are that rats and mice and other uninvited guests will steal a share. So fix your bird table out of reach of the creatures you would rather stayed away.

You don't need a large expensive table, with a fancy thatched roof, like garden shops sell. All that is necessary is a flat board, about eighteen inches square, nailed to the top of a six foot pole so that rats cannot climb onto it.

It is worth nailing strips round the edge, to prevent food blowing off, but leave about an inch space at each corner so that it drains satisfactorily.

Put a wide variety of food on it. Bread crumbs, grated cheese, cheese rinds, apples that have gone off, scraps from the table, bird seed and nuts. Tits and nuthatches and woodpeckers love fat so we hang up a lot of fat, but not in large hunks of expensive suet.

I ask our butcher to keep me the odd bits that customers discard because they only like lean meat. I put all these odd bits into a saucepan, melt them and pour them into basins or blancmange moulds. When they cool, I turn them out and stick a wire through the centre of the fat to hang it up. It looks much neater than shapeless hunks of suet, is certainly far cheaper and uses up all the bits which would otherwise be discarded. To help eke it out, I put a handful of chick crumbs or dog biscuits into thr fat while still molten and turn it into a cake.

If these little bits had been put onto the birdtable singly, they would have been pirated by large birds and probably dropped where rats could get them. Melted together in shapely moulds, the birds have to eat them where we can watch as payment for their meal.

Shelled peanuts in baskets or whole nuts threaded onto cotton attract tits and nuthatches, greenfinches and siskins. (It is said that siskins prefer their nuts offered in *red* plastic nut bags!)

Mealworms are irresistible to insectiverous birds and, if you want a robin to feed out of the palm of your hand there is no more likely bait than a few mealworms.

They are expensive and sold by the pound in pet shops but are not difficult to breed. Fill a biscuit tin with layers of bran divided by sheets of newspaper. If you put a few mealworms in, they will pupate, hatch out into beetles which will lay the eggs from which a whole batch of mealworms will hatch.

The whole cycle takes about nine months, but is influenced by temperature. If the tin is kept in a warm airing cupboard they hatch and grow a little quicker.

It is important to realize that your supply of food will attract an artificially high population of birds so that it is essential to continue the regular supply of both food and water when once you have started.

If you suddenly stop when the bad weather comes, the birds which are relying on you for their food supply will be short at a critical period and may starve.

Having persuaded most of the birds in your neighbourhood to come to dine with you, it is a small step to encouraging them to stay and breed.

It is quite easy to make nest boxes which will attract a very wide variety of birds far cheaper, and quite as good, as those sold in shops. The exact size of entrance hole and nesting cavity is most important and The British Trust for Ornithology, The Lodge, Sandy, Bedfordshire, issue an excellent booklet, including a do-it-yourself set of instructions, which covers nest boxes and bird tables.

It is cheap, comprehensive and includes instructions for erecting as well as making the boxes. If you do not want to make your own, the British Trust for Ornithology supplies ready made boxes and details of approved types.

15 Insects

Butterflies and moths are among the most beautiful and rewarding pets to keep. They have the added advantage that a successful brood of suitable insects can be liberated to replenish the population of some our threatened British species.

Although they are not supplied through the normal pet trade, it is now possible to buy a wide variety of both British and foreign species from Worldwide Butterflies Ltd, Over Compton, Sherborne, Dorset, who also supply breeding equipment and food plants.

The population of butterflies and moths has declined in England during the last twenty years or so because many have been killed by pesticides sprayed onto farm crops to prevent damage from other insects.

Selective weed killers have wiped out acres of vegetation on which harmless insects fed and the uprooting of hedgerows and mowing of roadside verges, in the cause of tidiness, has destroyed the foodplants many native butterflies and moths needed to survive.

So breeding British butterflies and releasing them in suitable habitat is a worthwhile hobby as well as being exciting.

The first thing to be certain about is that you will have sufficient foodplant to rear a brood of caterpillars. This is often very easy because common trees and plants such as buckthorn, lime and honeysuckle provide natural food for puss moths, brimstone butterflies, lime and elephant hawk moths.

Even stinging nettles are the favourite food of the larvae of peacock, red admiral and small tortoiseshell butterflies and tiger moths will do fine on sallow dock or dandelion.

The choice is endless and exciting and eggs can be purchased by the dozen, clinging to the leaves of pot plants on which the larvae will feed.

When they hatch out they are allowed to feed on the leaves of the pot plants or on plants growing in the garden. They are prevented from escaping by enclosing the whole plant in specially made fine muslin bags.

When the caterpillars are full grown, they change into chrysalids which are allowed to harden off for a few days and then carefully stored in emerging cages on peat or corrugated paper or under special conditions to suit the particular species.

They are normally sprayed, to keep them moist, if they are species of butterfly or moth which will emerge the same year, or kept in plastic boxes in a cool cellar if they will have to over-winter.

They will eventually emerge as immaculate butterflies or moths which can be put into muslin cages, to pair, after which they will lay eggs on their favourite food plant or can be released in suitable habitat to repopulate the countryside.

The whole process can be carried on in the near natural conditions of a spacious country garden or, equally well, in the smallest city flat.

For those with more exotic tastes, it is possible to apply exactly the same techniques with tropical Moon moths, nine inches or so across the wings, or even the Giant Atlas moth, from Asia, which is the world's largest species.

There is no limit to the choice, for not only are British and foreign butterflies and moths obtainable from Worldwide Butterflies Ltd, but a large selection of stick insects up to a foot or more in length.

It is most important that foreign species are *not* liberated or allowed to escape. Our climate is unsuitable for many of them, so it would be cruel to the insects, but also because 'introduced' species, which would be able to thrive here, could be very dangerous as potential pests because their natural predator controls would be absent.

Although they are not so glamorous as butterflies or moths, ants can make fascinating pets. There are about twenty-seven species in England and, on warm days, usually in late summer, the males and unmated young queens of a colony take wing and clouds of them fly in a nuptial flight where the queen is mated.

The interesting thing is that *all* the colonies of the same species in the area take flight at the same time on the same day, as if triggered off by telepathy. The more likely explanation is that they need very exact conditions for their nuptial flight, and when they do get the right conditions, they all take advantage of them at the same time!

After the flight, the males die and the females return to the nest where they can lay huge numbers of fertile eggs for years without being mated again.

Sometimes the female returns to her original nest and sometimes she starts a new colony where she tends her original batch of eggs herself. These will develop into the first workers which will take over the duties of nest building and feeding and tending young so that the queen can specialize in laying eggs. She may live for fifteen years or so and even the workers can live for several years.

A 'formicarium' or observation colony of ants is quite as interesting as an aquarium or vivarium. It is simply made by fixing two sheets of common window glass, about a foot or eighteen inches square, half an inch apart.

The easiest way to do this is to glue metal strips about half an inch thick, to the edges of the sheets of glass, making in effect a picture frame with a glass back as well as face, the face and back being held half an inch apart. The metal strip at the top must be only about nine inches long so that there is a couple of inches space at the top.

The sheets should then be mounted on wooden feet which support them upright.

Now fill the glass box with fine loamy soil through the space at the top to within two inches of the top, and it is ready for the ants.

Small red ants are best and, when you have found a colony, which will probably be under a stone or fallen branch, cut gently round the nest with a spade and lift it gently onto a white sheet alongside.

Scoop a hundred or so ants off the sheet and funnel them into a bottle which must be absolutely dry. You will do no good without a queen and you can recognize her because she will be several times larger than the workers and quite conspicuous. There will probably be several queens in the nest you have dug up.

Put the queen in a separate box, so that you know exactly where she is and return the spadeful of soil, containing the

249

rest of the nest, *very* gently to the hole in the ground you dug it from. The rest of the workers will soon repair it.

Now set your formicarium upright on a white soup plate surrounded by water. The kitchen sink with about an inch of water in the bottom is a good place for the soup plate. Tip the ants and their queen gently into the soup plate.

They won't like the plate and they will like the water even less so they will crawl all over the plate and formicarium, looking for more congenial quarters.

They will soon discover the space at the top of the formicarium and the attractive loam between the sheets of glass. When they are all safely inside, plug the gap at the top with cotton wool and leave them to settle down. They will soon start to tunnel and in a surprisingly short space of time they will have excavated a new nest in the soil in your formicarium.

Remove the cotton wool and smear a little honey on the glass inside the top of the formicarium.

They will also need a little water but do not overdo it because ants do not like soggy nests. Just enough tepid water to prevent the surface drying out and becoming powdery will suit them well.

The worker ants will lick the honey and store it in their crops to take into the nest and feed the queen and other workers.

If the formicarium is left uncovered it will be difficult to see what is happening becaue the ants' instinct is to tunnel in darkness, so that they will try to leave a wall of earth between them and the glass sides.

To avoid this, make a thick cardboard sheath to cover both sides of the glass up to the surface of the nest. This will keep all the underground area dark but leave the surface in daylight, as it would be naturally.

When you want to watch them, remove the sheath for a few minutes at a time and the tunnels will be exposed as clearly as if they had been sectioned with a knife. Put the cardboard back and return it to darkness before the ants start to redesign their tunnels.

If you have to go on holiday or grow tired of your formicarium, all you have to do is to empty it out by the nest where you got the ants originally and they will doubtless be delighted to return home!

Index